SKEPTOPOLIS ENDORSEMENTS

Freddy Davis, through his multiplicity of books and seminars, has been a champion for Christians to live with a Christian worldview. Now, he endeavors to demonstrate what that means through the life of the fictional character, Chris Bel, in his first novel, Skeptopolis. Freddy's ability to capture our attention in his nonfiction writings is now showcased in the fictional world. I am excited to endorse Freddy Davis and Skeptopolis.

Rev. Sean McMahon
Executive Director - Florida Baptist Association

"If you let it, this book will change your life. See how lives are transformed as a biblically informed believer speaks truth in love with confidence and humility. I want to do the same.

Jo Anne Arnett, Ph.D.
Co-Founder, Tallahassee Christian College & Training Center

Action, adventure, and a hero who stands on principle! Skeptopolis introduces readers to an evangelical worldview through the power of storytelling. What a fun way to do apologetics and a great discussion starter on how to engage today's culture with the gospel!

Ray Franklin
Professor Emeritus of Missions, Ouachita Baptist University

Dr. Freddy Davis has brilliantly written a novel, using a fictitious character, Chris Bel living in a Post Christian culture in Skeptopolis. The story demonstrates Chris's on-going battle to engage and to overcome the secular environment that seems to be smothering all Christians and opposing the spreading of the Gospel message. Dr. Davis has masterfully written about a fictitious situation and has made it relevant and eerily realistic for contemporary readers. If you are a Christian who longs to see the gospel shape your life and impact others around you. Skeptopolis is a must read.

Ken Dew, D.Min.
Every Nation Ministries
Equipping Evangelist, Apologist, Author

Freddy Davis is making waves in the fiction genre with the release of Skeptopolis. Known for his clear writing in non-fiction, Freddy now showcases his storytelling prowess in this engaging novel. Skeptopolis is more than just an entertaining read; it's a powerful educational tool that seamlessly weaves the fundamentals of apologetics into its storyline. Readers will gain a deeper understanding of various worldviews, delivered by an expert in the field. Freddy's creative approach delivers a compelling and timely message that is both thought-provoking and enjoyable.

Beverly Lewis
Executive Trainer and Business Coach

"An inspirational tale of a young man living out his faith and literally saving a town. At the same time, a practical guide to our great commission of sharing the teachings of Jesus and making disciples. Freddy weaves the two together in an evangelistic adventure, full of surprises, that will keep you on the edge of your seat. A must read for those who feel called to engage in our broken world and contemplating mission work, whether here or abroad".

Jim Kallinger
Senior Strategist at The Front Line Agency
President - National Association of Former State Legislators
Former State Representative - Florida House of Representatives

SKEPTOPOLIS

The Power of One Life

by

FREDDY DAVIS

Published by Leadership Books, Inc. Las Vegas, NV – New York, NY
LeadershipBooks.com

ISBN Hardback: 978-1-965401-03-3
Paperback: 978-1-965401-04-0
eBook: 978-1-965401-05-7

Scripture taken from the NEW AMERICAN STANDARD BIBLE®, Copyright© 1960, 1962, 1963, 1968, 1971, 1972, 1973, 1975, 1977, 1995 by The Lockman Foundation.

LEADERSHIP
Thoughtful, Relevant Leaders From Around The World
BOOKS

PROLOGUE

Most writers write novels primarily for the purpose of entertainment. They weave stories that engage the imagination and transport people out of their everyday lives and into a fantasy world that offers readers a pleasant escape from the burdens and boredom of everyday life.

Notably, there are exceptions, and this book is one of those. Of course, if you want to enjoy this work purely as entertainment, you may certainly do that, and you will enjoy the story! *Skeptopolis* does a great job as an entertaining story with fun and compelling drama. But, as they say, "there is more to the story" here for those who desire to take advantage of it – particularly for thoughtful Christian readers.

We live in a day where Christians and the Christian worldview face a great deal of opposition and even antagonism and hostility. Recent polling research has revealed that most Christians don't know how to engage society with their faith. In fact, most don't even have a solid grip on the essential elements of their faith.

As you read this story, you will follow a character who not only knows the essential basics of the Christian faith, but also how to effectively engage those who oppose him. He even knows how to do it in a way that reflects well on the faith itself.

So, jump in and enjoy. But also jump in and learn!

Editor's Note: Words in **bold** throughout the story have a corresponding entry in the Glossary at the back of the book.

TABLE OF CONTENTS

CHAPTER 1

BAM!

It was now all or nothing! A fight for the championship! As Chris entered the ring and looked across, before him stood the most feared fighter of the entire tournament.

Rock Hanson, a third-degree black belt, had won the annual city tournament for the last three years running. No one in Templeton seemed remotely capable of taking him out.

The dojos in town cooperated to hold a city-wide karate tournament every year. It was a chance for all the local students to learn proper competition etiquette and get experience in a live tournament environment. Today's tournament, however, was special. Sponsored by the North American Martial Arts Association, the annual winner of this tournament would go to the state tournament, which led, in turn, to regionals, then to nationals.

Rock's imposing figure – from his 6' 4" muscular frame, to his strong, pronounced square jaw, to his jet-black karate gi – projected a Darth Vadar-esque aura as he glared at the opponent he was poised to crush. Just looking at him caused most contestants to wither before even stepping into the ring.

To get into the championship round, Rock had easily won his bracket. All four of his opponents went down almost without a fight. It was hard to imagine anyone standing up to him.

Chris had easily made it through his bracket as well – though he didn't cast the same intimidating aura as Rock. While also tall, his slender frame and traditional white gi projected skill more than intimidation. Chris's one advantage was his extreme agility, speed, and precision. Using those qualities, he had worked his way into this final match ... all for the opportunity to face the prohibitive favorite in this winner-take-all match.

As Chris and Rock faced each other from opposite sides of the ring, spectators could feel the intensity radiating from their bodies. As they locked eyes, their breathing slowed, and their eyes narrowed as they strained to detect even the smallest weakness to exploit.

Chris had the blue ribbon tied around his left arm to signify he was in the blue corner, and Rock had the red. When the referee entered the ring, both contestants turned toward him and gave a low, deliberate bow to show proper acknowledgment and respect. They then turned and bowed to one another, as is the custom before each match. Next, Chris and Rock moved to the middle of the ring where the referee stepped between them to give his customary prefight explanation of the rules.

Once finished, he looked at each contestant and asked if they understood. After Chris and Rock nodded their heads in affirmation, they stepped back to the edge of the ring. Then, taking his proper position, the referee squatted slightly, and with a quick and forceful downward swipe of his hand yelled sharply, "Hajime!" ... and so it began.

As Rock and Chris faced each other, each was well aware of his opponent's skill. While they trained in different dojos, they'd had numerous opportunities to get to know each other at camps, workshops, and local tournaments. And, while they were not close friends, they had a healthy respect for one another, and were cordial when not in the ring.

Until this point, Chris had never been able to defeat Rock. Though he had come close two or three times, Rock still held a decided edge. Here they were again, facing each other in this high stakes, winner-take-all match for a chance to move on to the state tournament. This moment seemed to summarize what it was all about – the payoff for years of training and hard work were on the line!

Chris Bel came into karate almost by accident. When he was six years old, his mom, Sue, signed him up for a karate summer camp because he kept begging her. He was a huge fan of the Teenage Mutant Ninja Turtles on TV, and always ran around the house punching pillows on the couch and throwing karate kicks into his dad's easy chair.

Watching Chris' behavior, Sue was afraid one day he would hit someone, destroy a piece of furniture, or hurt himself. She was constantly trying to think of ways to channel his boyhood energy. After talking to Chris' dad, Fred, they finally got serious about making a plan. They thought, *Maybe by going to a karate camp, Chris could at least learn some proper technique, and maybe even gain a bit of personal self-control?* They figured it was at least worth a try.

As a six-year-old, Chris didn't stick to anything for long. Sue honestly believed he would lose interest soon after camp was over. But to her great surprise, not only did Chris love the sport, but it turned out he was a natural and quite gifted. He quickly picked up the foundational techniques and demonstrated a level of precision and coordination quite uncommon for his age.

Sue also had a high regard for Sensei Lance, the dojo owner. He was a friend from church, and she knew him to be a committed Christian. Beyond that, he had a keen ability to recognize the capabilities of the young people he taught and helped them advance to the highest level they were capable of achieving. By the end of the summer camp, Chris was way ahead of the other beginners, and Sensei Lance even had him working out occasionally with older, more experienced kids.

When karate summer camp was over, Sue and Fred sat Chris down at the kitchen table for a heart-to-heart talk. Fred looked him straight in the eye, "Chris, do you really want to continue karate? You know it's only gonna get harder, right?"

"Oh Yeah!!!" Chris nearly shouted with obvious excitement in his voice. "I love it!! I wanna become a black belt. Can I keep taking? Pleeease!?"

During Chris' summer experience, his parents had watched his progress carefully and noticed not only his innate ability, but also tremendous growth in his personal self-control. He no longer punished the furniture and threw random air kicks all over the place. They genuinely believed it was a good move and could even imagine the furniture lasting longer. After further consultation with Sensei Lance, they agreed to let him continue.

Over the next several years, Chris continued to progress, and in a relatively short time became the top student in the dojo. And by the time of this year's city tournament, he had, himself, advanced to become a third-degree black belt, and was unquestionably one of the best karate students in the entire city.

———————◆◆◆———————

When the referee started the match, the two began to circle the ring carefully and deliberately as they searched for weaknesses. Rock probed first with a fake low kick, then quickly turned and fired a roundhouse toward Chris' head. Chris saw it coming, though, and easily shifted out of the way.

Chris immediately shot his own roundhouse in an attempt to catch Rock while he was slightly off balance. But he was too good for that and easily ducked out of the way. Both fighters continued circling and probing with jabs and kicks, when suddenly Rock turned and threw a side kick that caught Chris square in the mid-section.

"Point red!" the referee yelled.

As he walked back to his corner to regain his composure, Chris knew he had to be more careful. He thought, *"The first one of us to three points wins, and I'm already down one. I've gotta be quicker!"*

"Hajime!" the referee yelled again to restart the match. The two carefully circled the ring once again looking for an opening. Suddenly, Rock faked a roundhouse kick to Chris' thigh, then quickly recoiled and shifted to strike at his head. Chris turned and lifted his leg to block the fake low kick, but when Rock turned and went high, Chris was not in a position to stop him, and the roundhouse head shot found its mark.

"Point red!" the ref shouted.

Chris was now down 0-2. At this point, it looked like Rock would take him out as easily as he had all the others. One more point and he would go home defeated.

Chris knew it was now or never. He had to do something dramatic just to keep himself in the match.

"Hajime!" the ref yelled out again.

In an attempt to catch Rock by surprise, Chris went straight in with a front kick to the mid-section. This time it was Rock who was caught off guard. No one expects that kind of direct attack right out of the gate because it's usually so easy to avoid. But this time it worked.

"Point blue!" the ref bellowed.

Getting even one point against Rock was never an easy matter, but this time Chris seemed to have done it so easily, and the shock of that point threw Rock completely off his game. And for some reason, Chris suddenly felt an entirely new level of confidence, as if a light bulb went off in his head. He consciously perceived a weakness he had not been able to capture before – and it was so clear. It was as if the fight started happening in slow motion. Suddenly, he could see Rock open up every time he shifted his weight.

With the score 1-2, the referee began the fight again. This time, Chris noticed how Rock would always take a double hop before throwing a roundhouse kick. If he hopped on his right foot, he would kick with his left, and vice versa. So the next time Rock moved in for a kick, Chris spotted the tell and twisted his own body to take advantage. When he saw Rock double hop on his right foot, he moved inside like a viper and struck with a left hook to the side of the head, catching Rock completely by surprise.

"Point blue," the ref yelled out.

It was now 2-2. Chris only needed one more point to take the match and win the championship.

With that second surprise, Rock totally lost his composure. He had never been in a position where someone had come back on him like that.

So when the referee started the match again, Rock, out of desperation, charged at Chris like a raging bull. That strategy is almost never a good one against an experienced fighter, and Chris simply blocked his attempted right hook and stepped to the side. Then, as Rock flew by, he threw his own backfist and caught Rock squarely on the side of the head.

"Match point blue," the referee yelled out.

Suddenly, the crowd went wild. It was an outcome no one expected, but many were excited to see.

Back in the ring, the fighters once again performed their ceremonial bows, then turned to face the crowd. The referee stepped between them, then raised his arm toward Chris, indicating he had won the match.

After the match was declared officially over, all of Chris' friends and family mobbed him in the middle of the ring. Everyone wanted a piece of the new hero. The local press also swarmed in to get their stories for the evening's local news. He then spent the next twenty minutes answering questions for the press while continually interrupted by his supporters. It was, perhaps, the most surreal moment of Chris' life.

The state tournament this year would take place just down the road in Skeptopolis. The thought of that location had a curious effect on Chris. He had been to Skeptopolis only a few times in his life, and always felt strange when he went. The city had been founded by committed Atheists and uber liberal Christian groups and was well known for its hostility toward Christians. Whenever Chris went there, he could actually sense an oppressive presence in the atmosphere.

But now, as he thought about going there to compete, another feeling arose – a totally unexpected one that shocked his senses. He began to sense that God wanted him to use this opportunity to somehow take the gospel to that God-hating place by way of his position in the tournament.

At first, he tried to dismiss the idea altogether. Why would anyone wanna spend time in that God-forsaken place, he thought to himself. Man, what am I thinkin'? I don't know anything about doin' that sorta thing, he reasoned as he tried to get his mind to change the subject. But the more he resisted, the stronger the sense of calling intruded into his mind. Finally, rather than continuing to push the thought aside, he decided he would seek the advice of some people he trusted. I know if this is of God, he reasoned, He'll open the doors for it to happen.

CHAPTER 2

AFTERGLOW!

After the tournament, Chris went home, cleaned up, and got dressed to go out and meet some friends to celebrate his victory. Their favorite place to meet was a park down by the river, dotted with colorful free-standing art, specifically crafted to express the wonder of God's creation. They especially liked to sit at a picnic table near the multi-colored metallic statue that looked like fire and ice spewing up out of the ground.

Abby, Zara, Levi, and Luke were Chris' closest friends and biggest cheerleaders. They had all been there to watch him win the title. On the way to the park, Levi peeled off and popped over to Joe's Burgers to pick up some of their famous steakburgers, along with Joe's famous homemade draft root beer.

As the crew walked together toward their favorite hangout, everyone was giddy. They couldn't stop talking about Chris' amazing victory over Rock. No one had ever bested Rock since he first took the city crown four years ago. They were ecstatic that their best friend had been the one to pull it off! Chris mostly just listened and smiled as his friends shared their blow-by-blow recollections.

"Yeah! What about that front kick!! Rock was totally caught off guard," Zara shouted out.

Luke chimed in, "And that backfist for the win … that was AWESOME!"

When the five arrived at the park, they found their usual picnic table under a giant oak that overlooked the river next to the fire and ice sculpture. As they quickly devoured their burgers, Chris' mood suddenly changed. A rather perplexed look appeared on his face as he seemed to drift off into his own little world. Rather than chiming in on the giddy celebration with his friends, he turned curiously silent. The dramatic shift quickly caught the attention of the others who turned to look at him with wrinkled brows. Seeing this, all four started asking Chris if he was okay. Chris hadn't even realized he had drifted off to never-never land – and their questions shocked him out of his trance.

As he snapped out of it and saw everyone staring at him, a wave of embarrassment swept over him and his face turned bright red. "Whoa, sorry 'bout that, guys. I don't know what came over me. All of a sudden I got lost in thought, and it just took me into another world."

"So what in the world were you thinkin' that zoned you out like that?" Zara asked, looking Chris straight in his eyes.

"Well, you know, guys," Chris replied, "I'm really excited about going over to Skeptopolis for the state tournament, but I've started feelin' a crazy compulsion to turn the trip into something bigger. I've been feeling God drawing me to use it as a personal mission trip and as an opportunity to share Christ. I've kinda been trying to resist the thought, but the more I do, the stronger God's calling seems to grab me. It's really makin' me nervous, and I don't know what to think – but I can't shake it."

All four were totally shocked. "Come on, Chris, you're not seriously thinkin' about bringing up religious faith over there, are you?" Abby stammered. "I mean, the people there *hate* Christians! No tellin' what they might try to do to you."

◆

Chris had long ago made a commitment to Christ that radically changed his life. He grew up in Templeton, and his family had been very active in church his entire life. Though, in his earlier years, the Christian faith hadn't been such a personal thing, it had still seemed like a normal part of his life.

In school, he was always one of the "cool kids." Known as a great athlete, and a straight-A student in class, everyone recognized his exceptional talent at whatever he tried. Even the not-so-popular kids liked him because he was nice to them.

Still, he remembered a time when he made some really bad choices that could've wrecked his entire future. In trying to be liked by everyone, he started hanging out with a beer drinking, pot smoking crowd. One day, after getting high with those friends, he nearly collided head-on with an oncoming car.

Fortunately, he was able to swerve out of the way at the last second, but his car spun around twice on the shoulder of the road before coming to a stop. When that happened, the profound shock kept him sitting there for an hour crying his eyes out and thinking, *What a stupid decision I made to get high. It just about got me killed.* While he knew what the Bible said about God and salvation, at that moment he began thinking about whether or not he would've gone to heaven if he had died – and right there on the spot, he told God he wanted to change his life. And from that moment he did – dramatically. He completely stepped away from the bad influences that nearly got him killed and recommitted his life to living faithfully for Christ.

———————◆◆◆———————

Abby, Zara, Levi, and Luke had been close friends with Chris since they were all young. They all lived in the same neighborhood and attended both church and school together. They also spent a lot of their free time hanging out and sharing their hopes and dreams. There wasn't much they didn't know about each other.

So when Abby so sharply voiced her objection about using the trip to Skeptopolis as a mission opportunity, Chris was taken aback – and honestly, the others were as well.

It was evident observing her life that Abby had a deep personal relationship with Christ. In fact, she often talked about the need for Christians to be more active sharing their faith. But Skeptopolis? That just seemed, at the moment, a bridge too far!

"So why the big objection?" Chris asked as he gave Abby a puzzled look. "I thought you, of all people, would be excited that someone was interested in going to that God-forsaken place to take the message of Christ. After all, you're exactly right, it's a place in desperate need of hearing about Jesus."

"I know," Abby responded feeling a bit ashamed that she came across that way, "but Skeptopolis is a really scary place. It has a reputation for chewin' Christians up and spittin' 'em out – both spiritually and physically. It's just not safe there and it makes me nervous for you."

Suddenly Levi broke into laughter. "Well, I feel pretty confident that Chris can take care of himself physically, so I'm not too worried about that. I mean, look what he just did to Rock." That comment refocused everyone's thoughts, and they all joined in the laughter at the absurdity of someone trying to take Chris on in a fight. "But tell me Chris," he said, "what in the world made you think that's a good idea? Now mind you, I'm not against you doin' it. But have you really considered all the implications of takin' on something like that? I mean, do you think you're ready for that kinda challenge?"

In some ways, it wasn't surprising that Levi would ask that question. After completing high school and college, he went to seminary to study for vocational Christian ministry. His dream was to one day become a pastor. But before going out on his own, he wanted a few years of being mentored. Their own pastor, Pastor Trumann, thought it a very wise decision, and offered him the opportunity to intern as a staff member at their church. So, when he finished his seminary training, Levi came back to their church and became an associate pastor.

Chris turned his head and looked up at the sky between the fire and ice sprays on the sculpture as he considered the best way to answer that question. He knew Levi was a deep thinker and wouldn't be satisfied with some superficial reply.

After a moment of collecting his thoughts, Chris responded, "You know, I've actually been thinking about this for some time now. I never thought about it deeply, or specifically what it might look like. I especially never thought about it in connection with karate. But the thought of makin' some kind of inroad into Skeptopolis has been a crazy thought I've had for quite a while. I'd sometimes even daydream about God doin' some kinda miraculous work to change that place. Honestly, I really haven't been willin' to talk about it to anyone until now because it's always seemed like a pipedream."

After a short pause to collect his thoughts, Chris continued, "I mean, I know the kinds of people who live there, and frankly it does seem like a scary place. But now that I have a genuine reason for goin' over there, the thought has bubbled back to the surface.

"Listen, I know there'll be people who'll try to trip me up intellectually. And I feel pretty certain there are others who'll throw out insults, and maybe even attack me physically. I know the shallow religious beliefs of the liberal churches there that basically just use religion as window dressing to promote social agendas. But there's also gotta be people who feel the emptiness in their lives and would be open to hearing a message that'll free their hearts. I honestly believe God has prepared me to reach out to them and given me an opportunity. I just feel this strong compulsion to do it."

"Wow, that's pretty compelling, Chris," Levi responded thoughtfully, starting to catch a little of the vision himself. "In some ways, that sounds a lot like the apostle Paul's experience in the city of Athens in Acts 17 when he spoke to the crowd gathered at the Areopagus."

Chris cocked his head to one side with a little grin and a nod toward Levi. "Yeah, that thought's actually crossed my mind a couple of times."

Hearing Chris share his vision, Zara, too, was moved by his sense of commitment to the people of Skeptopolis, and suddenly felt a compelling desire to encourage his vision. "Chris, what you're suggesting is scary to me, too. I definitely understand where Abby's comin' from. But wow, what a fantastic vision! And if God really is leading you to do it, then I'm totally convinced He'll take care of you. I can honestly envision God working a powerful miracle through you, and I want you to know you have my 100 percent support!"

When he heard Zara's moving endorsement, Luke also chimed in with unusual passion. "Me too, Chris! I'm totally on board. I think you'll do great things there!"

Hearing all the others put their support behind Chris, Abby chimed back in. "Chris, I still think you're nuts to even think about somethin' like that, and I hope I haven't put a damper on your vision. I know that if anybody can do it, it'd be you. It was just such a shock. But honestly, I'm really excited for you, too. I'm with the others. You have my 100 percent support."

All the affirmation from his friends moved Chris deeply. "Thank you guys for your encouragement. It means the world to me." So they all sat there for another thirty minutes finishing off their burgers and fries and re-living the day, then they headed back home.

CHAPTER 3

IN THE SWEET SHOP

When the group left the park, they had to walk past Merchant's Row, a brightly lit, popular hot spot in town with lots of local shops and eateries.

As they passed by, Amy looked to her left and saw the Sweet Shop's flashing neon sign begging her to get some ice cream. "Hey guys, I'm cravin' some ice cream. Wanna go to the Sweet Shop and get some with me?"

Everyone stopped dead in their tracks and looked at each other. "You know," Luke spoke out first, "ya got me on that one." The others immediately fell in line, and they turned and headed over.

When they opened the front door, the sweet aroma of ice cream and the bright décor instantly bombarded their senses. The playful and fun Sweet Shop welcomed their customers with colorful neon lights and posters of smiling people eating ice cream all throughout the shop.

When they walked in, no one was in front of them, so Chris walked straight up to the counter. He already knew what he wanted and ordered a two-scoop butter pecan sundae topped with butterscotch. "I love this place," he declared, as he paid for his frozen treat. "You can't get real butterscotch topping just anywhere." Chris immediately dug into his frozen treat and moseyed over to an empty table in the corner. The rest of the group followed suit, joining him there.

After everyone settled in with their frozen treats, Chris asked the group a question. "Guys, if you tried to tell someone about Jesus and they told you that you were stupid for believin' in Him, what'd you say?"

At first, no one responded, too busy eating their sweet treats.

But the thought of going to Skeptopolis weighed too heavily on his mind and he just couldn't let it go. He sincerely wanted his friends' opinions, so he asked again. "Hey guys, really ... what would you say if someone called you stupid for believin' in Jesus?"

---◆---

Chris was all too familiar with the history of Skeptopolis. Most of its original settlers had actually moved there from Templeton. Years ago, Templeton was known to be an especially God-fearing place where Christian values influenced the culture. Templeton had negligible crime, people were kind and honest, and that atmosphere permeated a society known to be generally prosperous and generous.

There came a time, though, when a large number of people from the outside moved into town to take advantage of such an idyllic place. This created a new problem however, as many of those new people had an entirely different set of values – which they brought with them.

At first, that great influx didn't cause much of a stir because the people of Templeton welcomed outsiders – for the most part. Beyond that, it seemed as though most of the newcomers self-identified as Christians, and naturally became active in the various local churches around town.

Over time, though, it became evident that most of the newcomers believed quite differently from the townspeople. While they talked about God and quoted from the Bible, theirs was more a "cultural Christianity," as opposed to the evangelical strain prominent in Templeton. Many were not remotely interested in sharing the Good News about salvation in Christ with people who didn't know Him. Instead, they began advocating for a primary focus on "meeting the material needs of their fellow man."

Of course, that kind of service to humanity has profound Christian value, but these newcomers did not focus on doing good deeds as a means for spreading the gospel message. They considered doing good deeds to be an end in itself, and over time many of them, while active in their churches, actually quit believing the message of Christ and salvation altogether. For them, the church was just another social action organization. As time passed, many even quit going to church at all. In fact, some even became hard core Atheists.

Others, however, remained in their churches and got involved – even to the point of becoming church leaders. Sadly, this focus on **social justice** and a **progressive ideology** created a great deal of internal strife and division in a number of the churches. Several even split over these newcomers' **liberal theological** activism.

At some point, though, the old timers, who had finally come to understand what was happening, began pushing back by clearly contrasting the true message of **historic Christianity** with the newly introduced false teachings. As more and more of the **faithful church community** woke up to the threat, they started calling out the **false teachings** and pushing them aside.

Seeing that the tide had turned against them, a large and influential group of the newcomers organized into a political block and attempted to take over what they could – not just churches, but political offices, businesses, and other local institutions as well. It didn't work out well, though. They didn't have the manpower to actually pull off the coup. On top of that, when they realized they would not get their way, many carried a grudge and began acting out in ways that alienated most of the townspeople even further.

One day, a small group of wealthy individuals decided on a different strategy. They found a massive plot of land about 40 miles away from Templeton and bought it for the purpose of starting their own town. They wanted a place where they wouldn't have to deal with the "narrow-mindedness" of the people of Templeton.

In relatively short order, the idea caught on and about 200 people moved to the new location. Over the next five years they organized themselves well enough to become their own town. They hoped – of course – to overtly contrast their "**paradise**" with what they considered to be the **narrow-mindedness** and **intolerance** of Templeton, deciding to name their town *Skeptopolis*. They actually wanted to be known for – and fly the flag of – their **skepticism** of traditional Christianity.

Over the succeeding years, as the new town's infrastructure developed, a steady trickle of people continued to flow from Templeton to Skeptopolis. In addition to "defectors" from Templeton, like-minded skeptics of Christianity came from surrounding areas, and over the decade the fledgling town grew into a sizable city with a current population of around 100,000, with its own college, town government, police force, public schools, businesses, entertainment establishments, and even its own skid row. While you could find a few churches in town, all were quite small and followed some form of extra biblical or non-biblical theology focused on progressive ideas about social justice.

The vast majority of townspeople, however, were Atheists – and mostly antagonistic ones, at that. They didn't like Christians at all – at least not **evangelicals**.

Over the years, many Christians attempted making inroads for the **gospel** in Skeptopolis. In fact, some Templeton churches even tried sending short-term missionaries; a few even making long-term commitments and moving to the city. Not a single person found success, however, or even lasted long enough to establish a beachhead. The hostility and oppression of the leadership and town's culture seemed insurmountable.

As the friends sat around finishing their ice cream, Levi finally answered Chris' question, "You know, right, that if you go to Skeptopolis and try to share your faith in Christ, you won't be welcome there? I mean, you'll probably get a cold reception just competing in the state karate tournament. But if you try to bring up Jesus, you realize they're gonna accuse you of bein' **ignorant** and **naïve**."

"I know," Chris responded, "that's why I asked the question. What would you say to 'em if they called *you* ignorant?"

Levi leaned back in his chair to ponder that thought. While he was thinking, Abby chimed in, "I have no idea what I'd say. That'd be really hard." Hearing that, Zara and Luke both pursed their lips together and nodded in agreement.

With that, Chris dropped his eyes and muttered in a barely audible voice, "Yeah, it wouldn't be a comfortable position to be in. But if I go, it's bound to happen, and I need to know how to respond."

"So what are you gonna do?" Zara asked. "If you go, you'll havta respond in a way that gets through to 'em or your entire effort'll be meaningless."

"Yeah, I know you're right, Zara," Chris answered. "I'm gonna have to put in some serious effort and get up to speed on all the things I need to know."

"So how're you gonna do it?" Luke asked, as he, himself, began to feel the mounting frustration.

"Well, would you mind if I brainstormed for a few minutes with you guys?" Chris replied, trying to create a friendly environment that would help him think it through. "I don't really know yet what I might say, but I need to organize my thoughts to begin figurin' it out. I need to come up with a plan. Would you guys mind bein' my sounding board?"

"Of course not," Levi replied, answering for the group. "Tell us what you're thinkin'."

Chris began, "Well, the first thing I prob'ly need to do is go to the library and do some research on Atheist beliefs, and probably read some books about it. I remember Pastor Trumann recently recommended one called *The Truth Mirage*. That might be a good place to start! I have a superficial sense of what Atheists believe from bein' in his **discipleship** training classes at church. He really does a great job equipping us to understand other worldview beliefs. But I need to go even deeper to learn specifically where the folks in Skeptopolis are comin' from. And more importantly, *why* do they believe what they do? Then, after I do my research at the library. I probably oughta go over and talk in more detail with Pastor Trumann and get his practical input. He probably has experience and insights that'll help me."

Abby jumped in, "Hey, here's another idea. You know, there are some people who actually used to live in Skeptopolis – people who've found Christ and had their lives turned around. You oughta talk to some of them, too. I bet people like that could give you some *really* good info – and they might even know some folks over there who would be nice to you when ya go."

"Hmmm., That's a great idea, Abby!" Chris replied enthusiastically. "That'd be Isaac and Joy Marvel. They're friends of mine, and I know they'd be more than happy to share their insights. I'll definitely do that."

After brainstorming a little while longer, they finished their ice cream, and headed home. By that time, Chris was ready to crash.

CHAPTER 4

FIRST STEPS

Before heading to the library to begin his research, Chris sat at the desk in his room and pondered the task ahead. *The first thing I need,* he thought, *is to clarify the specific things I need to know when I interact with people in Skeptopolis.* There were lots of things he *could* study, but he wanted to make sure he was going after the *right* things.

He pulled out a piece of paper and began to brainstorm. At the top of his paper he wrote: "Questions to Research: *I'm gonna think of everything I can and write those down, then refine the list,* he thought. So, he began writing down everything that came to mind.

So, what do I already know about the people in Skeptopolis? I know most of 'em are Atheists, so I need to know specifically what Atheists believe. I know they claim they **don't** believe in God, but what **do** they believe?

I also know they have different moral values from me, so I need to know what those values are and how they decide on the ones they follow. Beyond that, they must have some authority source for understanding what's right and wrong. What do they look to in order to determine moral beliefs?

Hmm, what else? As he kept thinking, he came up with some other ideas. I know they put a lot of emphasis on science. Atheists are claiming all the time that Christians don't believe in science. That's not true, but why do they have that misconception?

And are there other things? Oh, I know; I need to understand why they get so upset at Christian beliefs? I definitely disagree with their beliefs and want to share with them the truth about Christ, but I don't get angry just because they believe somethin' different – like they often do towards Christians. What's up with that?

And now that I think of it, there's one other thing that has me curious. I've noticed that not all Atheists believe all the same things. Are there different versions of Atheism?

After he finished brainstorming, Chris pulled all his notes together, wrote out a list, then reduced it to what he considered the most important questions. *Hmm, that seems like a pretty good list,* Chris thought as he looked it over once again. *If I can find out the answers to these questions, I should be in good shape to understand what I'm walkin' into.*

Questions to Research

1. What do Atheists believe?
2. Where do Atheist beliefs come from?
3. Where do Atheist values come from?
4. How do Atheists think about science?
5. How do Atheist beliefs affect their attitudes?
6. Are there different variations of Atheism?

With the list complete, Chris grabbed his backpack with all his stuff and headed over to the public library.

The library was downtown, about two miles from home. With nice weather on this afternoon, he decided to ride his bike and went out through the garage where he jumped on his bike and took off – enjoying the fresh air and exercise.

Chris pulled up to the bicycle rack in front of the library, got off, and chained it to the rack. *It's a shame to go inside on such a beautiful day,* he thought to himself. *Man, I sure would love to just sit down in the shade of that giant oak and enjoy the brisk air. But these questions aren't gonna answer themselves! I gotta go inside and do some research.*

When he walked in, Chris noticed there were not too many people around, so he headed straight toward the front desk to talk to the librarian.

Mrs. Chambers had been the public librarian for nearly 40 years. Over the years, Chris often went to the library to do research for school papers. He'd known Mrs. Chambers his whole life.

"Mrs. Chambers, how are you this afternoon?" Chris greeted her as he walked up to the counter.

"Why thank you for asking, Chris," she replied with a great big smile on her face. She was always happy to see Chris come in and hadn't seen him much since he graduated from college. "I'm doing very well. It's a wonderful day to be alive." Always ready with a cheerful comment, Mrs. Chambers made it easy to approach her.

"Mrs. Chambers, where might I find books about Atheism? I'm doing some research and need to study that topic a little deeper."

"Oh, is this to prepare for your efforts in Skeptopolis?"

Chris was shocked by her response, and it showed by the look on his face. He hadn't told anyone his plans except his friends. "How'd you know about that?"

"Oh, come on, Chris ... Templeton has surely grown a lot over the years, but it's still small enough to where exciting news spreads fast. Actually, your friends are VERY excited about what you're contemplating, and they're all talking about it. You're really lucky to have good friends like that."

"I should've known," Chris replied, with a chuckle in his voice. "So where would be the best place to start doing my research?"

Mrs. Chambers thought for a second, then replied, "Well, you might want to begin by looking it up in several of the encyclopedias in the reference section. That'll start you out with a good overview. After that, I'd head over to the religion section to get some more in-depth reading. There you'll find books written specifically about Atheism, some even written by Atheists themselves. That'll help you look at that belief system from a different perspective. And – while you're doing that – I'll look through some periodicals to see if I can find anything that might be useful."

"Thanks Mrs. Chambers, that'd be a great help. I'll check back with you after a while."

Chris headed over to the reference section and found himself a table. He set his backpack on the floor and pulled out a chair to sit and review his list of questions. Before going over to the stack, though, he pulled out his laptop and looked up some terms on the internet. After a little while, he went to the reference section and pulled out four different encyclopedias before heading back to his table.

After finding what he could from the encyclopedias, he walked over to the religion section. It took more time and effort there, as the information in those books went much deeper. But a bit of careful browsing led him to pick out three books with the type of information he was after. He took them over and laid them on his table.

After selecting the books he wanted, he walked back to Mrs. Chambers' desk to see what periodicals she might have found. She pulled out five magazines, and handed him two editions of *Free Inquiry* magazine, published by the **Council for Secular Humanism**, two editions of *The Humanist Magazine*, published by the **American Humanist Association**, and one edition of *Skeptical Inquirer Magazine*, put out by the **Center for Inquiry**. All had articles dealing directly with the values and mindset of Atheists written by Atheists themselves.

Chris took them back to his table, then sat down and began skimming through the books and magazines that seemed most pertinent to his search. When he finished, he packed up his things to leave. As he headed for the door and came to the front desk, he made a point of speaking to Mrs. Chambers one more time. "I really found some great stuff – thanks so much for your help."

"You're certainly welcome, Chris," she cheerfully responded. "Let me know if there's anything else I can do for you."

Chris had spent nearly four hours researching his list of questions and when he was finally done, he felt really good about it. Next, he wanted to organize the material and write up a summary report he could use as an outline to study more deeply. Once he did that, he planned to call his friends together again and share what he had learned.

It had, indeed, been a fruitful day.

CHAPTER 5

AT THE PARK AGAIN

"Hey Abby," Chris asked as they spoke on the phone, "do you suppose you could pull the gang together one more time and let me bounce a few things off you guys? I've been researching the beliefs of the people of Skeptopolis, and I'd like to get your feedback."

After pulling together all of his research from the library, Chris had taken about two weeks to compile and organize it – making it more useful for his in-depth understanding of Atheism. He had a ton of information, and it was a tedious task in putting it all together. But he finally felt good about what he had learned and was ready to get some feedback from his friends.

"Sure," Abby responded, "that'd be great. I'll call everybody and we can meet this evening at our usual place in the park after dinner. Say 7:00?"

"Perfect! Thanks, Abby. Look forward to seein' you guys then." After hanging up, Chris thought to himself, *This is really gonna help me get all my thoughts organized.*

At 6:30, Chris headed to the park. Since he was the first one there, he went to their favorite spot, sat down at the picnic table, pulled out his notes, and waited for his friends. The sun had begun to set, and the park lights began to flicker on as the sun crept below the tree line. All that, along with the soothing babble of the flowing river, created the perfect environment – a great backdrop for a discussion with his friends.

About five minutes later, Abby and Zara walked up together and sat down across the table from Chris. Shortly after, Levi showed up and sat next to Abby.

"Where's Luke?" Chris asked the group.

"Oh, he'll be here in a minute," Zara laughed out loud. "You know Luke." With that, everyone laughed out loud.

That really was Luke. And sure enough, about three minutes later, he came sauntering around the corner. "Hi guys," Luke shouted out as he slid in beside Chris, "what's happenin'?" Everybody started laughing again.

"What's so funny?" Luke asked with a quizzical look on his face. "Did I miss somethin'?"

"No," Abby shot back with a solid chuckle in her voice, "you didn't miss anything," which started a whole new round of laughter.

Luke wrinkled his brow and looked at everyone, wondering what was going on. "It's just you," Zara chimed in. "We were laughin' because we were just talkin' about how you'd be here shortly – and late."

"Sorry guys," Luke said through his sheepish grin as he started laughing with the rest of them. "I know. Somehow that's just me."

Finally, Chris jumped in to get things going. "Guys," he began, "as you know, I went to the library a couple of weeks ago and started researching what I might come up against when I go to Skeptopolis. I found *tons* of material and made lots of notes. When I finished, I organized it into several categories that I think make it easy to understand. I structured it around six questions and wanted to get your feedback. Here are the questions."

Chris then began to list them, from one to six, as follows:

1. What do Atheists believe?
2. Where do Atheist beliefs come from?
3. Where do Atheist values come from?
4. How do Atheists think about science?
5. How do Atheist beliefs affect their attitudes?
6. Are there different variations of Atheism? If so, what are they?

"So, using those questions, I wanna share with you what I've learned."

"Hey, that sounds like a really interesting way to do it," Zara responded. "Let's see what you got."

"Okay," Chris began. "The first question is, 'What do Atheists believe?' You'd think this would be pretty easy to answer, but it's actually more complicated than it seems."

"More complicated?" Levi interrupted. "What could be complex about that?"

"Well," Chris continued, "if you ask most Atheists what they believe, they generally just respond, 'I don't believe in God.'"

Abby gave Chris a puzzled look, "Well, that's exactly what I'd expect. What's wrong with that answer?"

"Well," Chris answered back, "that doesn't tell you *anything* about what they *do* believe. It only tells you what they *don't* believe. If you think about it, that's no answer at all."

"Hmmm! Now that you mention it, you're exactly right. That really is a nothing answer. So, what exactly *do* they believe, then?"

"As I dug a little deeper," Chris went on, "I discovered there are basically two different kinds of Atheists. One type is like **Hindus**, **Buddhists**, and other groups that hold **Far Eastern pantheistic** beliefs. They believe there is some kind of existence outside of our physical universe, but there is no actual **god**. They believe in a kind of impersonal **life force** – like 'the force' in Star Wars. But that's not the kind of Atheists who live in Skeptopolis."

"Hmm," Luke grunted out, "that's interesting. I never thought about that before, but it makes sense. So, what kind of Atheists are in Skeptopolis?"

"The Atheists in Skeptopolis are **naturalistic** Atheists," Chris explained. "Those are people who believe that the natural universe, operating by **natural laws**, is all that exists."

Abby interrupted, "Wait, let me make sure I get what you're sayin'. You're sayin' that since they believe God doesn't exist, then everything that does exist had to somehow come into existence based on the **laws of nature**, is that right?"

"Exactly!" Chris replied approvingly, nodding his head. "And for that to be true, there are four basic things that also *must* be true. First, the matter and energy that make up the physical universe has to be eternal or have somehow come into existence out of nothing. Second, life had to have emerged out of non-living chemicals. Third, all living things in the world had to come into existence by natural evolutionary processes. And fourth, consciousness had to naturally evolve out of non-conscious life forms. Those are the positive beliefs that make up the Atheism believed by the people in Skeptopolis."

"Wow, that's pretty heavy," Luke gasped. "I've never thought about it that way before."

"Ok," Chris continued, "that's the first question. The second question is, "Where do Atheist beliefs come from?"

"I'm all ears," Zara chimed in. "So where did those beliefs come from?"

Looking at Zara, since she asked the question, Chris explained, "Well, Zara, answering that question requires some historical background. I've already mentioned that the atheist beliefs in Skeptopolis come from **naturalistic Atheism** – the belief that the natural universe, operating by natural laws, is all that exists. Apparently, this particular belief can be nominally traced back to ancient Greece.

Chris continued, "But the way it's understood in modern times traces back to the beginning of modern science – during the Renaissance in the 15 and 1600s. The first people who really started getting into and developing the modern understanding of science were actually Christians who believed God created the universe in an orderly way, and that human beings are capable of studying and understanding it. You probably studied in school about people like Galileo and Sir Isaac Newton."

"Yeah, I remember studyin' about them in school, as well as about the Renaissance period," Abby chimed in.

"But over time," Chris continued, "as scientists began to accumulate more knowledge, some began thinking that if they could just advance enough, technologically, humans could learn *everything* there is to know about how the universe operates. And gradually, that led some to think that God wasn't needed at all for the universe to get going and continue. From that, a whole philosophy developed called **Naturalism**."

"It makes sense that Atheism would be a natural result of that kind of thinking," Luke remarked as he leaned in to get a more direct view of Chris. "I see how it could've developed that way. So how about the third question, 'Where do Atheist values come from?'"

"Now I found the answer to this question to be really interesting, Luke," Chris responded. "Once again, the answer flows naturally out of the belief that God does not exist. As Christians, we believe certain things about what is right and wrong don't we?" Chris asked.

Everyone took in that question and, after a moment of reflection, nodded their heads. Seeing their agreement, he went on. "So where exactly do our **moral beliefs** come from?"

Abby piped up, "From the Bible."

"Exactly right! That's our authority source." Chris paused a moment to let that sink in, then continued, "So that brings us to the third question. Since

Atheists don't believe in God, what could possibly be *their* **authority source** for determining what's right and wrong?"

At that, everyone just sat there staring at Chris. They were all searching their minds to come up with an answer. *What could it possibly be?*

After a moment, Chris explained. "Guys, since they don't believe God exists, they don't have an all-powerful, outside source they call on to tell 'em what's right and wrong. All they have is their own feelings or preferences. They have to make up their own moral beliefs as they go along. Now, what I personally find fascinating is that if you ask 'em about what's right and wrong, almost to a person, they'll tell you things like 'it is wrong to kill, or steal, or lie.' But they don't have any *reason* – outside of their own personal preferences – for judging those things wrong. So, for Atheists, their own personal opinions are the source of their **moral values**. Basically, they're their own god."

When Chris finished explaining that, everyone just sat there for a minute soaking it in. "That's totally fascinating, Chris," Zara finally said, breaking the silence.

"Yeah, really deep," Luke agreed. "That'll give me somethin' to think about for a while."

"Okay, so what's the fourth question again?" Abby asked.

Zara chimed in, "How do Atheists think about science?" She was the organized one and had written them all down.

"Exactly!" Chris exclaimed. "We've already touched on this a little, so I probably don't need to give a long explanation here, but there are some things worth mentioning."

"So, what else do we need to know about this," Luke asked.

"Well first of all, we need to make sure we're all on the same page about exactly what science is," Chris explained. "One of the things I discovered is that it's not at all unusual for Atheists to claim certain pivotal things are based on science, when they're really not. As for a definition, **science** is the use of observation and experimentation to discover things about the natural universe. Because Christians believe in miracles, Atheists often accuse us of not believing in science. Of course, that's simply false.

"The fact that Christians believe in God doesn't cancel out our belief in using the **scientific method** to study and learn things about God's creation. We absolutely *do* believe that. The difference between us and Atheists is that they believe the natural universe is *all* that exists, and that *EVERYTHING* can ultimately be learned through science – which is totally bogus."

"You know," Abby chimed in, "I've never heard anyone actually *say* that, but when I think about what's taught in a lotta schoolbooks – they explain things *as if* that were true. I've even had moments when that very thing has caused me to have doubts about my own Christian faith."

"Abby," Chris responded, "that's a *great* observation. And that explains the view of science that Atheists hold. They truly believe that everything, in all of existence, can ultimately be explained by science. So, they end up accusing anyone who believes in God of being **anti-science**. What they don't realize, though, is that their *own* belief – that the natural universe, operating by natural laws, is all that exists – is not a scientific belief. They actually believe it by **faith**."

"Whoa!" Levi blurted out. "Now that's heavy! And what a great insight! I never thought about it quite like that before, but that's exactly the way modern science books approach the subject. For instance, they teach *definitively* that the **Theory of Evolution** is true. In fact, many of 'em call it '**settled science**,' even though there's no actual scientific proof!"

"And," Luke added, "I'm readin' articles all the time in science magazines and newspapers where scientists simply assume there's life on other planets – again with no actual scientific proof. Man, this is great!"

That answer really caught everyone's imagination and they discussed its implications among themselves for several minutes. Finally, though, Zara felt they had dealt with it enough, so she interrupted the conversation and said, "So let's move on to the next question. I wanna hear more."

"Okay," Chris replied, "the next question is, 'How do atheist's beliefs affect their attitudes?' This question's important because – if I'm gonna go to their house and live among 'em – I need to have a handle on what makes 'em tick emotionally."

"Yeah, that *is* somethin' you'll have to deal with," Abby remarked as she pondered the implications of the question.

"Answering this question takes me back to what I said earlier about what's right and wrong," Chris continued, "and a little bit about what I said about science, as well."

"How so?" Levi asked, as he tried to fully absorb what Chris had just said.

Chris explained further, "You know how I said they have to make up their moral beliefs on their own, and how there's no actual science to back up their beliefs about the origin and development of the natural universe?"

Everyone nodded as his question brought to mind what they had just been talking about. "Well, putting it plainly, Atheism is a **religious belief**. It's a religion that promotes the idea that people who disagree with them about morality and about science are simply ignorant prudes.

"So, when I go to Skeptopolis and start sharing that God does exist, and that He's revealed right morality in the Bible ... and when I tell 'em their view of the natural universe is not based on science, they're gonna push back on me pretty hard. Those beliefs determine the entire foundation for their attitudes."

"You know, I think you're on to somethin'," Abby responded as Chris' explanation began to sink in. "Do you think you're ready to handle the blowback you're gonna get when you do that?"

Chris nodded, "Well, I'm sure I'm not gonna like it, but I think I'm ready. I really believe God is sending me on this mission, and His Spirit in me'll guide my steps."

"Okay ... last question. 'Are there different variations of Atheism?' And if so, what are they?"

"Wait," Luke blurted out as he remembered back to when Chris first started, "you already answered that one. You already told us about the Far Eastern variety of Atheism."

"You're right, Luke," Chris replied, "but there's another category of 'different' you also need to get."

Luke's brow wrinkled up as he gave Chris a quizzical look. "Huh? What's that?"

"You see," Chris continued, "there are different forms of *naturalistic* Atheism – different denominations, if you will."

"Different forms?" Levi blurted out. "Like what?"

"That's what I'm about to tell you," Chris chuckled realizing Luke and Levi were getting ahead of themselves. "Have you guys ever heard of **Existentialism**?"

Zara chimed in, "Yeah, we studied about that in English class. That's a belief that was popular in the 19th and 20th centuries. It emphasizes how individuals are responsible for creating their own lives by their own will."

"Right," Chris replied. "And what about **Secular Humanism**? Have you heard of that?"

"I have," Abby blurted out. "I have an uncle who claims to be a Secular Humanist. They believe human beings are able to know what is moral and not moral without believin' in God ..."

Suddenly, in mid-sentence, Abby stopped, then started back, "Hey, I knew I'd heard some of the stuff you were talking about before. My uncle is that kind of Atheist. Oh wow! Now this is all startin' to make sense."

"Perfect, Abby," Chris responded, glad she was beginning to make the connections. "So here's another one," he continued. "How 'bout **Postmodernism**? Have you heard of that one?"

"Oh I have," Zara spoke up. "We talked about that in my philosophy class in college. People who believe in that think everyone is right no matter what they believe. They believe that truth is individual and personal, so you can have your truth and I can have mine – and we're both right. Seems weird to me, but that's what they believe."

"You're exactly right, Zara," Chris acknowledged as he prepared to draw his conclusion. "So, do you know what all these beliefs have in common?"

Levi's eyes lit up and he jumped in, "I see it ... I think. All those beliefs are atheistic!"

"Exactly right," Chris affirmed Levi's observation. "But not just atheistic, they all represent **naturalistic Atheism** – and there are others, as well, like **Agnosticism** and **Marxism**. I think you guys are gettin' it."

With that, Chris was ready to wrap up his report. "Well, that's all I got," he said. "What do you think?"

"Man," Levi practically shouted, "I'm pooped! That was so intense it boggled my brain! I need to think about this a little more." The rest of the group nodded in agreement.

"Well Chris, is that everything or is there somethin' else you think you need?" Luke asked.

"Well, that's really about everything. What do you guys think?" Chris asked.

Levi responded as he spoke for the group and started to get up, "Chris, I think you've done a knock-out job with this – like you did to Rock in the tournament!" Amidst the chuckles from the comment about Rock, Levi continued, "Listen, I hate to be the party-pooper here, but I really need to head out. I have a counseling appointment in just a little bit."

The rest of the group followed his lead, and as they got up, Chris profusely thanked them for coming. "Guys, I think I've pulled this material together pretty well, but I wanted to make sure I was able to actually talk about what I found. Sometimes I can put a paper together, but not actually know the material well enough to explain it. This has been a great help. Thanks so much."

"No, thank you, Chris," Zara replied. "This has been exhilarating!"

Then, one by one, each of them expressed thanks to Chris for trusting them. It was a consensus feeling that they got as much out of it as he did. It would be a long time, if ever, before they would forget this pow-wow.

CHAPTER 6

ISAAC AND JOY

After talking with his friends, Chris felt the need to know more about the people who lived in Skeptopolis. The best way to get that insight, he figured, was to have a conversation with people who had actually lived there. As it turned out, a couple from church who were close family friends had not only lived there for 35 years but had once been Atheists themselves. Chris was sure they knew the lay of the land and could give him better insights into how best to go about interacting with the people of Skeptopolis. So he picked up the phone and called Isaac and Joy Marvel.

"Isaac, this is Chris. I'm sure you've already heard that I'm going to Skeptopolis for a while as a sort of mission trip. Would it be okay if I came over and picked your and Joy's brains about the people and culture there. I'm just tryin' to get as much insight as I can before I start."

"Of course, Chris. We've heard rumors of that and would be happy to share what we can with you."

Chris first met Isaac and Joy Marvel a number of years back when they started going to his church. At that time, they had just moved from Skeptopolis to Templeton because they came to know Christ and found it nearly impossible to continue living in a place where they were increasingly shunned because of their faith. In spite of the fact they were both very competent, highly educated individuals and held prestigious, good paying jobs, they were basically cancelled, forced out, and ostracized.

Isaac and Joy were both born and raised in Skeptopolis by Atheist families. They had attended school together all the way through 12th grade and became high school sweethearts their senior year. They dated throughout their college years and got married shortly after graduation.

After getting married, they continued their studies – both getting their master's and doctorate degrees at Skeptopolis University. Joy had studied Western Literature and took a job teaching at the university. Isaac earned his degrees in evolutionary biology and landed a job with an ecology firm doing research on sustainable energy sources. Both were highly respected in their fields.

Chris had heard each of them share their personal **testimonies** and their remarkable path to the Christian faith on multiple occasions.

Apparently, Isaac was the first to begin his search. It seems that while doing basic research in the field of evolutionary biology at graduate school, several things about the Theory of Evolution had made him a little uncomfortable and caused him to question what he had learned. At first, he simply tried to ignore the inconsistencies – and that worked for a while. After all, EVERY-ONE around him was fully committed to the belief. With all that brain power believing in it, didn't that mean it had to be true?

But one day, while working on a company research project they needed some outside expertise to complete the project. So they asked a consultant to come in and collaborate. While experimenting with some organic compounds in the production of electricity, the topic of the Theory of Evolution came up, and this visitor voiced his skepticism out loud in front of Isaac. The doubts he expressed made such compelling sense that, combined with his suppressed doubts, it caused Isaac's personal concerns to bubble back to the surface.

To satisfy his curiosity, Isaac reached out and invited this company guest to dinner at a local restaurant, just to hear his perspective. They ended up talking well into the night, and that conversation only served to produce even more doubt in Isaac's mind about evolutionary theory.

It bothered him so much that he spent the next six weeks digging deeper. By the end of that six weeks, Isaac had become completely convinced that what this "outsider" had said was true. When he finally arrived at that conclusion, it was such a shock to his system that he pretty much gave up on naturalistic evolutionary theory altogether. Of course, he didn't mention any of this to his co-workers for fear they would ridicule, or even shun, him.

But he did begin talking about it to Joy. She was a bit concerned when he first brought it up, but felt it was her wifely duty to help him work through it. So, they started discussing the topic every day, point by point, to try to get at the truth. But the more they talked, and as Isaac systematically expounded on the inconsistencies, the more doubt Joy began to experience in her own mind – until one day she said, "Isaac, you're right. Evolutionary theory simply can't be true."

At that point, Isaac did feel a certain amount of personal satisfaction that she had come over to his way of thinking. But their newfound conclusion left both of them with a huge dilemma. If they no longer believed in naturalistic evolutionary theory, what did they believe? Was it possible God really existed after all?

As hard as both of them found it to go that far, they felt they were already in too deep not to pursue the matter to the end. So, they decided to buy a Bible and just start reading it. In doing some of their research on the internet, they read one article suggesting that the Gospel of John was a good place to start. That seemed reasonable since it was a recorded history about the beginning of the Christian faith, so they started reading and discussing what they read.

After reading the Bible for a couple of weeks, both of them began experiencing something that neither anticipated. All of a sudden one evening, Isaac just blurted out, "I believe this! It comes across as truth." When he did that, Joy started bawling. Seeing her upset like that, Isaac put his arm around her and said, "What's wrong, honey? Why are you upset?"

"I don't know what's come over me," Joy responded, "but I believe it, too. I believe it's true."

After that, their lives changed dramatically. Over the next few weeks, they slowly began to mention their newfound beliefs in private conversations with people they trusted at work. In both situations, word began leaking out to their bosses. After a time, each of them was "called on the carpet" to be schooled by their respective higher ups who tried doggedly to talk them down from their "delusions" about belief in God.

While going through that process, Isaac and Joy searched all over for other believers they could connect with. They felt so alone. There were several churches in town, so they began visiting them one-by-one to get some support. They quickly discovered, however, that the people in those churches also didn't really believe what was written in the Bible. These "church people" had a different focus having little to do with the Bible. They spent their time advocating for social justice and for people "oppressed" by society. Content to focus all of their efforts on social service and political activism, Isaac and Joy just couldn't make themselves get onboard with it. It somehow just didn't seem right.

Not finding a single church that seemed to match up with what they read in the Bible, one Sunday they decided to drive the 40 miles over to Templeton "just to see" if they might find something different there. On that very first Sunday they visited Chris' church and were taken aback at the difference from all they'd experienced in Skeptopolis churches. They genuinely connected with the sermon – in a way they had not experienced at any church in Skeptopolis. After the service, they went and spoke to the pastor who invited them over for lunch.

After lunch they talked for the rest of the afternoon about their experiences and the nature of the Christian faith. In that conversation, Pastor Trumann clearly shared the gospel message with them, and they affirmed that they had genuinely received Christ into their lives. From that day forward, they began driving to Templeton to attend church every week and were baptized shortly afterwards.

In the meantime, the environment they faced at work continued to deteriorate. Their coworkers simply could not tolerate the fact that Isaac and Joy could believe that silly Christian stuff. About four weeks after being baptized, Isaac's boss called him into the office and gave him his walking papers. A week later, Joy's boss did the same thing.

To both of them, the blow seemed devastating at first. What they didn't realize at the time, however, was that God had it all worked out. When they shared their situation with Pastor Trumann, he immediately began networking with people he knew. Within a few weeks, both Isaac and Joy had new jobs lined up in Templeton: Isaac as a professor at Templeton University, and Joy as chief editor with a book publisher. Shortly thereafter, they themselves moved to Templeton. That was 20 years ago.

Having been just eight years old when the Marvels started coming to his church, Chris still remembered them from their early years at the church and got to know them very quickly. The people in the church community all rallied around them, and Chris' mom and dad often invited them over for dinner. Their families had become quite close over the years.

Because Chris had such a long-time connection with them and knew their story, he thought of them instantly while preparing for his mission in Skeptopolis. Chris was also friends with their two kids, Joe and Marilyn, a few years older than him. They had gone to college out of state and had jobs in other cities, so he actually hadn't seen them in a few years.

When Chris arrived at the Marvel's house, Joy warmly welcomed him in. They lived in a solidly middle-class development in the fastest growing part of town. They had moved there about five years previously when the developer had offered some sweet deals to entice buyers into his brand-new project. All the houses in that neighborhood were painted in very bright colors to make it look somewhat like a fantasy land – and making it a neat place to drive through.

Chris pulled up to their bright blue house and stepped inside. Looking to the right, he noticed the nice large living room and admired their open kitchen and dining room on the left. Straight ahead was a hallway leading to three bedrooms and a cozy den they had turned into a game room. You could also see the pool in their back yard through the windows.

Joy directed him over to the dining room table, then she and Isaac took their seats across from him. "Well, before we begin," Chris inquired, "how are Joe and Marilyn? I haven't seen 'em in a while. I hope they're doin' well."

"Thanks for asking," Isaac answered. "They're both doin' very well. Joe and his wife now have one child and he's workin' for an engineering company building parts for the Space-X booster rocket. It's quite exciting work. And Marilyn got married about a year ago. She and her new husband are looking to go overseas as missionaries in about a year. They're in training right now."

"I remember when you guys went to Florida for her wedding, "Chris remarked. "Sounds like everything's goin' well for both of 'em."

"Yes," Joy replied, "we're very proud and very excited for them both."

At that point, Isaac directed the conversation to the main topic Chris had come to discuss. "So Chris, tell us a little more about your plans for Skeptopolis."

With that, Chris began to share the details of what he felt led to do. Then he told them that his purpose today was to get as much insight as possible into the people and culture of Skeptopolis – so that he could be more effective.

"Chris," Joy exclaimed when she heard his story, "that's an *awesome* calling. You're also very brave to be willing to stick your head into the lion's mouth like that."

"Oh, I don't know about that." Chris responded. "It doesn't seem like that big a deal to me, though maybe I just don't know enough to be nervous."

Hearing Chris' response, Isaac and Joy both sat up straight and their eyes and mouths popped wide open. Then, after about three seconds of shocked silence, they both started laughing hysterically. Chris may not have known what he was about to get into, but they sure did. What he was about to enter was a *huge* deal. Chris' enormous understatement just struck their funny bone.

When they started laughing, a bewildered look came across Chris' face as he tried to figure out what was so funny.

In a few moments, Isaac and Joy began to regain their composure. Isaac took a deep breath to get to where he could talk again and then explained their response. "Chris, I'm so sorry for shocking you like that. We didn't mean to be disrespectful. It's just that when you said you don't know enough to be nervous, you really don't know how much of an understatement that is. What you're about to embark on is way beyond a big deal. Your comment just took us by surprise, that's all."

Then Isaac asked, "So how can we help? What kind of information would you like to get?"

Hearing them react the way they did was, in a way, quite sobering for Chris. If it caused that kind of reaction in Isaac and Joy, there certainly must be more to this than meets the eye. That response alone caused Chris to think more seriously about his research on Atheism.

"Well," Chris replied as he settled in at the table, "I've been doin' some research to prepare myself for this, and one of the things I've noticed is the different types of people who live in Skeptopolis, who have very different characteristics – but who are pretty much all still Atheists. I was hopin' you guys could help me understand some of the dynamics about the various groups that might help me make inroads with some of them."

"Well," Joy jumped in to address his question, "that's quite an astute observation. And you'll no doubt have to deal with different groups in quite different ways."

"Well, I came prepared," Chris chuckled as he pulled stuff out of his backpack. "I have my handy note pad and pen – and my fingers have been getting lots of exercise from writing so much these days!"

That's one thing the Marvels liked about Chris. He had a great sense of humor. They too joined in with Chris' chuckle, then got down to business.

"Okay, Chris," Isaac began, "let's just start with listing some details about the different types of people you'll likely run into, then we can give an explanation about each one. So, one group will be the folks Joy and I worked with – the academic types. Then there are the blue-collar workers. Next would be the students – both college and high school."

"Beyond that," Joy picked up, "you'll find small business owners – they're sort of a class of their own – and government workers. And don't forget people in the poor part of town. They tend to be a bit rough and lack much education. Unfortunately, they even have gangs in that area."

"Hmm," Chris interrupted teasingly, "I didn't think about havin' to use my karate skills for this."

"Yeah, hopefully not," Joy teased back with a chuckle in her voice, "but you never know."

"And you'll want to be aware of the media," Isaac interjected. "They can be very devious. When we were going through our struggles before leaving Skeptopolis, they found out about us becoming Christians and conspired to turn our situation into a public spectacle. That had the effect of adding even more pressure on our bosses to 'do something about us.'"

After Isaac mentioned the media, Joy tried to think if there were any others. "I think that's pretty much the main groups you might meet," Joy responded thoughtfully, "Oh. Well, you could also possibly end up meeting some of the wealthy people. There's not a whole lot of 'em, but they definitely have their own personality – and a *lot* of influence in town. If you start making waves, you might get their attention."

After writing down the different groups the Marvels listed, Chris began his probe. "Okay, let's dig in. I wrote down all the groups as you listed 'em. Let's start with the academics."

"Ah, yes, the academics," Isaac repeated as he thought back to his personal experience.

"Joy and I both came out of that world, so we have first-hand knowledge about what you could possibly face there. Some of those folks work for manufacturing and tech companies -- that's the world I was in. But I think you'll find that most are somehow connected to Skeptopolis University. You'll definitely need to be prepared for some hard-core opposition in that sector.

They're the ones responsible for getting both of us fired – just because we became Christians. Their opposition is 100 percent philosophical, and it's *very* strong. Along with that, you'll probably find much of the opposition they throw out is not very rational. Oh, they'll couch it in academic speak and throw out all kinds of 'peer reviewed' research to try and back up their point of view, but if you know how to respond, you can blow 'em outta the water pretty easily."

"I think I know what you're talking about, Isaac," Chris replied as he contemplated what they said. "I've been readin' about that very thing, and I think I'm up to speed on some of the issues they might throw at me. From my perspective, it seems that the main thing is not to be intimidated by their highfalutin vocabulary and pretentious attitude."

"Hmm, keen observation!" Joy interjected as she affirmed Chris' remark. "That'll definitely be a big part of dealing with them."

"Okay," Chris moved on, "how about the blue-collar workers?"

"Yes, that would be folks who do jobs that require some type of manual labor," Isaac jumped in. "In Skeptopolis, that would include agriculture workers, construction people, and those who work in various trades, like plumbing and electrical work. Normally you might think these folks would be more favorable to religion, but not in Skeptopolis. They also tend to be pretty hard core. The thing you'll find there, though, is that most of 'em are Atheists simply because they were raised that way. Very few have the ability to give an intellectual reason for what they believe, but they claim their Atheism, anyway.

"But don't let that fool ya! They'll still argue back and swear you're wrong – 'just because.' They can be a hard group to interact with because their faith in Atheism is mostly just blind faith. At the same time, if you make friends with them, they'll be nice to you. They're probably not ones to get into any kind of debate."

Listening to that, Chris wrinkled his brow. "Hmmm ... sounds like I'll need to walk a tightrope there. I'll have to give some thought about how to deal with people like that. I'm more used to interacting with people who have a more reasoned approach."

"So what about college students? What do you have to say about them?" Chris asked as he moved to the next group on his list.

"College students ... Yes, that can also be a challenging group," Joy acknowledged. Since she had been a professor at the university, she had a pretty good handle on what they were like. "You're not too far removed from being in college yourself, Chris, so you should remember what that was like. You'll run into a couple of unique dynamics with the students. First, they tend to be very idealistic; and second, they think they know more than they do. They have just enough education to make them dangerous – if you know what I mean."

All three laughed out loud when Joy made that comment. In spite of the fact that some students are highly intelligent individuals, college students are also well known for acting more out of emotion than from a solid intellectual base.

Joy continued, "Yes, what you have with students are some bright minds who've begun studying basic material on various subjects but haven't learned enough to understand the *implications* of what they're learning. They tend to soak up whatever their professors teach, but don't have the knowledge or experience yet to fully evaluate the depth of what they're being taught. And at Skeptopolis U, since virtually all the professors are Atheists, that's what they're soaking up. You'll need to do more than merely challenge their beliefs – you will need to provide very solid reasons *why* they should think a different way."

"So do you think it would be much different with high school students?" Chris asked as he moved on to the next category.

Joy pondered for a second then spoke in a more measured tone. "High school students have their own unique challenges. I've dealt with 'em more at church than in an academic setting, but I think I have a pretty good handle on their thinking. You know, they're also very idealistic but have even less knowledge than college students. Basically, all they know is what they've been taught at home and school – which in Skeptopolis is pretty much atheistic beliefs. They also tend to be very emotional – maybe even more so than the college students. If you can somehow get on friendly terms with a few of them and get into a non-confrontational conversation, you might make some headway there. But also remember, they're still under the influence of their parents, and for the most part, their parents will be very protective."

Chris was ready to move on to the next group and directed the conversation there. "Okay, what about the small business owners. Do you think they'll be a big problem for me?"

"Now that's a group that offers its own unique challenges," Isaac noted as he contemplated the business owners he had known in Skeptopolis, "but maybe its own unique opportunities, as well. You have to keep in mind that their first priority is to make sure nothing affects their business. At a customer level, they'll probably be very nice to you in order to get your business. Where you might possibly run into trouble is if you actually lead some of them to Christ. If that happens – and some of the really militant Atheists in town start making a stink – it could get dicey. On the other hand, a bit of tension exists between the business owners and the politicians. The political people are all into socialist ideas and like to soak the businesses by raising their taxes. You might actually find some allies in the business community if they sense you're somehow on their side."

Hearing that some Atheists might start deliberately causing him problems, Chris' ears perked up. "Causing a stink? What are you talkin' about specifically?"

"Well, the militant types can be real agitators. If they get the sense you're making headway with your faith in Skeptopolis, they might start tryin' to put pressure on the merchants by calling for boycotts or giving 'em bad press," Joy explained further. "Just something to keep in mind."

"On the other hand," Joy continued, "like Isaac said, with a bit of conflict between the business class and the political class, you might be able to use that in certain circumstances."

As he thought of the business owners and their sensitivity to public opinion, Isaac had another thought. "Oh yeah, that brings to mind another particular danger you'll wanna look out for, Chris – the media."

"The media?" Chris replied with a bit of surprise in his voice. "What about 'em?"

"There are a couple of things you need to know about the media in Skeptopolis – this includes the newspaper, and the radio and T.V. stations," Isaac noted. His thoughts went back to the ugly way they had treated him and Joy when it started leaking out that they had become Christians.

"First, they are, themselves, hard-core militant Atheists. When they find out you're there – and you can bet they'll find out – and particularly if you start makin' some kinda positive impact, I guarantee they'll give you all kinds of negative publicity. You'll need to be very shrewd when you deal with them. I don't know how you might do that, but maybe, somehow, you can make friends with one of the reporters. I don't know, though, that's a tough one. Just be aware."

"Hmm, I've never had to deal with anything like that," Chris replied as he tried to comprehend the significance of what Isaac was saying, "I appreciate that warning, though. I'm not sure I would've even thought about that. It seems hard to imagine they'd have any interest in me at all. After all, I won't be any kinda big deal there – in fact, I'm pretty much of a nobody I imagine. But since you've mentioned it, I'll game plan for that and see if I can figure out how not to get sucked in and beat down if they become aware of me."

"So, what about government workers in Skeptopolis?" Chris continued down his list. "What's special that I need to know about them?"

"Government workers? What do you think, Joy? Anything special about them?" Isaac looked over at Joy to probe her thoughts.

"Well, probably the thing you need to know most is that they are the establishment. They're the ones who've created the political status quo, and they don't like anything that gets things out of equilibrium," Joy explained as she tried to think about politicians and bureaucrats, she knew about. "As long as you don't create or cause any disturbances, they'll prob'ly leave you alone officially. But you do need to know that they, too, tend to be hard-core Atheists. If you do somehow get on their radar in a negative way, they can cause you all kinds of grief. Remember, they're in charge of the police, legal services, and all the regulatory agencies – so they can create problems in those arenas if they want to."

"Oooh," Chris replied reflexively, "I hope it doesn't come to that!" He thought about the prospect of getting in trouble with the law. "I've never been in trouble with them. I can't imagine how somethin' like that could happen."

"Well, just keep your antenna up," Joy responded to his uncertainty. "All kinds of things are possible where corruption exists."

Chris enjoyed all this great insight. He felt ready to move on to the next group, so he picked back up with his list. "Okay, just a couple more groups here on my list. What do I need to know about the poor people? I'm curious why they're even on the list."

"They're on the list because the poor part of town also contains a lot of gangs, criminals, and just plain rabble rousers. Remember, pretty much all these folks are Atheists, even the people on skid row. And if they don't like you, they don't need a reason to go after you. They just will. They'll consider you an enemy simply because you're a Christian."

"So what's the best way to reason with 'em?" Chris asked with a bit of concern in his voice.

"I don't know how much actual reasoning you'll get into with them," Joy replied. "For the most part they're not very educated, so intellectual arguments prob'ly won't go far. To really make headway there, you need to figure out a way to befriend some of 'em."

"Hmmm. Now that's an interesting thought," Chris reflected. "I get the feeling that a big part of this effort involves more than just having the right answers."

Hearing Chris' response, Isaac moved into counseling mode. "Chris, you know as well as anyone that sharing your faith is as much about building relationships as it is about sharing intellectual knowledge. You've heard the saying, 'People don't care how much you know until they know how much you care.' You're gonna have to implement that principle a lot where you're goin'."

Chris sat there and let that sink in for a second. "You know, I am so glad you threw that in here, Isaac. Sometimes it's so easy to get caught up in doin' the work that you sorta forget you're dealin' with real people. You're absolutely right. I first have to love them."

After a moment reflecting on that, Chris picked up his list again. "Okay, last group," he said with relief in his voice.

"Why have you put rich people on your list? Do you think I'll have occasion to interact with the country club set?"

Isaac wanted to answer that question, but also wanted to be sure Chris didn't misunderstand what he was going to say, so he chose his words carefully. "Well, to be perfectly honest, they're the ones who really control the city. It's more than likely they won't put themselves in the public eye if controversy arises, so you might not easily become aware of their influence. But you can bet your sweet bippy they will be the ones pulling the strings. Money talks, you know. They have just about everyone in their hip pocket. They donate large amounts of money to the university, they fund the campaigns for the politicians, they own the media outlets, control the school board, and even decide which businesses get the city contracts – and on and on it goes. You get the idea. If they get jittery, you can be sure you won't last much longer in town."

"Wow!" Chris almost flinched when he heard that explanation. "Sounds like fighting a ghost. I hope I can maneuver around that kind of intrigue."

At last, they finished going through the list. "Man, I'm exhausted!" Chris sighed as he took a deep breath. "This has been one intense discussion. I have lotsa things to think deeply about. But wow, what a great help you guys've been! Not only have you given me important information, but you've also given me a really practical things to think about regarding approach and strategy with these different groups. I can't thank you enough."

"Oh Chris," Joy responded with a huge smile on her face, "it's been our pleasure to talk with you. You're such an inspiration, and your passion for the mission is so moving. I don't think just anyone would be able to pull off what you're about to attempt. You can rest assured we'll be praying for you. If there's ever anything else we can do, just let us know."

"You don't know how much that means to me," Chris replied. "I feel quite sure things will come up where your advice will be invaluable. I'll definitely touch base when questions come up."

With that, Chris got up, shook hands, then turned toward the door. He knew for certain this would not be the last talk he'd have with the Marvels.

CHAPTER 7

PASTOR TRUMANN

Chris spent the next couple of weeks studying his notes. But before going to Skeptopolis, he had one more person he wanted to talk to – Pastor Trumann. All the knowledge he had gained about the nature and beliefs of Atheism, and the insights about the city and its people, was important, but this was, after all, a specifically Christian venture he would undertake. He also needed guidance about the spiritual nature of this effort. *I'm not going to Skeptopolis just to win intellectual arguments,* Chris reminded himself. *My purpose is to touch people's lives and encourage them to open up to a relationship with Jesus Christ.*

When he called the pastor and asked for a meeting, Pastor Trumann quickly accepted. Even though Chris had not yet sought his input, Pastor Trumann was keenly aware of what he was planning.

Sally, Pastor Trumann's secretary, welcomed Chris at the church office and walked him back to the pastor's office. Pastor Trumann got up from his desk, greeted him warmly, and invited him to sit in one of the brown leather upholstered armchairs facing his desk.

Chris and the pastor spent the first few minutes catching up on the latest happenings at church, along with updates about work and family. Then, after a few minutes, Pastor Trumann directed the conversation to the real reason for Chris' visit.

"Well Chris, we've all heard about what you're planning, and I must say, everyone's quite excited. What can I do to help?"

Chris had grown up in this church and under Pastor Trumann's leadership for nearly 20 years – from the time he first became its pastor. His solid teaching for all those years gave Chris a high regard for him. He was certainly a great preacher with a strong emphasis on teaching the Bible. Chris had never left a worship service feeling he had been short-changed. But the pastor had also initiated a remarkably strong emphasis on preparing his congregation to do the work of God out in the world.

Pastor Trumann's philosophy of ministry came out of Ephesians 4:11-13 – to "equip the saints for the work of ministry." He often explained to his congregation that the primary ministers in the church were not the pastors and church staff, but the people in the pew. He taught that those verses pointed to the fact that the main job of church leaders was to prepare their church members to do the work of God out in the world.

He reasoned that – for the work of God to reach the entire world – it would require all Christians to serve as "salt and light" in the world wherever they lived and worked. Comparatively speaking, there were very few church leaders, and their responsibilities necessarily kept them focused on caring for the community of believers. There just were not enough church staff to do the work of church organization AND going out to win the world for Christ. But if the church members could be trained to do the work, the Christian faith would spread like wildfire – like what happened in the early days of Christianity.

Pastor Trumann had set up his church to operate like a mini seminary and mission sending agency. Everyone received training in basic Christian theology, as well as in unique skills that enabled them to use their spiritual gifts to do the work of Christ in their everyday lives.

In fact, the very reason Chris felt so confident he could do mission work in Skeptopolis was because he had been so well coached under the pastor's leadership. But he knew he wasn't the only one prepared that way. The pastor had created a church environment and culture for the entire church body. On a regular basis, the church sent out missionaries, both to other countries and to other places in America. They also sent out a number of short-term mission groups – where church members could volunteer to use their training and serve, taking the message of Christ to different places in need.

"Pastor," Chris asked in response to Pastor Trumann's question, "what I want from you are your insights as to how to best interact with the people I'll be meeting. From the things I've learned at church, and in my personal preparation for this task, I think I'm ready for the questions and opposition I'll face in Skeptopolis. But I'm also aware that simply winning arguments won't convince people to turn to Christ. I've had lots of debates on social media about my faith with people who aren't Christians. And while I recognize there's great value in breaking down their false beliefs, not too many people would actually turn to Christ just because they're forced to admit that their false beliefs can't be backed up. Coming to Christ means entering into a personal relationship with Him. And to lead people to that place, I feel there's a personal element I have yet to get my head around."

"Chris," Pastor Trumann replied with a tone of excitement in his voice, "you probably have no idea just how profound a statement you've just made. I'm really excited to hear you ask that particular question. Yes, I think I can help you focus that thought in a way that'll help you be productive as you try to gain the good will of those you talk to."

"The truth is," Pastor Trumann continued, "it's not always possible to establish a deep relationship with those you try to engage concerning faith matters. You mentioned your encounters with people on social media. I know you write some Christian articles, and my guess is that at least some of the debates you've had with people have come from them attacking what you wrote in those articles."

"Well, that's exactly right," Chris acknowledged, confirming Pastor Trumann's speculation.

"Well," Pastor Trumann went on, "in situations like that, people often end up attacking you before you ever even have a chance to win 'em with your charm. In that case, you just havta hope that what you're sayin' is makin' 'em think more deeply, and that at some future date someone else'll be able to take advantage of your efforts. You can also hope that perhaps others who are just watching that conversation will be moved by your arguments. But when you have an opportunity for face-to-face encounters, you have an entirely different kind of possibility. There, you have a chance to actually develop some kinda relationship."

"Now mind you, a relationship won't always be possible," Pastor Trumann continued. "Even when you try to be nice and friendly, some people are just so anti-Christian that their bigotry won't let 'em open up to you. But you *can* make sure that when that happens, it's because of *their* attitude not *yours*. I'd say, as much as possible, before you ever engage people with the gospel message, or before you engage 'em in any kind of debate, make 'em your friend. Show an interest in their interests, take them out to eat, complement 'em on something they deem important – just do something to establish a connection. It's much harder for people to reject you outright when there's a personal connection."

"Wow, those are such profound insights, pastor," Chris said with a deep sense of wonder at his wisdom. "I know it won't necessarily be easy, but I can sure see how that could make a difference."

Then to encourage Chris even further, Pastor Trumann added another thought. "Indeed, it won't be easy. But as you maintain awareness of that principle, and actually get experience doing it, it'll become second nature. And for you, with your very winsome attitude and personality, I predict that you'll do quite well in that department."

"Also, there's one other thing you should be aware of, Chris," Pastor Truman added. "Do you remember in Acts chapter 17 when the apostle Paul went to Athens and shared Christ at the Areopagus?"

"Oh," Chris blurted out, "I know exactly what you're gonna say. I was discussing that very passage with Levi, Luke, Abby, and Zara just the other day. People responded to Paul in different ways. Some sneered at him, some were curious and wanted to learn more later, but some believed."

Pastor Trumann nodded and smiled. "Exactly right, Chris. And that's likely what'll happen with you, as well. So don't let the various responses affect your mood or your commitment to the task. The ultimate response people make will not be your decision – it'll be strictly between them and God. You'll be able to stay on an even keel to the degree you're able to take that to heart."

"That's exactly the kind of advice I was hopin' to get from you, Pastor," Chris responded appreciatively. "Thanks so much for your willingness to take the time and talk to me about this."

Pastor Trumann could see they were about to wrap up, but he had one more thing he wanted to say. "Before you go, Chris, what are your logistical plans when you get over to Skeptopolis? How long do you plan to stay? Where are you gonna stay? How are you gonna live financially?"

Chris really wasn't expecting to talk about money, but since Pastor Trumann had asked, he was glad to share it with him. "Pastor, this is a personal mission project I've decided to take on, and I plan to use my personal savings to make it happen. Over the last several years I've been able to put aside about $10,000, and I'm gonna use that as necessary to take care of lodging, food, and whatever else I need for as long as it holds out."

Pastor Trumann nodded approvingly, then began to share another thought. "Well Chris, I have a surprise for you. Several of the people on the missions committee have come to me and asked if it would be okay for the church to help you with that. You have no idea how excited they are about what you're planning. I doubt anyone would say something to you directly, but ever since word started getting out about you tryin' to penetrate Skeptopolis culture with the gospel, people have been asking me if they could contribute. If you're willing to accept their help, there's been about $25,000 pledged to back you up – and probably more comin'. What do you say?"

Chris was speechless. He sat there in stunned silence as he tried to process what the pastor had just said, then tears started rolling down his cheeks. It had never even crossed his mind to ask for help. He just felt such a strong sense of God's leading that he simply assumed using his own resources was the right thing to do.

After taking a moment to regain his composure, words began to stammer out of his mouth, "I … I don't know what to say. I never even considered that possibility. Why would they wanna do that?"

Seeing Chris' reaction, Pastor Trumann's eyes began to tear up, as well. "Chris, you're a part of this church family," he explained, "and the people here love and respect you. As you go out, they feel you're representing them, and they wanna be a part of what God's doin' in your life. You know, you've done the same thing for others when they went out on mission."

Hearing that, tears streamed down Chris' cheeks even more. He was moved beyond words. "Pastor, I don't know yet exactly how God's gonna use this, but maybe it's a bigger deal than I ever imagined. Nothin' would give me more joy than to be an official ambassador of this church in taking the gospel to a place that's so lost. I was excited about doin' it before, but this has moved my excitement level off the charts."

With that, Chris pulled a tissue from the box on the corner of the pastor's desk, wiped the tears from his eyes, and thanked Pastor Trumann for taking the time to mentor him. He also expressed his deep thanks to the church for their belief in him.

"Chris," Pastor Trumann responded, "I want you to know that I'm not only very excited for you as you embark on this journey, I'm also very proud. I can tell you that there'll be times when you'll get very excited, and other times when it'll be very hard. But God will sustain you through all of it. And you can be confident that I, and the church, will be praying for you as you take on this challenge."

Then, before Chris left, Pastor Trumann prayed for him and asked God to go before him to prepare the way. When the pastor had finished praying, Chris stood up, shook his hand, walked out of the building, and headed for home. He was now ready to begin the adventure.

CHAPTER 8

ON TO SKEPTOPOLIS

Today was a big day – the day Chris's championship team would drive over to Skeptopolis. Right on time, the Corvelle Tour Company's silver, 40-seat, luxury tour bus pulled in front of the city Civic Center. A small crowd lined the front of the pavilion to see the fighters off and cheer them on. After loading their suitcases in the baggage compartment underneath the bus, the members of the karate team boarded and headed off to Skeptopolis.

An hour later, the bus pulled up to the entryway of Hotel Skeptopolis, and everyone disembarked and went inside to check in. After going to their rooms and putting things away, the team met at the cafeteria to grab a bite for lunch, then went their separate ways. Chris went down to the pool with a book, found himself a lounge chair, and plopped down to read and relax.

This tournament had three weight divisions for the men: light, middle, and heavyweight. Plus three for the women: super light, light, and middleweight. In addition, they divided contestants into three age categories: 18-34, 35-59, and 60+, for both men and women. So, the Templeton team consisted of eighteen people altogether.

Chris competed in the men's, 18-34, middleweight category – the most competitive weight class, and also the most prestigious. Though the karate association would never make this distinction, the general public viewed the winner of that category as the best of the best. As a result, the champion in that class typically received the most media coverage.

Since Rock had been so prominent for so long at the state tournament, the minute Chris beat him in Templeton, the media in Skeptopolis took notice, and the typical David and Goliath media hype ensued.

While Chris enjoyed some time relaxing by the pool, a TV reporter tracked him down with her cameraman and asked him for a short interview. Not being busy at the moment, Chris put down his book and welcomed the interview. The reporter mostly asked him about his karate background – such as when he started training, how long he had been doing it, what style he practiced, and the like.

After the reporter left, Chris hung around the pool and read a little longer, then went back to his room to change clothes. Then, at 3:30, their team coordinator bussed them over to the arena to get a feel for the venue, receive an orientation, get their schedules and ring assignments, and meet some of the other contestants. After orientation, everyone was bussed back to the hotel to relax until dinner at the luxurious roof-top restaurant.

The next morning, Chris met his teammates for breakfast at the restaurant adjoining the lobby before going back to the arena for a final workout. Suddenly, Jennifer, one of Templeton's female competitors, ran up to the group and pointed at the TV on the lobby wall. "Hey guys, look!" she almost shouted. "It's Chris!" Sure enough, there he was being interviewed by the pool. The TV station was doing a segment on the upcoming tournament, and they used some of the footage of Chris from the day before.

In the report, the reporter included information about some of the other teams as well, but it was mostly about Chris. "Hey Chris," Ron joked, "I saw you talkin' to that female reporter yesterday by the pool. Did you charm her or somethin'?"

Chris was a bit embarrassed by the suggestion and mumbled back, "Aw, come on guys, I didn't do anything to encourage this. It was such a low-key interview, I thought they were interviewin' everybody."

As they listened to the report, Chris made an observation to the group. "Hey, there's all kinda information in this report that we didn't even talk about – and some of it's not even in the media packet. She must've done some research on me beyond that." Sensing his embarrassment, everyone piled on and hassled him all the more.

After breakfast, the team members went to their rooms to change into their karate gis, then met back in the lobby in preparation for going down to the arena. The bus was a bit late, so they all just milled around when a cute brunette with short bouncy hair walked by. When she spotted Chris, she shouted, "Hey, aren't you that karate whiz kid that was interviewed on TV?"

Oh no, not this, Chris thought. *Why me?!* Chris nodded meekly and flashed a shy smile. On confirming it was him, she yelled out to a group of nearby friends, "Hey guys, it *is* him. I told you it was him!" With that, a whole gaggle of young girls came running over asking for his autograph.

Chris had no idea what to do. The tournament hadn't even started. He hadn't done anything. *Why are they doing this?* he wondered to himself. But not to be impolite, he started signing autographs.

All the while, his teammates saw what was happening, and to further his embarrassment, they all started laughing out loud. Everyone thought it was hilarious, and several went over to him and started in themselves. "Hey Chris, can I have your autograph, too?" He would never live this down.

When he had finished giving everyone an autograph, Chris headed back over to join his group. They had all migrated to the other side of the lobby, leaving him to deal with the autograph seekers alone.

Chris was relieved to get through that experience, but before he could catch his breath, another crowd of young people saw Chris and suddenly swarmed over to the team. They also wanted to get Chris' autograph. As the bus was still running late, he had no choice but to navigate this new set of autograph seekers, as well. No one wanted the autographs of any of the other team members, so the teammates once again moved to the side and watched – laughing and shaking their heads.

Finally, the bus arrived, and Chris quickly excused himself and headed straight for it. Once on the bus, the team members teased him mercilessly all the way to the arena. "Hey, can I have your autograph?" "Can I get a selfie with you?" "Will you be my boyfriend?" At that point, all Chris could do was laugh, roll his eyes, and shake his head.

But it didn't end there. When he got off the bus, another group of mostly young ladies were waiting for him there – also wanting his autograph. Getting off the bus, he had to wade through them, too. As he moved through the crowd, he tried to be as polite as possible, but he had work to do and scooted into the arena as quickly as he could.

When the team had finished their workout and headed back to the bus, there was that group again. And once again Chris had to make his way through the crowd to get on the bus. Then, the same thing happened again when they got back to the hotel.

By that time, Chris was beginning to get a bit suspicious. *Who put these people up to this?* he thought to himself. *This is just plain weird.*

Later, after dinner, when he went back to his room, Chris called Sensei Lance and told him what was going on. When he heard Chris' story, he couldn't help himself – he just started cackling out loud – which got Chris a little ticked off. "Hey, this is serious. I don't like what's goin' on."

Sensei Lance quickly responded, "Hey Chris, honestly, I'm not laughin' at you. I'm laughin' at the situation. The people in Skeptopolis are scared to death of you."

"What?" Chris almost shouted back. "What are you talkin' about? They don't know anything about me."

"Remember, Chris," Sensei replied as he tried to explain, "you're in Skeptopolis. They hate Templeton. I'm tellin' ya, they did research on you, ran the story on TV, then gathered up that mob in order to distract you. They're either tryin' to shake you up or get you all cocky and overconfident so you'll lose focus. *It's all a ploy!* I've seen it before."

With that, it was as if a fog lifted. "Oh, wow!" Chris responded, "I did *not* see that comin'. They're out to get me. Dadgummit, I'm not gonna let that happen. Before – I just wanted to go out there and do my best. Now I wanna show 'em a thing or two."

Sensei Lance chuckled again, "Well, Chris, be careful how you handle this. Don't let it get under your skin, and don't let it get you out of your rhythm. You're one of the best I've ever seen at staying focused on the task at hand. Use that to your advantage."

Now, with a clear sense of what was going on, Chris felt more focused, and certainly more in control of his situation. "I can't thank you enough for your wise counsel, Sensei," Chris replied, feeling a deep sense of relief. "I definitely feel better. And that's exactly what I'm gonna do. I won't let 'em play me like that."

After hanging up, Chris began to focus on the task at hand. *I'm gonna win this tournament,* Chris thought to himself, *and I'm gonna win big!*

CHAPTER 9

THE BIG DAY

Finally it came – the big day. Chris rolled out of bed with a powerful sense of determination. He was always excited to participate in tournaments, but this was different. The fact that he was now aware of a deliberate plan to break him down caused him to have a more intense focus than he had ever experienced.

He took a quick shower, then met his teammates at 6:00 in the cafeteria. After breakfast, everyone went to their rooms to change into their karate gis, then came back down to the lobby to board the bus.

When Chris got downstairs, there was another throng of people wanting to crowd around him and get his autograph. "I'm sorry ... not now folks," Chris called out to the throng. "Right now, I'm only focused on the tournament. Catch me after it's over and I'll sign all your programs." With that he strode to the bus and got aboard. His teammates immediately noticed the change in his demeanor. He looked focused and ready to go.

When the bus arrived at the arena, Chris looked out the window, and sure enough, another crowd was waiting there as well. This one consisted mostly of "fans," but contained some media people, as well. They all wanted a sound bite from this new celebrity. But once again Chris put them off. "Guys, meet me after the tournament and I'll accommodate you then. Wish me luck."

As he strode toward the arena, most of the throng bowed to his wishes, but the press was not so easily put off. They came after him shouting all kinds of questions. Chris stopped and turned around one more time, "Guys, I'm sorry, but I came here to compete and it's time for that now. After the tournament I'll answer all your questions." With that, he turned and walked inside.

Once inside, the team huddled together to begin getting ready. "What in the world was that all about, Chris?" Jason asked. Jason was the middleweight male in the 35-59 age group. I've never seen anyone treated like you are."

Chris knew everyone was wondering the same thing, so he called the team together to explain. "Guys, here's the scoop. I thought all this was pretty weird too. So, I called Sensei Lance last night to get some advice. Here's the bottom line; this has all been a setup. You know the people of Skeptopolis don't like us. They'd never treat someone from Templeton like a rock star the way we've been treated – particularly one like me who's at his very first state tournament. It seems they've put together some kinda plan to try to get me to let my guard down. Sensei said he's seen this before. When he explained what was goin' on, it kinda ticked me off. But he told me not to let it get to me. He said use it as motivation to do even better. And that's exactly what I'm doin'. I'm gonna show 'em what karate's all about. I say we *all* use that as motivation."

When the others heard Chris' explanation, they, too, were a bit put off. "What a buncha garbage," Melinda snorted. "I say we all bust 'em up."

On hearing Melinda's response, Chris shared the counsel he had gotten from Sensei Lance. "Melinda, be careful not to let it get to ya. That's exactly what they want. Instead, internalize that feeling into an increased determination, and let's do our talkin' in the ring."

Just then the tournament director's voice blared over the loudspeaker. "Contestants, we are excited to welcome you to this year's state karate tournament. As you look around the arena, you'll find that the various rings are set up by age, gender, and weight class. Go find your place and register your presence at the table by your ring. We'll begin shortly. I wish all of you good luck."

With that announcement, the Templeton team huddled up one last time, and each person inserted their hand into the middle of the circle. Chris called out, "Templeton on three … one, two, three."

"TEMPLETON!" the team shouted in unison. They then separated and went to their respective stations.

At 8:30 am sharp, the tournament got underway. Rings were set up all over the arena, and, as the fights proceeded, eliminated contestants made their way into the stands surrounding the arena floor, while the winners sat in chairs around the rings to await their next opponent.

The entire venue pulsed with energy and excitement as the fans in the stands cheered for their favorite competitors. The largest and noisiest fan group was, of course, the contingent from Skeptopolis. Since their city hosted the tournament, lots of locals showed up to support the hometown favorites. And, since Templeton was not far away, the second largest contingent came from there. Overall, the Templeton team was doing quite well, so they had a lot to cheer about.

But about halfway through the tournament, the nature of the buzz began to change. Looking at the crowd, it became obvious that an increasing number of people were moving over into the area closest to Chris' ring. He was fighting like a man possessed! So far, through every single match, literally no one had even been able to lay a hand on him. To this point, he had won all of his matches on shutouts. That was unheard of.

As the tournament progressed further, Chris' streak continued. And the longer it went on, the more people crowded around his ring. Surely it wouldn't be possible for him to keep that up through to the end, would it? The longer the tournament went on, the stronger the competition became as weaker competitors were eliminated.

When it came to Chris' final match he was up against Bruiser – a competitor from Jackson. Like Chris, Bruiser had also won all his matches to make it to the finals. Could Chris fend him off too?

In this match, Chris wore the red ribbon, while Bruiser was wearing the blue. As the two faced each other across the ring, Bruiser glared at Chris as though he wanted to actually hurt him. In fact, he did have a reputation for playing dirty, and in a few cases he actually did injure some of his opponents. Even in this tournament he had used questionable tactics a few times and it had cost him points. But he was very shrewd. He used those tactics just enough to intimidate his opponents, but not enough to actually lose matches or get disqualified.

Chris had seen these dirty tactics before. It was not that common, but occasionally people came along who valued winning above sportsmanship, and they fought dirty like that. When it happened in the past, Sensei Lance would gather his students together and instruct them how to handle it. Because of that, Chris knew exactly what to do. Rather than be intimidated, Chris simply smiled and blew Bruiser a kiss.

As bullies don't generally have a lot of self-control and are mostly accustomed to getting away with intimidation tactics, they often lose their own focus when their bullying doesn't have the desired effect. And that's exactly what happened with Bruiser. When he saw Chris blow him a kiss, he took it as a taunt, and immediately his face flushed crimson with anger. *I'm gonna knock that sucker out cold!* he thought to himself.

As the competitors faced one another, the referee entered the ring from the side and the two turned toward him and bowed before bowing to one another. The referee walked to the middle of the ring, called the two together, and gave them their final instructions. He then stepped back, waited for the fighters to get into position, put out his hand and shouted,

"Hajime!"

In his anger, Bruiser immediately charged across the ring to bull rush Chris. But Chris was too good for that. He saw what was coming and threw a simple side kick right at Bruiser's neck and stopped him in his tracks.

"Point red," the referee shouted.

As the two contestants moved back to their sides of the ring, it was obvious that Bruiser was even hotter than before. He had a very angry look on his face and was beginning to make loud growling sounds. But Chris just kept his cool and stayed light on his feet.

"Hajime!" the ref shouted to begin the next round.

This time, Bruiser was much more cautious. He began dancing around the ring faking jabs and low kicks, but his growling became even louder.

Chris, for his part, stayed calm and waited for Bruiser to make a mistake. The way he was jumping around, Chris knew that sooner or later Bruiser would get himself off balance and he'd be able go in for the point. He didn't have to wait long. Suddenly, Bruiser spun around with a spinning backfist, and caught Chris on the side of his face. Immediately blood started dripping from his cheek. Bruiser, at that point, thought for sure that he had earned the point.

The ref, however, jumped in immediately and discounted the point. In this tournament, spinning backfists were illegal. He then walked straight up to Bruiser, looked him eye-to-eye and gave him a stern warning. "Another trick like that and you'll be disqualified!"

Bruiser wasn't actually surprised to get that warning, and he really didn't care at that point. He had a really smug look on his face and felt pretty confident that even if he didn't get the point, he'd done enough damage to Chris to intimidate him and get the upper hand.

The referee called time out and had the tournament doctor come take a look and clean the blood off Chris' face. Once that was taken care of, he came back over to Chris to see if he was ready to fight again.

If Chris had not been focused before, he was now. In fact, he had become so focused that everything around him seemed to be moving in slow motion. He nodded to the ref who then started the round again.

"Hajime!"

As Bruiser moved forward, he was growling and trying to present as intimidating a front as he could muster. Then, after dancing around a little, he suddenly cut loose with a spinning roundhouse kick toward Chris' head. But before he was able to fully get into his spin, Chris lunged inside and caught Bruiser with a sharp uppercut to the chin.

"Point red," the referee shouted out again.

He then moved back to his place, and when the fighters were back in position and indicated they were ready, he stuck out his hand again to start the third round.

"Hajime!"

At that point, it seemed all the wind had been knocked out of Bruiser's sails. He had done everything he could to will his way to victory but had become painfully aware that he was way overmatched. He seemed to have completely lost the spark that had always given him an edge. This time, he sluggishly moved forward with extreme caution. Having already seen his best tactics easily countered, he didn't have any appetite for taking Chris on. Recognizing Bruiser's ultra slow and off balance move toward the center of the ring, Chris spun to his right and let loose with a double action flying roundhouse kick that caught Bruiser completely off guard, right upside his head – and Bruiser went out with a whimper.

"Point and match, red," the referee shouted.

With the referee's call, the crowd erupted! Even those who were not Chris' fans couldn't help but be impressed with the masterful display they had witnessed. The whooping and hollering became so loud, in fact, that activity throughout the entire arena stopped for a moment as everyone looked to see what was going on.

With that, the fighters moved to the middle of the ring and the ref stepped between them. He then grabbed both of their wrists and lifted Chris' arm to declare him the victor. And with that, Bruiser turned and walked away with his head down, cursing under his breath.

Chris' record had remained intact. He had literally destroyed the competition – all of it. Not a single person got even one point on him the entire day. That had never happened before in the entire history of the tournament.

At the medal ceremony, the mayor of Skeptopolis, Jill Gadsden, came to the podium, congratulated all the winners, and personally handed them their trophies. Templeton received three gold, two silver, and four bronze medals. It was an outstanding showing for the team. But beyond that, Chris received the MVP medal for having the best record in the tournament. As they awarded the medals, the mayor took time to pose with each winner and have her picture taken with them. Astute politician that she was, she made a special point of praising Chris, and seemed to hang around him as much as she could – also getting extra pictures with him. She was sure that would translate into extra publicity for her.

Following the ceremony, the Templeton team gathered together once again to congratulate each other, but they were especially proud of Chris. They already knew he was special, and this confirmed it even more.

Immediately after the medal ceremony, the tournament director asked all the medal winners to go to the media area so the press could interview them. Obviously, Chris got a lot of attention. He was the star of the day. The members of the press had all kinds of questions for him. "How long have you been studying karate?" "How old were you when you started?" "What style do you study?" And the obligatory question by all the female reporters, "Are you single?"

But some of them wanted more. "Where do you get your inspiration?" one of the local *Skeptopolis Times* newspaper reporters asked. Chris thought for a second and answered, "You know, I get my inspiration from a lotta places. My sensei's a fantastic friend and mentor. He prepared me with the knowledge and skills to do well today. My family is also key – they're the ones who instilled in me the values essential for success in all the things I do in life. But I think the most important inspiration I have comes from my personal relationship with Jesus Christ. He's given me the inner peace and strength to live out my values in everyday life. I'd never be as successful as I am without Him."

After the interviews were over, everyone headed back to the bus to return to the hotel. Not surprisingly, a huge crowd awaited the Templeton team when they walked through the arena door. "Come on, Chris," one member of the crowd shouted out, "you promised autographs after the tournament."

Chris laughed out loud. "I did, didn't I? Okay team, let's please our fans." For the most part, people just wanted Chris' autograph, but since he included the whole team, the crowd went to all the team members. It took a little extra time, but everyone loved the opportunity.

When they finished, the team piled onto the bus and headed back to the hotel. After cleaning up and changing clothes, they met back at the restaurant and enjoyed the evening eating excellent food and reliving the day. No one really felt like staying a long time, though. It had been a long day, and everyone was exhausted. They returned to their rooms at about 7:30 to cash it in.

CHAPTER 10

A SURPRISE GUEST

By the time Chris returned to his room, he was completely wiped out from the tournament and didn't feel like doing anything. So, he took a quick shower and plopped down on the couch to unwind in front of the TV.

But then, right about 8:00, he was surprised by a knock at the door. He wasn't expecting anyone but figured it might be a teammate dropping in to chill for a few minutes before turning in. When he opened the door, he was shocked to see it wasn't one of his friends at all – it was the Skeptopolis mayor, Jill Gadsden.

"Chris, have you got a moment?" she asked as she quickly pushed past him and closed the door behind her. As she brushed by, he could smell the fragrance of exotic perfume following her into the room.

Jill was an extraordinarily attractive woman. Her shoulder length blond hair framed her face in a way that made her look like a beauty queen. And it wasn't just her natural features, her sharp, professional clothing made her look like a model straight out of a Parisian fashion magazine. And entering the room, she also had a large black tote slung over her left shoulder.

She was obviously quite self-confident. Most people would never make that kind of entrance into the room of someone they didn't really know. Of course, she pretty much had to be that way to become a successful politician in Skeptopolis.

In college Jill had studied political science and graduated at the top of her class. But in addition to being beautiful and smart, she was also quite the party girl. In fact, it was in her college social life, particularly her experiences in her sorority, Beta Phi Iota, that she gained her schmoozing skills. She could drink with the best of them, and rather enjoyed using her sexuality to gain favors, or put people in a position where she could influence them to advance her own agenda.

After college, she interned with the State Senate president for a year, then moved on to Washington, DC, as a political advisor for her district's congressman in the House of Representatives. While there, she fell in love with Harry, a seemingly up and coming political wonder boy, and the two of them married. It didn't work out very well, though, as both of them were so driven and competitive that they constantly fought. Apparently, he also didn't hold his liquor very well, and got rather violent when he was drunk.

They did, however, have a child together – a girl that Jill absolutely adored. On the other hand, Harry didn't feel he was ready to have a child and pushed very hard for her to have an abortion. The fight about that, the periodic abuse, and Harry's ambition finally became too much, and the couple divorced after just two years of marriage. Harry has had virtually no contact with Jill or his daughter since that time.

After the divorce, Jill returned to Skeptopolis to enter local politics. She was elected mayor the very first time she ran, ousting the previous incumbent who had held the post for 16 years.

She was also well known for being a totally ruthless politician. She knew exactly what she wanted and was willing to do practically anything to get her way. In the process of running the city, she had ruined the careers, and reputations, of many who had opposed her.

There was one other thing central to Jill's approach to life: she was a hardcore Atheist. Her dad was a lawyer with the American Civil Liberties Union, and himself, a dues paying member of the American Humanist Association. He had even been good friends with such people as feminist Betty Friedan and cosmologist Carl Sagan. In fact, these, and other prominent Secular Humanists, had often been guests in her parents' home, and she had the opportunity to listen in on some very deep conversations in her younger days. Over the years, her contempt for Christians had only grown. Until now, she tried to never miss an opportunity to disparage them.

When Jill came barging into Chris' room like she did, he was taken totally by surprise and just stood there for a long time gaping at her with his jaw wide open. She took notice of that and felt a sense of smug satisfaction that her entrance had its desired effect on him.

When Chris finally regained his composure enough to re-engage, he spoke politely, "Uh, well, this is quite a surprise. Is there something I can do to help you, madam mayor?"

Jill flashed a flirty look in his direction. "Oh Chris, there's no need to be so formal with me," she replied with as sexy a voice as she could muster. "Please call me Jill."

"Uh, okay, Jill," Chris stammered as he continued his attempt to regain his composure. "Uh, what can I do for you?"

She smiled sweetly and gave Chris another flirty glance. "I just wanted to tell you how totally impressed I was with how you fought today – and I wanted to do it in person. Your performance was unbelievably awesome! In fact, the entire city was impressed. I know the people of Skeptopolis and Templeton rarely see eye-to-eye on things, but in spite of the fact that you're from Templeton, from here you'll go on to represent our entire state – which means you'll be representing us, as well. I want you to know that we're 100 percent behind you and looking forward to you makin' us all proud at regionals."

Chris was still having trouble making sense of what was happening, and the very kind words only added to his confusion. "Well, uh, thank you, Jill," he replied, still stumbling over his words. "That's, um, very kind of you. I deeply appreciate your support, and I'll definitely work hard to make you proud."

"And to celebrate your victory," Jill continued her thought, "I brought a little surprise."

With that, she set her purse on the table next to her, opened it up, and pulled out a bottle of champagne and two champagne glasses. "I wanna drink a toast to your accomplishment," she announced.

Chris was again taken back, especially in light of the fact that he didn't drink alcohol. Trying to figure out how to get that idea across without offending her, he replied, "Jill, um, I feel a little awkward here. I'm totally flattered by your kind gesture. I truly am. And I hope you won't be offended, but I don't drink."

This time it was Jill's turn to be surprised. She had never met anyone who would turn down champagne to celebrate a great occasion. Even top athletes often did that when they won some kind of championship.

But she actually had an ulterior motive and was determined not to be denied. Thinking quickly on her feet, she devised a rouse to get around the objection. "Chris, I'm so sorry. It didn't dawn on me that my gesture might not be appropriate," she began talking fast to try to buy time to get out of this uncomfortable situation. "It's me that should be embarrassed, not you – please don't feel awkward. My intention was to celebrate with you, and I still wanna do that. There must be a way to get around this small obstacle."

"I've got it!" She suddenly declared. With that, she walked over to the room's mini fridge, opened the door, and saw that it was stocked with various kinds of beverages. Since she now knew he didn't drink alcohol, she skipped over the liquor and wine selections and went straight for the apple juice. After all, it had a similar color to champagne. She then opened it up, picked up the champagne glasses, and poured a glass for herself and one for Chris.

After pouring the apple juice, she handed Chris a champagne glass and held the other one in her right hand. She then raised her glass and offered a toast. "Chris," she opined, "congratulations on your fantastic victory today, and may your future karate encounters be even greater as you represent our great state." Having finished the toast, she reached over, clinked Chris' glass, and raised the beverage to her lips.

Chris was now feeling even more awkward than before, but out of a sense of not wanting to embarrass Jill further, he followed her lead, raised his glass, and also took a sip of the apple juice. He then smiled, and said, "Thank you, Jill, for the kind words. I'll definitely do my best to represent our state."

Jill then reached over, took the champagne saucer out of Chris' hand, and put both glasses on the table. Turning back around, she walked over to where Chris was standing, took him by the hand and pulled him over to toward the couch. When they got there, she sat down – then gently pulled him down beside her. After a short pause, she took a slow breath, and looked him straight in the eyes with a sexy smile on her face, as the fragrance of her perfume wafted across the space between them. "Chris," she said, "is there anything else I can do for you?"

At this point, Chris was starting to get the picture. He smiled, gently pulled his hand away, then turned more directly to face her so he could also look her straight in the eye. "Jill," Chris began to explain himself. "I think I see where you are goin' with this. Now I feel more awkward than ever. First, I want to say that there's no doubt that you're a very beautiful woman. I can see why anyone would be attracted to you. But the kind of encounter you're inviting would not be appropriate for me. I hope you understand."

"Oh," Jill replied as she reached up and put her hand over her mouth, "I'm so embarrassed again. Are you telling me you're gay?"

Chris' eyes got big from the shock of that statement. Oh my, he thought to himself, I can see how she might come to that conclusion, but she's getting' the wrong idea.

"No, nothing like that. I'm not gay."

"Oh, then you already have a girlfriend. Ugh, I should have known."

Chris chuckled and smiled as he gently shook his head. "No, it's not that either. I don't have anyone I am seeing seriously."

Rather confused at that point, Jill wrinkled her brow and asked, "Then why would you possibly turn me away?" And then in her sexiest voice, "We could have a VERY good time this evening."

Chris smiled back at her and once again looked her right in the eyes. He was finally feeling a little more in control. "Perhaps so," he responded, "but sexual relations outside of marriage doesn't fit within my moral framework. You see, there's someone I am not willing to disappoint by engaging in that kind of activity."

Now it was Jill's turn to feel confused. He had already said there was not anyone else in his life, so she couldn't imagine what the problem might be. With a perplexed look on her face, she asked, "So, who are you talkin' about then?"

At that point, Chris wasn't quite sure how Jill would respond, but it was clearly an opportunity to express his faith in Christ. "I've committed my life to Jesus Christ," he answered with a clear, steady voice, "and I'm just not willing to disappoint Him by embracing values that go against what He's revealed to be His way. As it relates to a sexual relationship, I made a conscious decision several years back that I'd be faithful to those **biblical values** and not have sexual relations with anyone until I got married. And when I do get married, I've committed myself to remain faithful to my wife until death do us part."

Hearing that, Jill became furious inside. She despised Christians to begin with, and this kind of prudishness was one of the main reasons why. She despised what she considered his "holier than thou" attitude. At the same time, she didn't want to lose face by allowing him to think his values were better than hers, or that he had caused her to even feel uncomfortable. But she did want to at least get in a subtle dig. So, she took a deep breath, gave him another flirty glance, and replied, "Ohhh, now I get it. I will say you've surprised me a little, though. I was honestly not aware that there were any people in our enlightened day and age that still held to those kinds of old-fashioned ideas. But I really didn't intend to do anything to make you feel uncomfortable, and I admire you for sticking to your guns. I hope you'll forgive my forwardness."

"Jill," Chris replied, hoping that the potential tension from that situation had been removed, "thank you for understanding. This whole thing's been a little awkward for me, as well. But you should know that there *are* still people who hold to those values and find very deep fulfillment in following them."

At that point, the wheels in Jill's mind began turning at full speed. She had actually come just to have a good time with Chris, but now her mindset had changed, and she saw this as a challenge. She always believed that Christians were prudish and hypocritical, and felt that if she could get Chris in the sack, it would prove he was a hypocrite, too. She had heard from some people she knew that he claimed to be a Christian, but really couldn't believe he, or anyone else, actually lived out the implications of **biblical sexual morality** in real life. She may not be able to get him now, but she wanted to leave the door open so that maybe in the future she could create that outcome.

"Well, I tell you what," Jill responded back with the sexiest voice she could muster as she reached into her purse and pulled out a business card, "here's my personal number. If you ever change your mind, I hope you'll call me. I really do find you very attractive." As she handed him the card, she glanced up at him once again with her most provocative "come on" look.

Chris blushed at her comment and gave her a shy grin.

Finally, Jill slowly stood to her feet and waited while Chris got up as well. She then reached out her hand to give him a handshake. But when he reached out and clasped her hand, she pulled him over gently and gave him a kiss on the cheek. "Remember, call me anytime," she whispered in his ear. "I'll be waiting."

With that, Jill walked over to the table, picked up her champagne and glasses, and put them back in her purse. She then made her way to the front door. Chris followed her there, then reached over to open it. As she walked out into the hallway, she glanced back and said, "Goodbye, Chris, ... until we meet again." She then walked down the hall and turned the corner out of sight.

CHAPTER 11

SHOCKED AWAKE

The next morning, Chris was startled awake out of a sound sleep. BAM BAM BAM!! It sounded like someone was trying to break down his door. "Chris!" He heard his name shouted through the door. "You've gotta see this!"

Chris looked over at the clock. It was only 6:00. *What in the world's goin' on?* he thought to himself. *There must be some kind of emergency.* He quickly jumped out of bed, staggered to the door in his pajamas, and peaked through the peep hole. It was his teammate, Randall. Chris quickly opened the door and shouted out, "What's goin' on? Is there a fire or somethin'?"

"No, nothin' like that," Randall responded, "but you've gotta see this!"

Chris looked in Randall's hand and saw he was holding a newspaper. "What?" Chris whined, audibly displaying his annoyance, "You woke me up for this? Couldn't it have waited 'til I got up?"

"Oh, I don't think you wanna wait that long. Look at this!"

Chris took the paper from Randall's hand and saw a giant headline that read: "**Templeton's Chuck Norris Destroys the Field.**" Below the headline was a rather impressive picture of him throwing a roundhouse kick at the tournament. On the left-hand side of the page was an article that gave a recap of the entire tournament. Right next to the recap was a second article that took up the rest of the space on the front page and bled onto page two – one that was completely about him.

The article about Chris contained some information that looked like it came from the team's media packet. But the bulk of it had obviously been researched by a reporter who must have talked to people in Templeton. There were also quotes from the post-tournament press conference. But there was one thing in particular Chris was looking for as he skimmed the article, *Did they put in my quote about my commitment to Jesus Christ?*

And there it was ... plain as day. *They did put it in!!* With that, Chris was jolted wide awake. This was exactly the big opportunity he had hoped for. *God's gonna use this,* he affirmed in his heart.

After reading the articles, Chris turned back to Randall and reached out to hand the paper back to him. "Hey, you kinda gave me a shock for a second, but I'm wide awake now. Thanks for bringin' that by. I'll have to get me one as a personal keepsake."

"Oh, you keep that one," Randall responded, "Jennifer already bought out the entire hotel supply. You know Jennifer. She's gonna take a bunch back to Templeton."

At that, they both laughed out loud. "Yeah, that's Jennifer, all right," Chris quipped.

After Randall left, Chris pulled out his cell phone and immediately called home. He knew his folks were early risers and would already be up. He wanted to share the news with them. When the phone rang, Chris' mom picked up and shouted, "Chris, congratulations! Looks like you've made quite a splash over there."

"Mom, you won't believe what they put in the Skeptopolis newspaper," Chris blurted out.

"Oh yes I would," his mom quickly responded. "Your dad and I've already seen it online. We're so proud of you. God is setting you up for what He sent you over there to do. That's a sign."

After talking for another ten minutes, Chris hung up the phone, got dressed, and went down to the cafeteria to meet his teammates for breakfast. For the next hour they talked about the tournament, and especially about the newspaper articles.

CHAPTER 12

MEET THE PRESS

As Chris and his teammates were about to leave the cafeteria, they heard a big commotion out in the lobby. A whole gaggle of reporters had just come into the building and were inquiring at the reception desk where they might find Chris. As the person behind the desk looked up, he saw Chris walking across the lobby toward the elevator and pointed, "There he goes right there." They all immediately rushed over.

"Chris, Chris," several called out, "could you take a few minutes for interviews?"

Chris was taken back with all the fuss, but consented, "Sure, I guess so. After all, before the tournament I promised you guys I'd talk afterward."

Then, one of the reporters who had remained to talk to the desk clerk ran over and informed everyone, "Hey guys, the front desk says we can use ballroom number two. It's right around the corner."

There had been a convention there the night before and it had not been cleaned up yet. Trash lay strewn around on the floor with tables and chairs scattered around but no one seemed to mind. So the reporters quickly grabbed some chairs and arranged them in a semicircle with Chris out in front. While they gathered their chairs, the TV cameramen set up their cameras, along with a backdrop to block out the messy room.

Chris had never done an interview like this before, but he had seen them on TV. He decided the best way to keep order was for him to take charge. So, he asked them to raise their hands and let him call on them as they proceeded.

A lot of their questions related to details in the Skeptopolis paper. However, as the press conference progressed, their inquiries got more detailed and personal, not only about karate, but about every aspect of his life, including his Christian faith.

After about forty-five minutes, the reporters exhausted their questioning. As they wrapped up, each came up to shake his hand and give him their business card, along with an invitation to connect back if he thought of anything else that might interest them. Then, the reporters gathered up their things and left.

Wow, that was pretty exhilarating, Chris thought to himself as he got up and headed back to his room, but it was also very tiring. I need to go rest up a while.

CHAPTER 13

CONNIE GRANGER

Before he could get out of the ballroom, though, one of the reporters came up behind him. "Uh, excuse me, Chris, may I have a word? I'm Connie Granger from the *Skeptopolis Times*," she offered as she handed him her business card. "I'm the one who wrote the article about you in today's paper."

Chris recognized her as one of the reporters who had been questioning him but didn't know until that moment that she was the writer for the article in the paper.

"Connie," Chris replied, "it's a pleasure to meet you on a more personal level. Besides today, I remember seein you among the reporters yesterday at the press conference. That was quite a story you wrote about me. I'm very flattered at your kind portrayal of me in the paper. I don't think I deserved such a stunning writeup."

"You're way too modest," Connie replied. "After yesterday's performance, you deserved every bit of that and more. That was most impressive. I don't think I, or anyone else there, has ever seen anything quite like it. And what you may not know is that the people of Skeptopolis absolutely *love* karate. Of course, most people aren't really thrilled that a person from Templeton won. As you probably know, there's not a lotta love lost here for you guys. At the same time, they do have a deep admiration for excellence when they see it, so at the very least you have their begrudging respect."

"Well, "Chris chuckled, "I appreciate the compliment, even if it's begrudgingly given."

Connie smiled at Chris' comment, then began to explain why she hung around after the others had left. "Listen, I'd like to do a follow up article on you. Would it be too much of an imposition for you to talk to me for a few more minutes?"

"Sure," Chris replied, trying to be especially gracious to someone who had been gracious to him. "It's the least I could do after you wrote such a flattering article about me."

Connie pulled up two chairs so they could face each other directly. As they sat across from each other, she shared that she wanted to do this article on a different part of his life. "Besides sports," she noted, "the people of Skeptopolis are very interested in religion and philosophy. I'd like to follow up more on your comments about your faith."

Connie's comment about faith caught Chris by surprise. "I thought most of the people here didn't like Christians or Christianity," he exclaimed with a look of bewilderment. "Is that not true?"

Connie looked at Chris with devilish grin and quipped back, "Well, I didn't say *what* philosophy and religion they were interested in now, did I?" From the look on her face, Chris could tell she was joking, and he let out a big laugh putting them both at ease.

"No. No you didn't," Chris conceded, "and I get it. So, what do you wanna know?"

But before Connie went on, she wanted to make one clarification. "Seriously, though, before we go on, I do want to be straight up with you. It is possible that you might not like this article as much as you liked the one today. This does get into a potentially more controversial topic. Are you up for that?"

"All I ask is that you be fair," Chris replied, "so I'll trust you on that."

So, for the next 30 minutes Connie asked Chris questions about his faith in Christ, what it meant to him, and why he felt it was important. Toward the end, she asked, "Well, what are you gonna do now? Will you and the team return to Templeton today?"

In answer to that last question, Chris began to open up a little about his future plans. "Well, the team'll return today, but I'm gonna hang around here for a while. I've heard all these negative things about Skeptopolis all of my life, and I don't believe you guys are as bad as all that. I wanna get to know you better."

With that, Connie's eyes bugged out in surprise. "What?!" she blurted out as her mouth gaped open. Then suddenly, a whole different set of questions began flowing. "Where you gonna stay? How long'll you be here? What are you gonna do? Do you know people here who you'll be hanging with?"

Chris laughed. "Whoa, gimme a chance to answer. Actually, I've made arrangements to stay for at least a month at an apartment complex over on Straight Street," he replied, trying to give her as much information as he could. "Maybe longer if it works out."

Truth was, Chris didn't really know yet what kind of opportunities might present themselves, so there wasn't much more detail he could give her. "You know," Chris reasoned, "maybe the people in Templeton and Skeptopolis have more in common than we realize. You guys aren't the only ones who are interested in philosophy and religion. Maybe our particular interests are not exactly the same, but in general there's prob'ly some convergence. I think it's fair for me to study you guys like you wanna study me, and maybe we could get some dialog goin'."

"Fair enough, Chuck Norris," Connie joked. That comment caught Chris' funny bone, and they both laughed out loud together.

Suddenly, a thought grabbed Connie's imagination. "Wait a minute! If you're gonna do that, another idea just popped into my head," Connie exclaimed as she began trying to convince Chris to go along with her. "If you're gonna be here, would you have any objection to me covering your 'research project'? I can't promise you I'll be sympathetic to your point of view, but I do promise I'll be fair. You know, this could be good for both of us. I'll get an exclusive, and this could open up some doors for you to meet more people and establish the kind of dialog you were talkin' about."

Chris thought about that for a moment. Hmm, she's right about this possibly opening up some doors. But it'll also likely put me in the crosshairs of the powers-that-be in town. It could get a bit dicey.

After pondering it for a moment, Chris replied, "Okay, you have a deal. This could be very interesting. I don't have a business card, but here, let me write down my phone number, and you can touch base periodically and get your intel."

"Fantastic!" Connie replied as she put Chris' info into her purse, "The more I think about this, the more excited I'm becoming about this possibility, actually."

"Well, I'm not sure yet whether I should be excited about it or not," Chris retorted, "but I'm sure that at the very least it'll be interesting. Connie, thanks again, for the kind article you wrote, and I look forward to seein' you again soon."

With that, Connie got up, they shook hands, and she turned around to leave. After a few steps, she glanced back over her shoulder and said, "Be sure to check tomorrow's paper. There might be something' there." Then she turned again toward the front door of the hotel and headed back to her office.

"What have I gotten myself into?" Chris mumbled under his breath. "I sure hope I'm ready for this."

CHAPTER 14

THE ARTICLE

Sure enough, the next morning's paper featured another front-page article about Chris. He was able to get a copy from the hotel desk clerk, then went to the cafeteria for some breakfast where he read it while he ate.

◆

𝕾keptopolis 𝕿imes

April 8   *Always There for You*   SkeptopolisTimes.com

Templeton's Chuck Norris

Knowing the Man

By Connie Granger

Monday, the state karate tournament saw the most amazing display of flawlessly executed martial arts skill ever witnessed in over 40 years when Templeton's Chris Bel finished the entire tournament without a single contestant scoring even one point on him. Regardless of whom you personally cheered for; you couldn't help being impressed by the outstanding skill that Chris displayed in the ring. It was pure poetry in motion.

In yesterday's paper *Skeptopolis Times* featured an overview of Bel's performance in the tournament, including a bit about his background. But who is this guy really? What is he like as a person?

This reporter had the opportunity to sit down with Chris to learn more about the man himself. Here is a recap of that interview.

Chris, first, for the girls, do you have a girlfriend?

Now that's a pretty funny way to start an interview. Actually, at this time I don't. I have some very close friends who are women, but no girlfriend at this time.

Ok, now that we have that important piece of information out of the way, what do you do for a living?

I finished college about six years ago and majored in business management. After graduation, I took a job with a large manufacturing firm in Templeton, Forester Manufacturing. Right now, I'm on a personal leave of absence to focus on karate and some personal projects.

So, speaking of karate, how did you get started doing that, and when did you realize you had such potential in this sport?

Well, I actually, sort of got into karate by accident when I was six years old. I begged mom to let me do it, so she signed me up for a summer camp. As a child I was crazy about the Teenage Mutant Ninja Turtles. I wanted to be Michelangelo. Mom really didn't think I'd stick with it, but I fell in love with the sport and have been training ever since. I've now advanced to third-degree black belt.

So what about other sports? Did you do anything else in high school or college?

You know, I actually did play a couple of other sports. I was on the wrestling team in high school. Then, in college, I joined the judo team for three years. But I never quit karate. That's definitely my first love. I got involved in the other sports only to improve my overall martial arts skills. And I must say, it's been of great benefit. The various contrasting disciplines have helped to hone my skill set, making a big difference in my performance.

So what was your childhood like?

Well, I grew up in a pretty average middle-class family, and am the oldest of four kids. My dad's a county school administrator, and mom's a homemaker. I grew up in a very stable family, and the older I get the more I appreciate how my parents raised me. My family was also very active in our church, which had a strong influence on my life.

So would you say you were the ideal child?

For the most part I think I was a pretty good kid. I certainly got into the normal mischief that most kids get into, but nothing really bad.

I will say, though, that when I was in high school, there was a time when I got involved with a wayward group of friends, and their bad influence nearly got me killed in a car accident. After that, I decided I didn't want that kind of life, so I changed friends and straightened myself out.

You mentioned you grew up going to church. Now that you're on your own, have you finally outgrown that?

To answer your question directly, no, I haven't outgrown it and don't expect I ever will. My church experience growing up was very meaningful to me. Most all my friends went to my church, and I have a lot of camaraderie with them still today.

I made my own decision to enter into a personal relationship with Jesus Christ when I was 11 years old. I must say, though, at that time it didn't mean a whole lot to me. That all changed when I was nearly killed in the car accident. That made me realize that the spiritual part of life was my anchor, and I became ever more involved with the church after that.

I expect many of your readers may not appreciate this part of my story, but that is my story. My relationship with Christ is, honestly, the most important thing in my life.

---————◆◆◆————---

Well, dear readers, at that point we were about to wrap up the interview when Chris shared something else with me. As it turns out, he will not be returning to Templeton with his teammates but has decided to stay in Skeptopolis for a little while. When he told me that, we continued our conversation, and I had the opportunity to ask him a few more questions.

But before we get back to the interview questions, I feel that a little more explanation is in order. What Chris told me was that his reason for staying in Skeptopolis is actually related to his religious faith. Let's not kid ourselves, we all know there's no love lost between the people of Templeton and Skeptopolis. We all know the history, and we all know the differences in our views on faith. But Chris seemed to honestly want to understand the people in our fair city better, to the extent that he's decided to stay here for a while. Upon hearing that, I imposed on him to ask a few more questions.

Chris, so are you staying here in order to try to win Skeptopolis to Christ?

Connie, that seems to be a pretty loaded question. Are you trying to get me in trouble? (*laughing*).

No, of course not. But based on what you have told me, that does seem like a pretty logical question to ask. After all, there have been a lot of folks over the years from Templeton who have come over here to do evangelistic rallies and street preaching.

Well, I promised that I'd be straight with you, and you promised to be fair with me, so I'm not going to dance around this. I honestly believe that the bad blood between Templeton and Skeptopolis is not good. I recognize our differences, but I don't see any reason why that should keep us from respecting each other as persons and creating friendships. I don't plan to wear my religion on my shirt sleeve, but, at the same time I'm not going to hide it, either. And if I do have the opportunity to make a few friends, I hope it will result in us being able to have some respectful and meaningful dialogs – not just about faith, but about all the areas of our lives where we share a common interest. I don't like the fact that there's tension between us, and I honestly hope to get to know the people of Skeptopolis and learn more about who you are.

So will you also work with a karate dojo here and give our folks some pointers?

Well, I'd never presume that they would want me to show up at their dojo. After all, we've had years of competing against each other. But if they'd like me to come and work out with them some, it would be my pleasure. We may compete with one another, but at the most basic level, we're brothers in the sport. So, it's up to them.

So, who else would you like to meet?

Honestly, I don't have a plan for that. I'd like to meet people from all walks of life. I hope I have the opportunity to do that.

Well, folks, this seemed to me to be a rather interesting prospect. And as I thought about the future, it occurred to me that you, our readers, might like to keep up with Chris, as well. So, I asked him if I could touch base with him once in a while and get an update, and he graciously agreed. So at least over the next few weeks, you can anticipate some follow-up stories on Chris Bel's quest. Let's see together where this might lead.

CHAPTER 15

MOVING DAY

When Chris woke up, it dawned on him that today was the day – moving day. He'd been on many mission trips in his life, so the idea of doing this was not new. But this time it was different. He was by himself and was here for the long term. On top of that, he had already put himself out there in a way that would mark him as a Christian in a city with a reputation for hostility toward Christians. Being certain that the newspaper articles would seal that label made him a little nervous about what might happen next. At the same time, he also felt quite exhilarated. He couldn't wait to see what God was going to do with this.

A couple of his friends had driven his car over to Skeptopolis, pulling the rental trailer with his things and parked it in the hotel parking lot before going over to watch the tournament. So, after Chris checked out of the hotel on Thursday morning, he went to the parking lot, put his suitcase in the car, and drove to his new apartment.

After finishing the paperwork at the apartment office, he unloaded his trailer and drove it back to the rental agency. He then went back to the apartment, walked into the living room, plopped down on the couch, and turned on the TV to relax.

CHAPTER 16

THE CALL

No sooner had Chris settled in than his phone rang. "Hey, is this Chris?" a voice inquired from the other end.

"Yes it is. Who is this?" He didn't recognize the voice or the number and didn't know who it could possibly be. Maybe it was a telemarketer. Getting those calls was certainly not unusual.

"Chris, this is Carl Jackson from CJ's Karate Dojo. Everyone calls me CJ. I'm the owner. Connie from the newspaper gave me your number. She said she didn't think you'd mind if I gave you a call."

Oh wow, this is a pleasant surprise, Chris thought to himself. I met some of the competitors from Skeptopolis at the tournament but haven't had a chance yet to check out any of the dojos.

"Not at all, CJ," Chris replied, "what can I do for you?"

"Well, I saw the article about you in the paper this mornin' and wanted to take you up on your offer. We'd LOVE to have you come work out some with us. Everyone at the dojo was at the tournament and saw your amazing skill – we would all consider it an honor to meet a karate celebrity."

With that, Chris' face turned bright red. He never thought of himself as a celebrity, and the very idea caused him to feel a bit embarrassed and self-conscious. He was really glad no one was there to see his face right now.

"Well CJ, I'd consider it an honor. I remember watching some of your competitors perform. They looked well trained and disciplined. I also remember goin' up against one of your guys ... Renaldo, wasn't it?"

CJ felt particularly pleased that Chris actually took notice of his dojo and was especially impressed that he remembered Renaldo's name. "Yeah, that's right. Renaldo was our sacrificial lamb for you. You took him out pretty easily. Well actually ... it looked like you took everybody out pretty easily," CJ responded with a chuckle in his voice.

"No, I remember him," Chris replied. "He was very disciplined. It took me a little bit to figure out the most effective way to approach him. He's very strong with quite a unique reverse roundhouse. I had to figure out his timing to get under it without getting' tagged."

Hearing Chris' comment gave CJ a real sense of pride and made a profoundly good first impression. "Well, he was certainly impressed with you, and I think he'd be thrilled to have the opportunity to work out with you and get some pointers. Listen, how 'bout it? Do you think you could come and work out with us sometime?"

"I'd love to," Chris replied. "So, gimme the details." At that point, CJ gave Chris the location of the dojo and various times the groups trained. As it turned out, it was actually on the same street as his apartment only a few blocks down.

"Hey, I had one other thought, too," CJ continued, "We would, of course, consider it a great honor for you to train with us at different times, but I'd also like to put another bug in your ear. From time to time we put on a city-wide karate workshop to provide special training for the city's karate students. I'd like you to consider the possibility of doin' somethin' like that, too. Obviously, you don't have to make a decision right now, but I did want to throw it out there and maybe we could talk about it later. What do you think? Might that be a possibility?"

Chris was a little taken aback by that suggestion, but the possibility intrigued him. His dojo back home periodically did trainings like that, as well, and often even invited other dojos to participate. They were normally not huge affairs but might have 30 to 35 participants. Chris found that he often picked up some great pointers at those opportunities.

"Sure, CJ," Chris replied, "I'd be delighted to talk about doin' somethin' like that if you think I might have something to contribute to the karate community here. What are you thinkin'? Do you have some particular topic in mind you'd like me to share with the guys?"

"Actually, I *was* thinkin' of something in particular," CJ confessed, "and in some ways it's a bit selfish on my part because I'd like to pick up some pointers from you myself."

Hearing that comment really piqued Chris' curiosity. He thought. What in the world could he be talkin' about? This is definitely unexpected.

"Okay, sure," Chris replied, "What do you have in mind?"

With Chris' receptive response, CJ began to get even more excited. "Well actually, you already alluded to it a few minutes ago when you were talkin' about your contest with Renaldo. You mentioned that you had to figure out the most effective way to approach him. You obviously have some pretty special skills for evaluating opponents, and I'd like for you to share how you go about makin' those kinds of evaluations and adjustments when you're in the ring. If my students could learn that kind of thinking process, I believe it'd help 'em become better *karateka*.

"You know CJ, you've just lifted yourself way up in my esteem for you," Chris remarked. "I'm very much lookin' forward to meeting you in person. Most people think that learning some new technique or move'll bring 'em success in the ring. In truth, the best increase in success comes from learning how to evaluate and take advantage of whatever situation you're in. I'd be delighted to share how I go through that process while engaged in *kumite*."

CJ could hardly contain his excitement. "Great! Here's what I'm thinkin', Chris. You have our training times, and I hope you'll take the opportunity over the next couple of weeks to come work out with us. That'll give you a chance to get to know our guys a little bit and build some excitement for the workshop. I'd actually like to set somethin' up fairly soon while the afterglow of the tournament's still in the air. How's that sound?"

"You know," Chris replied, "that actually sounds like a pretty wise approach. And I really don't have anything on my schedule right now, so I'm wide open. What are you thinkin'?"

Just in case he did get a positive response, CJ had already begun brainstorming some possible dates. "Well, before I called, I pulled out my calendar to look at some possibilities in case you were willing, and I think the *earliest* possibility would be Saturday after next. I know that's pretty quick, but it'd give my team here at the dojo time to get the publicity out for it. I think we could pull that off. How's that sound? Do you think that's too soon for you?"

Chris didn't even hesitate. "Like I said, at this point I don't have anything on my calendar, so that works for me."

"Listen, one more thing," CJ continued. "I hope you don't mind, but I think this would be a great marketing opportunity for the dojo, as well. Do you mind me using your name to help promote the dojo? I'm thinkin' it'd be really great for business, and at the same time maybe we can get more people interested in participating in the sport."

"Oh yeah," Chris responded enthusiastically. "I'm all for that. In fact, I hope it's somethin' that really can help your business. I think anything to help raise awareness for the sport's great."

CJ continued, "I think Connie'd be willin' to help with that, as well. I've known her for years. In fact, we went to high school together. And since she seems to have a special interest in followin' what you're doing, I think she could be instrumental in takin' our publicity to the next level. Are you okay with that?"

"Absolutely," Chris replied enthusiastically. "Like I said, anything to increase participation in the sport'll be fantastic. And based on what she's said to me, I think you're right. I believe she'll be lookin' for stories to feature me, and this could serve all our interests."

For CJ, this conversation was everything he dreamed it might be. "Well Chris, I can't thank you enough for bein' such a good sport with this. So many of the really good *karateka* I've met over the years are rather snobbish or arrogant, but I sense that you're not that way at all. I'm really lookin' forward to not just havin' you participate with us, but also getting to know you personally. You have our schedule. I hope you'll come as often as you can."

"Thanks for the kind words, CJ," Chris responded. "I look forward to seein' you soon."

With that, Chris and CJ hung up. Chris put his phone in his pocket, then walked over and laid down on his bed to ponder what had just taken place. *I have no idea where all this'll lead,* Chris thought to himself, *but I've asked God to open doors for me, and I think this might be the first one.*

CHAPTER 17

AT THE DOJO

Chris showed up at CJ's dojo about 30 minutes before the beginning of class just to get oriented to how they did things. As he approached the building, he was shocked to see how big the facility was. It literally took up an entire city block. He had no idea there was any karate dojo in the entire state this big. It really got his curiosity up as to what it looked like on the inside.

When he walked through the front door with his gear, Chris could see an expansive workout area through the open door on the other side of the lobby. At the reception desk on his right, students signed in when they arrived, and staff could answer any questions that they or others might have.

As Chris made his way over to the desk, CJ saw him through the open door of his office. He immediately recognized him from the tournament and made a bee line to the area behind the counter. Then, without stopping, he went straight through the swinging door that opened from the office area into the lobby where Chris stood. "Chris!" CJ exclaimed with a great big smile on his face, "So glad you're here! I know this is the first time we've met formally, but somehow, I already feel like I know you. You don't know how much I appreciate you takin' the time to share yourself with us."

Even though this was the first time Chris had met CJ in person, he did remember seeing him at the tournament. Chris grinned, "Well, the pleasure's all mine. I wasn't sure I'd find a home away from home here in Skeptopolis, but I believe maybe I have. I must say, I'm totally blown away by your facility. I've never seen anything like it."

"Well," CJ responded, "I must say I'm very fortunate. We've actually only been in this building for about a year. Before that, my dojo was a couple blocks down the street, and was about a fourth this size – probably more like what you're used to seein'. I'm particularly fortunate that this city loves karate, and I just happened to be in the right place at the right time. I also have some very gifted staff who've been instrumental in promoting the dojo and helping it grow.

In some ways we were forced to make a move. The dojo had grown to the point that the old place could barely accommodate more students. This place came open and the owner was havin' a hard time selling it. It came on the market at a really good price. I don't know what possessed me, but I caught a vision to go big and see if we could turn this into the premier dojo in the state. It's been a lotta work, but we're really proud of what we're buildin' here."

"Well, I can certainly say I'm impressed," Chris responded with all the enthusiasm he could muster, "and I think you've prob'ly pulled it off. I tried to get here a little early to get myself oriented. Ya have a few minutes to show me around?"

"Absolutely! I'd love to. Follow me."

As they walked through the door on the other end of the lobby and into the workout area, CJ bypassed an explanation of that area and took Chris straight to the locker rooms on the other side of the building. They were magnificent and looked like what you would find in professional arenas.

CJ then led Chris around the corner to another part of the dojo that had been set up as guest quarters. "Back here we have four rooms that are available when we have visiting teachers come in to do workshops and such. I'd offer one to you, but it appears you already have your own place. This is usually for people who come from out of town. To be honest, when I have family or friends come into town, this is also a place they can stay to keep from havin' to rent a hotel room. And listen, if you ever have guests come over, you're definitely welcome to use those rooms as well."

Chris hadn't even considered the possibility that he might need guest accommodations for people who might come to see him, but he filed that invitation away in his mind. "Well thank you CJ. That's very kind of you."

Continuing the tour, CJ took him through the training area. It was huge and looked like a gymnasium divided into four distinct sections, each covered with the kind of padded flooring that was specially striped to accommodate karate training.

Additionally, on one sidewall were special training devices like heavy bags, wooden punching boards, torso training bags, and the like. On the other side were assorted weight machines and a large cabinet to hold various martial arts weapons. Again, Chris couldn't help but comment on how nice the dojo was. "CJ, you've really put together an unbelievable training facility. I'm totally impressed."

"Comin' from you, Chris, that's a real complement. Thanks for the kind words."

"Straight ahead, of course, is the office suite you've already seen," CJ continued. "Let's walk over there for just a minute and let me introduce you to the staff. We have three people who work here."

When they walked back into the lobby, CJ pushed open the swinging door that led behind the counter and invited Chris to follow. Behind the reception desk were four offices – his and one for each of his staff. As they walked in, CJ poked his head into each office and called everyone out. When they arrived, he said, "Everyone, I'd like you to meet Chris Bel. I told you he'd be comin'. And – as I shared with you – he'll be leading the workshop we'll sponsor in a couple of weeks. Chris, I want you to meet Dolly, our receptionist, Jack, our bookkeeper, and Diane, our business manager. I'm proud to say they are some of the best business talents in town, and the key to our business success. And all of 'em also train here at the dojo."

Chris walked over to greet each one individually and shook their hands. "It's a pleasure to meet all of you. I must say, I'm so impressed with what you guys have accomplished. This is without a doubt the finest dojo I've ever seen. You guys are unbelievable! I look forward to getting' to know you better."

Chris then glanced over at CJ as a way of getting his attention to ask permission to share his thoughts about his participation at the dojo. "CJ, while your staff is here with you, this is probably a good time to just mention my thoughts about participating with you guys. Tell me what you think. What I'd like to do is to attend each of the classes once over the next week leading up to the workshop. That way I can get to know your students a bit, and they can see me too, and hopefully that'll encourage more of 'em to come to the workshop."

"I love that idea!" CJ responded enthusiastically. "And to make it even more effective, I'll make sure everyone knows what you're doin'. That'll probably encourage more of 'em to make a point of attending class. Dolly, start making calls to all the members and tell 'em what's happening, and tell 'em to be sure to come to class."

Then Diane chimed in, "Perfect! This'll also give the rest of us somethin' concrete to work with as we create publicity for the workshop. From the staff side, we consider this a great marketing opportunity to grow the dojo even more."

She then turned to Chris," I guess CJ mentioned this is a "city-wide" event, right ... and that there'll be people from other dojos as well?"

Before Chris could respond, CJ jumped in, "Diane, I've been thinkin' a little more about that. You know, normally we host our workshops right here at the dojo. But I have a sneaky feelin' this event's gonna be way larger than what we're used to. I'm wonderin' if it might not be wise to rent a larger facility to hold all the people." He then turned to Chris, "What do you think, Chris? Would that put too much pressure on you?"

Chris replied without hesitation, "Listen, I'm game for anything that'd help you guys out. If you think that's the best thing to do, it's certainly fine with me."

CJ could hardly contain himself. "Wow, this is gonna be better than anything I'd even imagined. Diane, book the downtown arena and start getting' the publicity out immediately – whatever you need, just do it."

"We'll get right on it boss, "Diane replied. "This is gonna be really good."

With that settled, CJ turned to Chris one more time, "Listen, class is set to begin in about 10 minutes. Why don't you go ahead and change, and we'll begin shortly."

"Sounds like a plan," Chris replied. "And if it's okay with you, for this class, I'll just basically hang around in the back and observe how you guys do things. Then you can sorta pull me in as appropriate."

"Perfect," CJ responded, "see you in a couple of minutes."

Over the next week and a half, the number of participants coming to class picked up considerably, and Chris had the opportunity to meet and work out with most of the students who trained at the dojo. CJ had done an excellent job of getting people of all ages, and walks of life, involved in karate. As a result, Chris got to meet many of the local politicians, business people, government workers, technicians from many different trades, as well as students ranging from elementary school to college.

And as word got out about the workshop, all the other dojos in town made a special point to promote it as well. They were used to participating when CJ held his annual event, but this time most of them even called to see if they could co-sponsor. It was turning out to be one of the largest local sporting events Skeptopolis had seen in a very long time.

CHAPTER 18

THE WORKSHOP

"Holy Cow!" CJ exclaimed as he and Chris watched people enter the arena for the workshop. "So far, we've had over 300 registrations. I never in my wildest dreams thought anything like this could happen. It's sure a good thing we decided to move to the Arena. Looking at the registration cards, it appears most of these people are already training in karate, but there are a good number who aren't. I think we'll get some new students from this."

Chris nodded his head and smiled. He thought to himself, *Only God could orchestrate something like this.*

Chris then turned to CJ, "CJ, it looks like we'll begin in about 20 minutes. At the beginning, I'll let you do the introductions to get everything started. Then when you're ready you can turn it over to me. Sound good?"

"Perfect!" CJ responded.

Christ nodded and smiled, then went over to his private corner to wait.

At 10:30 sharp, CJ took the microphone and proceeded to get everyone's attention.

"Good morning, everyone! Let's gather around and get this show on the road. As you know, we have a karate celebrity leading our workshop today. The newspaper has called him "Templeton's Chuck Norris," which I think embarrassed him a bit, but I know him as Sensei Chris Bel. And I feel pretty certain that before the day is through, you'll know him more personally as Sensei Chris, as well.

"Just for a little background, Sensei Chris is a third-degree black belt in Shaolin Goju Karate and has been studying martial arts since the age of six.

I'm sure you're all aware of how he won the recent state karate tournament in record setting fashion. And, by the way, we are privileged at CJ's Karate Dojo to have Chris working out with us as he prepares for the regional tournament in Missouri." Being the businessman that he was, CJ couldn't help but put in a plug for the dojo in hopes that those who were not already taking karate might consider joining his in order to work out with Chris.

"And by the way, we also have a reporter here from the *Skeptopolis Times*, Connie Granger. She'll probably write an article about this for the paper when we're done, so if she asks you a question sometime during the day, please cooperate with her. We don't want to get on the bad side of the press." With that comment everyone in the arena chuckled out loud. There was just too much truth in that remark.

CJ continued, "I don't wanna take a lot of time away from the workshop, but we need to get organized a bit in order to make the workshop run smoothly. In discussing this with Sensei Chris, I asked him to focus his teaching on something I believe'll help you become a more effective fighter. Today you'll want to pay special attention as he is going to share with you probably the number one secret to his success in the ring. You won't regret having come today; I assure you.

"So what you're gonna learn is somethin' very practical. In the process, you're also gonna get a lot of actual practice working on the techniques he'll teach. That means we need to get everyone into groups by age and experience. As you look around the arena, you'll see signs that designate the various groups we want you to break into. Go now and find your proper place.

It took about ten minutes, but everyone moved to their spots as quickly as possible, then sat down on the floor facing CJ. When he saw that everyone was in place, he picked up the microphone again and addressed the participants,

"Okay folks, now what you've all been waiting for, Sensei Chris Bel."

To a huge applause, Chris walked out onto the arena floor where CJ was standing, took the mic, and began to speak. "Greetings everyone. I wanna thank you for comin' and am very much lookin' forward to our time together today. First, I wanna thank CJ for his vision in pulling this workshop together. Before you leave today, you'll want to thank him and his incredible staff for their fantastic work in doing that. I also wanna thank all of you for your warm reception. I consider it a great privilege to be here with you today. It was truly an honor and privilege to compete in the recent Skeptopolis state tournament. You guys were fantastic hosts.

"Now I know that during that tournament you were rooting for your own guys to win, and I'm sorry to have messed that up for you in my division." Chris expected that to draw a laugh, and he paused appropriately as the laughter flowed.

When it died down, he continued, "Well, not really. I have to be honest. I definitely wanted to win." That brought even more laughter than before.

After a short pause to let things quiet down again, he continued, "But with the state tournament over, and as we look forward to regionals, I now consider myself part of *your* team, and I hope you'll cheer for me as I represent our state." With that there was another round of applause. It seemed Chris was already starting to win them over.

"So, let's not waste any more time. Let's get the workshop under way and get to the heart of our training for today."

The workshop continued all the way until late afternoon, with only a break for lunch. At the end of the training, when Chris had finished working the students out, he once again picked up the microphone and addressed the group. "Guys, that wraps up the workshop for today. But we still have about 30 minutes before we dismiss, so I wanted to give you a little bit of time to just ask me any questions you have on your mind. If you have a question, raise your hand and I'll call on you. When I call on you, say your name, and ask your question."

Immediately, hands went up. "Okay," Chris called out. "Let's start with you on the right side over there."

"Thanks, Sensei Chris for the workshop today. This has been fantastic. My name's Marshall. My question is, 'How often do you train?'"

"Great question, Marshall," Chris replied. "It hasn't always been the same. As I've gotten older, I've increased my training schedule. When I first started, it was a summer camp, and we went every day. But when the camp was over, I went to class twice a week. I was six years old at that time. I continued that schedule until I became a teenager, and at that point I started getting a desire to compete. So, to further improve my skills, I started training four to five times a week, and have mostly kept that workout schedule since that time. Of course, I do take breaks from time to time, but that's my usual schedule. Who else has a question?"

"My name is Joanie," a young teen girl called out. "Do you have a special diet?"

"Another good question, Joanie," Chris responded. "I can't say I have a special diet that I go by, but I will say that I do watch what I eat and when I eat it. At this point in my life, I don't have to really watch my calorie intake because I work out so much. But I've found there are certain foods that slow me down or make me feel less than optimal – and, unfortunately, some of those things are foods I really like. That doesn't mean I never eat 'em anymore, but I do watch carefully when I eat 'em, and I'm careful not to eat too much when I do. In talking to my friends who also practice karate, I've found that a lotta times the foods that work for people are not always the same. As you continue your training, keep track of what you eat and when you eat it, and it won't be long before you figure out what works best for you."

"Is there another question?" Chris asked the group.

"I have a question. My name's Steve. As you can see, I'm a bit older than most of the folks here. I'm a professor over at the university. My question is not exactly about karate, but I've read the newspaper writeups about you and it stuck out to me that you're deliberately promoting your religion through your celebrity. Why are you doin' that?"

"Steve," Chris began his reply cautiously, "first I wanna thank you for your question. Indeed, my faith is very important to me, and is somethin' that really does provide me with an inner peace and calmness that helps center my life. I'm certain you feel your own faith provides benefits for your life, as well. Everyone has a spiritual element to their life that needs to be fulfilled. If you don't get that peace, it can create all kinds of tension and distractions in your life ...."

Before Chris could finish his sentence, Steve interrupted, "Listen, not to be crass or anything, but I think your religious stuff is a crock. You're obviously very good at karate, and I think you should just stick to that."

That comment came as a bit of a shock to Chris and had the potential to throw a sour mood over the entire workshop just as they were about to wrap up. CJ took a step forward and was going to stop Steve from continuing, but Chris raised his hand to stop him, and spoke directly to the attack.

"Steve, listen, I don't wanna be confrontational here, but your comment's just not appropriate for what we're doing right now. That subject wasn't even a topic here until you brought it up. We've been focusing entirely on karate. I'll tell you what, though, if you wanna talk further about that, I'll be glad to have that discussion with you at an appropriate time. What's say, after we dismiss here, let's talk and set up a time to get together. Does that sound like a plan?"

"You're right, Sensei," Steve apologized. "That was inappropriate for here. I'll catch you when we're done."

"Great! Thank you, Steve, for your consideration."

After that, Chris answered a couple more questions, then closed things out by addressing the entire group. "Well everyone, on your feet and face me. I don't know about you, but for me it was a fantastic day. I hope the workshop's been everything you hoped it would be. Now, let's bow out and we'll be finished."

After bowing, the students spontaneously began clapping and shouting. It turned into a full two-minute ovation. There was whooping and hollering everywhere. "Thanks, Sensei! That was awesome!" a voice from the crowd shouted out. "Yes it was!" several more yelled.

After the applause died down, CJ took the mic, and after a few parting words dismissed the workshop. At that point, everyone slowly began to file out.

CHAPTER 19

NEW RELATIONSHIPS

"Chris, what a fantastic workshop!" CJ gushed. "I never in my wildest dreams imagined that somethin' like this could happen in the first place. And I never imagined it could be as successful as this was. And people's comments as they were leavin' … WOW! Everyone's as high as a kite. You did a fantastic job! Thanks."

Chris blushed and flashed a smile. "Yeah, it seems to have worked out really well. I always try to give people my best, and it's really gratifying when they're pleased. And your team did an awesome job pullin' it all together."

"And oh, I almost forgot," CJ blurted out as another thought came to mind, "Steve's waitin' over by the arena office complex to talk to you. I'm not sure I envy you with that. By the way, you handled that situation with him really well. There's several other people with him also – including Connie – just a heads-up."

"It's okay, CJ. I'm glad to talk to him. He seems like a nice enough guy." So Chris turned toward the office complex and headed in that direction.

As he approached Steve, Chris noticed there were three other people standing next to him – one of which was Connie. *I guess she sees a story in this,* Chris thought to himself. *I don't believe I've ever seen the other two, though. In fact, I don't even remember them bein' at the workshop.*

Chris walked up to the group and reached out to shake hands with Steve. Not to be impolite, he also greeted Connie, then introduced himself to the other two. "Hello, I am Chris. Are you guys here with Steve?"

The person closest to Chris reached out her hand. "Hello Chris, I'm Sybil, and this is my friend Colleen. We know Dr. Craven, but we're not here with him. We were just hopin' to have a word with you."

"Well, ladies," Chris replied, "it's a pleasure to meet you. I was actually meeting Steve for a short appointment, so if you don't mind waiting, I'll be glad to come over and talk when we get done."

"That's fine," Sybil replied. "We don't wanna impose, so take your time."

Chris glanced over at Connie to see if she wanted something in particular. "I'll wait, too, Chris. You go ahead and take care of your business." Chris smiled at her and nodded.

Then, just to get a little more privacy, Chris and Steve walked a few steps down the hall before Steve spoke up. "Sensei, I want to apologize again for speakin' outta school durin' the workshop. I obviously wasn't thinkin' clearly at that moment. By the way, your training was superb – best I've experienced."

"Thank you, Steve," Chris responded. "I appreciate your kind words. Now, what can I do for you?"

"Well, Chris, you know Skeptopolis is not very friendly toward Christians. Now I'm not a bigot that way, but I do want you to know up front that I also don't have a favorable view of your religious faith."

Chris smiled, "Well, I sorta gathered that from your question in the workshop."

Steve nodded, flashed an embarrassed smile, and continued, "What you probably don't know, though, is that I'm a sociology professor over at the university. One of the classes I teach is *The Evolution of Religion*. Since you've made such a public show of your Christian faith, I assume you truly believe the Christian faith is real. Would that be a correct assumption?"

Chris pursed his lips and nodded. "Yeah, that'd be correct."

"Well," Steve proceeded, "I was wondering if you'd be interested in sharing about your faith in my class one day?"

Steve's request came as a quite a surprise after the incident at the workshop. Chris thought, *If he was so outspokenly against my Christian faith, why would he want me to speak to his class?* But even with that doubt, Chris didn't hesitate. He just assumed God was opening a door for him. "Sure, I'd be glad to do it. Tell me more about what you have in mind."

"Well," Steve went on, "you need to be aware that it could be a bit uncomfortable for you. You already know that my views about Christianity don't correspond to what the Bible teaches, and I teach what I believe. But you also need to know that the students in my class agree with me, and that they'll be itching to show you how your faith is wrong. Now I wouldn't blame you for not wantin' to get caught in the middle of something like that, but what do you think?"

As Steve was talking, Chris processed the situation in his own mind. It's pretty obvious that Steve is very anti-Christian, and he's just itchin' for a chance to put me down in public. He's prob'ly thinkin' that if he can make me back down, he can crow to his colleagues that I was too afraid to express my faith in public. And if I do take the opportunity, he doubtless thinks his students'll be able to break me. He prob'ly also thinks he has me in a no-win trap. And I'm sure he'll also have Connie there to document it. I believe he wants her to write about it, so I'd be humiliated in front of the whole town. But I also believe I'm prepared. I think he'll be surprised to have his own beliefs effectively pushed back against. But regardless, I know God's called me to this and will reveal himself through it.

"Well, I can't say that you've exactly made your offer sound enticing," Chris responded with a chuckle in his voice. "But okay, Steve, I'm game. I'd be happy to share with your class. At this point, my schedule's pretty flexible, so just let me know when a good time would be."

"Well, how about next Tuesday at 10:00 in the morning?" Steve inquired. "My class will be all ready to hear you. We meet at the University's Darwin Hall in room 224. Does that work?"

Chris pulled out his cell phone and entered the date, time, and location into his calendar. "That'll be great, Steve. Thanks for the invite."

Having that settled, Chris and Steve turned and walked back toward the office complex where the others were waiting. Chris stopped when he got to them, but Steve kept on walking.

"Good day, ladies," Steve said as he headed toward the exit. "Chris, see you next week."

Chris then looked at Sybil and Colleen and asked, "Well, what can I do for you ladies?"

With that greeting, Sybil jumped right into her explanation. "I'm sorry that we're bargin' in on you like this," she said apologetically, "but we saw in the paper where you're a Christian, and we wanted to invite you to come visit us at our church. We go to Southside **Universalist Church** over on Fourth Street."

When Chris first heard them say they were from a church, he was somewhat caught off guard. He knew there were not very many churches in Skeptopolis, and the ones that existed were likely to be theologically liberal and didn't have much of a reputation for inviting people to visit. But when they told him the church's name, it all made sense. Universalist churches believe that everyone automatically goes to heaven when they die – a very different teaching from what is taught in the Bible. Beyond that, they tend to be extreme social liberals, advocating for abortion and homosexual marriage. Most Universalist churches follow theologically liberal and postmodern forms of theology rather than New Testament Christianity, the way the Bible defines it.

"Well Sybil, I'm very flattered that you'd invite me, but I'm sure you're aware of the differences between what I believe about the Christian faith and what you believe. The two views are not very compatible. Why would you want me to come to your church?"

"Yes, we're very aware of that," Colleen jumped in, "but we think we can change your mind. Our church isn't very big, but we wanna share with you the great work we have goin' on in the projects with our food distribution, education ministry, and pregnancy counseling services. And our pastor is so gifted at sharing about the love of Christ. We believe when you see how Christ is working in our congregation, you might wanna be a part of us. We also think your presence would be a great witness, and that more people might come to church if they heard you're comin'."

"Well, thank you for being so straightforward," Chris replied. "You know, one of the reasons I decided to stay for a while in Skeptopolis was to get to know more people. I'd be delighted to share fellowship with you at your church. But I wanna be as honest with you as you've been with me. I'm very committed to my evangelical faith, and I don't think you'll change my mind. If I come and we can talk about this, will I create problems for you? I don't wanna be a problem."

Sybil replied, "Chris, we're completely aware of the differences, but we love everybody and just wanna love on you, as well."

"In that case," Chris replied, "I'd be delighted to come. I look forward to seein' you soon and meeting your friends. Thanks for the invitation."

As they left, Chris couldn't help thinking to himself, Wow, I didn't expect that. I wonder what'll come of that invitation.

Suddenly, a tap on the shoulder broke Chris' chain of thought. When he turned around, there was Connie still waiting to see him.

"Oh hey, Connie," Chris chuckled. "You startled me."

They both giggled and she quipped, "Well, how about little ol' me sneaking up and surprisin' Chuck Norris."

They both laughed out loud and Chris bantered back smiling, "Yeah, you got me on that one. What can I do for you?"

"Oh, you know," Connie responded. "You promised I could observe and write about you, so I just want to stay in touch to collect on that promise."

"I know, and I'm a man of my word," Chris replied back. "But you also said you'd be fair, so I'm counting on that."

"Hey, you'll see another article tomorrow. I'm gonna write about the workshop. Now you do realize, don't you, that everything I've written so far has been pretty glowing. And the article tomorrow will be no different. I was here the entire day, and I've already interviewed CJ and several of the other karate senseis – as well as a few of the participants. Everyone had nothin' but good to say about you. You seem to be the golden boy in karate circles around here."

Chris smiled. "Maybe, but I don't have any illusions about what you're capable of. I keep waiting for the other shoe to drop."

"Hey, I promised I'd be fair, and I will. I'll call it as I see it with honesty and integrity," Connie countered. "It does look like it's gonna get a little harder for you, though, as you step out of the karate arena and into interactions with other demographics. I'm very curious how you're going to handle Dr. Steve. He's a brilliant professor. And while he can be very nice and civil on the outside, he despises Christianity with a passion and can't wait to tear you apart. You realize that don't you?"

"Did he tell you that?" Chris inquired.

"No, not in so many words. But I've known him a long time, and I'm tellin' you, he's comin' after ya."

"Actually, I did discern that," Chris affirmed, "but the confirmation's helpful."

"And interacting with the people in the Universalist church'll also be a challenge," Connie continued. "You realize they invited me to observe that, too, right?"

"Well, I wasn't aware of that, but I can't say I'm surprised," Chris replied. "You come across to me as someone who's very thorough, looking in every nook and cranny."

Connie gazed at Chris with a very determined look, "You don't know the half of it!" Then, to let him know she was just playing with him, she let out a huge laugh.

The next day, sure enough, just as Connie had promised, there was another very positive article about Chris and his performance at the karate workshop. It contained glowing reports about how many people participated, how it was such a positive influence on the business environment, how the participants were excited to learn some ways to improve their karate, and, overall, how Chris handled the training in such a positive and professional manner.

She also wanted to make sure there was at least a little controversy mixed in, so in addition to all of the positive feedback, she mentioned Steve's question and had a few comments from him, as well. Overall, Steve's comments about the workshop were positive, but he couldn't help but get in a dig or two about Chris' faith. Connie also noted that Steve had invited Chris to speak to one of his sociology classes and that he had agreed to do it.

As Chris read the article, he was pleased with the overall tone and content, but also felt a little nervous. Up until now, Connie hadn't introduced anything controversial about his faith into her reporting. Now, though, there was the potential for that. In some ways he felt she was being straight with him, but also had the feeling it was possible he was being set up. He knew he'd have to handle this whole thing very carefully.

CHAPTER 20

AT THE CHAMBER

"Hey Chris," it was CJ on the phone, "what's happenin'?"

"Hey CJ, how's it goin'? Everything's fine here. Actually, I don't have any major plans today. I was just gonna chill. Somethin' goin' on?"

"Well, both yesterday and today my phone's been ringin' off the hook, but it's not exactly been what I expected."

"Oh yeah? Well, you've got my curiosity up. Who's been callin' ya?"

"I've been gettin' calls from other business people in town. They wanna meet you. We actually have a Skeptopolis Chamber of Commerce breakfast meeting tomorrow mornin,' and these guys were askin' if I'd bring you as my guest. So, I told 'em I'd ask. Would ya like to go?"

A little shocked, Chris asked, "Why do they wanna meet me? I'm not even in business."

"I know," CJ replied, "but you're a pretty hot commodity these days. They like to be in the know about what's goin' on in the community. Some even think that somehow bein' associated with you right now might give them some kinda business advantage. Who knows what might develop out of knowing some of 'em – but meetin' more people can't hurt."

"Well, you're absolutely right, CJ. I think it'd be great to meet some of your colleagues in the business community."

"Great! Can you be ready by 7:30 tomorrow morning? I know that's a little early, but it's a breakfast meeting. I can come by and pick you up if you like."

"Super," Chris replied. "I look forward to seein' you then."

The next morning, CJ pulled up in front of Chris' place right at 7:30 in his fire red 1966 Ford Mustang. Chris was watching for him through the front door window, and when he saw the car pull up, he exited his apartment, locked the door, and walked over to CJ's Mustang.

"Mornin', CJ." Chris said as he got in and closed the car door. "Sweet ride. '66 isn't it?"

"Yeah, I'm kinda partial to this car. I got it about five years ago. It was in pretty bad shape when I got it, but I fixed it up and returned it to its former glory. I'm the envy of the town with this baby."

"I bet you are," Chris responded. "So, how's it goin' this mornin'?"

Doin' great!" CJ replied enthusiastically. "I'm still in the afterglow of the workshop. That was one of the most exciting days of my entire career as a dojo owner."

"It was definitely cool," Chris replied. "I still have a hard time believin' that many people would show up to train with me."

"You're way too modest," CJ quipped. "You're the coolest thing to ever happen to karate in this town."

The rest of the way to the meeting, Chris and CJ exchanged small talk about karate and the possibility of CJ getting some new students from the workshop participants. "We've already signed up 10 new students because of the workshop," CJ shared, "and we've fielded about 20 other calls. I'm sure some of them'll also sign up."

About five minutes later, they pulled into the parking lot of the local country club where the Chamber held their monthly Monday breakfast meetings. It was not due to start until 8:30, but CJ wanted to get there early to introduce Chris around before things got busy.

As they walked towards the front door, Denise Norton, a local realtor, came up beside them. She was all decked out in her "realtor uniform" with her company's logo on the shirt. "Hey, Denise," CJ greeted her, "let me introduce you to Chris Bel. Chris, Denise is actually one of those who called me over the weekend to see if I could talk you into comin'. She's a local realtor. Denise, this is Chris."

Chris reached out to shake her hand. "It's a pleasure to meet you, Denise. Thank you for extending the invitation. I still don't know a lotta folks around here, and this is a great opportunity to meet some more people."

"Great to meet you, too, Chris," Denise replied. "You've become quite the celebrity in town. Everyone wants to meet you."

As the three of them walked into the building, Chris was still rather mystified. *How is this happening?* he thought to himself.

When they walked in the front door, they ran into Butch Grissom, a local contractor and this year's Chamber president. "Chris," CJ volunteered by way of introduction, "I'd like you to meet Butch Grissom. He's the president of the Chamber this year and he'll be running this morning's meeting. He owns the largest construction company in town and has built a good majority of the newer buildings you see around our fair city. He also does renovation work. He was another one of those who urged me to invite you to the meeting this morning."

As Chris' hand gripped Butch's to shake, he immediately noticed the calloused hands and firm grip of a person who worked in construction. As Butch spoke, his deep voice, fast talking, huge sense of self confidence, and smooth delivery gave Chris a clue as to why he had been selected to be chamber president this year. He also surmised that Butch was a great salesperson.

"Chris, what a pleasure to meet you. I've been followin' the articles about you in the Times with great interest. You've created quite a sensation in the community since you arrived."

Chris was still not used to being a celebrity, and once again felt somewhat awkward at the notoriety. "Well thank you, Butch," Chris responded. "It's a pleasure to meet you, as well ... and thank you for the kind words."

Before Chris could respond further, Butch jumped back in, "Listen, I don't wanna be too forward here, but I do want to put a bug in your ear before you get inundated by a bunch of other folks. If you have an interest in pickin' up a sponsor, I'd like to talk to ya later. It'd put some resources in your pocket and give me some good publicity – a win for both of us, I think. Just think about it and we can talk later."

"Well thank you, Butch," Chris replied. I look forward to talkin' with you more."

At that point, more people began walking up to the group. As Butch had already put in his plug, he backed away to make room for the others. After about 10 minutes of standing around and being introduced to a number of other people, it was about time for the breakfast to start, so everyone moved toward the tables. CJ led Chris over to a table on the right side of the room where they claimed their chairs, then walked over to the buffet line. While going through the line and filling their plates with eggs, hash browns, bacon, toast, and fruit, CJ went along introducing Chris to several more business leaders in the community. Then, after going through the line, they made their way back to their table.

Sitting at the table with them was Mark Johnson, a local lawyer, Bradford Nicholson, the owner of Carlile's Building Supply, and Janine Zorn, who owned a general store called Zorn Mercantile. They had some time to eat before the program started, so Chris took the opportunity to get to know the people at his table.

"So Mark," Chris inquired, "what kinda law do you practice?"

"Well, I specialize in fightin' for people's civil liberties. We deal primarily with cases that involve discrimination against women, the LGBT community, minorities, reproductive rights, and the like. In fact, we're closely affiliated with the ACLU – the **American Civil Liberties Union**. You familiar with that?"

"Of course," Chris replied. "You guys are in the news all the time." Chris didn't want to pursue that conversation too deeply because he was well aware that many of the values of the ACLU were completely contrary to his Christian values. After all, this was a time for meeting people, not getting into debates. There would surely be opportunities for that later. Chris continued, "So I'd think there wouldn't be a lotta those kinds of cases in Skeptopolis. Do you work much in other cities?"

"Well," Mark replied, "I do work with cases in other parts of the state, but you might be surprised just how much there is here, as well." Mark then leaned over and half whispered in Chris' ear, "I don't wanna say this too loud, but there's a certain amount of corruption in the local government, and I actually do have a fair number of discrimination cases I engage with the city, and with the county. But overall, this is a great place to live."

While Mark's comment was half whispered, it was intentionally loud enough so the others at the table could hear it, too. So when Mark made his comment, CJ inserted himself into the conversation, "And Chris, you don't wanna find yourself pitted against Mark. He has a reputation as a 'take no prisoners' kinda guy. You don't wanna get on his bad side." While Mark was a very pleasant person to know, everyone knew what CJ said was absolutely true, and his comment elicited some nervous laughter from the others at the table.

Mark also knew it was true, but he put forth a lotta effort to make his friends not feel nervous around him and spoke up to respond to CJ's comment, "Well, all of you here are the good guys, and I only go after the bad ones. All of you are definitely on my 'good side.'"

Hearing that, everyone laughed out loud with CJ chiming in once again, "Thank you for that, Mark. I'll sleep better tonight, now." And the cackling grew even louder.

When the laughter died down, Chris turned and spoke to Bradford, "So Bradford, tell me about your store. What's your story?"

"Well, Chris," Bradford replied, "First, please call me Brad. It's mostly my mother and people who knew me when I was a child who call me Bradford." And the laughing broke out again.

Chris, too, laughed and quipped, "Well, I certainly wouldn't want to be mistaken for your mother." And the laughter grew even louder.

Brad continued, "Carlile's is actually a franchise. We're part of a chain of stores located throughout the entire state."

"Yeah, I thought I recognized that name," Chris chimed in. "I've actually shopped at the one in Templeton. Building supplies, right?"

Brad nodded his head, acknowledging Chris' observation, then picked back up, "I used to be in the construction business myself, but saw a need and an opportunity to go into business for myself and I jumped on it. The store here in Skeptopolis has actually been here for quite a number of years, but when the former owner was ready to retire, he sold it to me. I actually used to work for Butch Grissom. I saw that you met him when you came into the building. In fact, he's my biggest customer."

"That's pretty cool, Brad. So is the building business good in Skeptopolis?"

"Well, it's like any other business, it has its ups and downs. But right now, the construction industry's in a good place, so I'm feelin' pretty optimistic at this point. Butch, in particular, is workin' on a new housing development on the north side of town, and that has things hummin' along pretty well right now."

There was one more person at the table and Chris turned to Janine. "Well, what about you, Janine?" Chris said as he turned his attention to her. What's the story of your store?"

Janine smiled and began, "Well, Chris, first let me also welcome you to the community. I think everyone here's intrigued by your big splash in town."

"Well thank you, Janine, that's a very kind thing to say."

She then proceeded to answer Chris' question. "Zorn Mercantile's a family-owned business started by my grandfather. I'm the third generation to run it. It started out as a small-town general store but's grown now to be a much larger operation. When Zelmart moved into town, we had to adapt or die, so we decided to compete by expanding and carrying a much more extensive inventory. We're still the primary supplier of supplies and equipment for the surrounding farming community, but we also go head-to-head with the big box stores selling hardware, housewares, work clothes, and the like – and I think we do a pretty good job. I believe the community really appreciates the fact that we didn't just give up and go away, and they go out of their way to support us. I'm very proud of the fact that we hold our own against the national chains."

"Wow, that's a pretty cool story, Janine," Chris exclaimed. "I look forward to doin' business with you myself."

"Well thank-you Chris," Janine responded with a smile on her face. "You're welcome anytime. And when you come, pop on in to see me and we can sit on the front porch of the old buildin' and have an RC Cola and a Moon Pie."

Everyone laughed again. When the store expanded, they kept the wooden facade of the old store intact, complete with the front porch, in order to maintain that "old fashioned" general store ambiance – and it was still a popular gathering place where the townspeople could just sit and talk.

CJ chimed in, "Actually, Chris, you might wanna take her up on that. Everyone in town *loves* that place, and it does hold a lotta nostalgia for the people around here. I think you'll like it."

At that point, Butch moved to the podium and called the meeting to order. Before introducing the guest speaker, however, he made a point of introducing Chris as CJ's special invited guest. In doing that, he encouraged those who had not yet met him to take the opportunity to do so after the meeting. That met with a round of applause, so Chris briefly stood and waved to the attendees. With that, the meeting continued as normal.

Every meeting has a guest speaker who gives a talk on something that would be of interest to the business community. Today's guest was the head of the state retail federation who had come to town to lobby city hall on behalf of easing the zoning regulations. They wanted it to be easier for businesses to expand in Skeptopolis. He gave a report on what they were trying to accomplish and about how the negotiations were coming along.

At the end of the meeting, a big rush of the business leaders in attendance headed toward Chris to shake his hand. He ended up standing around and talking for another entire hour. Fortunately, CJ had anticipated something like that, and made sure his karate classes were covered during that time.

When CJ finally had the chance to take Chris back to his place, the conversation centered on all the morning's events. When they arrived back at the apartment, the two continued to just sit in the Mustang and talk. "CJ, I wanna thank you for takin' me to the meeting this morning. That was, honestly, an unexpected pleasure."

"Chris, you don't realize the favor you've accumulated around town," CJ replied. "It's very real. But also, don't be fooled into thinkin' you have no opposition. There is an undercurrent of people who aren't really thrilled about you bein' here – some of 'em very powerful and influential. It's quite possible that you're not gonna be as well received by certain parts of the community as you were by the business leaders. In fact, one of the reasons the people at the Chamber like you is because they know certain others don't – and they're actually hopin' you'll be able to shake some things up a bit."

"Ooh?" Chris responded. "I'm not sure I like the idea of bein' part of a proxy fight. I don't like creating enemies. What's that all about anyway?"

"Well, here's the deal," CJ began to explain. "The business community's the more conservative element of the community. When I say conservative, I'm primarily talkin' about economics and politics. They want laws and regulations to be eased to make it easier to do business and make money. Let me clarify one thing for you though, I know you have a particular interest in religion, and in many places, conservative religion and conservative politics kinda go together. That's not really the case here. For the most part, those in the business community aren't interested in religion at all."

"On the other side of the spectrum are the government types and the university. Most of them are very liberal – both politically and economically. And for the most part, they HATE Christians. To them, political and economic liberalism revolves around promoting socialist economic policies and spendin' tax money on social welfare projects. The business community and those other interests are always buttin' heads."

"While the business people really don't care much about your religious opinion, they do recognize that your views overall align more with their values, and they honestly think your interaction with the community will shake out more favorably in their direction."

"One other thing," CJ went on, "the reason you're getting' a pretty fair treatment in the Times is that the media has to be careful to walk a tightrope between the two sides. The balance of power's pretty even in the city between the liberals and conservatives, and both sides lobby the paper pretty hard. The editors at the Times know if they come out too hard on one side or the other, it could hurt *their* business. They really do try to maintain some semblance of objectivity. That said, do be prepared for an occasional hit piece to balance some of the nicer things. They do have one editorial writer whose job it is to balance out Connie."

"Wow," Chris answered back. "I haven't seen that dynamic at work in the short time I've been here. That's really good to know. I'm still not sure I like the idea of being in the middle of that fight, though."

"Well, like it or not," CJ explained, "the dynamic exists. You don't getta choose how other people feel, and you can't guide their aspirations. You've already put yourself in a position where people are watchin'. Just a heads-up."

Chris thought about that for a moment, then answered back, "I see what you're sayin', and I really appreciate your insights about the community dynamics. But you're absolutely right. If I'm gonna be a visible person in the community, I at least need to know the dynamics that are playin' out around me. I really appreciate the heads-up."

CHAPTER 21

SOCIOLOGY CLASS

When his alarm went off at 6:00 AM, Chris rolled over, reached for his phone that was on the bedside stand, and turned it off. *Tuesday – today's the day. Darwin Hall. Ten o'clock,* Chris thought to himself. *Today'll be a huge challenge and a massive opportunity.*

After hopping out of bed and making it up, Chris took his time shaving and getting dressed before grabbing a bite to eat. After breakfast, he grabbed his Bible from the nightstand and spent a little time communing with God. Finally, he pulled out the notes about Naturalism and the Christian faith he had written before leaving Templeton and looked them over one last time.

The university was only a 10-minute drive from Chris' apartment, so about 9:15 he headed toward the school. He wanted to make sure he could find a parking place and be at the classroom in plenty of time.

Chris found a parking spot easy enough and headed over to Darwin Hall. After walking up the stairs to the second floor, he quickly found room 224. It was good timing. The bell rang to end the previous class just as he got to the classroom, and he just stood beside the door while that class emptied out.

Right as the bell rang, he saw Connie walking up from the opposite direction. "Hello Chris," she called out. "Great to see you this mornin.'"

Chris smiled, "Well, did you come to see the massacre?"

"Oh, come on Chris," she responded. "I've already learned not to underestimate you. I do, though, anticipate this'll be … let's just say, *interesting.*"

Chris and Connie decided to wait outside the door until Steve arrived. Just then, he heard a voice behind him. "Chris, glad you were able to make it,"

Steve called out with a lilt in his voice. "And hello to you, too, Connie. Good to see you."

"Hello, Dr. Craven," Connie responded. "My pleasure to be here."

That was the first time Chris had heard Steve's last name. At the workshop he was just Steve, and he had heard Connie call him Dr. Steve. *I should call him Dr. Craven in front of other people,* Chris thought to himself. *I need to show the proper respect for him in his own classroom.*

As the students began drifting into the room, Steve led Chris inside to the front near the lectern. Connie spotted a chair next to a side-wall whiteboard and made her way over there. It was out-of-the-way enough that she could fly "under the radar" as much as possible. All the while, the rest of the students made their way into the room and over to their desks.

There was an audible buzz in the room. Steve had told his students Chris would be coming, and what he would be talking about. He also gave them an assignment to come up with questions they could ask Chris – not just about himself, but about the Christian faith in general. He hadn't actually told them to be hard on Chris, but he didn't have to. He had already expressed his own opinion about Chris' beliefs to the class – that generally speaking, Christians were weak minded people who needed faith as a crutch. To be sure, his students got his drift. He didn't want to make any direct attacks but did what he could to create a passive-aggressive, adversarial atmosphere.

Then, just before the bell rang, three other professors strode into the room and made their way to the very back where they could observe. Seeing that, Chris looked over at Steve wondering what they were doing there. Steve took the cue and explained, "Don't worry about them. They're not gonna involve themselves in the discussion at all. Those are just some of my colleagues. I mentioned to 'em that you'd be comin', and they wanted to hear what you had to say. Those are doctors Everson, Gray, and Albritton. Everson's an evolutionary biologist, Gray teaches philosophy, and Albritton's a professor of religion. You might also be interested to know that Albritton's the pastor of the Universalist Church in town.

Whoa, Chris thought to himself, I can see they're rollin' in the heavy artillery to try to intimidate me. But I've got this. I bet they have further plans to come after me if they don't get what they want in this class. They probably wanna see where they think my weaknesses are so they can have a possible advantage later. I hate to have these kinds of conspiratorial thoughts, but I've already seen how these folks work, and I need to be on my toes.

Right then the bell rang, and Steve walked to the front of the class. As he looked around, he began, "Well, class," he said sarcastically, "glad you all could make it. Usually only about two-thirds of you can be counted on to be here on any given day, yet today we don't have an empty seat in the house. Looks like we have nearly 100 people today. I guess you're here to listen to our special guest.

"You all know I study karate, and actually met Chris Bel when he led the karate workshop at the arena the other day. Perhaps you've been reading about him in the newspaper over the last few weeks. He's become quite a celebrity in town. Let me also introduce you to Connie Baker with the *Skeptopolis Times* sitting over there at the side of the room. She's the one who's been writing about Chris." Connie smiled and lifted her hand so people would know who she was.

Steve continued, "Today, Chris is going to tell us about his Christian faith. Since this is a class about the evolution of religion, I thought it'd be good to have you hear firsthand how the Christian faith has evolved to the present time. Chris is gonna share his story, then some of you will have the opportunity to ask him questions." With that, Steve turned to Chris and said, "Chris, welcome to the class. You have the floor."

As Chris strode to the lectern, those in the class gave him a polite applause. Rather than just jumping into the meat of his presentation, though, he thought it would be good to begin with a more neutral topic to break the ice. And since he was known for karate, he decided to open with an introduction that featured his sport.

"Greetings everyone. It's a special privilege to be here with you today. How many of you have at least heard about me over the last few weeks since the karate tournament? Virtually everyone raised their hand. There had been a lot of talk about karate lately because of him. "So how many of you have read some of the articles Ms. Baker has written about me over the last few weeks?" About two thirds kept their hands up. Chris continued, "So have any of you ever studied karate yourself?" About one fourth of the class kept their hands up. "Well, how about now? Are any of you continuing your training?" All of the hands went down except for two guys sitting on opposite sides of the room. "First, let me express a special congratulations to the two of you. I hope you find the sport as rewarding as I do. So did either of you attend the karate workshop?" Both kept their hands up ... then in unison replied back, "It was great!"

"Well thank you, gentlemen, for the kind affirmation. I'm delighted to hear that."

Chris then turned his attention to the task at hand. "Dr. Craven kindly asked me to share with you about my Christian faith, and it's certainly my pleasure to do so. As I begin, I also want to acknowledge that I recognize it's quite likely that very few, if any, of you share my faith. In fact, not only do you likely not share my faith, but perhaps even hold to a faith that's diametrically opposed to mine. As I progress through my presentation today, I just want you to know that I intend to be completely respectful to you, and hope you'll show the same respect for me – just as Dr. Craven has done."

With that, Chris plunged into his presentation. "I was raised just down the road in Templeton. I'm sure you're aware, at least to some degree, of the religious background of Templeton. It was founded by Christians and a *very* strong Christian tradition remains to this day. In some ways it's similar to the founding of Skeptopolis with its very strong atheistic tradition. I was raised in a home where both parents were committed Christians, and they took me to church from the time I was born.

"I don't know how much you know about the Christian faith, so I want to give you at least a little bit of background. People may be born into a family where the parents are Christian, but that doesn't make the child a Christian. The Christian faith has to be individually accepted when a person gets to a place in life where they can understand what it's all about, then make a personal decision to accept it. Though I grew up going to church, I didn't personally make my own decision to enter the faith until I was a young teenager.

"There's another thing you also should know about the Christian faith. Deciding to become a Christian is not a matter of joining a church. Now as I share my story with you, you need to realize that, because of time constraints, I'll need to do so in a very abbreviated fashion. I could go into much more detail, but I honestly want to leave time for you to ask some questions, as well."

Chris continued, "The Bible teaches that God created mankind for the purpose of having created beings with whom He could share love and fellowship. When He created the first man and woman, they enjoyed that kind of fellowship. But one day, it was shattered when they did something that broke trust with their Creator. This not only caused a rift between them and God individually, but actually caused sin to enter the world where it had not existed before. This rift actually changed the very nature of man in a way that produced a sinful nature to be passed on to succeeding generations.

"The reason for the rift in the first place is because God, by His very nature, is holy and will not dwell in the presence of sin. So when sin entered mankind, it created a division between man and God that had eternal consequences.

"But God loved His creation so much, that he determined to create a fix for the problem. He would do this by implementing a plan whereby man's sin could be forgiven. But while being willing to forgive man's sin, justice still demanded that the sin be paid for. The truth is, sin is so grievous that the person who sins should die – not just physically, but spiritually, as well. And spiritual death means the eternal separation of man from God.

"But there's an eternal principle that's also revealed in the Bible that allows for a substitute to take the place of the one who has sinned. However, the substitute had to be someone worthy – one who had never sinned.

"As God assessed the situation, He was fully aware that no human being could ever achieve that requirement. So, He decided that He Himself would incarnate as a man, live that sinless life, and then offer Himself as a legitimate substitute. That incarnation was the man, Jesus Christ, and His death on the cross was that act of substitution. But that's not all. On the third day after His crucifixion, Jesus raised Himself from the dead to demonstrate that He had power over sin and death.

"There's one more thing you need to know. The fact that Christ sacrificially offered Himself does not mean that every human receives the benefit of His sacrifice. People must individually make a decision to receive God's forgiveness in order for it to be applied to them.

"So that brings me back to my own story. When I was a young teen, I made the decision to turn my life over to God based on the forgiveness for sin that He offered me. When I did that, God did forgive my sin and brought me into a personal relationship with Himself. Now I not only know *about* Him, but I know Him *personally*, and we enjoy fellowship with one another. So that's the basic story of the Christian faith and how my story connects to it."

After giving that brief overview, Chris then opened himself up to questions. "Okay, so who has a question they want to ask me?"

With that, hands went up all over the room. Chris saw all the hands and didn't know where to start. So he turned to Steve and said, "Dr. Craven, I don't know all your students, and don't know where to start with answering their questions. Perhaps you could be my intermediary here and manage that part for me."

Steve was more than happy to oblige and stepped up beside Chris. He had a pretty good idea who would be most likely to ask questions that might trip Chris up, and was glad to be put into a position where he could select the people he thought best to pull it off. "Okay, let's begin with Mary on the first row," Steve said as he pointed to her. "What question do you have, Mary?"

"Thank you, Dr. Craven," Mary responded, then turned her attention to Chris. "Chris, you know that the name of this class is *The Evolution of Religion*. We've been studyin' the evolution of religion and have learned that there was a time in the early evolutionary history of man when he didn't have religious beliefs at all. Then gradually, as the human species evolved, humans began acquiring an awareness of spiritual feelings, called Mana. As evolution progressed, religion also began to evolve to more complex forms – from Animism to polytheism to henotheism – the belief in many gods but the worship of only one – then finally to monotheism. So here's my question: Your description of the Christian faith started with monotheism. I think you skipped a bunch of steps. How do you account for the higher steps of evolution occurring before the lower steps happened?"

"Thank you, Mary, for that question," Chris began. "And let me say that you've asked a very good, and I believe a very important, question. Let me begin my answer by noting that the evolutionary theory of the development of religion is not **settled science**. In fact, it's actually not a scientific theory at all. Science is a methodology that is based on observation and experimentation. To arrive at the evolutionary model for the development of religion in human history, science can't even be used. Rather, the theory is based on **naturalistic presuppositions** – it is **philosophy**, not science. Rather than begin with scientific observations, advocates of that theory begin with the philosophical assumption that religion had to develop based on the evolutionary model.

"Let me propose to you another theory – the '**original monotheism**' model. This approach says that monotheism was first as God revealed himself to Adam and Eve in the beginning. Then, in later times, as human societies developed and spread out around the world, that initial truth devolved into the other forms that you just mentioned as people moved further from God. I personally believe that the original monotheism model has more to commend it than the evolutionary model."

When he finished answering Mary's question, Chris looked over at Steve and nodded that he was ready for the next one. Steve then stepped forward and said, "Okay, who else has a question for Chris?"

Again, hands went up all over the room. Steve looked across the room and said, "Alright, let's get someone this time from the back. Joe, what's your question?"

Joe stood up so he could be clearly heard. "Chris," he began, "in your explanation, you alluded to the Garden of Eden story, and talked about it as if it were actual history. But we all know that the Eden story was not actual history but was a **myth** that was orally passed down through generations during the period of pre-history. How can you believe it?"

Chris moved back to the center of the room behind the lectern and began his reply. "Thank you, Joe, for another very good question. I appreciate it because it's a question that gets right to the heart of many people's doubts about the truth of the biblical narrative. What I wanna do, though, is answer your question with another question. How do you know it's a myth? How do you know that the story was not accurately transmitted through the period of pre-history to successive generations through a particular family line? You see, once again we have a situation where the evolutionary model is assumed to be true without any way to verify its validity. People who advocate for that theory believe it because they can't bring themselves to believe in a supernatural reality, not because there's any kind of objective, scientific verification. If God really does exist and is the kind of being described in the Bible, it's actually not unreasonable at all to believe the story. And I believe that what I just shared with you is true."

Chris again looked over to Steve to indicate he had finished answering and was ready to move on to the next question. Steve once again came to the front of the room and said to the class, "Okay, who else has a question?"

Again, hands went up all over the room. "Let's see," Steve pondered as he looked over the class, "how about Janice. Janice, what do you want to ask Chris?"

"Thank you, Dr. Craven, and thank you, Chris, for taking the time to share with us today," Janice began.

"My pleasure, Janice. I deeply appreciate the invitation. What's your question?"

Janice continued, "In your presentation, you talked about your own spiritual feelings. However, people from other religions have spiritual feelings, too. Why do you dismiss their religions? What makes your beliefs better than theirs?"

Chris looked at Janice, nodding his head in approval at her question, then responded, "Thank you for that very thoughtful and insightful question. And Dr. Craven, I want to complement you, as well, for helping these students think deeply and critically about faith matters. The issues being addressed here are truly worthy of discussion."

Turning his attention back to Janice, Chris went on, "Janice, in order to evaluate the validity of a religion, you can't go by feelings. I could actually ask you the same question about your own feelings. You have certain things you believe, and those feel right to you. But how can you know that your beliefs are better than another, or that they are true or right?

"Rather, we have to evaluate beliefs by how they match up to the way human beings experience reality. That's actually a rather in-depth topic, and, unfortunately, we don't have time in this short period to deal with that. But I will say that I've studied it quite a bit, and I believe that the Christian faith matches up with human experience better than any other faith system. So just to summarize my point here, yes, you're right that everyone has feelings about their faith system. That said, feelings are not a valid criterion for evaluating the truth or falsity of a belief. There is a way reality is actually structured, and any belief that does not align with that actual structure is false. Feelings actually have no place at all in making that determination."

Once again, Chris looked over to Steve and said, "I believe we have just a little more time before class ends. Shall we entertain one more question?"

Steve stood up, walked to the middle of the room and said, "Yes, I believe we probably have time for one more. Who'd like to ask it?"

Again, hands immediately went up all over the room. Steve was hoping that someone would be able to trip Chris up at least a little, so he thought to himself, *Who's the sharpest student in the class who might be able to get in some kinda dig? I know, Martin's just the person.*

"Martin," Steve pointed as he called out the name, "why don't you take the last question. Make it a good one."

Martin stood up, cleared his throat and said with a firm confident voice, "Dr. Craven, thank you for this privilege. And Chris, I too want to thank you for coming and sharing with us today. Here's my question. In your last answer, you implied that everyone has religious feelings. Well, I don't have any religious feelings because I don't have any religious beliefs. Why do you think your last answer's reasonable?"

As Martin sat down Chris nodded his head, then thoughtfully and deliberately responded. "Another very insightful question. Thank you, Martin, for asking that one. Let me begin by saying that you may think you don't have any religious beliefs, but you do. Every person's most basic beliefs are their worldview beliefs. And without exception, worldview beliefs are accepted by faith. Let me see if I can explain that for you, using your beliefs as an example.

"A lot of people who are Atheists have a particular way they define their beliefs – and based on your question I'm assuming that you claim to be an Atheist. However, before I go any further, I do want to make sure that I'm interpreting you correctly. Have I read you right on that?"

Martin nodded and spoke up, "Yes, that's correct. I'm an Atheist."

"Let me confirm one other thing with you, as well," Chris continued. "Most Atheists I interact with define Atheism as a lack of belief, and object to me even saying that Atheism's a belief. Would that also characterize your thoughts correctly?"

Again, Martin nodded and responded out loud, "Yes, that's *exactly* what I believe."

"Thank you for that clarification," Chris responded. "I don't wanna be answering a different question from what you're asking. Okay, so I want to propose for you a different definition for Atheism. It's my contention that it's not a 'lack of belief' at all. Atheism is just as much a faith system as my Christian faith. Let me explain.

"While you may not believe in God, you do believe in something as it relates to matters of religion – and whatever that 'something' is, you believe it by faith. This goes for everyone in the world. It's not unique to any particular religious belief system. The way you define the essential elements of a person's religious beliefs is to ask three simple questions:

"One, what is the nature of ultimate reality?

"Two, what is a human being?

"And three, what is the ultimate one can achieve in this life?

"In fact, I believe that these three questions are so important, I wanna write 'em on the board so you can copy 'em down for yourself and think about their implications later." With that, Chris went to the whiteboard at the front of the room and wrote them down.

Essential elements of every religious belief

1. What is the nature of ultimate reality?
2. What is a human being?
3. What is the ultimate that one can achieve in this life?

"Now let me lay out for you the Atheist answers to these questions. By the way, Atheism is an expression of a naturalistic worldview, and the atheist answers to them are the same as the naturalistic answers. Here's how they're answered. And let me write the answers down on the whiteboard as I list 'em.

"Question one is: 'What is the nature of ultimate reality?' Atheism answers that question by claiming that ultimate reality consists of the natural universe operating by natural laws. There is nothing else.

"Question two is: 'What is a human being?' Atheism answers that question by claiming that human beings are naturally evolved animal creatures that have the most complex brains of all creatures in the animal kingdom.

"And question three is: 'What is the ultimate one can achieve in this life?' Atheism's answer to that question is that the ultimate one can achieve in life is survival and the fulfillment of personal desires – as this life is all that is acknowledged to exist."

Essential elements of every religious belief

1. What is the nature of ultimate reality?
   Ultimate reality consists of the natural universe operating by natural laws.
2. What is a human being?
   Human beings are naturally evolved animal creatures that have the most complex brains of all creatures in the animal kingdom.
3. What is the ultimate one can achieve in this life?
   The ultimate one can achieve in life is survival and the fulfillment of personal desires.

Before moving further, Chris interrupted himself and addressed Martin again, "Now Martin, once again I wanna be sure my answer aligns with the intent of your question. Do I seem to be on track with my answer so far?"

Martin once again nodded and replied, "Well, I'm interested to see where you go with this, but so far everything you've said seems to be reasonable."

"Thanks, Martin," Chris continued. "Now let me make a very profound statement. When people answer these three questions, they answer 'em based on their beliefs. There's no way to get at these answers based on **empiricism**. Science simply can't answer questions like this. There's nothing to experiment on or observe. What that means is that the Atheist answers are not based on any kind of objective data. They must be answered based on a person's **faith in their underlying worldview beliefs**. As for Atheism, there's no way to know empirically that the natural universe, operating by natural laws, is all that exists. There's no way to know, using any scientific methodology, that human beings are naturally evolved animal creatures. And there's no way to know, using any objective criteria, that the highest aspirations possible for human beings are tied to matters related to our physical existence. You *must* believe your Atheist beliefs based on faith that your answers to the three questions are correct. There is no science to back it up. Thus, your Atheism is a religious belief.

"Now, to complete the circle and give closure to your question, you asked why I believe that my beliefs are reasonable. Here's my answer. My belief in God is not merely an intellectual belief. As I shared before, I believe God is an objectively real person whom human beings can know in an objectively real personal relationship, and that He has revealed Himself to humanity. Based on what is taught in the Bible, I've opened up my own life to Him, and entered into a personal relationship with Him.

"Now I know you're thinking, 'Hey, how can you know that's true?' But here's the deal – if reality actually exists as I have explained, then there is an objectively real God who exists in a place outside the natural universe. And if He is as I've described Him, then it's not unreasonable at all for everything I've said to be true."

When Chris finished answering that question, he noticed there were only five minutes left in the class. That being the case, Chris turned to Steve and said, "Dr. Craven, I see there's only five minutes left in the class, and I don't think we have time to take any more questions, so I'm turning everything back over to you. As I do, I want to thank you for inviting me. I hope it was everything you and your class members hoped it would be." With that, Chris turned and walked over to the side of the room to let Steve take back over.

Steve then walked back to the lectern and addressed the class for the last couple of minutes. "Class, first let's show our appreciation to Chris for coming and sharing with us." At that, the class gave him a big round of applause, which Chris acknowledged with a smile and a nod. Steve continued, "Over the next few days we'll have the opportunity to discuss some of the things we've heard today." Then he continued with a sarcastic grin on his face, "I hope you'll make the effort to actually be in class for these discussions."

Just as he finished, the bell rang, and the students began filing out of the room. Steve walked over to Chris, shook his hand and said, "Honestly, thank you for sharing with us today. I must say you surprised me a little. I was certainly not expecting the kind of intellectual heft you shared with the class. This'll give me an opportunity to deal with some things in class that I normally only get to talk about with my graduate students. Very well done."

Chris didn't really know what to say. He was quite surprised himself that Steve would complement him that way. He knew that he initially had intended to try and embarrass him – and maybe that motivation was still there. But at least for now, he was satisfied that he had made a favorable impression. He also hoped sincerely that some of the things he'd said would help students consider the possibility he was right.

CHAPTER 22

THE FIGHT

After the class let out, Connie went up to Chris and asked. "What are you gonna do now? That was quite an interesting exchange you had with the students. If you have some time, I'd like to follow up and get your take on the class experience."

"Well," Chris responded, "I'm actually getting ready to go over to the dojo for a karate workout. I'm gonna drive to my place, pick up my gear, and head over there right now. But, if you have the time, you can ride with me back to my place and walk with me over to the dojo. We could talk while we're traveling. Then, if you still have time, I don't have any plans for after the karate class ... and you might enjoy seein' that part of my life, as well."

"Sure, I could do that," Connie replied. "Your exploits have now become a significant part of my job. The more I can get the better. My office is close to the campus, so I walked over here. Ridin' with you'll be fine if you can take me back to the *Times* office after we're done."

"Sure," Chris responded, "that wouldn't be a problem at all. My car's this way."

The two of them walked to where Chris had parked, got in, and headed over to his place. As they drove along, Connie spoke, "Chris, that was quite an impressive presentation you gave. But I think I was even more impressed by the way you handled the students' questions. How'd you learn all that stuff?"

"Well," Chris replied, "I've actually been studyin' those things for a number of years. I guess to really understand it, you havta have at least a little bit of understanding about what a church is and how it works. Do you have any background with that at all?"

Connie thought for a second and replied, "Well, I guess I don't really have any firsthand experience. I've been to a few church services here in town when there was some kinda story to cover, but as far as actually attending and learning the inner workings of one, not really. What do you think would be helpful for me to know?"

"To begin with," Chris began, "I feel pretty certain that my experience in my own church is gonna be rather different from what people would experience at any church here in Skeptopolis. All of the churches here, without exception, follow a form of theology that puts a focus on social justice and social action, not on teaching the Bible. We understand the Bible to be an actual revelation of God and His ways to mankind. So, while we do involve ourselves in helpin' our fellow man, the main thrust is on knowing God personally and allowing Him to work in and through our lives. It's an entirely different mindset."

"Okay," Connie responded, "I'll bite. So how has that difference put you in a position to learn all the stuff you shared in the class today?"

"Well, it all has to do with emphasis. Different churches have different things they focus on. As I mentioned a moment ago, the churches in Skeptopolis are focused on social justice and social action, so they tend to involve themselves in things like political activism and social services. The churches in Templeton are almost exclusively evangelical churches, and they focus more on such things as evangelism, teaching the Bible, caring for the people in their congregation – and also creating a meaningful worship experience for those who attend. All those things are actually very important. And really, every church should be working toward all those things all the time.

"But my pastor has a little bit of a different focus, and it all goes back to his philosophy of ministry. He takes his primary philosophy from Ephesians 4:11-13 in the Bible. Those verses indicate that the essential job of church leaders is to 'equip the saints for the work of ministry.' He firmly believes that its the everyday Christians, not just church leaders, who have the most potential for impacting the world with the message of Christ, so he works diligently to implement that philosophy by the way he leads his church.

"By the way, just in case you were wonderin', the biblical concept of 'saints' is slightly different from the average person's stereotype. It actually refers to every believer, not just to special, extra-holy people.

"So my pastor puts an extraordinary amount of effort into makin' sure that the people in the church learn as much as they can about the Bible, and how to effectively reach out into the community to share Christ. He provides all kinds of classes to teach us. He teaches some himself, and others are taught by various experts who are either members of our church, or who he brings in from the outside.

"As for his own experience, he was able to attend a seminary to get specialized theological education. But most Christians don't have that opportunity. So he determined to structure our church's programs in a way that would sorta make the church our seminary. With that, we could become equipped to do what God's called us to do in our own lives in the context of our personal life situation. So that's mostly where I learned all this stuff."

"I must say, I'm quite impressed," Connie responded. "I think you must have a very wise and gifted leader."

Just then, they arrived at Chris' apartment. "Connie, if you'll hang on for just a second, I'll run inside and get my gym bag. I already have it packed and ready to go. Then we can walk over to the dojo. It's only a couple blocks down the street."

"No problem," Connie answered as she opened the door to get out of the car. "I'll be right here." Chris quickly went inside, picked up his gym bag, then came back to the car to get Connie, and they then began walking toward the dojo.

As it happened, Chris' apartment was not in the best part of town. In fact, there were two rival gangs that had their headquarters in the vicinity. Chris had seen various gang members hanging out in the yard of one particular house he had to pass on his way to the dojo, but up until now no one had bothered him as he walked past it. But for whatever reason, one of the gang bangers, Gino, when he saw Chris and Connie coming down the road, decided he was not going to make it easy this time. As Chris and Connie approached the gang house, Gino stepped onto the sidewalk right in front of them. "Hey, where do you guys think you're goin'?" Gino snarled. He was the leader of the Red Flag Pack.

When that happened, Connie was terrified and quickly slipped in behind Chris. For his part, Chris quickly sized up the situation and said to Gino, "Listen, we don't want any trouble. We're just headed to the karate dojo on the next block to work out. You don't mind that, do you?"

Gino squinted his eyes, gritted his teeth, then walked straight up Chris so their chests bounced off each other. He then stuck his mug right in Chris' face – they were literally nose to nose. "If you wanna get by, it'll cost ya 20 bucks. Pay up right now!"

Chris didn't even flinch when that happened, but after a moment took one step back. "I'm sorry, I don't believe I got your name," Chris responded. "I'm Chris, and this is my friend Connie. She's a reporter for the *Times*."

"I don't give a rip who you are. Pay the 20 bucks or you'll pay for it with your hide," Gino responded back with a threatening growl in his voice.

By that time, about 10 other gang members had heard the commotion and came out of the house to see what was going on. When they saw the situation, thinking they'd have some fun with this, they began to cheer Gino on. "Hey Gino, why don't you wipe the sidewalk with his face?" one called out. "Tear him up, Gino!" another yelled. "He's disrespectin' you."

"Oh, so you're Gino." Chris spoke calmly and confidently as he tried to defuse the situation. Well, Gino, it's a pleasure to meet you. Now you don't really wanna make any kind of a big deal outta this do you? Just let us go by and everything'll be cool."

"Hey dude," Gino replied gruffly, "do you know who I am?"

"Yeah, you're Gino," Chris responded with a smile on his face.

"Hey, I'm Gino Chrysler – head of the Red Flag Pack," Gino growled ominously. "You really don't wanna mess with me."

As the taunting got louder from the other gang members, a couple of students getting ready to head into the dojo heard the ruckus and saw what was going on. They immediately ran inside to tell CJ. When he heard what was happening, he flew out the front door of the dojo and ran down the street to where Chris was, followed by the two who had reported it to him. CJ was, himself, from this neighborhood, so he knew these guys and their families. "Hey Gino," CJ called out as he walked up to the gang house, "what's goin' on?"

"CJ my man," Gino responded back, "you're not gonna get in my way, are ya? These two strangers came into my hood and I think they should have to pay to go through."

"Well why didn't you say so!" CJ retorted. "Are you gonna take him out?"

"I am if he doesn't pay me 20 bucks," Gino replied.

"Well, can you wait just a minute? My guys at the dojo don't get to see a real fight very often. Can I get 'em here to watch? I know who this guy is, and I feel pretty certain he won't be willin' to pay your 20 bucks."

Gino thought CJ's response was a bit strange, but also thought having an audience might be kind of funny, so he said to CJ, "Yeah, go get your guys. They're fighters. I think they might enjoy watchin' a real fight."

Turning his attention back to Chris, Gino said, "Is he right? Would you rather get your face beat in than pay my 20 bucks?"

"Gino, I really don't wanna fight, but I'm sorry, I won't pay your 20 dollars," Chris replied.

"Alright then, go get your people, CJ," Gino growled. "This should be fun."

CJ told one of the kids who had followed him there to go back to the dojo and get the rest of the people who were there for class, and to get back ASAP. Everyone watched as he ran to the dojo and quickly reemerged with about 20 others trailing behind. When everyone had arrived, all the other gang members and the karate students formed a circle around Gino and Chris.

"Now Gino," CJ called out, "before you begin, I wanna ask you a question."

"Yeah, what is it CJ?" Gino asked.

"You heard about the karate tournament we had just a couple of weeks ago, didn't you?"

"Sure," Gino replied. "Everybody's heard about that."

CJ continued, "Well you know the guy that won and was all over the papers?"

"Yeah, what about him," Gino replied, kind of annoyed that CJ was talking about something that didn't pertain to what was going on.

"Well, this is the guy. And here's the deal. If you beat him, he'll pay the 20 bucks. But if he beats you, you never bother him again."

Gino was rather shocked at the revelation, but that only made him more irate. CJ had lured him into a trap, and he couldn't back down now – even if he wanted to. "CJ, you're a scum bag. Now I'm gonna beat him up even worse than I planned to before."

But before anything further could happen, Chris chimed in with his conditions. "Wait, Gino. That deal's not good enough for me. If I lose, I'll pay your 20 bucks. But if I win, not only do you not hassle me when I walk by in the future, I want us to be friends. And, I have one further part of the deal … if you beat me, Connie'll make you a hero in the newspaper by writin' about how you whupped up on a karate champion. But if I win, she won't write anything that'll embarrass you."

With that, Chris looked over at Connie, and she gave him a really dirty look. "You think you can control my writing like that?" Connie scoffed.

"That's the deal Connie, if you want further access to me."

"Oh, all right, but I don't like this," Connie blurted back.

Chris just smiled, then turned back to Gino, "Deal?"

At that point, Gino knew that was about as good a deal as he was going to get, and he nodded his approval.

"Alright then," Chris exclaimed, "let's do this."

Gino immediately charged at Chris in an attempt to knock him to the ground. He planned to start by pounding in his face. But at the last second, Chris easily sidestepped him and pushed him down to the ground.

Gino jumped back up and came after Chris again, this time swinging both fists. But Chris simply dodged his flailing arms.

Gino charged again. This time Chris stepped to the side, grabbed Gino's wrist, whipped his arm high into the air and pulled backward. Gino's feet flew out from under him and he went straight down on his back. Chris then drew back and punched toward his rib cage in a way that would crush three or four of his ribs. But just before hitting him, Chris pulled his punch, just barely touching his chest. Then he quickly swung his body around and went to his knees with Gino's head between them. When he got in that position, he put his thumbs in Gino's eyes and yelled, "Don't move or I'll gouge your eyes out."

Immediately, Gino froze. He knew the whole time Chris was only toying with him. He could've put him in the hospital at any moment.

"So what do you think, Gino?" Chris spoke calmly to him. "Do you think we can just be friends?"

No one knew quite what to expect at that point. Would Gino try to keep fighting? Would he call on his gang buddies to crash in and begin a brawl that would pull in CJ and the kids from the dojo? Would someone pull a gun?

Then, after just a few seconds, Gino burst out laughing. He'd never seen anything like that and was totally impressed. "Let me up, you dog face!" Gino shouted as he continued laughing.

Chris wasn't sure exactly what to expect if he let him up, but he did know that if Gino tried anything else, he could handle himself easily enough. So, he let him up.

With that, Gino jumped up, still laughing uncontrollably. He then took a step toward Chris, stopped and looked him straight in the eyes, then reached out to shake hands. "A deal's a deal." Chris smiled and reached out his hand, as well, and the two shook.

With that, Chris looked Gino in the eye. "Gino," he said as he began working to collect on the bet, "now that we're obligated to become friends, I think we need to get to know each other a bit. Here's what I propose if you're willin'. I'd like to take you out to dinner this evenin' so we can learn some things about each other."

Gino couldn't believe what he was hearing. "What?" Gino giggled, "Are you asking me out on a date?"

At that, everyone began to laugh uncontrollably. Chris, too, just laughed and shook his head. "You're just weird. I don't want us to get too serious on our first date, so we'll just go down to the Burger Barn. I'll pick you up at 6:00."

Everyone cracked up again at hearing Chris actually make his offer.

Then Gino responded in a way that completely defused the situation. "You know, maybe you aren't so bad after all. Okay, it's a date."

With that, the gang members all filed back into the clubhouse, and CJ, with all his students tagging along behind, headed back to the dojo with Chris and Connie bringing up the rear. Once inside, there was not enough time to have an actual class, but Chris thought this might be a great teaching moment. "CJ," Chris asked, "since there's no time to have a complete class, would it be okay if I just talked to the class members and shared with 'em some things about dealin' with situations like that?"

"Wow, that'd be awesome," CJ responded. "I wanna hear what you have to say, myself."

CJ then turned to the class members who were, at that point, just standing around. "Class, I want everyone to go to the middle of the dojo and have a seat. Chris is gonna share with you some deep karate wisdom."

When everyone had settled in, Chris moved to the front of the class and began to share some important life principles. "Class, you all saw what went on today. Make no mistake about it, that could've easily turned into somethin' very ugly. Someone could've been seriously injured."

"Yeah, Gino," one of the students yelled out. Everyone laughed.

"Please don't laugh at that situation," Chris implored the class. "While I have the skills to have hurt Gino badly, I didn't do it. Why do you think that was?"

Without waiting for anyone to answer, Chris continued, "In spite of the fact that Gino was not nice to me, I still consider him to be a person of worth. Y'all know that I'm a Christian, and my faith teaches me that every person, even mean people, are persons made in the image of God. If God can look on 'em with love, then I oughta be able to do it, too. If Gino had ultimately not been willing to respond to my request for friendship, and was determined to truly hurt me, or any of you, I would've defended you. I was fully aware that Miss Connie over there, and you guys, as well, were potentially in danger. But how much better is it now that I can be friends with him? And who knows, as our friendship grows, I might even be able to help him get his life goin' in a better direction. You just never know.

"I know that as you watch various TV shows and movies," Chris continued, "karate's mostly used just to beat up on people. But it can do so much more for you. If you learn it well and develop good character in your own life, it can be a tool to build you into a person who can positively influence other people. I hope you'll think deeply about that going forward."

When Chris finished, it was time for class to be over. CJ moved to the front of the class, had them all stand and bowed them out.

Chris then called over to Connie to get ready to head back to his place. As she came up, CJ also walked over to where he was. "Wow, Chris, that was just too impressive – what you did with Gino, *and* what you shared with the class."

Chris responded, "You know, what you did by bringin' out the whole class was kinda dangerous. Someone could've gotten hurt."

"I don't think so," CJ replied. "I grew up with most of those guys and I know 'em pretty well. First, I know their fighting capability. They're bullies, but they have nowhere near the skills you have. I knew Gino couldn't hurt you. But beyond that, I've come to have a great deal of faith in you. I don't know exactly what it is, but I just knew you'd somehow make that come out in a positive way. I've seen you do that already in more than one situation. And you confirmed my faith in you. You're just a good all-around guy. I think you really may be able to have a positive influence on Gino. I'm pullin' for that."

"Gee, I don't know what to say," Chris replied. "I really hope you're right."

Chris then looked over at Connie, "Well, Connie, are you ready to head back?"

Connie nodded her head and they both headed toward the door. "See you soon, CJ," Chris called back. CJ waved as they walked out.

Connie hardly said anything as they walked the couple of blocks back to Chris' place and was actually a little nervous when they passed in front of the gang house again. When they arrived at the apartment, Chris quickly put his unopened gym bag in the apartment, then both of them jumped into his car. Chris had promised to take her back to her office.

As they drove, Connie opened up, "You know, when Gino jumped out in front of us like he did, I was really scared. I mean REALLY scared. I don't know whether or not you noticed, but I immediately got behind you."

Chris chuckled, "Yeah, I noticed. But that's okay. I wasn't gonna let anyone hurt you."

"Chris," Connie continued, "you're such an unusual person. I don't think I've ever met anyone quite like you. I'm having an increasingly difficult time knowin' what to write.

"Let me be totally honest ... I've seriously been lookin' for a way to criticize you for somethin'. I've particularly been lookin' for a way to report negatively on your faith. I haven't told you this, but that's actually part of the assignment my boss has given me. I thought for sure I'd get some good fodder in Dr. Craven's class this morning. I didn't. And then, to watch how you handled Gino, and particularly the lesson you gave the students in the karate class ... I am feelin' a bit conflicted right now."

"Do you really think I didn't know what you were up to from the very beginning?" Chris replied. "But I also want you to know that I don't hold any animosity toward you, your boss, or anyone else who's skeptical about me. If I was concerned about that, I wouldn't have opened myself up to you in the first place. I want you to know that I truly, from the bottom of my heart, believe the things I've been sharin' with you and others – particularly where it concerns my faith in Jesus Christ. I'm certainly not perfect, and if you hang around me long enough and keep tryin', I have no doubt you'll find that thing you can criticize me for. But I also know God doesn't love me because I'm a perfect person. He loves me because I'm his child. And because I love Him back, I want to imitate that character trait in my life by lovin' others – even people who don't like me. That allows me to be as transparent as I am. What you see is what you get to the highest degree possible."

Connie paused for a moment before responding. "I must say, Chris, what you've just said is very moving. Again, I don't know what I might end up writing in the future about you, but I do appreciate your openness to me. And I promise I'll keep my original promise to be fair in my reporting. You've given me a LOT to think about today. I have a little more follow up to do, but'll prob'ly have another article about you in a couple of days."

Just then, Chris pulled into the *Times* parking lot and drove Connie up to the front door. "Well, thanks for the ride, Chris," Connie said as she opened the door and got out. "This has been one interesting day. I look forward to seeing you again soon."

Connie then walked to the front door of the building, turned and waved goodbye, then disappeared inside.

CHAPTER 23

THE DATE

At 6:00 sharp, Chris drove up to the front of the gang headquarters to pick up Gino, just as they had agreed. When he stopped, Gino exited the front door of the house, sauntered to the car, and got in the front seat with Chris. "Hey, Gino, how's it goin'?"

Gino looked over at Chris with a smile, "Well, I'm ready for our date." Both cackled at Gino's joke. Then Chris pulled away heading toward the Burger Barn.

The Burger Barn was probably the most popular greasy spoon in town. Two brothers had started it 25 years ago who just loved hamburgers. Over the years, before beginning their restaurant, they had perfected the art of making gourmet burgers. They had something for just about any palate, with about 25 different kinds of burgers. They had even become a national sensation after being featured on one of the Food Channel's greasy spoon shows. They always had a full house and usually a wait to get in – even on weekdays. Besides the burgers, they had fabulous onion rings, five types of seasoned fries, and sold their sweet, iced tea by the barrel.

Chris pulled the car into the parking lot, then the two of them got out and went over to get in line. Luckily, the wait was only about 10 minutes.

As they approached the window, Chris commented to Gino, "You know, I've heard about this place for years. It's pretty well known, even in Templeton. But this is the first time I've ever come here. What would you recommend?"

"You can hardly go wrong with anything they make," Gino responded, "but my favorite burger is 'The Gobsmackum.' That's a half-pound burger topped with nacho fries, jalapeno peppers, and bacon. Queso cheese is on the nacho fries, so you don't need to ask for cheese. And if you also order a small fry, that'll be plenty for the both of us. They pile so many extra fries in the bag that orderin' more than one's a waste."

"Holy Moly!" Chris exclaimed, "I've never heard of anything like that before. Sounds awesome! Since you're the expert here, I'm gonna follow your lead."

"I promise, you won't be disappointed," Gino declared. "You're gonna love it."

When they got to the order window, Chris ordered two Gobsmackums, two large, sweet ice teas, and one small fry. After Chris paid, they moved to the pick-up window and waited for their number to come up.

"Number 427 ... order's ready," shouted a voice at the pick-up window.

Chris and Gino walked up to the window, picked up their order, and made their way to an empty table. "427 – is that the number of customers they've served today?" Chris asked Gino. "It seems like the numbers they're callin' out are pretty much in consecutive order."

Gino nodded. "Yep, that's the way they roll. I'm telling ya, they sell a ton of burgers here."

After sitting down, Chris dug into his burger. After a moment of chewing and savoring his prize, he gushed, "Wow! This thing's fantastic! Where've you been all my life?"

Gino flashed a huge grin, then dug into his, as well. It made him feel good that Chris approved of his choice.

As they ate, Chris scanned the restaurant. As he looked around, he noticed a lot of people looking over at him and Gino. "Hey Gino, does it seem to you that a lotta people are lookin' at us?" Chris asked.

"Oh yeah, you can count on that," Gino responded. "You know you're a celebrity around here, right? I mean, your story and picture's been in the paper a lot since the tournament. On top of that, there's a bunch of folks in town who don't like me. They notice when I'm around. I think I scare a lotta people. Combine the two of us, and you can count on a lotta stares and whispering. But there's something else, too."

"What's that?" Chris asked with a bit of curiosity in his voice.

Gino continued, "Word's gotten out that we're here together. I don't know whether or not you've noticed, but there's extra cops in the corner over there, as well."

"Well, I did notice that, but didn't think anything of it. You think they're here because of us?"

"Actually, it's probably mostly because of me," Gino responded. "I always seem to draw extra scrutiny."

"But that's not all," Gino continued, "Did you notice who's sittin' over in that other corner tryin' to conceal her presence? It's Connie. She's here to spy on us."

Chris hadn't noticed, but when he looked in her direction and saw her sitting there, he couldn't help himself – he began cackling out loud. And when Chris started laughing, Gino couldn't contain himself, either. They were both laughing hysterically – which caused even more stares. Chris thought to himself, *I'm sure this is not a coincidence. She's here to get more intel for her next story.*

"Hey Chris, you wanna have some fun with everyone here? Let's pretend to start a fight right here in the restaurant."

With that, Chris laughed even harder. "Well," he answered after he was able to catch his breath again, "I'm absolutely sure that'd get both our names in the paper – but prob'ly not in a way either of us would like. I'm sure those deputies would have us cuffed and in their patrol cars before we could bat an eye."

"Oh, I know," Gino replied as he grinned ear to ear, "but it'd be a great gag."

"Well, I'm not so sure about that," Chris answered back. "Maybe you're used to that kinda thing, but it'd definitely be somethin' different from what I'm used to."

"You know, Chris, you're not such a bad dude. I honestly didn't know what to expect meetin' you here this evenin'. Readin' about you in the paper, I was sorta spectin' a kinda strait-laced, religious stick in the mud. You actually come across as pretty normal."

"Well, thanks for that ... I think," Chris replied smiling. "I am just a real person. My Christian faith is an integral part of my life, but that doesn't keep me from liking people and enjoyin' life. In fact, it gives my life even greater meaning. I have somethin' beyond myself to strive for that gives purpose and joy to my life.

"But you know," Chris continued, "the reason you know somethin' about me is because Connie's been publicly reporting about me and my life. Tell me somethin' about yourself. How'd you end up gettin' in the gang?"

"Well," Gino began, "it's really not a very pretty story. I never knew my dad, and my mom was a hooker. She got pregnant by some John. I'm not sure she even knows who it was. I don't know why she didn't abort me, but she didn't. So, I grew up in the hood in the home of a hooker, with drug pushers and addicts all around. The gang was here way before I was, and it's actually pretty hard to stay out of it when you live in my neighborhood.

"In spite of all the bad influences, though, mom really did try to take care of me. I honestly think she wanted me to avoid the gangs. She pushed really hard for me to get my education. Would it surprise you to know that I have a college degree in wildlife management?"

When he heard that, Chris' jaw dropped, and his mouth gaped open. "You have what?" Chris gasped. "Yes, you have now officially blown my mind."

Gino smiled. "Yep, got my degree right here at Skept U."

"So why didn't you leave the gang and go into the wildlife management field?" Chris blurted out.

"Well, I thought about it," Gino went on, "but the gang's like my family. They're pretty much the only family I have. A few years ago, mom finally died because of the hard life she lived, and I didn't have anyone else. And because I have a college degree, I was the most obvious choice to lead the gang. It didn't take long for me to actually become the leader. Besides, the business enterprises I have with the gang allowed me to make a lot more money than I could ever make doin' wildlife management."

Chris was really curious at that point and asked. "So, in effect, you've become the father of all of the other kids in the gang. Would that be a fair assessment?"

"Well, I hadn't really thought of it that way," Gino replied, "but I guess there is a certain amount of truth to that."

Chris continued, "It really makes me feel bad for you that you had such a rough childhood. Is yours a pretty common story with the other kids, as well?"

"Yeah," Gino replied, "I suppose my story's not that unusual – except for the education, of course. Most of the kids don't even finish high school."

Chris focused in and looked Gino straight in the eye in order to probe into his inner soul, "Gino, do you really care about the other kids in the gang?"

"What kinda question's that?" Gino responded defensively. "I already told you I'm responsible for 'em."

"Well Gino, I know you know in your heart of hearts that for nearly all your kids, the gang's a dead-end street. How many of 'em will spend years in prison, or maybe even be killed in feuds with other gangs? Don't you aspire for them to have a better life?"

With that, Gino's demeanor changed, and he looked down at the table with a dejected look in his eyes. "Chris, you don't realize the futility of what you're sayin'. We're trapped in this life. There's no way out. We've just accepted it."

Chris looked back at Gino recognizing he had hit a very raw nerve. "Gino, at this point I don't know what I can do for you, but even in this short time we've had together, I'm beginnin' to feel like a brother. I'd like to help you somehow better the life of your gang family. Let me know if there's somethin' I can do for any of 'em. And I want you to know that I'm gonna be prayin' for you, as well. I think you have some kind of greatness in you." Then Chris chuckled, "It may be really *waaay* deep down, but I believe it's in there some-where."

Hearing that, Gino gave Chris a sideways glance and started laughing again. "You're just too much Chris. You know, I haven't been able to have this kinda conversation with anyone in a long time, and I feel a strange kinda con-nection to you, too. I hope we can somehow keep this friendship, though it's pretty hard to do in a gang context. You always have to keep your 'radar' on. Can't really trust anyone."

"Gino, I have a thought," Chris changed the subject. "I don't wanna start a pretend fight to get attention, but I would like do somethin' to have a little fun. You up for it?"

"Whatcha got in mind," Gino answered.

"Let's go surprise Connie. She's by herself over at that corner table next to the entrance to the bathrooms. There's a couple of chairs beside her. I'm sure she's tryin' to keep us from knowin' she's here. So, if you go around to the right toward that direction, she'll probably think you're goin' to the john and'll duck her head down hopin' you won't recognize her. – so she won't really be watchin' your movements. When I see she's not lookin', I'll circle around on the left side. Then, when we get right at her table, you sit down in the chair on her right and I'll sit in the one on her left. Let's embarrass her for her spyin'.

Gino laughed again. "I like your thinkin', kid. Let's do it."

The plan worked to a T. They both arrived at Connie's table at the same time and plopped down beside her before she even knew what hit her. "Hello Connie," Chris spoke first. "You do realize they'd never hire you to be 007, right?"

Immediately, when Connie looked up and saw both of them sitting beside her, her face turned blood red and her jaw dropped open." Chris and Gino both began laughing hysterically.

"Thought you could spy on us without us knowin', huh?" Gino spoke up.

Connie stammered, "Uh ... uh ... what're you guys doin' here? What a surprise to see you."

With that, Chris and Gino burst out laughing again, causing Connie's face to turn even more red – if that were possible. "You're so funny, Connie. Did you really think you could spy on us without us knowin' you were here?" Chris laughed. "We've been watchin' you watch us."

"Well what if I was," Connie replied defiantly. "I'm just doin' my job!"

Chris and Gino burst out laughing again. "Yeah," Gino mocked sarcastically, "just doin' your job."

Chris patted Connie on the shoulder, "Don't worry, we're not mad. We just thought it was funny. Can't wait to see the story."

With that, Chris and Gino stood up and headed toward the door still laughing. Just as he got to the door, Chris looked back at Connie and gave her a wink. She still had that flustered look on her face over the shock of that encounter.

Chris and Gino walked across the parking lot, got into the car, and Chris drove Gino back to his place. But before going inside he confided to Chris, "You know, I don't know when I've had this much fun. I know we didn't do much, but just hangin' out and havin' a regular person to talk to was really nice. Now if you tell anybody I said that I'll deny it, and I'll come beat your tail. But for this evenin' it was really nice."

Chris smiled. "Me, too. I think this was the most enjoyable time I've spent with anyone since coming to Skeptopolis. Thanks for reachin' out in friendship."

Gino nodded and smiled, then turned and headed into the house. Chris turned the car around and went back to his apartment.

CHAPTER 24

NEXT EDITION

Connie raced to meet the deadline for her next article on Chris. These updates had become quite the talk of the town, and businesses wanting their ads associated with the articles had tripled. She had already written most of the current one, but before she could finish, there was one further detail she needed to follow up on. She wanted to interview a few of the university students who had been in the classroom when Chris talked to Dr. Craven's class.

So that evening she spent a couple of hours at the school chasing down a few kids in their dorm before racing back to her desk at the *Times* to complete the story before the deadline.

She was able to get interviews with five of the students. In interviewing them, it turned out to be a mixed bag. A couple of them thought Chris' explanation was totally bunk, one was rather neutral, while the other two were really intrigued and would like to hear more.

Armed with that information, Connie went back to her office, finished the article, and had it ready for the next morning's edition.

———————◆◆◆———————

𝔖keptopolis 𝔗imes

May 6   *Always There for You*   SkeptopolisTimes.com

Templeton's Chuck Norris Continues to Impress

By Connie Granger

A lot has happened since our last update on Templeton's karate whiz kid. In our last article, it was noted that one of the participants in Chris' karate workshop was Dr. Steve Craven, a sociology professor at Skeptopolis U. Following the workshop, Dr. Craven invited Chris to speak to his *Evolution of Religion* class – which Chris accepted. I had the opportunity to sit in on that class and observe the interaction. Thus, this article will not be about karate, but about some of the things Chris is doing outside of that arena.

I must say, Chris made a real impression on the class. He began by sharing some about his own religious background, then opened the floor for questions. The questions he was asked were very substantive, which is a great credit to Dr. Craven. In some ways it appeared that some of them were designed to trip Chris up, but he was totally respectful to all the students and able to respond in a very competent way.

The first thing Chris did in the class was to give an overview of the Christian faith. It was a very traditional rendering asserting that Jesus Christ was God who incarnated as a man and became the Savior for those who would accept Him into their lives. He then allowed some of the students to ask questions. Here are the questions that were asked and a brief synopsis of Chris' replies.

The first question was: Your description of religious faith started with monotheism and didn't account for the evolutionary development of religion. So how do *you* account for the higher steps of evolution occurring before the lower steps happened?

Chris answered by explaining that he did not believe in the evolutionary model – that monotheism came first, and the emergence of other religious forms was a gradual corruption of that.

The second questioner asked him to explain his belief in a literal Garden of Eden. He was asked how he could believe it.

Chris responded that if God actually did exist, as he believes, the Garden of Eden story is not as farfetched as some may think.

The third questioner asked how Chris could be so sure that his spiritual feelings about his faith were true, when other people from other faiths have equally strong spiritual feelings.

Chris answered that by commenting that the validity of a religious belief cannot be determined based on feelings – that the beliefs themselves must match up with the way human beings actually experience reality.

The final question asked was, perhaps, the most hard hitting of all. The questioner asserted that he did not have any religious beliefs, and wanted to know why Chris thought his own answers about the nature of faith were reasonable.

Chris responded by stating that everyone has religious beliefs, even people, like the questioner, who believe they don't. His reasoning was that there is no science able to deal with questions about God and ultimate origins. Thus, even what Atheists believe about those things are based on faith in their underlying belief system.

I later asked Chris if he had learned about this topic at some theological school, but he assured me that he did not have that kind of professional training. However, he also shared that his church in Templeton puts a premium on training their people to be conversant about these kinds of topics – something I personally found rather interesting.

I also wanted to get a sense of how the class responded to Chris, so later I took the opportunity to interview some of the students about their reactions. In those interviews, I got several divergent responses. First, to a person they were impressed with Chris' poise in front of the class and the respect he showed to the students. As for their responses to the content, it was a mixed bag. If the admittedly small sample size is anything near accurate, 40% were very skeptical of what he shared, another 40% were quite impressed, while the other 20% were neutral.

Future articles will continue to deal with what is going on with Chris' life. You will definitely want to stay tuned as I can assure you that there are some very interesting things coming up.

———◆◆———

Connie desperately wanted to include the incident with Gino and his gang. After all, that was a story she knew would sell a massive number of papers. But she didn't feel she could run with that right now. She had made a promise to Chris not to print anything that might embarrass Gino, and she was afraid that she would lose access to him if she didn't keep her word.

At the same time, she also felt sure there would come a time when the opportunity to write about it would present itself – and she would be ready when it happened.

She did, though, take the occasion to drop an anonymous line in the paper's gossip section. Most people don't take what is written there all that seriously, but at the same time, most also could not resist reading it. While it did often cause some people a certain amount of heartburn, it was one of the more popular sections of the paper, and advertisers were willing to pay a premium to have their ads on that page.

The gossip item Connie anonymously put in was **"Templeton's karate kid seen whooping it up at the Burger Barn with gang member Gino Chrysler."**

Short and sweet, but it did create an opening for future articles should the possibility open up.

CHAPTER 25

CONSPIRACY

"We've got to do something, and do it soon," Steve fumed to his professor colleagues – Everson, Gray, and Albritton. "This thing with Chris Bel's gettin' completely outta hand. I was sure that by getting Chris to talk about his 'magic Christian faith' in my class, he'd totally humiliate himself. It completely backfired. We can't have this Christian humiliating us like that. Did you see yesterday's paper? I'm mortified. That stupid reporter made him out to look really good at *my* expense."

"Well wait just a minute, Steve," Dr. Everson responded back. "I agree that somethin' needs to be done. I have as low a view of Christianity as you do. But we won't accomplish anything good if we lose our heads. I've seen how some new philosophy can sweep over a group of people and become a big fad – especially among impressionable college students. What we need to do is come up with a concrete plan to turn this thing around."

"That's easy for you to say, Everson," Steve shot back. "You're not the one who was made to look like an idiot in front of the entire city. You read that article. It was a pure puff piece on that punk."

"Calm down Steve," Dr. Gray jumped in. "Everson's right. We have to keep our cool and develop a plan to turn this thing around."

Steve fired back, "Guys, I don't think you realize how bad this is. You should've heard the discussion in my class yesterday. It's gonna take me the rest of the semester to undo the damage that kid did. Nearly half the class were fallin' all over themselves tryin' to defend him. What do you think we can do?"

Just then, Dr. Albritton piped in, "Why don't we challenge him to a debate and invite the city to watch. I'm sure that between Everson's expertise as an evolutionary biologist, Gray's as a philosopher, yours as a sociologist, and my background in religion, we can put him in his place."

"Wait," Dr. Gray chimed in, "we need to be careful here. We have to be very sure we don't turn him into a martyr. The four of us challenging him to a debate are likely to come across as really heavy handed. Even people that might be inclined to agree with us could get offended if we just pile on him like that. Rather than a debate, why don't we set up a roundtable discussion on religion and invite him as a guest participant? What do you think about that?"

"YES! That's genius!" Dr. Albritton almost shouted. "And I have exactly the right venue to pull that off. Over in the religion department, we have those kinds of roundtable discussions all the time. We don't even havta play this up as a big deal. What'll make it a big deal will be the newspaper writeup the next day that exposes him as a lightweight."

Dr. Everson spoke up, "Do you think that might be a little dangerous? After all, so far, the paper's been pretty soft on him. This could backfire, as well."

"I don't think so," Steve jumped in. "The kid's actually pretty smart, and rather likeable. But I don't think he's been put in a position yet to really fail. That reporter's certainly made him look good. But if you read the articles carefully, she's been tryin' to do her job and be as objective as possible. She actually has slipped in a few negative things here and there. There just hasn't been a situation where the flaws in his beliefs have had a place to break through. I think the roundtable could be just the thing."

"Okay Steve," Dr. Albritton responded. "But we need to do this in a way that makes it come across as natural. Let's think a little more deeply about it and develop a plan."

They all agreed to give it some more thought and meet again in a few days to brainstorm some ideas. With at least the ice broken on the need, and an agreement to get back together to actually do something, they all felt a little better as they picked up their things and left the building.

Three days after their first meeting, the four professors met again in Steve's office to put together a specific plan to, once and for all, put Chris in his place in public. Steve started the meeting, "So, has anyone thought of a way we can do this?"

Dr. Albritton spoke first. "When we met the other day, I proposed that we use the religion department's public forum series to put Chris on display. I've been givin' that a little more thought and I think it has the potential to work for us."

"Okay, tell us what you're thinkin'," Dr. Gray interjected.

"Well," Dr. Albritton continued, "first of all, this is an ongoing program, so it won't come across as something we've specially designed to trip him up. It'll be in a natural setting. We do these every week during the semester to expose the students to different beliefs.

"What I'm thinkin' is that we can do a forum on the evolution of religious beliefs. In a way, it'll be an expansion of what he did in Steve's class, so there's that tie in, as well. It'll be a natural setting for Steve to invite his class, and it'll provide another opportunity for Chris to crash and burn in front of 'em.

"But this time, instead of letting *him* control the topic and have students do the questioning, we can have professors who know their stuff be his opponents – and the professors involved should be us. It'll be a natural fit."

"Keep going," Dr. Everson encouraged as he indicated that he liked the direction this was moving.

"So here's what I'm thinkin'," Dr. Albritton continued. "Steve'll be able to talk about the topic from a sociological point of view, Gray from the perspective of philosophy, and Everson from a biological view. I'll be the moderator. It'll be three against one from a wide perspective without it seemin' like we're just trying to pile on. I feel pretty certain we'll be able to hold our own against this relatively uneducated kid. What do you guys think?"

"I love it," Steve responded enthusiastically. The others quickly nodded their agreement.

"The only thing left is to get Chris to agree to do it," Steve chimed in.

Dr. Albritton responded. "Well, since it's my program, I'll figure out a way to make that happen. Give me a little bit of time to come up with a plan."

CHAPTER 26

THE OPENING

"Hey Chris, this is Gino. Can we talk?"

Chris was just finishing his dinner and getting ready to settle in for the evening, and maybe watch a little TV, when the phone rang. He was a bit surprised to get a call from Gino but was glad to hear his voice.

"Of course, Gino, it'd be my pleasure. When would you like to meet?"

"Would it be okay if I came over right now?" Gino responded with a sound of urgency in his voice. "I have somethin' I need to talk to you about."

This really got Chris' attention. *What in the world could be this urgent for Gino?* he thought to himself.

"Of course, Gino. You know where I live, right?"

"I do," Gino responded. "I'll be there in about 10 minutes."

"Perfect! I'll see you in a few."

After just a few minutes, Chris heard a car pull into the parking lot and stop. Directly, a car door slammed, and a few seconds later came a knock on his door. Chris looked through the door window just to confirm it was Gino, then opened it and invited him in.

"Gino, my man!" Chris greeted his newfound friend by clasping his right hand and moving in for a chest bump. "Come on in. What a treat to hear from you. I had such a good time the other day at the Burger Barn. In fact, I don't remember when I've had so much fun with someone."

Gino grinned. "Yeah, me too. That was a blast."

Chris pointed to the couch. "Have a seat. Can I get you somethin' to drink?"

"Nah, I'm good," Gino responded as he walked over to the couch and plopped down.

Chris likewise walked over to an easy chair across from the couch and sat down. "Well, what can I do for ya, Gino? You sounded on the phone like there was somethin' a bit urgent."

"Chris," Gino began, "remember the other night when we were talkin' about my guys and their futures?"

"Of course, Gino. You expressed a very deep sense of care and concern for 'em. I was really impressed with that." Chris responded thoughtfully.

"Well, that got me thinkin'," Gino continued. "I really do care for those guys. Truthfully, they're the only family I have. And as I thought about it more deeply, I began to realize that in gang life, I could never give 'em what'd be best for 'em. All I have to offer is a life of crime. And you were absolutely right, many of 'em will wind up in jail, and some'll even end up dead. And that's been weighin' heavily on me ever since we talked. For the most part, these guys don't have anywhere else to go. Their families are dead, or they've been abandoned. And they don't have an education that could give 'em a better life. They're stuck. Honestly, I don't even know why I came to you about this. I don't know what you could do to help. But for some reason I felt a sense of hope radiating out of you. And ...."

Chris interrupted, "Gino, what a great guy you are. The concern you've just expressed is about the most moving thing I've heard in a long time. What are you thinkin'?"

"I don't know," Gino responded. "I honestly don't know what I thought you might be able to do. But here's what I did. The next day after we met, I pulled the whole gang together and we just sat around and had a heart-to-heart. I told 'em what I was feelin' and that I wanted to be able to help 'em. I talked about gettin' an education and we went around the room letting each person just dream about what they'd do if they could. Did you know that to a person they all wanted to further their education? And you know why? They knew I had a college degree and thought if they could get some kind of credential it'd give 'em a leg up. Then they started talkin' about how they'd always dreamed of bein' in the military, or ownin' a business, or workin' on cars, and on and on. Every one of 'em had some kinda dream. We had never talked about that kinda thing before, and I was really surprised by what I heard.

"But then, as we talked more, everyone began to give reasons why it could never happen. And while there was a moment of energy and excitement, just as quickly the air went out of the room. None of 'em saw a way out. Chris ... ," Gino went on with a sense of pleading in his voice, "Is there a way out for my guys ... or is this just a pipe dream?"

Chris sat there for a moment, stunned and wide eyed, just taking in what he'd heard. He would never in his wildest dreams have imagined he was going to hear what had just come out of Gino's mouth.

After a few moments of silence, Chris began to respond, "Gino, let me ask you a few questions and let's think more deeply about what you're askin' and what might be possible. You know, right, that to do what you're suggesting will be a monumental task. It's not just a matter of goin' to school or goin' and gettin' a job. We're talkin', here, about a massive lifestyle change. We're talkin' about learnin' an entirely new way of thinking and acting. Do you think you and your guys are up to a challenge like that?"

Gino raised his head and looked Chris square in the eye, "Chris, I know we could do it if we saw there was an actual possibility. Right now, though, no one believes it's even possible."

"Okay," Chris responded, "let me talk about the first step that's required to accomplish somethin' like that. I know for my life it all begins with my inner spirit. I have to have somethin' within my own heart that gives me enough personal strength to withstand any adversity that comes my way. And I guarantee adversity will come. That's just life. Without that spiritual strength, I'll just be knocked down when I meet opposition ... you know, just give up. Does that make sense?"

"You know," Gino replied, "it actually does make sense. I've seen that in you. I saw it in you when we first met out on the road. It showed itself in a level of confidence I've never seen before. And I saw it in you when we were at the Burger Barn – when you were willin' to be with me out in public and didn't care what anyone else thought. Is that the kinda thing you're talkin' about?"

"Yeah, I guess it is," Chris replied thoughtfully, "I think those things prob'ly were an expression of that strength in my own personal spirit. What I need you to understand, though, is that there's a specific source for that inner strength – it's my personal relationship with Jesus Christ. He's the source of my inner spiritual strength. Has anyone ever explained anything about that to you before?"

Gino suddenly lurched forward and fired back, "Hey, you do realize, right, that you're in Skeptopolis? No one talks about that kinda stuff here. The people in the school system are very bold in their teaching of Atheism. All I ever heard about Christianity was skepticism and jokes."

"Oh, I didn't mean to touch a nerve, Gino. But I can't give you the truth about the source of my strength without dealin' with my faith in Christ. You see, Christianity's not merely a religious tradition. It involves the understanding that God's a real person who has personally revealed himself to humanity in order to show us how we can know Him in a personal relationship. It's based on the fact that God is holy and requires holiness for people to enter His presence. At the same time, it recognizes that human beings have an inner, evil nature and don't qualify to do that. I mean, the things you've been sharin' with me about you and your guy's lives sorta play that out, I think. Would you agree that human nature kinda naturally takes us down that road?"

"Listen Chris, I'm sorry to be a little touchy on this topic. I'm fully aware of the bad things we do. But we're not the only ones. Those people downtown and out in the burbs look down their noses at us, but they're a bunch of liars, cheaters, and hypocrites themselves. You'd be shocked to know how many of 'em look to us to supply 'stuff' to feed their vices."

"Exactly right!" Chris affirmed Gino's observation. "It doesn't matter who you are. If you're a human being, you have this sin problem in your life. I have that problem in my life. And because it exists, *everyone* is separated from God. God Himself is the only one who's perfectly holy."

Hearing that, Gino relaxed a bit, leaned back and settled his body into the couch. "Well, that doesn't sound too promising," he responded. "What can anyone do, then, to change that and get the inner spiritual strength you're talkin' about?"

"That's exactly the right question, Gino. According to the Bible, God did provide a way to fix that dilemma. You see, the sin problem had to be taken care of. Sin is an offense against God, not just some bad act a person does. And God's justice requires that the penalty for sin be enforced. It's kinda like when you break the law – which I think is somethin' you're very familiar with. If they catch ya, the justice system takes over and you get punished for your offense. But the penalty for sin is death. We're not talkin' here about physical death, but spiritual death – which is separation from God. It's that separation from Him that causes us to have the inner spiritual weakness we've been talkin' about. So to solve that problem, someone had to pay the penalty to satisfy God justice system.

"But God's desire is that we not have to pay that penalty. He doesn't want us to be separated from Him. So He created a fix by providing a substitute for us – someone who should not have to pay the penalty, but who's willing to accept it on other people's behalf. It had to be someone who was not guilty of sin, but who'd step in willingly and pay the penalty for our sin for us. No human being could ever meet that qualification. It'd require someone livin' their entire life, from birth to death, without ever committing a single sin. Since no human could pull that off, God Himself came to earth as a human being to accomplish that purpose. That person was Jesus Christ. He was not guilty of any sin during His entire life, but he willingly received the death penalty by dyin' on a Roman cross. You're familiar with that form of capital punishment back in those days, right?"

Gino nodded his head. "Yeah, I remember studyin' about that in school in our ancient Roman history class. So you're sayin' – that when they executed Jesus, it wasn't just a regular Roman execution?"

"That's right," Chris continued. "It was, of course, a physical execution, but the significance of that killing went far beyond any civil crime. You see, Jesus wasn't guilty of anything. He was an innocent man. But He allowed Himself to be killed anyway. It served as a spiritual sacrifice of His life in order to pay the penalty for our sin."

Gino just sat there taking in what Chris was saying.

Chris went on, "But you need to realize one more thing, Gino. Receiving the benefit of Christ's sacrificial death is not automatic. You havta keep in mind God's purpose for doing it in the first place. It was to take care of the sin problem so human beings could enjoy personal fellowship with Him. So, to make it personally apply to our life, each individual has to admit their own sin and ask God's forgiveness. They must then invite Christ to be a part of their life. When an individual does that, God forgives the person, and a personal relationship with Him is established. In fact, He adopts us into His family as His child."

"Wow," Gino exclaimed as his eyes grew wider, "that sounds too good to be true. Does that mean a person doesn't ever sin again after that?"

"Oh man," Chris replied shaking his head, "I wish that were true. No, we still have that sin nature within us that makes us have a tendency to continue to sin. But God does change us. In fact, He actually enters into our life with His very Spirit. This does a couple of things. First, it seals the relationship. But second, it puts in us a new nature that gives us a deep desire to put aside sin. Unfortunately, we still have the old nature, which is why we will still struggle with the sin problem. But we also have the new nature to help us fight back. Then one day, when we finally die physically, our human sin nature will no longer be a part of us. When that happens, we'll experience an absolutely perfect and unrestricted relationship with God in eternity. But until then, the struggle will continue.

"There's more, though. God's Spirit in us is what gives believers the spiritual strength I told you about earlier. That's what you saw in me that's caused you come here and ask me these questions."

Gino repeated what he thought Chris had just told him to make sure he was getting it right, "So all I have to do is just admit my sin to God, ask Him to forgive me, and invite Him into my life? Is that what you're sayin'? That's it?"

"Yep, that's it," Chris replied. "It's a very simple process, but it's also a very big decision. It's life changing, but some people are totally freaked out about it. So, what do you think?"

"Chris," Gino chose his words carefully, "you've given me a lot to think about. If I do this, I realize my life'll havta go in an entirely different direction. I don't know if I can do that."

"Oh, you can do it, Gino," Chris countered. "Literally millions, maybe billions, of people throughout history have had their lives changed like that. The real question is, 'Are you willing?' How bad do you want it?"

Gino sat quietly on the couch for a time contemplating what Chris had just shared with him. And Chris just let him think until Gino was ready to speak again.

"Chris," Gino finally broke the silence, "what about my guys? If I do this by myself and leave 'em, they'll be totally lost. I don't think there's anyone who could take over leadership of the group successfully. And I don't know if any of 'em would want to take the step to receive Christ."

"Well, Gino," Chris responded thoughtfully, "I think you need to have another heart-to-heart with your guys to talk about it. If they really do have dreams that go beyond bein' part of a criminal gang, they're also gonna have to make some personal choices."

"Yeah, you're right," Gino replied. "But I don't know how to have that conversation. You were really eloquent tonight explainin' all that to me, but I don't think I'd be able to do it."

"Well Gino," Chris spoke into his hesitancy, "if you wanna explore this, let's make a plan. I'll give you a way to have that talk, and a way to follow up with it. Are ya game?"

"So what do you have in mind," Gino inquired.

"I have a short little booklet that basically explains everything I've just shared with you," Chris responded. Here's what you do. First, go back to your guys and share with 'em our conversation. Tell 'em that you heard 'em share their dreams and aspirations, as well as their doubts about any possibility of pullin' it off. Tell 'em you talked to me about it, and I shared with you that there's an inner spiritual strength that's necessary to make it happen, and that we talked about that, too. Then, ask 'em if they wanna hear about it. If they agree, then you guys can read through this booklet together. After you read it, let 'em talk about their dreams and aspirations again. Finally, tell 'em that if they want to go deeper and hear more about possibilities, you'll have me come over and I'll talk with 'em about it. What do you think?"

"I'm gonna do it," Chris. "If they reject it outright, I'll just let it go. But if they wanna go deeper, I'll call you over."

Gino continued, "I'm just not sure, though, how this can possibly work out. I honestly do see how this inner spiritual element has to be in place first, but that still leaves a huge problem I'm not sure can be dealt with."

"What problem's that, Gino?" Chris asked.

Gino laid it out as directly as he could. "Suppose they do decide to go for it? Logistically how are we gonna help 'em move to another level? Our criminal activity's our means of supporting ourselves. It's gonna take resources to shelter and feed everyone. And if they're gonna further their education, there are issues that havta be dealt with there, too."

"You're absolutely right, Gino," Chris responded. "Right this minute I don't know logistically how that might work out. But I do know some people who might be able to help, and I'm willing to go to bat for you guys. While you're having your talk with the guys, I'll check out some things on my side."

"And Gino," Chris added with heartfelt sincerity, "I want you to know that I'm deeply moved by your desire to help your guys this way. It's one of the most selfless acts I've ever witnessed in my life. And no matter how this turns out, I'm glad to be able to call you my friend. Thanks for bein' willin' to trust me this way."

Gino smiled and nodded, "Yeah, me too. Thanks for bein' there."

At that point, Gino stood up, reached out his hand to Chris, and they once again clasped hands and chest bumped. Gino then turned toward the door and left.

CHAPTER 27

OFF TO CHURCH

Chris had been thinking about taking Sybil and Colleen up on the offer to visit their church but had not done it yet. Following the karate workshop, they had been very gracious about inviting him to visit for a Sunday service, and he promised he would. Being a man of his word, he felt he ought to keep his promise. He also thought they might have connections to some resources that could help Gino and his guys. So, the next Sunday, he decided it was a good time to make good on his promise.

No sooner had he gotten out of his car in the church parking lot, than he saw both Sybil and Colleen making a beeline toward him. They'd been hoping he would show up one Sunday and had been on the lookout for him.

"Chris," Sybil called out as she approached the car, "how are you?" We're so glad you've come to visit us."

"Yes we are," Colleen echoed. "How ya doin' these days?"

"Well, hello ladies. I'm doin' great. Thanks for askin'. And how 'bout you guys?"

"We're doin' very well," both responded in unison.

"And even better now that you're here." Sybil gushed. "We're so excited. And you got here in plenty of time. Let us take you inside and help you get situated. You can sit with us if you like."

"That'd be great," Chris replied. "It is always more comfortable to actually know somebody when goin' into a new place."

"Yeah, that's definitely true," Colleen replied. "And we really do want you to feel comfortable. The folks here are very kind and'll want to make you feel at home." Chris really did appreciate Sybil's and Colleen's attention, and it definitely made him feel more relaxed.

They walked together across the parking lot and into the front door where the ladies began introducing him to a few of the church members who happened to be in the foyer. Then, as Sybil looked around, she spotted, on the other side of the building, Dr. Albritton, their pastor.

"Oh, there's Dr. Albritton over there," Sybil remarked. "Let's go over and introduce Chris to him."

"Oh yeah. Dr. Albritton," Chris repeated. "I actually met him over at the university. It was only a brief introduction, but I was told he's the pastor here."

"Great," Colleen replied with an excited smile, "that'll make it even better."

The two ladies escorted Chris over to meet Dr. Albritton, and Sybil spoke up as they approached him. "See, Dr. Albritton, I told you he'd come."

With that, they all smiled. Chris thought to himself, *Oh, they've been talkin' about me.*

Dr. Albritton reached out to shake hands and as Chris reciprocated, he said, "Chris, great to see you again. Welcome to our humble abode."

"Dr. Albritton, it's my honor. It's great to see you again, as well."

"I see our welcoming committee has already got you trapped," Dr. Albritton joked, which caused everyone to chuckle out loud.

"Yeah, they surrounded me out in the parking lot just as I was getting outta my car," Chris teased back. "They're very efficient." Everyone laughed again.

Dr. Albritton couldn't believe his luck to have Chris show up at his church on this particular day. He'd been struggling to figure out how to rope him in on the roundtable without it looking like some kind of conspiracy. "Listen Chris, it's about time for me to head to the platform for the service, but I'd love to have some time for us to chat a bit. Can I invite you to lunch? My wife's already prepared a feast, and we'd love to have you over." Then looking over at Sybil and Colleen, he continued, "In fact, if you two are available, we'd love for you ladies to join us, as well."

Chris was rather surprised at the invitation but was delighted. "Sure," he responded, "I'd love to."

Then looking back over at Sybil and Colleen, Dr. Albritton asked, "And ladies? How 'bout it?"

They, too, were rather surprised, but both looked at each other, nodded, and said, "Yeah, we'd love to come."

"It's settled then," Dr. Albritton replied. "I'll let Martha know we'll be having guests."

"Thank you for the invitation," Chris responded. "I was hopin' to find out more about your church, and this'll be a great opportunity for that, too."

After shaking hands once again, Dr. Albritton excused himself and went inside the worship center to find his wife and let her know about the new plans and get ready for the start of their service. Chris followed Sybil and Colleen into the worship center behind Dr. Albritton. It was beautifully decorated with two isles. The paneling around the platform area was red oak, which matched the chairs on the platform, and in the choir loft. The chairs' green padding matched the padding in the pews, making it all look quite elegant. Sybil and Colleen found a place for them to sit in the middle section of the auditorium that seated about 250 people. They took their seats there. Looking around the auditorium, it appeared there were around 90 - 100 people in attendance.

The atmosphere of the service was a little different from what Chris was accustomed to. While the actual structure of the service was familiar – church announcements, singing, and a sermon – the songs were mostly unfamiliar. They sang different words to the hymns he did know, but most of the songs had to do with nebulous expressions about "love" and social justice messages about helping the needy and oppressed. The small choir loft had only 10 people, but they harmonized beautifully and set the atmosphere for the service rather nicely.

The sermon sounded quite strange to Chris' ears. Dr. Albritton preached on Matthew 25:40 from the **New Revised Standard Version** (NRSV).

"And the king will answer them, 'Truly I tell you, just as you did it to one of the least of these who are members of my family, you did it to me.'"

When Dr. Albritton announced the Scripture reading came from the NRSV, Chris thought back to a study he had done several years back with Pastor Trumann on Bible translations. There are so many English translations these days, and he wanted to get a sense of what the differences were, so he took that special training. He recalled that this version was an update of the Revised Standard Version (RSV) published by the **National Council of Churches** (NCC), and that the NCC is a worldwide ecumenical organization comprised of churches from many denominations that pretty much all follow some form of **liberal theology**. They put a priority on such things as ending racism, ending mass incarceration, and interacting with Christian and non-Christian religious groups to try to bring world peace. The Bible translation itself is recognized as a scholarly work but does use gender neutral language by not referring to God as "He," and replaces masculine pronouns that refer to multiple people with words that are more "inclusive."

In his sermon, Dr. Albritton made the point that the very purpose of Christ, and thus of the church, was to help the down and out. He noted that in this world, there are two basic classes of people – those who are oppressed, and those who are the oppressors. In order to be on Jesus' side, we have to side with the oppressed against the oppressors. His final point was that in order to be on the side of the oppressed, we have to identify who they are and do what we can to help them. He concluded the message by asserting that the reason their church has a special focus on doing food distribution, education services, and pregnancy counseling was because of Jesus' teaching. Then, to close out his message, Dr. Albritton encouraged the church members to go to one of the ministry tables out in the foyer after the service and sign up to serve in one of the ministries.

Following the sermon, the congregation stood for a last song, then began filing out of the worship center. As they left, several people came up to Chris, introduced themselves, and told him they were pleased he had chosen to visit with them for the service.

When those people left, Sybil turned to Chris and asked, "Well, what did you think? Wasn't that an awesome sermon?"

Chris didn't really think so, so he smiled and responded to Sybil's question in a way that didn't really answer her question, as he didn't want to offend her. "I really do want to thank you for inviting me to visit your church today. Everyone's been so kind."

"Chris," Colleen chimed in, not really recognizing what Chris had done, "it'll be about 15 minutes before Dr. Albritton finishes up and is ready to leave. Can I answer any questions for you about the church?"

"Well, actually yes. Since we have a few minutes, I'm very interested in hearin' a little more about the church's ministries that Dr. Albritton was talkin' about."

"Oh, absolutely!" Sybil nearly shouted in her excitement. "Let's go to the ministry tables and let us tell you about 'em."

So, the three of them made their way out of the pew and walked back to the foyer. The closest display table was the pregnancy counseling table.

"You know Chris," Colleen jumped in, "one of the most difficult situations many young girls find themselves in is when they get pregnant. This is particularly a problem with coeds on the college campus. So, we have a partnership with Planned Parenthood to counsel these girls and help 'em deal with that crisis in their lives."

Chris was not expecting that answer. He knew Planned Parenthood was the number one abortion provider in the nation. *Why would a church partner with an abortion provider?* he thought to himself. "So," he asked out loud, "just what kind of counseling do they get?"

Colleen picked up her explanation, "Oh, we help those ladies with whatever they need. Most of 'em wanna get an abortion without their family ever finding out. So, we're able to help facilitate that by hookin' 'em up discreetly with our Planned Parenthood partner. But that's not the case for everyone. Some people decide to keep their babies and just need various kinds of help. And occasionally someone wants to carry the baby to term and put the baby up for adoption. We help the young girls sort through all that, then get 'em the help that meets their particular need."

Chris could tell Colleen was very excited about the pregnancy counseling ministry and asked, "So Colleen, are you involved in that ministry?"

"Oh yes," Colleen responded enthusiastically. "It's one of the most fulfilling things I've ever done in my life. I get to help so many young ladies. And they're so appreciative."

Chris still couldn't get over the fact that they had a partnership with Planned Parenthood. *Yes,* he thought to himself, *the mindset of the people in this church is very different from my church.*

At that point, Chris was almost hesitant to ask about the other ministries, but since he had started this process, he felt it would be bad form to not find out about the rest. So he asked, "Okay, tell me about the education services."

"Now that is my favorite," Sybil chimed in. "Walk over here with me to the education table."

The three of them walked over to the table where Sybil introduced Chris to Melanie. "Chris, meet Melanie. She's the head of the education ministry."

Melanie reached out to shake Chris' hand. "Very nice to meet you, Chris."

Chris shook her hand and said, "Likewise Melanie, it's my pleasure."

"Melanie," Sybil spoke up, "perhaps you've read about Chris in the *Times*. He's the karate master who broke the state record at the karate tournament a few weeks ago. Colleen and I invited him to come visit us, so here he is. We're just sharin' with him a little about the church and wanted him to hear about the education ministry."

"Yes, of course. I've been reading about you. You're the talk of the town! It's very exciting for us to have a celebrity visit our small church."

This very kind complement embarrassed Chris and caused his face to turn bright red. He lowered his eyes and said, "You guys ... you're embarrassin' me. I'm no celebrity."

The ladies smiled at each other and responded almost in unison, "Oh yes you are. You have no idea."

"So, tell me about the education ministry," Chris spoke up to change the subject.

"Well," Melanie began, "we started this ministry about 15 years ago. At that time, I noticed there were a lotta kids, particularly in the poorer sections of town, who were droppin' outta school, or getting way behind in their class-work. So, I came up with an idea to begin a tutoring operation. I went to a couple of the poorer schools and talked to the administrators to see if that was somethin' that'd be helpful for the school and for the kids. Well, they jumped on it. So I got three other people, including Sybil here, and we just started doin' it. It was such a huge success that we began expanding it to reach more kids. It started just in the elementary schools, but soon expanded to the middle and high schools, as well. Then, we found that there were lots of kids who had dropped outta school and still wanted to get their GED, so we began workin' with them, too. We actually average working with about 100 kids a year."

"Wow, that's amazing," Chris enthusiastically remarked. "You guys are doin' a great work. Thanks for sharin' it with me. I'd actually love to hear more, but there's one more ministry Sybil and Colleen are gonna share with me. Maybe there'll be a time to talk later, Melanie. Thanks for your time."

"Absolutely my pleasure," Melanie responded. "I'd love to share more anytime."

Sybil and Colleen then pointed over to the food distribution services table and guided Chris over to that one. "You know, we call this the food distribution ministry because that's what it started out as, but it's actually become somethin' much larger," Sybil explained.

When they got to the table, Sybil said, "Chris, this is Jacob. Jacob, Chris."

"Nice to meet you, Jacob."

"Nice to meet you too, Chris. I recognize you. You're the one who won the karate tournament. My younger brother was in the tournament, and I went to watch him fight. When you started racking up all those points – and wins – everybody went over to watch you. That was a really impressive performance."

Chris was again embarrassed, but attempted to be as gracious as he could. "Well thank you, Jacob. Thanks for your kind words."

"Jacob," Colleen jumped in, "we only have a few minutes before we gotta go but tell Chris a little about the food distribution ministry. I already told him we actually do more than just hand out food."

"Sure," Jacob responded. "Well, it actually did start out as distributing food to needy people. The city doesn't have a food bank, so the church decided to start one. We started out primarily by helpin' poor families in the city who needed help with food and groceries. In the beginning, we mostly connected with the schools that partnered with our education ministry to get the names of struggling families. Then, once we got it established, the newspaper did a writeup on us and other people started askin' us for help. So, we started expanding. Before long, it got to be more than we could handle alone, so we began sharing about the ministry to the rest of the community. Everyone got behind it and it has become a pretty big deal.

"But as we began helping those poor people, we also started comin' into contact with folks who had other needs – homeless people, abused spouses, abandoned children, and the like. So, we began creating a network to help those people, as well. So now we have a homeless shelter, a jobs program, a number of housing units, and a counseling center to help disadvantaged people get on their feet. We're really proud of what we've created."

"And rightly so," Chris replied. "I know you help a lotta people in need."

Chris then turned to Sybil and Colleen. "Thanks so much for sharin' these ministries with me. It's very rewarding to know there's people here who care about the needs of others."

At that moment, Dr. Albritton walked into the foyer and over to where Chris, Sybil, and Colleen were standing. "Well, folks," he called out, "I've finally finished all the things I needed to do. You guys ready to head over to my house?"

"We're ready," Sybil responded. "This is gonna be great."

CHAPTER 28

SETTING THE HOOK

After leaving the church, the group headed to Dr. Albritton's house as planned. Since Chris didn't know the way, he followed Sybil in her red Corvette.

When Chris and Sybil arrived, the others were already there, so they made their way to the front door of the house. "Nice car," Sybil. "I didn't take you for a hotrodder," Chris remarked.

"That old thing?" Sybil laughingly replied causing them to both laugh out loud. She then explained, "Actually, I inherited it from my uncle when he passed away. He was really into sports cars and had five different ones. I got the Vette. Oh, and did I mention he was rich?"

"Well, it's an impressive machine," Chris responded. "You're really fortunate to have a car like that." Sybil smiled and nodded, acknowledging the complement as they walked up to the front door.

From the outside, the Albritton's home was quite impressive, a two-story house painted white. It looked like an old plantation house with a beautiful front porch and columns. Rocking chairs on the front porch totally completed the look. This was, obviously, one of the nicer parts of town.

When they got to the front door, Sybil knocked, and Colleen immediately met them at the front door to let them in. Entering the house, they walked through the formal entry hall and turned to enter the living room on the right. Once inside, Dr. Albritton greeted them and offered Chris the overstuffed recliner directly across from the large screen TV. He then took his seat in an attractive blue swivel chair, and Sybil and Colleen made their way to the couch.

Looking around the room, Chris admired the refined furnishings. The high ceiling boasted an elegant plantation style ceiling fan in the middle and the large brick fireplace on the end wall, flanked with bookcases, presented an air of old-world distinction. Chris also noticed the beautiful artwork on the walls in massive, ornate frames.

"Lunch'll be ready in about 30 minutes," Dr. Albritton explained. "The food's already been prepared, and Martha is just warming it up and getting the table ready."

Just then, Martha Albritton entered the room to greet her guests. "Hello, everyone. I'm so glad you've come over to join us this afternoon. We absolutely love havin' guests for Sunday lunch. We do it quite often, so I always get up early to prepare something and have it ready after church. Because of our work schedules, we aren't able to do this durin' the week, so we try to make it happen on Sundays."

Sybil spoke up, "Chris, you don't yet realize what a treat you're in for. Mrs. Albritton's a master chef. In fact, she's the head chef at the convention center downtown."

Martha smiled, "Sybil, you're just too kind. I really do love to cook and feel very fortunate to have the opportunity to work at the convention center. I get a great deal of personal satisfaction bringin' a bit of joy into people's lives with food."

After greeting her guests, Martha requested their indulgence, "Well, if you'll excuse me for a few more moments, I need to finish up in the kitchen." With that, she turned and walked back to finish her preparation.

"Chris," Dr. Albritton inquired, "what did you think of the church service?"

With that, Chris used the same formula he had used with Sybil earlier. "Well, I can honestly say I am very glad Sybil and Colleen invited me to come. Besides them, I met some really nice people, and I particularly enjoyed learnin' about your church's various ministries. It appears you guys have great participation from the people in your congregation."

"Yeah, I was quite glad to see the ladies takin' you around to the various ministry tables to share that with you. We're all very proud of the social justice work we do in the community," Dr. Albritton noted. "Was there somethin' in particular that interested you?"

"Well," Chris replied as he pondered his response carefully, "at this point I'm not completely sure. I actually am workin' on somethin' that might potentially plug into what you guys are doin' – that is, if you find it to be worthy of takin' on."

Dr. Albritton, Sybil, and Colleen were all surprised at that comment. What in the world could he possibly be workin' on that'd interact with our church ministries, they all thought.

"So, what do you mean?" Sybil blurted out.

Chris' face turned serious, and he leaned forward to share what he was contemplating. "It's really too early to know anything for absolute certain," Chris answered, "but recently I've had the opportunity to interact with some gang members down by the karate dojo."

Colleen interrupted, "Yeah, I saw in the paper where you were seen with one of 'em at the Burger Barn. That's actually created a buzz around town. Have you actually become friends with some of 'em?"

Chris continued, "Well, at this point, I really don't know exactly where this relationship might go, but I've discovered that many of those folks haven't completed their schooling, and some have an interest in doin' so. I'm hopin' to encourage at least a few of 'em to go back to school. In fact, I hope I might even be able to influence some to get outta the gangs altogether. If I'm able to pull that off, they're gonna need some help I don't have the resources for. Your church ministries got me thinkin' that you guys may be able to gimme some guidance, and maybe even help materially in that arena if the opportunity opens up."

Upon hearing that, Sybil immediately sat to attention, "Seriously? You really think you might be able to do somethin' like that? We've been tryin' for years to break into those gangs to help 'em – without even the slightest hint of success. Listen, if you're able to pull somethin' off, you can definitely count on us. We'll help you any way we can."

"Well, like I said, at this point I am not sure of anything. I anticipate it'll be at least a couple more weeks before I know anything for sure. But thanks for that encouragement and offer of support. If it does work out, I'd love to plug in with you guys on that."

Dr. Albritton was also a bit surprised and intrigued to hear what Chris was sharing. He certainly didn't anticipate him being interested in any kind of social services ministry. His stereotype of evangelicals like Chris was that they were only interested in "getting people saved" and promoting "tradition- al American values." What he had heard him share with the students in Dr. Craven's class certainly didn't give him any reason to break his stereotype. He thought to himself, *Maybe there's more to this guy than I realized.*

"Well, Chris," he said out loud, "you let us know if there's some way we can help. Our church is all about helpin' 'the least of these,' and the people in the city's gangs clearly fit into the 'oppressed' class that we focus on."

After pausing for a moment to allow that topic to conclude, Dr. Albrit- ton casually changed the subject in a way that would allow him to probe and see whether he might make some inroads with his personal agenda – getting Chris to participate in the roundtable. "So Chris, to shift the focus just a little, I did wanna tell ya that I thought your presentation to Dr. Craven's class was very interesting, and quite well done."

"Well thank you, Dr. Albritton. I must say it was a bit nerve wracking. I'm well aware I was expressing ideas that were not, shall we say, the most domi- nant beliefs in the room. And I was particularly aware of the professor contin- gent in the back of the room. I did feel quite nervous."

"Well, you didn't show it at all," Dr. Albritton responded. "You shared and answered questions with seemingly great confidence."

"Well thank you for the kind words," Chris replied. "I did enjoy doin' it and felt pretty good about it overall."

"Listen," Dr. Albritton continued, "what would you think about partici- pating in another presentation at the school – one that would actually tie into what you did for Dr. Craven, but in an expanded forum? A number of times each semester – actually every week – the religion department sponsors a roundtable discussion where we invite people from outside the school to interact with some of the professors. We often try to invite people who hold non-traditional points of view to expose our students to different perspectives on various subjects. And in Skeptopolis your beliefs definitely fit into that cat- egory. We actually have one comin' up next week, and the person scheduled to participate called me yesterday and had to cancel. I was thinkin' we'd have to cancel the whole thing, but then you came to my mind –and I was wonderin' if you might like to take his place."

Suddenly Chris' "danger" antenna popped up. *Hmm*, he thought to himself, *I wonder if I'm bein' set up here.*

"So tell me somethin' about it," Chris replied.

"Well," Dr. Albritton went on, "you've already met all the participants of this one. Since it's sponsored by the religion department, I'll be the one moderating the roundtable, but Dr. Craven, Dr. Everson, and Dr. Gray will be the other panelists. The topic actually relates to the focus of Dr. Craven's class you spoke to the other day. That's what made me think of you. This roundtable will be about the social and personal evolution of man. As you might guess, the three of them firmly believe in it. You'd be the only voice in opposition.

"The way the roundtable works is that you'd be interacting with only one of the professors at a time, and it'd be a back-and-forth discussion, not a debate. You'd be dealing with each one of them based on their particular specialty as you talk about how evolutionary theory interacts with their discipline. I know this is rather sudden, and you might be a little hesitant to put yourself in that position ... and I'd completely understand if you didn't feel comfortable doin' it."

At that, Chris' mind started whirling. *I absolutely know this is a set-up. Steve and Dr. Gray teach in the social sciences and believe that individual human beliefs, and those of society, evolved through history. And Dr. Everson's an evolutionary biologist. Then there's Dr. Albritton himself. He's definitely nice enough, but his liberal theology inclines him to also believe religion has its root in evolutionary human development. And here I am, not even an academic – no title of doctor in front of my name. But if I turn it down, that could shoot my credibility, as well. And, after all, I did come to Skeptopolis knowin' this sorta thing could happen – and I prepared for it. I can't pass this up.*

"Wow, Dr. Albritton. I don't know what to say," Chris responded. "I was definitely not anticipating this. You know I'm not an academic. I'm really not sure how much credibility I'd bring to a panel like that. Are you sure havin' me do it would meet the needs of your roundtable?"

Dr. Albritton replied, "Oh, you don't need to worry about that. This is not for a class or anything. It's just somethin' we do as an enrichment activity for the students to let 'em hear different perspectives. In fact, we often have people with non-academic backgrounds participating in these. After all, it's people like you who represent most of the people in the world. But like I said, you don't need to feel any pressure about it. If you don't feel comfortable, I definitely understand. It wouldn't be the first time we had to cancel one of these."

Chris took a deep breath, looked Dr. Albritton in the eye, nodded his head up and down a few times and cautiously replied, "Okay, I'll do it. So when and where will it take place?"

Dr. Albritton felt giddy on the inside but carefully maintained his stoic outward demeanor. "It'll be comin up on Friday, June 4th, in the main lecture hall of the religion building," Dr. Albritton responded with a big smile on his face. "I know this doesn't give you much time to prepare, but I'm really glad you'll be participating in this with us. I've been pretty bummed at the prospect of canceling. And because of your recent celebrity, I think it'll be of great interest to the students. We might even have a few more than usual."

"Well," Chris responded, "I hope I can live up to your confidence. Would you mind writing down the details for me so I can be sure to get it on my calendar?"

"Absolutely, glad to do that," Dr. Albritton responded. "I'll give it to you before you leave."

Just then, Martha entered the room and announced, "Lunch is served. The dining room's across the hall over to the left. If anyone needs to wash up, the bathroom is just down the hall on the right."

The five of them spent the rest of the mealtime with everyone asking Chris questions about himself – just to get to know him better. "Are you actually from Templeton? How did you get interested in karate? How did you get so good? What's your church like?" … and on and on. Chris managed to fit in a few questions about each of them, as well. Their conversation at the table ended up lasting about two more hours.

When it came time to leave, Chris thanked his hosts for their wonderful hospitality. "Mrs. Albritton, that was one of the most delicious meals I've ever eaten in my life. Thank you so much for having me over," he said shaking her hand. "And thank you, too, Dr. Albritton. I deeply appreciate your kindness to 'one who's a stranger here.'"

Both responded, "It was our pleasure. Thank you for coming."

"Oh, and Chris," Dr. Albritton spoke up as he pulled a piece of paper out of his pocket and handed it over, "I wrote down that information about the roundtable for you. Here it is."

"Oh, right," Chris responded. "Thanks."

Sybil and Colleen also said their goodbyes and the three of them walked outside together, got into their cars and went their separate ways.

CHAPTER 29

BREAKTHROUGH

"Chris, can you come over to the house right now?" Chris was just settling in for the evening, but Gino's voice had a certain urgency to it.

"Uhhh, I guess so," Chris replied, a bit concerned. "What's up?"

"Well, I finally got all the gang together and shared with 'em what we talked about the other day. They're willin' to hear what you have to say, but it needs to happen right now. Can you come?" Gino repeated.

Chris immediately recognized the urgency of the situation. "Gino, I'll be there in five minutes." So, he jumped out of his chair, grabbed his car keys and headed out the door. "Lord," he prayed as he got in the car, "I feel so inadequate for this. I'm not sure I have any idea what to do. Please guide me in this process."

True to his word, Chris arrived at the gang enclave in five minutes, got out of the car and briskly walked to the front door. Before he could even knock, Gino swung the door open and invited him in. As he looked around the room, he saw that all twenty gang members were there – 17 guys and three girls. This was the first time he had seen the whole group together. Usually there were only six or seven there at a time. They really did look like a tough bunch, and Chris was thinking that if he were not there under friendly circumstances, this is not a place he'd want to be. But since he was Gino's friend, everyone greeted him warmly, though he could tell there was a certain amount of tension in the room.

"So," Chris spoke first, "what would you like from me?"

Gino invited Chris to sit in a chair at the front of the room and said, "Chris, I shared with the gang what we talked about the other day. I didn't hold anything back. I told 'em how much I cared for 'em, and that I wasn't sure if I was really doin' right by 'em by leading 'em down a path that would certainly be the cause of many of 'em goin' to jail or gettin' killed. Then I told 'em about our talk, about your offer to help anyone who wanted to get an education and move in a different direction in life, and what you said about how just doin' it without having a new focus on life would probably not be enough to cause that to happen – that it'd require a spiritual element to be introduced, as well. So I shared with 'em the booklet you gave me. Now to be honest, about half the group are very curious, but the other half are rather skeptical. So, I asked 'em if I could invite you over to answer any questions they might have. So that's where we are."

Chris surveyed the room to see if he could detect where the opposition might be coming from. It was hard to tell at this point as everyone seemed to be holding back to see what would happen next.

"Okay," Chris began, "it seems Gino's already pretty much laid things out. What do you guys want to know from me?"

Selena was the first to jump in. She was quite a cute girl, with short brown hair and a petite frame but was also extremely tough – you could see it in her eyes. In fact, she was pretty much considered second in command behind Gino. She was never one to take anything off of anyone. "Chris," she declared in a snarly voice, "this all seems kinda hokey to me. Now I appreciate that you wanna do somethin' nice for us, but this religion stuff just doesn't ring true to me. Now mind you, I respect you, and I'm willin' to hear what you have to say. But I'm not sure this is a good thing for our gang. What are you tryin' to do here?"

Chris listened to what Selena had to say, then carefully gathered his thoughts before he spoke. "Selena, I get it. And I want you to know that I'm not tryin' to pull any stunts. I know we don't know each other very well at this point, but I do hope by now you've at least been able to see that I don't have any kind of agenda to cause you guys problems. As I look at all of you and your situation, it's obvious to me that I've had opportunities, just because of my life circumstances, that you haven't had. Most of you've had to look out for yourselves for most of your lives – in circumstances that no one would consider good. As it is now, I find myself in a position to do somethin' good for some people, and I'd like to do somethin' good for you guys if I can. I personally don't get anything out of it except the personal satisfaction of helpin' you.

"Now all of you know how I ended up making a connection with you guys in the first place. Our first contact could've ended up a bloody mess. But I personally didn't want that. And while there may be a lotta people who look down their noses at you because you came from this part of town, and because you're part of a gang, I don't feel that way. In fact, I consider it a privilege to have met you – and hopefully you also look at me as a friend.

"So when I made the connection with Gino, I wanted to do anything I could to help you guys out. I don't have money, and I don't have criminal connections to further your business enterprise. But I do have connections and a way to help you change your life direction if that's something you'd like.

"But Gino's right, everyone, and that means every single person in the world, has to make a personal decision about what kinda life they want. So if any of you want a life that goes outside of what you'll ever get from gang life, you'll have to make a decision that'll turn your life in a different direction."

When Chris paused, Blade jumped in with another question, "Yeah, but what's this religion stuff all about? Why have you introduced somethin' like that?"

"That's a legit question, Blade," Chris replied, taking it as seriously as he possibly could. "So let me see if I can give you a solid answer. To do that, let me ask you a question. Is there anyone you love so much that you'd do anything for 'em?"

"Of course. I'd do anything for my mom."

"Okay, one more question," Chris continued. "If you saw one of the Checkers gang members in a dark alley by themselves one evenin', what'd you do?"

Blade responded with a chuckle, "I'd show 'em why I'm called 'Blade.'"

Everyone laughed out loud at his obvious gang humor.

Chris smiled at the joke, then replied back, "So what makes the difference in the way you see your mom and the way you see the Checkers gang?"

"My mom's family," Blade smirked, "and the Checkers are enemies."

"What you're saying, then," Chris went on, "is that your attitude toward your mom – or toward the Checkers – makes all the difference. So, what would have to happen for you to have the same attitude toward a member of the Checkers as you do toward your mom?"

Blade glared back at Chris, "That'd never happen!"

"Well, maybe not," Chris replied, "but if it *were* to ever happen, what would be necessary?"

Blade thought for a moment, "Well, I suppose somethin' would havta happen to change my mind."

"Exactly!" Chris replied approvingly. "That's precisely the right answer. If something like that were to ever happen, there'd have to be a complete change of attitude. Now here's the reason I asked you those questions. If you ever decided you wanted to change your way of life, the exact same kind of attitude change would have to happen – and the only way that ever happens in human beings is for somethin' to occur that changes our attitude.

"So here's the deal – the only one with the power to change your attitude that way is God. If you wanna go a different direction in your life, it'll be necessary to follow the path Gino shared with you in that little booklet.

"I can tell you from my own personal experience that God is real, and He loves you. In fact, He loves you so much that He created a way for you to get the kind of attitude change we're talkin' about."

Chris continued, "Listen, it's not just gang bangers who are in the situation of being enemies of God. Every human being in the world's in that situation – you, me, the Pope, everybody. The cause of that is what we call sin. Every human being has a sin enemy in their heart that rules 'em and is out to kill 'em – kinda like an enemy gang member inside of you. That's the source of all of your bad thoughts and deeds – and God just won't keep company with people who are ruled by this sin enemy. To get on God's good side, that enemy has to be eliminated. The only problem is, no human has the power to overcome it. Only the power of God can do it.

"But God set things up where it had to be done in a certain way. In this life, that internal enemy'll never be totally eliminated, but God has made the possibility for another warrior to enter your life that's powerful enough to defeat it – and that warrior is God Himself, in the form of His Spirit. It is His Spirit in you that gives you the ability to live out the new attitude that'll motivate you to pursue, and keep on goin', in the new life we're talkin' about.

"So here's how it works. First, you actually deserve to be separated from God because of your sin. You're the one who acts on it, and you're guilty before God. That's true for everybody in the world. But He loves you and doesn't want you to have to be judged for it. His solution was to have someone else receive the judgment you should receive. It'd be like you bein' convicted of a crime, but someone else volunteered to go to prison for you so you could go free.

"But for God's requirement to be met, there had to be a worthy person – one who was not guilty of any sin – who'd be willing to take that punishment for you. Since there wasn't, and never has been, any human able to live a perfect life like that, God decided that he'd do it Himself. He came to earth in the form of the man Jesus Christ. He lived a perfect, sinless, life, then sacrificed Himself when He was executed on the cross as a sinless man. That was Him taking the punishment for sin that was rightly yours. On the third day after that, He rose from the dead to prove that He actually had the power to overcome sin and death. What's important to recognize, though, is that Christ didn't have to die on the cross. He was God in the flesh, and He had the power to get out of it if He wanted. But he also knew that Him dying in the place of guilty sinners was the only way to take care of the sin problem. So he did it.

"But just because He sacrificed Himself like that doesn't mean all of us are automatically off the hook. Every person has to decide for themselves whether they'll accept Christ's sacrificial death or not. So now the choice is yours. If you do it, God'll pronounce you not guilty of sin and put His Spirit in your life to give you the spiritual power to overcome the evil enemy in your heart. If you decide not to, you'll continue on as you have been. So, is there anyone here who'd like to invite Christ into their life and let God change 'em?"

After Chris asked that question, there was a long silence in the room. Then suddenly, Gino spoke up. "Guys, I've been agonizin' over this ever since Chris shared it with me the other day. I want my life to change. I wanna have a life that goes beyond just makin' money and wieldin' power. I'm gonna follow Christ. Who's with me?"

Carl quickly spoke up, "Guys, you know I had a horrible family life, and that I had to get in the gang just to survive. But I've always had dreams of makin' a better life for myself. In thinkin' about it, I honestly believe this is the only way to make that happen. Gino, I'm with you.

One-by-one, eight others chimed in, "I'm in, too."

The remaining 10 gang members just stared. They just were not able, at that moment, to pull the trigger. Finally, Selena spoke up, "I can't do this. I'm outta here. Anyone else who doesn't wanna be part of this joke can come with me."

With that, Selena abruptly stood up, turned around, and stormed out the back door. The other nine who had not stood with Gino got to their feet and followed behind her.

After they left, Gino asked Chris, "Well, what do we do now?"

Chris looked at the ones who remained and began to explain, "You've all indicated your desire to invite Christ into your life. All that's left is for you to actually do it. When I told you God is a real person, I was serious – He really is. And when you talk to Him, He hears and responds to you. And if you invite Him into your life, His Spirit actually enters your life and begins the life change I was talkin' about. So how 'bout each one of you tellin' God you want Him to enter your life. Let's do it one by one. Gino, would you like to go first?"

So Gino prayed and invited Christ to come into his life. Following him, one-by-one, the rest did the same. As they did so, they felt a powerful sense of God's presence in that place. Some were so moved that tears began spilling out of their eyes.

So, for the next two hours, Chris began teaching them the essential basics of the Christian life. He went into more detail about the things he had already shared, and answered all the questions they had about Christ and the Bible.

When he finished, Chris got up to leave, and Gino walked with him out to his car. He then asked, "Chris, we've made this first step, but now comes the hard part. You're gonna havta deliver on helpin' us start a new life. What's the plan?"

"Gino," Chris responded, "you're absolutely right. Obviously, I don't have anything already lined up because I didn't know what would happen here. But I do have some leads and I'll get right on it. I'll give you a call tomorrow and we can begin to put the wheels to this in motion."

"Sounds like a plan," Chris, "and I wanna thank you for what you've done tonight. I really believe it's the right thing."

"Gino, my heart's full. I'm gonna do everything I can to help you and your crew have the best life possible. I count it a privilege to call you 'my friend.'"

CHAPTER 30

WHEELS IN MOTION

The next morning, Chris immediately got to work to put into motion the things that would be necessary to support the new believers who had invited Christ into their lives the night before. The first call he made was to Pastor Trumann back in Templeton. When he called, he shared in detail what had happened and the circumstances that lay before him. Then he asked, "Pastor, what do you think is the first thing that needs to happen?"

Pastor Trumann didn't even hesitate. "Chris, those kids are comin' out of a life where God wasn't even a consideration. Beyond that, they live in an environment where they've never had the opportunity to be around people who believe in God. Skeptopolis doesn't even have a true Bible believing church. The first thing those guys need is a shepherd."

"Well, I know you're right, Pastor. So what can we do? I can help 'em some, and I will. But I don't have the background, the training, or the experience, to set up a long-term framework for them to grow in their faith. Besides, my time here'll be somewhat limited."

Pastor Trumann paused a moment as he thought about Chris' situation. Then he said, "Chris, I have a thought. But before I can actually do anything, I have to talk with some people. Here's what I'm contemplating. What would you think if our church sent Levi over to Skeptopolis to start a church there with your gang buddies being the first members?"

"Holy moly!" Chris exclaimed. "Do you think somethin' like that's really possible? That'd be awesome!!!"

"Chris, that would be awesome," Pastor Trumann responded. "But to make it happen several things'll have to fall into place – not the least of which would be for Levi to agree to it. Then, I'd have to bring the idea to the church to get 'em behind it. A startup like that'll need significant backing – and possibly for an extended period of time. I think I know how this'll play out, but I have to go through all the right channels to make sure we can finish this if we start it."

"I'll tell you what," Pastor Trumann continued, "I'm gonna get on this immediately to see if we can get the ball rolling. I'll call you later this afternoon and give you a progress report."

"Wow! This is way more than I expected," Chris nearly shouted. "And while you're doin' that, I'm gonna to get to work on some of the other pieces that have to go into this puzzle. Thanks so much! I can't wait to hear back this afternoon."

"Perfect," Pastor Trumann responded. "I'll talk to you then."

After he hung up, Chris dialed Sybil. He needed to see if she might be willing to help explore possibilities for some further education for those who wanted it. "Hey Sybil, this is Chris Bel. How ya doin' today?"

"Chris? Oh wow, I wasn't expectin' to hear from you. This really is a pleasant surprise!" with the shock clearly resonating in Sybil's voice. "What can I do for ya?"

"Umm, you remember the conversation we had over at Dr. Albritton's house about some of the gang members possibly wanting to further their education?"

"Yeah," Sibil replied with some hesitancy in her voice.

Well, it seems that this has become an actual possibility – and much more quickly than any of us expected. I have ten gang members who are quitting the gang and would like to do somethin' to move their lives in a new direction. I don't know their specific needs just yet, so that'll have to be assessed. Some of 'em may want to get their GED, and others might wanna learn some kinda trade. So do you guys wanna get in on this?"

"Do we?!" Sybil almost screamed. "Like I told you the other day, we've been tryin' for years to make inroads with that community. This would be a dream come true for the education ministry."

"Well," Chris continued, "I don't know yet exactly what steps'll be next with these folks. This possibility has *just* opened up. But before I went any further, I wanted to know if you were the ones I should deal with about this."

"Absolutely!" Sybil responded with excitement continuing to rise in her voice. "In fact, I'll go ahead and touch base with Melanie and get some things rolling. Then when you're ready, you can let me know and we can start gettin' things underway."

"Perfect!" Chris responded. "And there's one other thing."

"What might that be," Sybil replied wondering what else could possibly be in the mix.

"Well again, this is somethin' where it's too early to know exactly what's goin' on, but it's possible we may need housing and other living support for some of these kids. If that becomes necessary, do you guys have resources to help in that arena, as well?"

"Uhhh, actually, it might be possible," Sybil replied. "Let me get with Jacob, the head of the church's food distribution ministry, and see what the possibilities are. And Chris," Sybil continued, "I have no idea how you've done this, and obviously no idea how it'll all turn out, but in the short time you've been in Skeptopolis, you sure are makin' a difference in a lotta people's lives. This is just amazing!"

"Well Sybil, I really don't believe I can take credit for this. It seems to me God's doin' somethin' really unique among us, and I'm just excited to be riding this wave."

Chris' last statement caught Sybil totally by surprise. While she was very active in her church, she was definitely not used to hearing God get credit like that. That's just not the kind of thing that was expressed in her church. But it also put a spiritual thought in her mind that she found strangely exciting. "Me too," Sybil replied. "Me too."

"Well listen Sybil, I'm still workin' on figurin' out the situation here, but as soon as I know more, I'll get back to you. Thanks for checking out the possibilities."

"Absolutely my pleasure!" Sybil replied with obvious excitement still in her voice. "I'll talk to you later."

So far, this is goin' great, Chris thought to himself. He couldn't wait to see what would unfold next.

Now, he thought, I need to talk to Gino again. I've gotta find out from him exactly what the needs are.

When Chris dialed Gino's number, he picked it up right away. "Hey Gino, this is Chris. How ya doin' this morning?"

"Chris, I'm so glad you called," Gino responded with noticeable anxiety in his voice. "We need to talk. There's some things happenin' that are somehow gonna to have to be managed."

"Sure," Chris replied. "Tell me when and where."

"Well, the sooner the better," Gino replied. "What are you doin' right now?"

"Gino, I am here for you, 100 percent. Where ya wanna meet?"

"Can I come over to your place? If so, I'll be there in 10 minutes," Gino said with the sound of urgency still in his voice.

"Absolutely! Come right on over. "I'll be waitin' for ya."

Ten minutes later, Gino pulled his car in front of Chris' place, hopped out, and hustled to the front door. Before he could knock, Chris already had the door open and invited him in.

After clasping right hands and doing their traditional chest bump, Chris invited Gino to have a seat on the couch. "Can I get you somethin'?" Chris offered.

"No thanks," Gino replied, "I don't care for anything right now."

"So, tell me what's goin' on. I can tell there's a certain urgency here."

"Yeah, there is," Gino replied. "We need to handle a particular situation or there could be some serious trouble. I had a meeting with Selena this morning. She's really ticked off about the gang splittin' up, and she's decided she's gonna to take over with the ones who left with her. Blade'll be her number two.

"Basically, she's given me an ultimatum. She wants the gang house and is willin' to fight to take it over. I told her I didn't wanna fight and wanted to stay friends with her and the other members, but she wasn't havin' any of it."

"So what'd you tell her?" Chris asked, rather concerned at this potentially explosive turn of events.

"I told her to give me three days to talk it over with my guys and I'd get back with her."

"And how'd she respond?" Chris asked.

"She said to let her know tomorrow ... and that if she didn't hear back, they'd come guns blazin'," Gino groaned, dropping his eyes as he thought about what was happening.

"Here's the deal," Gino continued, "I can't back down from her or I'll lose all credibility with my guys, and they'll just return to the gang. They won't be willin' to lose face that way. I do think I can manage this, but I have to have some options in play to make it work."

"So what kind of options do you need?" Chris asked.

"Well, after I talked to Selena, I went and had a sit-down with the guys. I was flat out honest with 'em. I told 'em I had their backs and that I'd help 'em take the next step to their dreams with honor, but that they'd have to be strong and trust me. I told 'em that the house was the gang house and had been for nearly 50 years. Also, that if we weren't gonna be in the gang, we needed to make other arrangements. They're willin', but they need to have somethin' concrete to hang their hats on. You said you thought you could help. Is there anything you can do?"

Chris nodded his head and pursed his lips together to signal that he understood the gravity of the situation. "Gino, I've already begun talkin' to some people that believe they can help. They're havin' to consult with their people, though, and I think to actually begin rollin' some things into place I'll need at least another day. If you think it's an emergency, all the guys can come and crash a couple of days here in my house, but if I understand you right, they won't be willin' to do somethin' that looks like they are runnin' away."

"That's exactly the situation, Chris," Gino confirmed, "but if you think you can pull off somethin' within two days, I think I can buy us another day."

"I'm on it, Gino," Chris replied. "I'll get back to you as soon as I know somethin' more. In the meantime, see if you can get us that extra day."

With that, Gino pulled out his phone and called Selena. When she answered, he said in a very gruff voice, "Selena, let's meet. Be at the park by the river in two hours. Come alone, and don't stand me up!"

Selena couldn't back down at that point, so she responded with a growl in her own voice, "I'll be there."

Gino nodded and looked at Chris with a determined look in his eye. They both stood up, gave each other another chest bump, and Gino headed out the door.

About three hours later, Chris' phone rang. It was Pastor Trumann. "Chris, I have somethin' to report back to you. It's still preliminary, but I think we have some good news.

"First, I talked to Levi, and he was beside himself. I've never seen him this excited about anything in my life. He *absolutely* wants to do it."

"Oh wow!" Chris exclaimed with utter exhilaration in his voice, "That's fantastic! You know Levi and I are best friends, and there's nothin' I'd like more than to be able to work on this with him."

"I thought, you'd be pleased," Pastor Trumann responded. "But there's more. I talked to the elder chairman, Jim Scott, and shared with him what was goin' on with you, and the possibilities that lay before you. He was also beyond excited. Obviously, he can't speak for the entire board – but he's calling an urgent meeting tonight after everyone gets off work to talk about it. He believes that everyone else'll be as excited as he is, and that they'll recommend to the church that we send Levi and give financial support to your efforts. But you know these kinds of things take a little time to work through the process. We'll have to call a church business meeting, and in order to put some financial backing behind it we'll have to wait a couple of weeks before we can vote on it in accordance with the church bylaws. I'm thinkin' you might not have that kinda time before you have to begin acting."

Chris chimed in, "Well, you're right about that. There are some things going down where time is of the essence." Chris then shared with Pastor Trumann about the talk he just had with Gino.

After hearing the explanation, Pastor Trumann picked up where he had left off. "Well Chris, we do have a bridge plan to help you out immediately if necessary. Jim told me that if things did have to move faster, he'd personally foot the bill for this project for a year. I'm sure you know he has the means to do that if he wants to. His personal view is that the church will be as excited about it as he is, and'll want to back it – and that it'll be better to have the whole body behind it if that's possible. But he also said that he'll do it personally if he has to – and he believes there are others who'd get involved, as well.

"I also shared that with Levi and asked him how quickly he'd feel comfortable movin' on this? He indicated he could be ready to go in about five days. Can he stay with you until he's able to get his own place?"

"Oh yeah!" Chris exclaimed. "There's nothin' I'd love more than that. Tell him to come right on over."

"Well then," Pastor Trumann responded, "looks like the wheels are in motion. I'll keep you posted."

"Pastor," Chris responded with tears running down his face, "this is one of the most powerful movements of God I've ever seen in my life. When He's ready to move, things really happen."

"Yes indeed," Pastor Trumann replied, "that's our God. Chris, you take care, and we'll talk again soon."

"Fantastic! Thanks Pastor," Chris replied as they ended the call.

In the meantime, Gino met Selena at the park. She walked up to him with a steely look in her eye as if she were ready to take him out right then and there.

"Quit it, Selena!" Gino barked. "You're gonna get what you want, so quit being a snot rag! I recognize that the house is the gang house, and that if we're no longer gonna to be in the gang, we won't stay there. But you know how this goes. No one's willin' to back down. If you're determined to try to make my guys lose face, then a bunch of people are gonna go to the hospital or die. And right now, if you lose a bunch of people, you probably won't have enough to even continue havin' a gang – and certainly not enough to stand up to the Checkers when they see you've been so weakened. So let's end this thing amicably. I need two days. Back off and let us take care of the arrangements we havta make."

That sharp tirade caught Selena a little off guard. She honestly thought she'd have to fight to get the house – which is why she was coming across so tough in the first place. But now, after realizing she wasn't gonna have to fight after all, she smiled at Gino and said in a rather sultry voice, "Gino, you know I'd never fight you. We've been through too much together. We've fought and shed blood together for 10 years. We'll always be brother and sister. But I really am surprised that you're walkin' away like this. How could that happen?"

"Selena, I know right now you're findin' this hard to understand, but the change of heart we were talkin' about the other night ... it's real. God is real and Jesus Christ really has given us a new direction in our lives. I can't explain it myself, but it's real."

"Okay, Gino, whatever!" Selena interrupted. "I'll give you the extra day and we'll stay outta the way. No confrontation, and no hard feelins. You're right, though, I don't get it. I wish it could be true, but I just don't see it."

With that, Gino and Selena went their separate ways to let the process play itself out.

When Gino got to his car, he picked up his phone and gave Chris another call. "Chris, we have two days. Work your magic."

"Workin' on it, Gino. There's already some pieces beginnin' to fall into place."

Later that afternoon, Chris received a call from Sybil. "Chris, I have some partially good news. Jacob's been hustlin' and we have some opportunities. He wasn't able to get living space for all 10 of your guys this quickly, but he was able to get some housing for seven. In our housing unit, there are two side by side cabins that are currently unoccupied. One has two rooms and the other has five. They could be ready to move in tomorrow. We can also provide food for everyone for a while. Does that help?"

"Sybil," Chris replied excitedly, "That's perfect! I actually just talked to Gino, the gang leader who's instrumental in makin' all this happen. It looked for a little while like this rift in the gang could've turned violent about the housing situation, but he was able to buy another day. That'll be perfect. I've also lined up some help from my contacts in Templeton, so that'll also help. There's obviously still work to do, though. I havta make some kind of arrangement for three more. Let me get on that and I'll talk to you again later."

"Sounds great, Chris," Sybil replied excitedly. "This is so exhilarating! I can't wait to see how it all plays out. Talk to you soon. Bye."

"Great!" Chris responded. "Talk soon."

Suddenly, Chris had another idea. I wonder if CJ'd be willin' to house a couple of the guys for a while. Since that's his neighborhood, he prob'ly even knows some of gang members and their families. A couple of the guys might even wanna take karate. I'm gonna go ask him.

Chris immediately got in his car and drove down to the dojo. No classes were going on at the moment, so CJ was just hanging out in his office.

When Chris walked through the front door, Dolly greeted him with a great big smile. "Hey, Chris, how ya doin'?" she said enthusiastically.

"Doin' great, Dolly, good to see you, too. Listen, is CJ available? I'd like to talk to him for a second."

Before Chris even got all of the words out of his mouth, CJ walked into the room. "Heard your voice," CJ said as he stuck out his hand. "It is always great to see you. I didn't expect you to make it over today."

"Well, somethin' unique's come up," Chris responded. "You got a second?"

"Always got time for you, Chris. "Come on in my office."

Chris walked in and CJ closed the door behind them. "What can I do for ya?"

"CJ, you know I've been having some interaction with the Red Flag Pack, right?" Chris began.

"Do I know?" CJ replied laughing out loud. "I remember you nearly got us all killed with 'em."

Chris, too, started laughing at the memory of that day. "Well, since that time, Gino and I have actually become pretty good friends, and I've had a chance to interact with him quite a bit. In fact, I've convinced him and nine of his guys to actually quit the gang and go straight."

Hearing that, CJ's jaw dropped, and his eyes bugged out. "What?! "Are you serious?"

"Dead serious," Chris replied. "They wanna go to school and turn their lives around to live a normal life."

"I can't believe it," CJ responded. "That's incredible! I don't know what to say."

"Well, I do have one little problem," Chris continued. "In order to pull this off, I'm havin' to arrange various kinds of help for 'em. I've managed to find some housing for seven of 'em, along with some food support. I haven't asked him yet, but I'm gonna ask Gino if he'd like to move in with me. That leaves two that I still need to make arrangements for. I was wonderin' if you might be willin' to put up a couple of guys in your rooms for a little while. I don't know which two right now, but I know you know a bunch of those guys, and maybe even know a couple that might like to train in karate – a couple of guys you could also provide a good influence for. Think that might be a possibility?"

"Wow, Chris," CJ blurted out, "you never cease to amaze me! Everywhere you turn you're makin' a difference in people's lives. I don't know how you do it."

"You're too kind, CJ," Chris replied, "but I really can't take the credit for this. I don't know what God's doin', but He's the one who's workin' all this out. So, what do you think?"

Not being a religious person, CJ didn't really know how to respond to Chris' God talk, but he did like and trust Chris. "You know, if it was anyone else askin', I'd be very hesitant. But for you, I'd do nearly anything."

"CJ, besides being a great businessman and sensei, you're just a great guy. Later when I talk to Gino and the guys, I'll first see who might actually know you. I know if you knew at least one of the guys it'd be a lot more comfortable. Then I'll see who might actually be interested in takin' karate."

"That's perfect," CJ responded. "I just bet there's a couple that know me and my family who'd like to do it."

"Great," Chris responded as he got up from his chair. "I'll get back with you soon." With that, the two shook hands and Chris left.

When he arrived back at his house, he sat down in his easy chair, pulled out his phone and called Gino. When Gino answered, Chris said, "Hey Gino, I've got some great news for ya."

"Oh yeah?" What's happenin'?"

"Well, I've almost got all the initial logistical issues taken care of," Chris went on. "I've secured a place to live for nine out of the 10 guys. There's one cabin that houses five, and another right beside it that houses two. Then – and you won't believe this one – CJ has two rooms in his dojo that he's willin' to let a couple of guys live in for a while. I was thinkin' maybe there's a couple of guys that actually know him and his family who might even want to take karate."

"Chris, are you serious?" Gino responded in amazement. "I can't believe it. I know I really put myself out there to commit to this thing, but honestly, I did kinda believe it was all gonna fall apart. You're magic!"

"Well," Chris responded, "that does still leave one more. But I have an idea on that, too."

"What's that?" Gino responded.

"Well, first let me tell you another thing that's happenin'," Chris interrupted the flow of the conversation. "One of my best friends in Templeton is gonna be moving over here to Skeptopolis. He's around our age and has a seminary degree. You know how we talked about the need for new Christians to grow in their faith? Well, he's coming over to help you guys with that. Sadly, there's not a Bible believing church in all Skeptopolis. He's gonna to work to change that."

"Wow, Chris," Gino replied, "the hits just keep on comin', don't they? Is there anything you haven't thought of?"

"Well," Chris went on, "I did say there's one more thing that needed to be taken care of. My friend's name is Levi, and when he comes over, he's gonna move in with me for a time until he can get his own place. But my place has two bedrooms, and I think we could make a third person fit. It'd be just a little crowded, but I'd like you to move in with us, too. That'd take care of all 10 guys."

With that, there was silence on the other end. This gesture caught Gino so by surprise that he was overcome with emotion, and tears began rolling down his cheeks. Never in his life had anyone cared about him or expressed genuine love the way Chris was doing. "Chris," Gino responded through his tears with a choked-up voice, "I accept."

CHAPTER 31

ZORN MERCANTILE

Chris had yet to make it over to Zorn Mercantile to take advantage of the "front porch experience," and had wanted to do so ever since meeting Janine Zorn at the Chamber of Commerce meeting. He finally had some time today, so decided this would be the day.

Zorn Mercantile was started by Janine's grandfather when the town was first founded. He was among the group that left Templeton to establish Skeptopolis. In those early days, besides being the go-to place for general supplies, it was also the place where people would come and socialize. It had a huge front porch with a bunch of rocking chairs, and ceiling fans rotating above. People would come and sit for a while just to shoot the breeze while drinking their RC Colas and eating Moon Pies.

When her grandfather got ready to retire, her father took over the business and ran it himself for 25 years. Janine had been around the store since she was an infant, and actually started working there helping her father when she was only six years old. Her father grew the Mercantile into a fairly large operation, but when Zelmart opened a store on the outskirts of town they were in danger of going out of business.

Being a shrewd businessman, however, her father immediately recognized what he needed to do to compete with the big box store. So, he began taking steps to transform Zorn Mercantile into something that could one-up Zelmart and win over the locals. The first thing he did was to identify the key factors and merchandise that would entice customers to prefer shopping with Zorn over Zelmart. While he couldn't compete on price for most of the cheap, made-in-China stuff sold at Zelmart, he found suppliers willing to give him a very competitive price for much higher-quality, American-made products. He also stocked the shelves with a huge variety of unique items people couldn't find at Zelmart. The townspeople quickly recognized the difference in quality and selection and maintained their loyalty to Zorns – rather than abandon them for the cheaper stuff and generic experience at the big box store.

Next, he chose to massively expand the store. Fortunately, the original store was on a large tract of land, so they tore down the old building and built a huge new store which communicated to the townspeople that Zorn was in business to stay and wasn't about to shrink back and disappear.

But there was one more thing her father wisely decided would make Zorn more desirable. He wanted to make it a fun place. He wanted kids to beg their parents to go to Zorn. And he wanted the everyday townspeople to remember it as the best social gathering spot in town. So, when he tore down the old store, he preserved the front porch and attached it to the front of the new building. From the front, it looked like the same familiar store with the same nostalgic feel. But on the inside, it was as modern and attractive as any big box store anywhere. To add that unique quality, they had designed a whole section to attract the kids, with old-fashioned candies and treats, a soda fountain, and lots of one-of-a-kind toys.

And it worked! Now, Zorn Mercantile carries practically everything you could get at Zelmart, not only with better quality and selection, but a better experience and a store with personality – just a fun place to go.

Janine had only taken over the store herself about two years earlier when her father decided he was ready to retire. Besides her experience working in the store most of her life, she also earned a degree in business management at Skeptopolis U, and after that an MBA.

When Chris parked in the lot and walked up to the front of the store, the front steps seemed to reach out and draw him into yesteryear. He also noticed a ramp that came in from one side to accommodate those with disabilities. As he walked up the porch steps, the store was bustling! On the porch, several groups of locals sat in the rocking chairs drinking RC Colas, eating Moon Pies, and just "chewing the fat." As he walked toward the front door, to his right he noticed an old-timey drink box full of soft drinks, including Nehi Sodas, Orange Crush, Dad's Root Beer, and, of course, RC Colas. Next to that was a rack with Moon Pies in a variety of flavors. They even had a friendly cashier on the porch ready to greet customers, so they didn't need to pay inside the store. The inside of the store was clean and modern, but at the same time retained a nostalgic vibe – and the place was full of customers.

Chris thought he'd just browse the store for a while to see things for himself, so he began wandering the isles. As he looked around and walked past the kids' section, it really did give him a warm, friendly feeling of just wanting to slow down his pace and hang out.

After wandering around for about 15 minutes, he suddenly heard a voice behind him. "Chris, is that you?" It was Janine. She had spotted him through the glass window of her office.

Hearing his name, Chris turned around and saw her coming up from behind. "Janine, great to see ya. I hadn't yet had a chance to come over to see the store, but it's been on my mind ever since we met."

"I'm so glad you came," Janine responded. "Hey, have you got a few minutes? I wanna give you the true Zorn Mercantile experience."

"Absolutely," Chris replied with a certain amount of anticipation. "I don't have anything else planned this afternoon. I reserved it just to come here."

"Well great! Let's go find a place to sit on the front porch."

Janine led Chris back to the front of the store and out onto the porch. On her way out, she picked up two RC Colas and popped their tops. With those in hand, she picked up two Moon Pies, then led him down to the left where there were several empty rocking chairs. When they sat down, Janine handed Chris his own RC Cola and Moon Pie and the two began to chat.

"Well Chris, I've continued to read about you in the paper. Sounds like you've been havin' some interesting experiences. I knew you were into religion, but I didn't realize you were an intellectual in that arena. What's this about you debating the sociology class at the university?"

Chris laughed. "Well, it wasn't exactly a debate. One of the university professors I met through karate teaches an Evolution of Religion class. He asked me if I'd share my religious beliefs with the class because they're quite different from what he teaches at Skeptopolis U. He thought it'd be an enriching experience for his students. That's all. It definitely was an interesting experience for me, though."

"Well, it sure sounded like a lot more than that from the newspaper article. Sounded like you sorta stumped 'em."

Chris smiled. "Well, I don't know about that, but it definitely was different from what they were used to hearing."

"And what about that comment in the gossip section that said you were seen with a gang member at the Burger Barn? Was that true?" Janine continued questioning.

Chris chuckled again. "Yeah, that's actually true. I've begun a friendship with the leader of the Red Flag Pack. Now *that's* turning out to be quite a story."

Janine's eyes got big. "So it really is true. What's with that?"

At that point, Chris told her the story of how he and Gino met, and that because of a commitment to Christ he and nine of his gang members were leaving the gang to turn their lives around. As he shared, Janine was mesmerized by his story.

When he finished, Janine just shook her head. "Wow, that's an incredible tale, Chris. I'd like to hear more about how everything ultimately turns out. That's just amazing!"

At that moment, Butch Grissom walked up. "Hello Janine, how's it goin'?" He then looked over at Chris and reached out his hand to shake. "I thought that was you, Chris. And how ya doin'?"

"Chris immediately stood up to shake hands. Hey Butch. Great to see you. I'm actually doin' great. Janine here has been givin' me the famous Zorn Mercantile experience, and I must say it's better than I ever imagined."

Butch answered back, "Oh yeah, this is definitely the happenin' place. I love it here. I just came by to pick up some hardware for a construction job we're workin' on. Janine here is my go-to supplier for all things hardware. My guys are loadin' it on the truck as we speak."

"Chris, you might be interested to know that Butch, here, is largely responsible for the new look of the store," Janine interjected. "He's the one who worked with my dad to come up with a plan and design the store to make it competitive with Zelmart. Then, his company actually built it. It's truly a work of art."

"You're too kind, Janine. But your father's really the genius behind this place. Anyhow, I just wanted to pop out front here to see if there was anyone I knew. Glad I ran into you, Chris. And by the way, that sponsorship opportunity still stands. I like what I'm readin' in the paper about how you're takin' on some of those elites in town."

Chris smiled again. "Well, Butch, I'm not sure what the sponsorship might mean at this point, but there really might be a possibility. You know I'm gonna be competing in the regional karate tournament in July. Some support at that point might be helpful."

"Well, you just let me know, Chris. I'm pullin' for ya."

Butch then began turning to leave. "Sorry I havta run, but there's no rest for the weary. Gotta get back to the job site. See you guys later."

"See you later Butch," both Chris and Janine called out at the same time.

"And Chris," Janine said with some lament in her voice, "unfortunately, I need to get back to my office, too. But it was so much fun talkin' with you. I hope you'll come back. I really do wanna hear what happens with the gang thing."

"You got it, Janine," Chris replied. "And thanks so much for the Zorn Mercantile experience. This has been really great. I already love this place."

Janine smiled in appreciation at Chris' compliment, and the two of them headed back toward the store entrance.

CHAPTER 32

MOVING IN

Chris saw the car pull into his apartment parking lot and immediately went outside. "Levi – it's so great to see you my friend," Chris shouted, smiling from ear to ear. Levi had just pulled into town to begin working with Chris and his new friends. He didn't bring more than his clothes and a few personal things as he figured staying with Chris would be temporary. If it all worked out as he hoped, he'd soon be moving into his own place.

Levi got out of the car and the two friends gave each other a great big hug. "Great to see you too, Chris. I'm so excited to plug in to what you have goin' on here. It sounds really exciting."

"Man, exciting is a massive understatement. God's workin' so fast it's makin' my head spin. Here, let me help you get your things outta the car."

Levi opened the trunk and back doors of the car and the two began grabbing suitcases and boxes and carrying them into the apartment. "Let's take these into the master bedroom. You'll be sharing that with me," Chris said sort of matter-of-factly.

Levi didn't mind, but thought that was a little odd, tilting his head to the side and giving Chris a quizzical look. He had a two-bedroom apartment, after all.

Chris smiled about the surprise he was about to deliver. "Yep, change of plans. You're gonna have to put on your missionary pants and be adaptable."

"Okay ... I'm up for that," Levi replied with a little hesitancy in his voice. "So what's goin' on?"

"You know how I just mentioned that things are happening really fast?" Chris began his explanation, "Well, since we last talked, there've been some new developments. Turns out, we're gonna have another housemate."

"Oh, okay," Levi responded. "Who is it?"

Chris continued his explanation. "Well, you know the gang leader, Gino, I've been tellin' you about? It's him. We needed a place for one more person – to move out of the gang house – so I offered for him to live here with us for a while."

"Wow, VERY cool!" Levi responded enthusiastically. "Since he's such a key person in all this, having an opportunity to develop a deeper friendship with him'll be fantastic."

"I thought you'd approve," Chris replied. "He'll actually be here shortly to move in. I told him you'd be moving in, too, and he's also anxious to meet you."

Just then, they heard another car pull into the parking lot. Chris looked out the window and there was Gino. "Well, would you look at that? I told you he'd be here shortly – and this is definitely 'shortly.'"

The two of them chuckled and Levi quipped, "Yeah, that's shortly alright."

Chris and Levi went outside to greet Gino. As he got out of the car, Chris immediately made the introduction. "Gino, this is my friend Levi Berger. He's the one I was tellin' you about who's come over to help you and your crew on the spiritual side. He wants to help you guys grow in your new faith. Levi, this is Gino."

When Gino heard Chris' introduction, he grinned from ear to ear and reached out to shake hands. "Levi, I'm so excited to meet you. Chris has told me a lot about you, and I have to say, any friend of Chris' is a friend of mine."

"Well thank you, Gino," Levi responded. "I can say the same thing. I think we have a mutual admiration society when it comes to Chris."

"Well, Gino," Chris chimed in, "let's get your stuff outta the car and get you moved in."

Gino didn't have much in the way of worldly possessions, so it didn't take long for the three of them to get his stuff out of the car and into his room. "You know, I feel kinda bad takin' a bedroom for myself and makin' you two share a room," Gino said as they put the last of his things away."

"Hey, don't think a thing about it," Chris replied. "Levi and I've been best friends for a long time, and we're both excited to be roomies. Besides, it's only temporary. As soon as things settle out a bit, he's gonna to be lookin' for his own place."

While Gino began getting his room organized and putting his stuff into the closet and dresser, Chris was helping Levi get settled in too. After an hour or so they had basically finished, and Chris walked to Gino's room and peeked in. "Hey Gino, we need to get the whole group together this afternoon to talk about the housing situation. Think we can do that?"

"Absolutely," Gino replied. "I think everyone's anxious to know what's happenin' next. They're actually all over at the gang house right now. Would this be a good time to go over and talk to 'em?"

"Now's good," Chris responded. "We can go in my car."

So the three of them piled into Chris' car and headed over to the gang house. When they arrived, they got out of the car and walked up to the front porch. Gino opened the door, walked in with Chris and Levi tagging along behind, and shouted so everyone could hear, "Hey everyone ... meetin' in the main room, right now!"

The other nine exiting gang members quickly made their way to the main room and took a seat. "Okay," Gino began, "first I wanna tell ya that I have some really great news. Everything's comin' together with the housing. You don't have to be concerned any more about what happens next. The machine's in motion."

You could feel the collective sigh of relief all over, and everyone in the room began to clap and shout out their approval.

Gino continued, "I brought Chris over so he could work out the specifics with everybody. But before I turn it over to him, I wanna introduce you to Levi Berger. He's Chris' close friend from Templeton, and he's a pastor. He's actually movin' here to Skeptopolis just for you guys.

You know Chris has already spent a lotta time helpin' us understand the basics of our new Christian faith. And I don't know about you, but the more I hear the more excited I get about growing in my faith in Christ."

When he said that, comments of affirmation reverberated across the room.

"Well, Levi's even more qualified than Chris in that department, if you can believe that, and he's agreed to become our own personal Christian life mentor."

"Hi guys," Levi jumped in to greet the gang. "I'm really excited to work with you and take you on an exciting faith adventure!"

Once again, the room erupted with everyone whooping and hollering their approval.

"So," Gino continued, "let me introduce all of you to him."

With that, Gino began introducing all the gang to Levi. "First, on the front row here, we have Damon. He does have a family in the hood, but all of 'em are really messed up. Beside him are Dexter and Cason. These guys are brothers, and they actually have a very good family who are really concerned about them – but there's a lot of alienation there. I hope you can help 'em fix that. On the next row, startin' on the left side, is Titus. Frankly, I was surprised he decided to accept Christ. He may be the toughest guy in the whole group. I can tell you, though, I'm really happy for him. I think he has the potential to really make a name for himself.

"Next is Maximus. Maximus has brains. He's smart enough to go to college, and even get an advanced degree if he wants to. The first two on the back row are Zander and Axel. Too bad these guys left school. They're unbelievable athletes, and probably could've made college teams in some sport. Next to them is Gunner. Gunner's great with his hands. He can fix nearly anything, and we've depended on him to keep the house in good repair. Then finally, at the end is Delta. She's also very smart and has actually been our bookkeeper. There were two other girls in the gang, but both of 'em decided not to join us – Selina who'll probably now become the boss of those stayin' in the gang, and Dominique, whose boyfriend didn't wanna come along."

Suddenly, Gunner timidly raised his hand. "You have a question, Gunner?" Gino asked. "What's up?"

"Well, I hope this doesn't throw a monkey wrench into the situation, but there's somethin' you need to know."

"What's that, Gunner?" Gino inquired with a little concern in his voice. The last thing they needed now was something new to gum up the works.

"Well, you know Delta and I've been a thing for a while. We just found out yesterday she's pregnant. I think that'll affect what we're talkin' about."

No one was too shocked to hear that news, but a collective groan could be heard throughout the group. At that point, Chris jumped to his feet and stepped to the front to talk to Gunner and Delta. "So guys, what do you wanna do? Do you really love each other?"

Delta and Gunner both turned to look each other in the eyes, then Delta spoke up. "We really do, and we'd like to get married. But we don't know how that's gonna work now."

Chris responded back, "Delta if you and Gunner are serious, we'll make it happen. In fact, Levi'll be able to perform the wedding for you."

Chris then turned to Gino, "Gino, today's Friday and I think it is too late to do anything now, but do you think you can take 'em to the courthouse Monday and let 'em apply for their marriage license? That is, if they're ready to take that step."

Chris looked back over at the couple to get their response. And when he looked, both of them sat there wide-eyed with their jaws gaping open in surprise. Then spontaneously they both shouted out, "YES!" and embraced each other with wild excitement. "That's exactly what we'd like," Gunner shouted, "but we had no idea it'd even be possible."

"Then it's settled," Christ responded. "You'll apply for the license on Monday, and we'll have the wedding next week."

Hearing that, everyone clapped and cheered.

When the noise died down, Chris brought the discussion back to the task at hand. "Okay guys, now that we have that taken care of, let me share with you the housing situation. First, Gino's movin' in with me and Levi – at least for the time bein'. Beyond that, we have three other places. Two of 'em are next door to each other. Of the two that are side-by-side, one has two rooms, and the other has five. In light of the fact that we're about to have an old married couple among us, with a child on the way no less, I'm thinkin' Gunner and Delta should have the two-room cabin. That way when the baby comes, they'll also have room for the little one. How's that sound to everybody?"

"That's a great idea," Titus piped up. "That's exactly what they'll need."

"Before I go further," Chris continued, "let me tell you about the other place that's available for two people. In this place there are actually two rooms, so you'd each have your own privacy. This one's in CJ's karate dojo. There's four apartment style rooms in the building that he uses for guests, and he's agreed to let a couple of you use two of 'em. Now I'm gonna let you guys make the final decision on this, but here's what came to my mind. Whoever lives at the dojo's gonna have the opportunity to study karate if you want. CJ said he'd be willing to train you. Are there any who'd especially like to live there?"

Zander and Axel's hands shot up like a rocket. "Chris," Zander spoke up, "we've actually studied with CJ before – when we were younger. Our family lived right down the street from him, so we actually know him. We ended up goin' a different direction in life than he did, so we haven't been around him for a while, but we'd love to be able to study with him again."

Chris smiled, "You know, somehow I thought the athletes would like that opportunity. And I had an idea there'd be some of you who'd know him, since he also grew up in the neighborhood. Is everyone good with that?"

The others nodded in agreement – obviously a good choice.

Chris continued, "Now this doesn't eliminate the possibility for any of you others to study at the dojo as well if you want. CJ's willing to take on any who'd like to do it."

"So," Chris went on, "that leaves the other five in the other cabin. There's five rooms in that one, so each of you'll have your own private room. Does that sound okay?"

Simultaneously, comments of "that sounds good," "that's fantastic," and "that's great" reverberated around the room. Everyone was really excited now.

With that settled, Gino had one other thing he wanted to mention to the group. So, he stood back up, moved to the front, and quieted everyone down. He then proceeded to give one more announcement. "Guys, what I'm gonna tell you now is on an entirely different subject. Next week, Chris has somethin' comin' up that'll be rather unique. He's gonna be a panelist in a discussion with some of the professors at the university. It's gonna be basically him against everyone else as they talk about faith stuff. I think we all oughta show up – for two reasons. First, we need to support Chris. Like I said, this is a big deal. There's people in the city who wanna put him down because he's a Christian. We need to have his back. But there's a second reason, too. I have a pretty strong feelin' this'll be somethin' we can all learn from – and not just stuff about living out our new faith. We've all watched how Chris has handled a LOT of very dicey situations where there's no love lost for Christians. He just has this way of handlin' that. And since we live in this environment, too, I believe we'll get some great insights into how he does it. Is everyone in?"

Without hesitation, the room erupted with, "Chris! Chris! Chris! Chris! Chris! Chris!" then everyone broke out in spontaneous cheers and applause.

Gino then turned to Chris, "You've had our back, man, and we got yours."

Hearing that, Chris pursed his lips together, and smiled as tears welled up in his eyes. "Guys, I really hope I've been able to give you hope for your lives, but I want you to know that you give meaning to mine, as well. I'm really excited for all of us." Then wrapping things up, he thanked Levi for joining them on such short notice and gave them one last instruction. "Okay everyone, I know you've already started packin' to leave. Get it all together right now. We have a truck that'll be here in about 30 minutes to take your gear over to your new digs."

CHAPTER 33

WEDDING BELLS

It took a few days, but Gunner and Delta received their marriage license the Thursday after their Monday application at the courthouse. They were anxious to get married. In the days while they had waited, Levi met with them and gave them some very sound Christian marriage counseling so they could at least begin by looking at marriage through a Christian lens. Neither of them had ever seen good husband and wife role models growing up, so they eagerly absorbed everything Levi shared with them.

But Levi went one step further. He, himself, was a single guy and knew his limited perspective meant he wasn't fully equipped to help them. So, he called Pastor Trumann who gladly drove over to Skeptopolis with his wife, Lisa, that evening and gave them personal – and more in-depth – marriage advice. After those sessions, Gunner and Delta's excitement grew even more – especially as their new knowledge about being a real Christian family began to develop.

Sybil and Colleen didn't know about the upcoming wedding until a couple of days before the event. Just to check on how things were coming along with the former gang members, the two of them went over to the cabins and ran into Chris, who was talking about wedding plans with Gunner and Delta. When they overheard the discussion, Colleen blurted out, "Chris, why didn't you tell us this was happenin'!?"

"Oh my, Colleen," Chris stammered apologetically, "that never even crossed my mind. But ya know, you're right. We definitely should've invited you guys. This has been such a whirlwind thing that we just haven't made any real formal plans. Levi's gonna do the wedding, and we were just gonna have an intimate little gathering at Gunner and Delta's house with only the guys there. Neither of their families care anything about it, so it was just gonna be us."

"That's what you think, Chris!" Colleen exclaimed. "Delta's gonna have a proper wedding in a church. I'll make the arrangements with Dr. Albritton to use our chapel. And we'll find Delta a wedding dress, too ... and get Gunner a suit."

Upon hearing this, Delta could hardly contain herself. She suddenly broke down sobbing. As was the case with most young girls, she had always dreamed of getting married in a real wedding dress and all the ceremony, but in her situation, she never even entertained the thought it could really happen.

Seeing that, Colleen immediately went over and put her arms around Delta. "Listen, we know you've had a tough life," she said as she hugged her tighter, "and we're so proud of how you're tryin' to turn your life around. This is a big thing you're doin', and we're gonna support you one hundred percent. You're a special person."

Delta couldn't help herself, but just continued bawling like a baby as she hugged Colleen and thanked her profusely.

Colleen then walked a few steps away, pulled her cell phone out of her purse, and called Dr. Albritton to make arrangements for the use of the chapel. He gave his blessing right away and said it could be available at 2:00 on Saturday. She thanked him and went back over to the group to deliver the news. "Guys," she said, "2:00 Saturday at the church chapel. It's all set. Delta, you and Gunner come with me and Sybil right now. We'll go over to the warehouse and find a wedding dress and a suit. I know there's some over there. Chris, we'll see you in a little bit."

As Delta and Gunner got into the Vette with Sybil and Colleen, everyone just watched in shock, not knowing what to think. Everything at this point was totally surreal.

Just over an hour later, Sybil brought Gunner back to the cabin with a suit in hand. After he got out of her car, she yelled out to Chris, "You guys, take Gunner to the barber shop and get him a haircut. When we finish with Delta, we're takin' her to the beauty shop to get her hair done. She then turned her car around and sped off again. It was left to Gunner to explain that Sybil and Colleen weren't going to allow him to see Delta trying on wedding dresses.

After another hour, Colleen and Sybil brought Delta back. "Well, let's see it," Chris shouted across the way. "We wanna see the dress."

The three girls got out of the car giggling and grinning from ear to ear. "Hey," Sybil called back, "that's not allowed! Gunner can't see her in her wedding dress until the time of the wedding. That's tradition, and that's what we're gonna to do."

"Now, one more thing!" Colleen proclaimed as they got close enough to the group to lower her voice. "Tomorrow evening at 5:30, be at the chapel. We're gonna have a wedding rehearsal. This is only for those who'll be participating in the wedding itself. Will there be a best man and maid of honor?"

They hadn't really thought about that. The wedding party was only going to be the bride, groom, and preacher. Gunner called over to Gino, "Hey, will you be my best man?"

Gino grinned from ear to ear. "You bet! I'd be honored."

Delta then looked dejectedly down at her feet. "I'm not sure about a maid of honor," she said quietly. When I joined the gang, all my friends abandoned me, and the other two girls I was close to in the gang stayed in when I left. They don't wanna have anything to do with me now."

Sybil immediately jumped up. "Delta, I'll be your maid of honor – if you'll have me. I'd be honored to do it."

"Would you really?" Delta responded, once again choking back tears. She couldn't remember any of her girlfriends ever caring for her like that."

"It's done then," Colleen declared. "You got that Levi?"

Levi was more than a little shocked to be ordered around that way, but so excited for Gunner and Delta that he was more than happy to oblige. Levi stood to attention, saluted Colleen and replied, "Yes ma'am! Got it! I'll be there tomorrow with bells on – 5:30."

"Oh," Colleen continued, "and don't anyone make plans for after the rehearsal. After we finish, we'll have a rehearsal dinner in the church fellowship hall. The whole group's invited."

When the next evening arrived, the wedding party met at the Universalist Church chapel for the rehearsal – which went off without a hitch. Then the whole party made their way to the fellowship hall where several church members had prepared a veritable feast for the young couple. Martha Albritton herself managed the entire dinner. It was definitely a night to remember.

The next afternoon, at 2:00, Levi pronounced Gunner and Delta "man and wife." For the first time in his life, Gunner looked and felt handsome in a new suit and fresh haircut, and Delta radiated with beauty and joy in her elegant wedding dress and the fanciest hairdo of her life! Altogether, a small but enthusiastic crowd witnessed the ceremony including Chris and the entire newly engineered gang, plus a good handful of the Universalist Church members who'd been tapped to help. Pastor Trumann and his wife also drove over for the event, and Dr. Albritton even slipped in to show his support for the great work his people were doing for this young couple.

After the wedding, all the participants made their way back to their homes. Gunner and Delta were especially excited to start a new life – and a new way of life – together. As everyone watched, they walked over to their house, and just as they got to the front door, Gunner picked up his bride and carried her over the threshold.

CHAPTER 34

ON THE HOT SEAT

Chris drove to the university campus after having a light dinner with Levi and Gino at the apartment. He found a parking spot near the religion building. It was Friday, the big day for the roundtable where he would dialog with the university professors. He arrived a little early so he would have time to find the Hawking Auditorium and get himself oriented. After parking, he got out of his car and went inside Freud Hall.

On entering the Hall, he found himself in a wide corridor. Straight in front of him, on the wall, he spotted a map showing the location of all the rooms in the building. Chris walked over and checked out the location of the Auditorium, where the roundtable would take place. He located the space, went down the breezeway to his left, made his way there and went inside. From that door he could see all of the seating and the stage down in front. It looked like the room would hold about three hundred people.

Down at the front, Chris could see Dr. Albritton was already there directing the stage set-up, so he went down to find out what he needed to do. As he made his way toward the stage, Dr. Albritton spotted him and shouted out. "Chris, great to see you. Welcome to the School of Religion."

"Great to see you, too, Dr. Albritton," Chris replied. "Looks like I'm in the right place."

"Indeed you are," Dr. Albritton responded. "Come on over here and I'll give you an overview of how this is all gonna work."

Chris walked over to where Dr. Albritton was, then followed him onto the stage. "You can see that we're putting a table here on the front of the stage with two chairs facing one another across the table. When we get all set up, there'll also be microphones, so everyone'll be able to hear clearly. This is where the dialogues will take place. We want this to be as informal as possible, so it'll basically be a one-on-one discussion between you and the various professors who'll be participating. Each of the discussions will last about 20 minutes. We don't have any pre-determined questions. We want this to be just a free-flowing conversation between two people. I'll be moderating and will introduce the topic in each session. Then you guys can simply begin discussing the topic. How's that sound?"

"Sounds good," Chris replied. "This should definitely be interesting."

"The other participants should be here any minute, so if you just want to have a seat down on the front row that'll be fine. I have a few more details to attend to, and the people comin' to watch should start arriving in about 10 to 15 minutes. Usually at these things, the auditorium's about 25% full. Just make yourself comfortable and I'll be back in a few minutes."

"Thanks," Chris replied. "I'll be right over here." He then went and sat down at the end of the front row on the right side and waited.

After about five minutes, Dr. Gray and Dr. Craven walked in together and made their way down front. They had participated in these roundtables many times, so they already knew the drill. When they got to the front, they saw Chris and walked over.

When he saw them coming, Chris stood up, took a couple of steps in their direction, and reached out his hand to shake. They all shook hands and exchanged pleasantries for just a moment, then saw Dr. Everson walk in from the side door. When he saw all the others together, he walked over to where they were, and the greeting cycle continued. About a minute later, Dr. Albritton also came down and joined them.

After a few moments, Dr. Albritton invited everyone onto the stage where he went through the agenda once again. "Gentlemen, we've put four chairs over here on the side of the stage. When we first go out, all of you can take a seat there. Then, when I call you up, you can walk over to the table in the middle. The first two to come to the table will be Chris and Dr. Gray. You men'll talk about the evolution of philosophical thought. When you're finished, Chris will simply remain at the table while Dr. Gray returns to the chairs on the side and Dr. Craven comes to the table. You two will discuss the evolution of religion in society. The last will be Dr. Everson. Everson, when it's your turn, Dr. Craven will return to the side chairs, and you'll move to the table to discuss the Theory of Evolution proper. I'll monitor the time and direct the movement of the roundtable as appropriate. Does anyone have any questions?"

No one said anything, so Dr. Albritton proceeded to give them one last instruction, "There's a green room back behind the stage where you men can go and relax until it's time to begin. Professors, you know where that is, so you can lead Chris back there. I see people startin' to make their way in, so go ahead and I'll be with you in a few moments." With that, they went back to the green room to wait.

The roundtable was set to begin at 7:30 pm, so Dr. Albritton made his way back to the green room at about 7:20. As he walked in, he gave a sly wink and nodded to the three professors. They seemed very confident that their plan to discredit Chris would work. *This will be the night,* they thought, *we will destroy his influence in front of the entire town.* As he entered the door, he said to the group, "Men, I believe we're gonna have a record crowd tonight. We didn't advertise this beyond what we usually do – mostly at the school – but somehow, word got out to the entire community and there seems to be a huge interest there, as well. The auditorium's already nearly full. We're gonna have standing room only, and we're scramblin' to set up an overflow room where we can put up a large screen TV. I've never seen anything like this before at one of our roundtables. Chris, it looks like you're a pretty big draw."

Chris looked up at Dr. Albritton and replied, "I sure don't know why. I know I haven't done anything to make this happen."

"Well, Chris, regardless of how it happened, this ought to be an exciting night."

After about five more minutes, Dr. Albritton led the group to their chairs on the stage of the auditorium. Then, when it was time to start, he walked up to the moderator's mic and began speaking to the crowd. "Welcome, everyone, to this evening's religious roundtable discussion. Tonight, we have a very special guest who will interact with our faculty specialists. The topic for this evening's discussion relates to evolutionary theory. As most of you know, the Theory of Evolution has implications far beyond the mere physical evolution of man. That's one part of it, of course, but the principles of evolution apply to virtually every aspect of human development. In today's roundtable we'll be looking at evolutionary theory as it relates to philosophy, to society, and then finally to physical human evolution.

"Our guest today has become quite the celebrity in Skeptopolis, particularly as it relates to his karate skills. As it turns out, Chris Bel is not only an expert in karate, he's also a Christian and believes the Theory of Evolution is not true. As our guest this evening, he will be advocating for the Christian point of view as he discusses the topic with Skeptopolis U professors who believe it *is* true.

"For those of you who don't know how the roundtable works, Chris, as our guest panelist, will interact with each of our three professors one at a time for about 20 minutes each. He'll interact with Dr. Gray from the philosophy department regarding the evolution of philosophy, with Dr. Craven, our resident sociology professor regarding societal evolution, and finally with Dr. Everson concerning biological evolution. Dr. Everson teaches biology, and his specialty is evolutionary biology.

"So, if you're all ready to begin, let me introduce the panel and we'll get underway. First, we have Dr. Gray. Dr. Gray please stand." As he stood, the audience gave him a round of applause. One particular section on the right side appeared to be especially enthusiastic. It seems he had invited his classes to come, and these were his students.

Dr. Albritton continued, "Dr. Craven, would you stand?" As he stood, the crowd also gave him a round of applause. This time, an even bigger section of students cheered him on. As Dr. Gray had done, Dr. Craven had also invited his students to attend – since Chris had actually spoken before some of them, they had a heightened interest in tonight's roundtable.

Dr. Albritton picked up the introductions again, "Then we have Dr. Everson. Dr. Everson, please stand." He also received a nice round of applause with a section of his students making some extra noise.

"And finally, we have our guest panelist, Chris Bel. Chris, please stand."

As Chris stood, notable sections in different parts of the auditorium not only applauded but began whooping and hollering in support. The noticeable ruckus, in fact, shocked most everyone, including Chris. And all those not there to support Chris craned their necks to see who could possibly be showing up with such enthusiastic support.

As Chris looked out over the audience, he saw a section taken up by Gino and his troupe. Another group included CJ and a number of students from the karate dojo. In another area was a cadre of business people whom Chris recognized from the Chamber of Commerce meeting – including all the ones who sat at his table. Chris even recognized a few from the Universalist Church, including Sybil and Colleen. Chris had no idea all these people were coming – since it was pitched as a university event – and felt a sense of pleasant surprise, and even relief, that he had at least some support in the audience.

As he continued looking around, he also noticed Mayor Gadsden was there, along with a sizable contingent from the city government. They were clapping politely, though it was obvious they were not doing so out of eager support for him. Finally, he saw in the upper right corner, an entire media contingent, including Connie, who were diligently noting the crowd's response.

Dr. Albritton was also quite surprised at the enthusiastic response Chris received. Not to acknowledge it would have been awkward and impolite. So, he looked over at Chris and remarked with a smile on his face, "Well, Chris, it looks like your fan club's here in force."

He then addressed the entire audience once again, "Folks, let's give our entire panel another round of applause and we'll begin."

After the brief applause, Dr. Albritton spoke again, "Chris, you and Dr. Gray please come to the table and let's begin."

The two of them walked up to the table and sat across from one another in front of their microphones. When they had settled in, Dr. Albritton addressed them and said, "Gentlemen, modern scholarship recognizes that human thought has evolved based on an evolutionary pattern from its beginning as a very simple set of beliefs to increasingly more complex ones. Christianity doesn't believe that. Would you two discuss this topic?

After Dr. Albritton asked his question, Chris spoke up first. "Dr. Gray, before we go any further with this discussion, I'd like for you to explain exactly how you believe this evolutionary process happened. Since we've not had any personal discussions on this topic, I'd like to have at least a brief explanation of your take on it so that, when we discuss, we'll be on the same page."

Dr. Gray was slightly taken back by this request. He wasn't really expecting to have to explain his point of view since he felt pretty sure most everyone already understood and agreed with his view. But since Chris had asked, he didn't have much choice. Chris had made the explanation the very basis for moving the discussion forward.

"Well sure," Dr. Gray responded, "it's actually not very complicated at all. You see, in their very early evolutionary stages, human beings were not capable of the kind of complex thought we are capable of today. They had much smaller brains and began, pretty much, like most of the other animal species we see in the world – without the ability to think self-consciously. But over millions of years, the life forms that ultimately did evolve that ability began to develop a reasoning ability in ways the other animals did not. This capacity gradually increased until we have what exists in today's world. So, at each stage of evolutionary development, as they were able, various thinkers came up with new understandings about the topics that philosophy deals with – reality, knowledge, and values. So, in a nutshell, that's how the process occurred. So, Chris, as a Christian, how do you believe it happened?"

At that point, Dr. Gray was sure that Chris was going to begin talking about how God created man complete, and that he could easily and totally debunk that Christian point of view.

"Dr. Gray," Chris responded, "it appears to me that what you've described is an explanation based on naturalistic worldview beliefs. Am I correct with that assessment?"

"Uh, well ... define for me what you mean by 'naturalistic worldview,'" Dr. Gray stammered. "That's not terminology we typically use, and I wanna make sure I'm on the same page with you."

"Of course," Chris responded. "By naturalistic worldview, I'm referring to the belief that the natural universe, operating by natural laws, is all that exists. So, my question is simply, 'Does the explanation you have just given me depend on a naturalistic worldview being true?'"

This was not at all the way Dr. Gray had envisioned the discussion going. He was not accustomed to having to justify his worldview beliefs. In fact, he had not even seen anyone bring up alternative worldview beliefs before. After all, *everyone* knew that human philosophy emerged in the human animal based on an evolutionary process.

"Uh, Chris," Dr. Gray blurted out as he tried to regain control of the conversation. Turning one shoulder away from Chris and crossing his arms. "I really don't see what this has to do with the validity of your view. How does that even address the Christian belief about God and whether or not He has revealed truth to man concerning reality, knowledge, and values?"

"Well of course it's relevant," Chris replied, looking Dr. Gray in the eyes. "I understand that you don't believe that the biblical point of view is correct, and you do believe that naturalistic worldview beliefs are true. My question is, 'How do you know that the naturalistic point of view is true?'"

In an attempt to turn the conversation, Dr. Gray responded, "Well Chris, how do you know your beliefs are true?"

Chris remained calm and leaned in to respond, "Dr. Gray, here's the deal. I believe God actually exists as a person, capable of revealing Himself to mankind in general, and to individuals in particular. The reason I believe it is not because I can demonstrate it empirically, but because God is personal in a way that makes Him able to engage human beings in a personal relationship. I actually have personal experience engaging that relationship, and it's based on that relationship that I believe what I believe."

"So," Dr. Gray tried to pounce, "you're saying that God speaks to you?"

"I'm saying that God has revealed Himself to mankind in numerous ways," Chris replied, "and one of those ways is by engaging me personally. I don't believe it simply because I've had some kind of nebulous mystical experience, but because my personal experience corresponds to the other forms of revelation God has made to mankind – things such as the teachings of the Bible, the corresponding experience of other Christians throughout history, and the historical record itself. So, God's revelation is not like what you just tried to characterize it to be, it is much more than that."

"But you're attempting to make the case that your human experience is the basis for your beliefs, is that right?" Dr. Gray countered.

"That is partially right," Chris responded, "and I get the point you're trying to make. But you never answered my question. 'How do you know that your naturalistic point of view is true?' Do you have some empirical verification that Naturalism is true, or do you believe it by pure faith?"

At that point, Dr. Albritton broke into the conversation. It was immediately clear to him that Chris was about to paint Dr. Gray into a corner that he would not easily get out of, and he absolutely wanted to avoid that – particularly this early in the roundtable. "Gentlemen, I'm sorry to say that our time is up on this exchange. This has been very interesting, and I would hope that at some point in the future there might be an opportunity to explore this topic further."

With that, both Dr. Gray and Chris stood up, reached across the table, and shook hands – thanking each other as they did so.

"Dr. Craven," Dr. Albritton spoke once again into the microphone, "would you please make your way to the table to begin part two of this discussion?"

As he made his way to the table, Dr. Albritton continued, "This second topic will be about societal evolution. So here is the discussion point. Modern social science research has demonstrated that human societies began as small bands of people but found that the survival of the species was enhanced when they banded together in groups. Thus, over time, societies developed in complexity based on evolutionary principles to the forms we now see in modern times. Christianity seems to have an entirely different belief about the development of societies. What light can you gentlemen shed for us on this topic?"

Dr. Craven had a definite advantage over Dr. Gray in that he had seen Chris express his beliefs about this very topic in his classroom and had also noted how Chris dealt with Dr. Gray. He was determined not to get caught in that same trap. In an attempt to go on the offensive, he chimed in first. "Chris, I had the advantage of hearing you share your beliefs with my class, so I'd like to get you to clarify something about your Christian beliefs for me."

"Sure," Chris replied, "what might that be?"

Dr. Craven lifted his shoulders and gestured with his hand toward the audience while leaning in. "As a guest in my class, we were discussing the evolution of religious belief – which is, obviously, one aspect of societal evolution. Modern scientific theory proposes that societies evolve from less complex forms to more complex. Based on that, the progression for religious development should naturally be from more primitive animistic forms to the more sophisticated forms such as monotheism, and ultimately Atheism. On that day, however, based on your Christian beliefs, you proposed a very novel idea that monotheism, the more complex, was the original form, and the other forms resulted as the more complex devolved into the more primitive. What evidence do you have to back that up?"

Dr. Craven thought he had set up a 'gotcha' question – much like Chris had asked Dr. Gray about his evidence for a naturalistic worldview. Certain that he had put Chris in a box that would be difficult to work his way out of –

he did not realize how he'd actually given Chris an opening to challenge his beliefs.

"Dr. Craven," Chris responded, "I think you've done quite a good job of contrasting our two beliefs. You believe that religious beliefs evolved from more primitive forms to more complex ones, while I believe that monotheism was the original and devolved to what you have described as more 'primitive' forms – as people moved further away from God. So let me propose something to you. What if the Genesis account of the creation of man is true? What if God created man and put him in a place where He, and the human beings He created, could have personal interaction with one another. In that scenario, the human beings would have gotten to know God and understand Him based on what He directly shared with them. If that original revelation revealed a monotheistic God, would my proposed theory be an unreasonable conclusion?"

"Well, based on that presupposition, I suppose that wouldn't be unreasonable," Dr. Craven replied, "but there's simply no scientific evidence to back up that scenario."

"Dr. Craven," Chris continued his inquiry, "You're a sociology professor, is that correct?"

"Yes," Dr. Craven responded, "that is correct."

"And sociology is a social science," Chris continued. "Is that also correct?"

"Again, correct," Dr. Craven replied, adjusting his glasses.

"And tell me if I am also correct in this assessment," Chris went on, both palms on the table. "Sociology is an attempt to apply the scientific method to the study of human social behavior. Is that right?"

"I think you have it, Chris," Dr. Craven replied affirmatively.

"And one last question," Chris continued. "The scientific method is the use of observation and experimentation in an attempt to understand the natural universe. Is that also correct?"

"That's also correct, Chris," Dr. Craven responded – this time allowing a little bit of sarcasm to emerge as he began getting a little irritated with the barrage of 'simpleton' questions."

Finally, Chris brought his questioning to a head. "So, what observation and/or experimentation do you have to prove that your evolutionary view of religious development is true? It seems to me that your belief in evolutionary development is as much a religious belief as mine."

The 20 minutes for this session were nearly over, and Dr. Albritton quickly recognized, once more, the devastating implications of that last exchange. So, in order to save Dr. Craven from the embarrassment of fully exploring those implications, he decided to end that session and begin the third. "Dr. Craven, Chris, it appears that time is up for this part of the discussion. I want to thank you both for your very engaging interaction."

With that, both of them stood up and reached across the table to shake hands. Dr. Craven strode back to his chair on the side of the stage.

"Now it's time for Dr. Everson to make his way to the table," Dr. Albritton announced. "This session will be about biological evolution."

Dr. Everson saw how easily Chris had cast doubt on the positions of the other two professors. Although he didn't like to see that happen, he could admit to himself the weakness of their arguments. He knew that – even though social scientists attempted to use the scientific method to back up their research – they really didn't have a true scientific methodology for making definitive scientific claims, especially since they could not experiment on or directly observe the past. His specialty, however, was biology, which he considered a hard science. He felt very confident he could effortlessly put Chris in his place.

Dr. Everson walked over to the table, sat down, then smiled at Chris and nodded a greeting. Chris smiled and nodded back.

Dr. Albritton once again stood before the mic and began introducing the last discussion of the evening. "Gentlemen," he began, "modern science acknowledges that all life forms began in a very simple state, and over millions of years has evolved into the complex tapestry of life that we now see on earth. In fact, most scientists now recognize the Theory of Evolution to be a scientific fact. That said, Christians don't recognize that to be true, and insist that God created the various life forms, and created man to be special and unique. What do you gentlemen have to say about your points of view?"

Feeling he had the upper hand, and full of cool and cocky confidence, Dr. Everson jumped in immediately to go for the jugular, "Chris, hardly any scientists at all believe in Creationism, and virtually all of them believe in the Theory of Evolution. In fact, if you actually looked at the many peer-reviewed scientific journals, practically all of them are filled, month after month, and year after year, with scientific evidence that it's true. Who do you think you are to dispute the accumulated knowledge of practically the entire scientific community regarding this?"

Chris immediately recognized not only the hard ball tactics Dr. Everson tried to employ, but also the venom with which he made his attack. Way before this evening at the roundtable, he had determined not to act that way or mirror that kind of hateful attitude. He intended to make his point, to the best of his ability, by demonstrating Christian love and patience.

"Dr. Everson," Chris responded, placing his palms on his lap and leaning into the microphone, "I deeply appreciate the passion you have for your belief in the Theory of Evolution. But you do realize, don't you, that so far, the argument you've made is not a scientific argument at all? In fact, it's a pure attempt at intimidation. Rather than make a scientific argument, you've tried to shame me into backing down because my belief is a minority position based on those who are in the scientific community.

"Let me make a few observations about your comments. First, it doesn't matter what some, or even most, scientists believe if they can't back it up with actual science. Science is not based on consensus; it's based on experimentation and observation. Second, the fact that there are many peer-reviewed articles attempting to prove the theory, also, in itself, is a meaningless fact. If all the peer-reviewed scientific journals are controlled by people who believe the theory, and if all of the people doing the peer reviews believe in it, then what kind of slant do you think will result? What if a scientist who believes in creation were to submit an article to one of those journals? What do you think would happen? I think we both know it would be rejected out of hand because its conclusions don't match the assumptions of the various periodicals. That rejection would not be based on science, but on the beliefs of the journal editors. Finally, you stated that the consensus of the scientific community is that the Theory of Evolution is a scientific fact. If that's so, then why is it still called the *Theory* of Evolution? The reason is because it has *not* been scientifically proven to be true."

You could see Dr. Everson becoming increasingly angry with Chris as he clenched his hands, pursed his lips, and redness flushed up his neck in stark contrast to his white collar. He immediately shot back, "Chris, what gives you the credibility and the right to stand before this crowd and spout your ignorance? Do you have any degrees to back up your arrogant words? Have you studied and written on this topic? All you have is an unsupported religious belief that is born of ignorance and superstition!"

Seeing this antagonistic situation develop, Dr. Albritton became intensely concerned that things were about to get out of hand and started to make a move toward the microphone. Chris saw him start to take a step in that direction, but immediately put out his hand and gestured for him to stay put. *Lord, help me represent you well,* he thought prayerfully, then took a deep breath and responded to Dr. Everson in a calm and deliberate voice. Chris had grown very adept at calming tense situations. Although he had not practiced being in an environment like this one, his training in karate had proved itself by equipping him with exceptional self-control and skills for de-escalating tense situations.

Chris first spoke his name, "Dr. Everson." Then, after a short pause, he very slowly and deliberately addressed the situation by acknowledging the obvious. "You are right that I don't have a degree in this topic. You're also right that I haven't written on this subject. And additionally, you're right that my religious faith has a profound influence on my beliefs about this. But once again you've just based your argument on an attack on me, rather than on any evidence from science. Let's just take this as quickly as we can to the bottom line. Share with me and the audience the science that proves the Theory of Evolution to be true. You don't have to give us everything, just explain the actual science proving that it's possible for a life form, any life form, to evolve from a less to a more complex form."

Dr. Everson immediately jumped in. "First, we see natural selection working all the time. Look at the many types of any plants or animals, and you can see it at work. In fact, scientists, farmers, animal breeders, and botanists use that evolutionary principle all the time."

Chris interrupted, "But you're not describing evolution from less complex to more complex life forms. You're only describing micro-evolution – what you have identified as natural selection – where small adaptive changes take place within the same kinds of living things."

"Yes," Dr. Everson responded, "but given enough time, those evolutionary changes are capable of evolving to more complex forms. Just look around the world and see the great variety of life forms that exist."

"So, are you sayin' that the macro-evolution you are describing, where less complex forms can evolve to more complex forms, can be shown using actual science?" Chris queried.

"Well, first of all, science doesn't use the terms 'micro-evolution' and 'macro-evolution.' They are one and the same process and are dealt with simply as 'evolution.' Now, of course, there are several theories about how the evolution from less to more complex life forms might happen, as it has not yet been demonstrated in a lab. After all, these things take thousands of years. You're asking an unreasonable thing."

"So, what you're saying then," Chris interjected, "is that you are making an assumption about evolution that does not have any actual scientific backing, but you believe it to the extent that you *deem* it to be true. You reject the terms 'micro-evolution' and 'macro-evolution,' not because you have a scientific basis for doing so, but because it doesn't fit your evolutionary belief presuppositions. It seems to me that you're also saying that you, and your fellow believers in naturalistic evolution, are continuing to investigate ways to try to prove your *belief* to be true. Is that what you are saying?"

"I'm sorry, Chris, that your feeble mind is not able to comprehend the complexities of the science of life. The fact is, there is simply no other possibility."

"Ah," Chris responded, "no other possibility? Well, *IF* it is true that the only thing that exists is the natural universe operating by natural laws, then perhaps there is no other possibility. But what if God *does* exist as He's described in the Bible? Would it be possible then?"

"Well, if fairy tales were true, then of course magic is possible. But it's simply not true," Dr. Everson barked back.

"Well, it seems to me, Dr. Everson, that you're not advocating for actual science at all," Chris replied. "You have a philosophical belief that you're trying to prove. What you've proposed is just as much a religious belief as my Christian faith."

With that, Dr. Albritton briskly stepped up to the mic and began his conclusion. "Ladies and gentlemen, it seems that our time has come to a close. With such interesting exchanges on such a fascinating topic, time just seems to have flown by too quickly. I honestly wish we had more time for all three of these discussions. Chris and Dr. Everson, thank you for such a stimulating discussion." At that, Chris and Dr. Everson stood up and made their way back to the row of chairs with the other participants.

"Now before you go," Dr. Albritton spoke once again to the audience, "I want to thank all of you for coming this evening and enjoying this very entertaining exchange. And I'd like to remind you that we do this every week while school is in session. How great it would be if we had a full house like this every week. And I particularly want to thank our panelists, Chris Bell, Dr. Gray, Dr. Craven, and Dr. Everson. Gentlemen, you have made this a very memorable experience for all of us." Let's give our panelists one more round of applause. After the applause died down, Dr. Albritton dismissed the crowd.

When Dr. Albritton had finished speaking, the three professors politely shook hands with Chris one more time, then turned and exited quickly and unceremoniously. Dr. Albritton then also walked over to Chris, thanked him again for participating, then, also left.

As Chris exited the stage in the front, all of his friends and supporters flocked to meet him. Gino and his group, along with Levi, CJ and others from the dojo, a good contingent from the Chamber of Commerce membership, and even a number of students who had been in Dr. Craven's class when Chris spoke, came down to greet him. Jill also made a rather public display of shaking his hand and telling him "Nice job." Additionally, quite a number of others who didn't even know Chris lined up to shake his hand.

After a few minutes, Connie also made her way to find Chris. "Chris, I know you must be pretty tired," she acknowledged, "but you know there'll be another article in the paper tomorrow. Could you give me a few minutes for an interview before you leave?"

All of his friends wanted to go out with Chris to celebrate and asked him if he would go with them. "Guys," Chris called out to them, "where we goin'? Burger Barn?"

"Yeah, Burger Barn," they all called out.

"Okay," Chris responded, "I need to give Connie a few minutes here. I'll meet you over there in just a little bit, alright?"

So, all his friends left, and Chris stayed a few minutes more for his interview with Connie.

CHAPTER 35

DAVID SLAYS GOLIATH

The next day when the newspaper hit the street, it created an unusual buzz for Skeptopolis. Typically, the townsfolk didn't entertain controversies over the subject of religion, especially since hardly any of its residents believed in God. Before the recent stir, they easily dismissed out of hand all religious claims in news articles, or religious themes in art and entertainment works. With the latest headline, however, that dismissive point of view seemed to nearly evaporate.

While most people in the city had little expertise in the foundational beliefs of Atheism, they knew enough to make them feel smug in their beliefs. One way the *Times* supported these beliefs – and added a layer of assurance – was to feature articles by the "actual experts," even producing podcasts, documentaries, and the like. The residents and leaders of Skeptopolis could always count on the *Times* to provide good PR and technical backing when needed – often leaning on the professors at Skeptopolis U.

Based on this uninterrupted narrative which had been orchestrated and guarded for decades, the headline hit readers like a blow from Chris' fist. When the headline announced that some lowly "non-expert" like Chris had just bested the experts at their own game, it came as a shock to most everyone. For some, it only angered them and increased their resolve to do anything necessary to squelch Chris' influence in the community. For others, it generated confusion – many for the first time – about the confidence they felt regarding their atheistic beliefs, and even what they'd been told about Christians. Then, and even more troubling, a small but not-so-insignificant group of people were becoming even more curious about Chris' Christian faith.

———————— ◆◆ ————————

𝕾𝕶𝖊𝖕𝖙𝖔𝖕𝖔𝖑𝖎𝖘 𝕿𝖎𝖒𝖊𝖘

May 29   *Always There for You*   SkeptopolisTimes.com

David Slays Goliath

Templeton's Chuck Norris Does It Again

By Connie Granger

Last night, the City of Skeptopolis witnessed one of the most fascinating happenings this reporter has ever seen. Many of you are, perhaps, unaware that the religion department at Skeptopolis University conducts a weekly academic roundtable for students during the semester. The roundtable is designed to give the students an opportunity to hear varying opinions on subjects relating to religious beliefs in society. You need to understand that this roundtable is not set up as a debate but as an informal discussion so professors and guests can discuss the topic at hand. Each roundtable centers on a particular theme.

Generally, the University invites a guest from outside, who is knowledgeable about the subject at hand, to sit down and interact with professors whose area of expertise intersects with the topic. Last night's topic had to do with the evolutionary development of ideas, society, and man, and how they stand in opposition to Christian beliefs about those subjects. The man I've called, "Templeton's Chuck Norris," Chris Bel, was invited by Dr. Albritton to represent the Christian point of view, while doctors Gray, Craven, and Everson from the university faculty represented the evolutionary argument.

The Hawking Auditorium, I am told, holds about 300-400 people, which is typically about one-quarter full for these roundtable discussions. Last night, however, the auditorium was filled to capacity and the staff had to set up an overflow room with a large screen TV to accommodate those who could not fit into the main auditorium. Typically, only students who have some academic connection to the field of study or major related to the discussion are in attendance. Again, uncharacteristically, a huge contingent from outside the university, in the community at large, packed out the event.

As this reporter watched the roundtable unfold, it turned out very differently from what I expected. Frankly, I was expecting both sides to simply present their beliefs and argue back and forth about them for a bit – kind of like a debate. What happened, though, caught me totally by surprise. Rather than debating the pros and cons of the different positions, Chris challenged the very basis of evolutionary points of view in the varying fields of philosophy, biology, and sociology.

As this discussion unfolded, none of the three professors provided evidence for their points of view in a way that put Chris on the defensive – or even showed the Christian view to be unreasonable.

Following the roundtable, I wanted to get a sense of people's thoughts as they left the auditorium, so I stood outside the door for about 10 minutes sampling people's opinions. My survey was unscientific, of course, but several comments represent the overall sentiment of those who attended. I heard such comments as:

- "I can't believe that the professors couldn't out match that guy."
- "That kid blew the professors out of the water."
- "What a disappointing performance by people who are supposed to be experts."
- "Wow, I heard things I've never heard before."
- "Shocking, just shocking!"

Next, I hoped to interview the participants, but none of the professors had time to speak to me. However, Chris courteously was willing to indulge me for a few minutes to ask a few questions.

Chris, that was quite a performance. I think most people were rather shocked that you were able to hold your own with the professors. How do you feel about that?

Well, I was very pleased to have the opportunity to interact with the community this way. It was very gratifying to see the interest people have in the topic. And I was grateful for the invitation to participate. As far as a performance, I don't see it that way at all. It was a discussion of ideas, not a performance. All of the professors who participated are very accomplished teachers and researchers, and the school should be proud to have such people on the faculty.

Well, I must say your response is quite gracious, but let me share with you some of the comments I got from people as they were leaving the auditorium. (At that point I read him the comments above.) What do you think about that?

I really hope your paper doesn't portray the roundtable in that light. This wasn't a debate; it was a discussion. People who have a reaction like someone won, or that someone had a disappointing performance, doesn't really understand what was going on there. I believe that kind of reaction shows more about the people making the comments than about the roundtable participants. It shows that they themselves are looking for affirmation of their own personal point of view rather than trying to learn something.

The approach you took to the discussion, I thought, was quite fascinating. Rather than try to defend your Christian beliefs, you went after their beliefs. What was your thinking on that?

Well, that's a little bit of a mischaracterization. In spite of what you might have thought, I was not "going after" their beliefs. What I was trying to do was merely demonstrate that naturalistic worldview beliefs are just as much a faith point of view as my Christian beliefs.

Seemingly, most people look at the beliefs of a naturalistic worldview as somehow being objective facts, while Christian beliefs are subjective. That's simply a wrong approach to classifying them. When taking that approach, people tend to put science on one side and religion on the other. But those two are not the same. Science is not a belief system; it is a methodology. As Christians, we believe in science just as much as those who hold a naturalistic worldview. I absolutely believe that the scientific method is a valid approach to investigating and understanding things that relate to the natural universe. The difference is, I believe that not everything in reality can be evaluated using the scientific method. Things do exist outside the natural universe. Naturalists believe that the natural universe is all that exists. But that assumption can't be demonstrated by science. It is a faith assertion – a religious belief. So, when people try to say that their understanding of things such as philosophical beliefs, societal development, and life's origins and development can be known *scientifically*, they must be able to produce some actual scientific evidence to show that it's true. And if there is *no* actual science, then what they believe is a faith assumption, not a scientific certainty.

In the various discussions, my beliefs were characterized as *religious* while they assumed that their beliefs were based on *science*. That is simply not true – and my entire point was that the basis for their beliefs is *faith* just as much as my beliefs. Once that fact is established, then it becomes possible to discuss the data that might support one side or the other in a constructive manner. Until then, you can't even have a fair discussion.

Chris, I want to thank you for taking the time to talk to me about this. Good luck as you go forward from here.

Thank you, Connie, it was my pleasure.

As I conclude this article, I will make one final personal observation. In spite of the fact that Chris did his very best to put a gracious twist on what happened at this roundtable, the vast majority of people in attendance did view it as a debate, and the overwhelming consensus of those present seems to be that David did, indeed, slay Goliath.

If you were not able to attend the roundtable but would like to view it, it was recorded by WSTK TV and is now available online. If you go to the *Skeptopolis Times* website, www.skeptopolistimes.com, you will find a link there.

————◆◆————

When Chris saw this article, the irony – that the headline in this Skeptopolis paper used a biblical metaphor – was not lost on him.

CHAPTER 36

SETTING UP SHOP

While some things in Chris' life put him in the public eye, a lot was also going on behind the scenes that few people knew about. All of the former gang members had to be moved to their new quarters and helped to settle into their new lives. Obviously, Chris was a key figure in that process. Most people also didn't know he had started working hand-in-glove with the Skeptopolis Universalist Church to help his new friends.

Sybil and Colleen had worked diligently with their church's ministry teams to get the former gang members all the clothing they needed to begin their new direction in life, and actively helped them start their new way of living by furnishing their quarters with the necessary furniture and food. The church's operation was, obviously, very sophisticated from many years of experience. Life for Gino's crew quickly began to settle into a new routine.

Sybil and Melanie then began the process of exploring the right educational and job opportunities for them. They had so much to do in order to give such a large and diverse group the individual attention they needed.

Because of their local connections, however, Sybil and Melanie soon managed to get Gino a job interview with the city's park service in their animal services division. It was an entry level job, and with his degree in wildlife management he was way overqualified. But he knew that if he could get his foot in the door and prove himself, there would be opportunities to move into higher level positions in the future. When he went for the interview, the officials were so impressed that they hired him right on the spot.

Only three of the crew, besides Gino, had actually finished high school – Gunner, Delta, and Maximus. The rest needed to work on their GEDs and get a job.

It was pretty easy for Melanie to get everyone who had not finished high school into a GED class. Since six of them needed to go the same route, she found a teacher to form a class just for them. So, Zander, Axel, Dexter, Damon, Cason, and Titus formed that class.

While Melanie made arrangements for their education, Sybil went about trying to find them jobs. At this point, they didn't need anything fancy, just something that would give them a little bit of spending money and allow them time to study. She found a local manufacturing company willing to hire Dexter and Damon to do custodial work. Zorn Mercantile had a need for two stock boys, so Cason and Titus agreed to take that on. Butch Grissom's construction company could really use a couple of physically fit young men to assist their skilled laborers, so Zander and Axel landed those jobs.

Even though Gunner had finished high school, he didn't have any specialized training to be hired as a specialist. However, he really wanted to study to be an electrician, so Melanie secured him a spot in the local technical school to study that trade. Butch connected them with a local electrician desperate to find new workers who agreed to take him on as an apprentice, and even pay for his schooling, with the condition that he would agree to work for them for at least three years after he graduated – something he was very excited to do.

In some ways, it was a little more difficult to help Delta. She loved working with numbers and would have liked to do bookkeeping, but her experience was rather limited. And with her background as a gang member, it was a struggle to find someone willing to take her on in that capacity. Melanie easily got her enrolled at the local community college so she could begin working on her A.A. degree, with the hope of then transferring to Skeptopolis U to get a degree in accounting. But Sybil didn't give up, and finally found a local CPA who would be willing to hire her as an entry-level bookkeeping assistant where she could be carefully monitored.

As Sybil saw everything falling into place so smoothly, she remembered back to what Chris had said about God orchestrating the circumstances. *Could it possibly be that Chris' understanding of God is true after all?* she thought to herself as she began feeling a strange stirring in her own heart.

That left Maximus. He had this dream to get into astronautical engineering. He had been intrigued with rockets from the time he was a small child, but as he grew up, he had pretty much given up on the possibility of going into that field. With this new opportunity, his dream was rekindled, and he shared that with Melanie. At first, she was quite doubtful. *How could anyone with his background get into a field like that?* she thought to herself. But to humor him, she took him to the university and arranged for an aptitude test – which he passed with flying colors.

Melanie was more than shocked when Maximus came out in the 99th percentile on the test! So, with that encouragement, she immediately began setting up the necessary testing to get him into the school – which he also aced. In fact, when the Dean for the school of engineering saw his test scores and heard his story, he offered him a three-quarter scholarship if he would agree to come to Skeptopolis U. Then, after talking to a local engineering firm who contracted with NASA, she not only got them to cover the rest of his schooling, but also hired him as a paid intern while he was in school. It was a win-win for everyone.

For the next two weeks or more, everyone worked intensely and with great dedication to get Gino and his gang set up with housing, jobs and education. Each of the "kids" were excited at their future prospects. No one could have ever believed they would be able to start new lives doing things they had dreamed about but never believed possible.

And while most of the Universalist church members weren't all that excited about Chris' beliefs and his growing influence on people in the city, they were excited about the turn of events with the former gang kids – and even more excited that they got to see their social justice ambitions accomplished of "helping the least of these." This win, at least at this point, was enough to allow them to overlook things they didn't like. It appeared they had smooth sailing ahead.

CHAPTER 37

PLANS FOR A NEW CHURCH

hris and Levi finally had a chance to unwind and watch TV in the living room after a full day. Chris had spent several hours at the dojo helping teach classes and working out in preparation for the regional tournament. Levi spent the day at the kitchen table – prayerfully working on plans for how to develop the group into a church.

After a few minutes, Gino walked in and sat down with them. "Guys, I have a couple of questions for ya. Got a second?"

Chris immediately muted the TV, as he and Levi turned to hear what Gino had to say.

"Listen, since the situation with all the guys is beginnin' to settle down, and everyone's gettin' into a regular routine with school and work, we've all been talkin', and were wonderin' if it might soon be possible to set up some kinda Christian training opportunity for the group. All of us are new at this Christian thing, and there's so much we still don't know.

Hearing Gino's request, Levi quickly jumped in. "Gino, you had no way to know this, but that's exactly what I've been workin' on. I've only been here a short time, so I've been spendin' a lotta time tryin' to get myself oriented and gettin' to know everybody. But doin' somethin' like that is exactly what I came here for. In fact, I'm already workin' on a comprehensive plan for teachin' you guys all the basics of the Christian life. I still have a ways to go to get it all together, but I have a good start on it already, and we could actually begin somethin' immediately – if y'all are up for it."

"That'd be awesome!" Gino responded enthusiastically. "Everyone'll be excited to hear that. Can you tell me what you're thinkin'?"

"Sure, Gino. There's actually different ways people think about doin' this, and I have a particular philosophy that I plan to carry over when we start a church in the future. But until we're able to take that step, I wanna mainly work with just you guys.

"My plan is to teach you in a way that'll help you be self-sufficient in your Christian walk. The Christian life's not just about receiving Christ into your life then goin' to meetings and classes to learn more. When you invited Christ into your life, His Spirit entered into your body to create an actual personal relationship with you. The entire rest of your life should be learning how to live in that relationship."

As Gino listened to Levi's explanation, he was all ears. "Yeah, that's exactly what Chris shared with us when we first came to Christ. I remember him sayin' that."

"Exactly!" Levi went on. "So, I wanna teach you in a way that'll help you become increasingly mature in your faith, and able to have confidence as you express your faith out in society – and that's a pretty big deal here in Skeptopolis where there's a lot of opposition to the Christian faith."

"I can see the logic in that." Gino responded nodding his head. "I like that idea."

Levi picked back up on his thought. "So that's the philosophy in a nutshell. Now to implement that philosophy I needed to decide what topics to include in the training. I'll start with the very basics like Christian doctrine and worldview concepts, how to pray, how to study your Bible, the meaning of worship, and things like that. I'll also teach you how to share your faith with other people, and how to answer their questions when they ask you – which'll include how to deal with people who attack your faith.

"YES!" Gino shouted, pumping his fist. "I've seen how Chris does that and I wanna be able to do it, too."

Levi smiled and nodded. "Yeah, Chris is pretty good at it. He's been at this for a long time."

Levi then looked directly at Gino and asked, "So when do you think we oughta start?"

"Levi," Gino responded with a focused look in his eye, "I say we start right away. Everybody wants it. Ya think we can start this week?"

"Well, Gino, I don't see why not. How about next Wednesday? We can do it at 6:00 PM, after everyone's finished with school and work. That'll give us time to let everybody know. Does that work?"

"Absolutely! I'm goin' to my room and calling everybody right now. So where should we meet?"

Levi looked over at Chris. "Well, what do you think?"

Chris thought for a second, "The place we have access to right now that'll hold the most people is the five-room cabin. It has a large living room. How 'bout doin' it there? And it doesn't have to be limited to just our group. If you or your guys know anyone else that'd like to come, they're welcome, too."

"That's perfect!" Gino replied excitedly. "Let's do this!"

Gino hopped back to his room and started calling everyone. Levi looked over at Chris chuckling out loud, "Well, I didn't see that comin' today. Those guys are excited! I better get to work."

Chris nodded, also chuckling, "Yeah, I'd say you better quit goofin' off and get goin.'"

CHAPTER 38

SPIRITUAL BABY STEPS

Chris and Levi both greeted everyone as they mingled in the living room of the five-room cottage. Of course, all the former gang members were there, but there were a few surprises, as well. Chris had been especially busy getting in touch with people who had shown an interest in the Christian faith.

First, he called Connie to see if she'd like to see what was going on. He didn't expect her to write anything about the class right away, but it would give her some more insight into what Chris was doing, and he thought she might go for it.

He also called Sybil to see if she would be interested. She hadn't given any indication that she actually wanted to engage Chris' faith in a deep way, but at the same time she had shown some interest in some of the things he said, and he thought she might at least want to find out more. He told her she could bring Colleen, too, if she was interested.

There were also five students at the dojo who had asked Chris a lot of questions about his faith, and he invited them to come. Two were students from Steve's Evolution of Religion class who had indicated they still took karate. Chris had made sure to connect with them at the dojo. The other three were high school aged karate students. Chris wasn't sure their parents would allow them to come, but he offered anyway.

When it was time to begin, the room was pretty full. Chris was particularly gratified that all those he had invited had come – even Connie and Sybil. Sybil had asked Colleen, but she wasn't interested.

The couch and all the chairs were full, and several people were even sitting on the floor. When everyone was seated, Chris walked around and passed out some pens and notepads. "As we do this, you guys'll probably want to take notes. This'll be somethin' you can keep and refer back to in the future as you participate."

Then, right at 6:00, Levi began. "Greetings everyone. For those of you who don't know me, I'm Levi Berger and I'll be the one leading this group. Our plan is to eventually start a new church here in Skeptopolis, and when we do that, I'll be the pastor. Chris and I grew up together and have been friends since elementary school. We also went to the same church in Templeton. After we finished college, I went to a seminary to study theology. A seminary's a special school for people who want to go into Christian work. Theology's the field of training where we study the Bible and other courses that help people become church leaders. After that, I returned to Templeton where I became an assistant pastor in our church.

"The plan is for us to meet right here every Wednesday at this same time. Of course, I know all the former gang members, but today's the first time I've met some of you. In the future, our study'll be open to anyone who'd like to come. So any of you who have friends you think would like to participate, you're welcome to bring 'em.

"Here's the format we'll use. We'll begin every week singing a few songs. In the Christian faith, our singing is not just about enjoying the music, but is a way we can express praise to God. It's always a good way to get ourselves focused on being in God's presence. I play the guitar a little, so I'll play and teach you some of the songs. I didn't bring it today because I knew we wouldn't have quite as much time because of getting organized. But beginning next week that's what we'll do.

"After that, I'll lead a Bible study that'll help you begin learning what's in the Bible. What's in the Bible has been revealed to us by God specifically to teach us about Himself and what He desires for our lives. We actually have some Bibles here for any of you who don't have one. If you don't have one, would you just raise your hand?" Everyone raised their hand. "Okay, that looks like pretty much everyone. Chris, could you pass those out for me and make sure everybody gets one? Thanks. And if you don't have a Bible of your own, you can keep the one you just received. It's our gift to you.

"After the Bible teaching, I'll spend a little time teachin' you some things about living out the Christian life. A life in Christ is not just a matter of coming to a meeting and learning new stuff. God is actually a real person who we can know in a real personal relationship. But since He's a spiritual person, we havta learn how to live in that relationship. The reason it's even possible is because the essence of our own being is also spiritual. Our spirit can connect with His, so we'll spend some time every week also dealing with that.

"Today we're gonna look in the Bible at John 1:1-14. We've given all of you the same version of the Bible so I can just give you page numbers right now. As we go along, you'll learn where the various books of the Bible are located, and eventually be able to find 'em without me havin' to give you page numbers. But for now, turn to page 1073. Here's what's written there.

[1]In the beginning was the Word, and the Word was with God, and the Word was God. [2]He was in the beginning with God. [3]All things came into being through Him, and apart from Him nothing came into being that has come into being. [4] In Him was life, and the life was the Light of men. [5]The Light shines in the darkness, and the darkness did not comprehend it.

[6]There came a man sent from God, whose name was John. [7]He came as a witness, to testify about the Light, so that all might believe through him. [8]He was not the Light, but he came to testify about the Light.

[9]There was the true Light which, coming into the world, enlightens every man. [10]He was in the world, and the world was made through Him, and the world did not know Him. [11]He came to His own, and those who were His own did not receive Him. [12]But as many as received Him, to them He gave the right to become children of God, even to those who believe in His name, [13]who were born, not of blood nor of the will of the flesh nor of the will of man, but of God.

[14]And the Word became flesh, and dwelt among us, and we saw His glory, glory as of the only begotten from the Father, full of grace and truth.

"Some of you may have heard about Genesis 1:1-14 before. That is the very beginning of the entire Bible and tells how God created the world. It starts out, 'In the beginning God created the heavens and the earth.' John 1:1, that we just read, feeds off that and says, 'In the beginning was the Word, and the Word was with God and the Word was God.' As you think about that, what do you think John was talkin' about? What is the 'Word' that was in the beginning with God and was God?"

"Before we look at the answer to that, I wanna tell you that this section of Scripture is so deep that I could literally go on for several hours talkin' about it. But this is the first time we've been together, so I just wanna give you a taste of how rich it is. Here are some of the things John said about the Word in this passage.

- Verse 2 - He was in the beginning with God.
- Verse 3 - All things came into being through Him.
- Verse 4 - Life came from Him.
- Verse 4 again - Light, that is understanding about God, came from Him.
- Verse 5 - God shines the Light in the darkness – that is the places in the world that don't understand about God – and the darkness doesn't understand it.
- Verse 10 - The Word was in the world.
- Also in verse 10 - The world was made through Him but did not know Him.
- Verse 11 - He came to His own, and His own did not receive Him. Now the people who were 'His own' that John is talking about here were the Jewish people of His day.
- Verse 12 - But all who did receive Him – that is, those who believed in Him – were given the right to become children of God.
- And finally, the key verse – verse 14: 'And the Word became flesh and dwelt among us.'

"The Word bein' talked about here, if you haven't already figured it out, was Jesus Christ. All the things I just mentioned are about Him: Jesus is God – the creator of everything; He came to the world to reveal Himself; Most people reject Him; But those who believe in Him can enter into a relationship with Him as His child.

"What I want you to do during this next week is to reread just these verses once per day and write down any questions you might have about 'em. Next week, we'll take some time to answer all your questions. Does that sound like a plan?"

As Levi shared this Scripture passage, every eye was transfixed on him, as the group sat spellbound taking in what he had said. And when he finished, they sat there – dead silent. While not everyone fully understood the depth of meaning, Levi's message found a home deep within the hearts of everyone there – and they were all deeply moved.

After pausing a moment in order to make a transition to his next point, Levi picked back up. "Now I wanna take just a moment to pray. Prayer's not a ritual, but a means of communication. It is how our spirit talks to God – who is, Himself, Spirit. Since God is a real person and we are real persons, that kind of communication is possible. So now, let's bow our heads together and speak to our heavenly Father. 'Father, thank you for revealing yourself to us in the Word, Jesus Christ. Thank you for revealing to us that we can know You in a personal relationship and become Your child. As we look over these verses during this next week, speak to our spirits through them so that we can grasp the profoundly deep meaning found in them. In Jesus' name I pray. Amen.'"

When he finished praying, Levi moved on to the next part of his training. "Guys, the next thing we're gonna do is talk about the most central core of the Christian faith. If you wanna understand Christianity, and if you wanna share it with other people, this is what you'll need to know. Be sure to take careful notes here.

"First, we can explain the core of the Christian faith by answering three simple questions based on what is taught in the Bible. By the way, we won't go into a deep explanation of this right now, but you can use the exact same three questions to find the core beliefs of any faith in existence – including Atheism. The questions are:

1. Who is God?
2. What is a human being?
3. What is the ultimate a person can receive from this life?

"So how does the Bible answer these three questions?

"To answer question one: The true God is the God revealed in the Bible. You'll need to explain that He is a person, He is holy, He is just, and He is love – all four. You can't leave any part of that out.

"The answer to question two is: Human beings are persons made in the image of God but fallen. Just write that down right now and I am gonna explain it more fully in a moment.

"And the answer to question three: The ultimate people can receive from this life is to know God in a personal relationship.

"Now obviously, these are the short answers. Over the next few weeks, we'll dive more deeply into the implications of each one. But for now, you have the bottom-line answers.

"Next, we need to know the story behind the Bible's answers to the three questions. Now I know all of this is new to most of you, and there's a lot here. So if you're not fully getting all of it right off the bat, don't worry. We'll be goin' over all of this many times in the future and breakin' each part of it down. Over time, it'll all come together for you.

"So, we can break the story down into five parts. Here is how that story goes:

"Part 1: Creation - God created the world, then created mankind – Adam and Eve. He made His creation without sin, so it'd be possible for people to have a personal relationship with Him. God is Holy and cannot fellowship with sin.

"Part 2: The Fall - Here's the part where we see what it means that man is fallen. God gave instructions that there was one thing the humans could not do – eat the fruit of the Tree of Knowledge. However, Satan appeared to Adam and Eve and tempted them to do what was forbidden. So in spite of God's command, Adam and Eve gave in to the temptation and ate the forbidden fruit. That act of disobedience brought sin into the world and broke the fellowship God had with them.

"Part 3: Life after the Fall - The sin that entered the world corrupted the human heart and made it unholy, thus unworthy to fellowship with God. If the problem could not be fixed, man would have to pay a steep price as the penalty for his sin – eternal separation from God.

"Part 4: Redemption - God determined that He would not be defeated by Satan, so He revealed a way that the Fall could be overcome. The ones who commit sin should have to pay the penalty for their own act. But God had a law that said if a sinless person would sacrifice himself in place of the sinner, He would forgive the sin. That's what is meant by redemption. But, of course, there was no human able to do that. So, since no human could meet that requirement, God came to earth in the form of a man, Jesus Christ, lived a perfect life that made Him qualified to be the sacrifice – that is, to be the redeemer – then He died on the cross to become that sin sacrifice. So now, anyone who is willing to ask God's forgiveness and invite Christ into their life can receive forgiveness for their sin.

"Part 5: Eternity – At death, those who have received Christ will enter eternity with God, and those who choose not to will spend eternity separated from Him.

"Now I want you to understand that this is just a skeleton outline of the story. Over the next few weeks, we'll dive deeper into this as well. But that's the message you can share with people to tell 'em about Christ.

"Well, I believe we're outta time for this evening, but I hope you'll ponder your notes over the next week and come back next Wednesday when we'll continue. Let's close with prayer. 'Father, thank you so much for providing us with a way to know you. You're truly a gracious and loving God. Guide us through the rest of this week and lead us back next week. In Jesus' name I pray. Amen.'"

Some of those who came had to leave right away, but those who were able hung around for a while and asked Levi and Chris all kinds of questions. It was a massively successful kickoff.

CHAPTER 39

TACKLING THE GANG CULTURE

"Do you have any dreams to do anything with your life beyond working for a gang?" Gino asked Eunice and Marshal as they stood on the corner selling drugs. They were members of the Checkers Gang.

Gino had been particularly challenged by the training opportunity a couple nights before. It gave him a vision to go out and share with other gang members how they could get their lives turned around. Between that day and now, he had spent countless hours picking both Chris' and Levi's brains to master the material. He was determined to make a difference in some people's lives.

When Gino approached Eunice and Marshal, they knew exactly who he was, and Marshal quickly walked to the other side of the street and just watched what was going on. He didn't want anything to do with Gino.

Eunice stayed, though, and allowed Gino to talk. After Marshal left, Eunice thought for a moment and said, "You know, when I was younger, I always dreamed of being a hair stylist, but you know how it is in this neighborhood ... it just never worked out."

"And why didn't it work out?" Gino responded.

"Well, mom and dad got divorced and I ended up on the street with my mom. It was all we could do just to survive. I dropped outta school to help us get by, and sellin' drugs for the gang became an easy way to make enough money to buy food. When my mom died of pneumonia, I was by myself. My dad was a drug addict and didn't want anything to do with me. The gang was all I had."

Gino had heard this story too many times before. In fact, there were members of his own gang who had almost identical stories. It was people like Eunice that made him want to help if he could.

Normally, gang members wouldn't even talk to members of other gangs. But word of Gino having quit gang life, and the story of how he was getting help for other former gang members, had spread like wildfire. Because of his reputation for having been a gang leader himself, and the latent dream many gang members had of leading a normal life outside of a gang, there were quite a few people who were willing to listen to him.

"Well, what if I could show you a way out of gang life?" Gino continued.

"I don't know," she replied. "I'd like to think it was possible, but I'm afraid. I don't believe it'd work."

"Eunice," Gino went on, "you've heard my story, right? About how I quit the gang and have gotten my own life turned around?"

"Everyone's heard your story, Gino. But I don't see a way for me. I don't have anywhere to go, and no means to make a new start."

"But have you heard my whole story?" Gino continued. "You know, when I left the gang, I didn't leave alone. There were 10 of us – and all of us were in the same boat you're in. The reason we were able to pull it off was because some people were willin' to help us. They helped us with a place to live, with food, and even helped us get jobs and get into school. Do you still dream of being a hairdresser? It's not an impossible dream. I know people who'd help you just like they helped me."

"It all seems too good to be true," Eunice protested. "Why would anyone wanna do that? We're not, after all, considered to be the *elite* of society."

"Eunice, you may find this hard to believe, but there are people who wanna help you just because they love you. In fact, they love you even though they've never met you personally. They love you just because you are a fellow human being."

Hearing that almost brought Eunice to tears. No one had ever really cared for her since her mom died – even people she knew – even other family members. "I wish I could believe that," Eunice sighed. "It just doesn't make sense. Why would a stranger care about someone like me? I have nothing to offer anyone."

"Eunice, why do you think I've been willin' to come down into your gang's territory to talk to you? We'd never met in person before today, yet here I am risking my own life to tell you how special you are and that you can turn your life around. I'm an actual example that the kind of special love I'm talkin' about really exists. You see, I didn't used to know that kinda love either until someone showed it to me. A person I didn't even know pushed himself into my life and not only showed me it existed, but how I could find it for my own life, as well. He told me about how God loved me so much that he sent Christ to earth to provide me a way to know Him.

"At first it didn't seem like it could be true to me either, but my friend challenged me to release my doubts and trust that God really did care like that. At that point, I figured, 'What've I got to lose?' If I did it and it didn't make any difference, I wouldn't have lost anything. But if something did happen, I'd be able to follow my own dream. So I did it ... I invited Christ into my life. And when I did, I experienced the presence of God in a way that I never imagined even existed. I mean, I didn't even believe in God, but He revealed His existence in my own life and literally changed me. It changed how I felt toward Him and how I feel about other people. I now feel love for you, for instance, just as I felt God's love for me. You can have that heart change too if you want."

Eunice just stood there with her mouth open. Hearing about God the way Gino was describing Him was mind boggling. She had never even imagined anything like that. Yet Gino was right. Here he was standing before her, obviously an entirely different person than he had been when he was a gang leader. Her mind was spinning. *Is it really possible?* she thought. *Is there life beyond the gang? Could I have the life I dreamed of as a child?* She felt a powerful desire to believe Gino, but she was also petrified. *What would her gang leader think? Would Gino's friends really come through for her like they had the others he was telling her about?*

Finally, she asked, "So what would I have to do?"

"If you'll come with me today," Gino replied, "I'll get you set up. But before we do, would you like to take the spiritual step I talked about – the one that'll change your heart – the entire way that you look at life? Me helpin' you's not dependent on that, but I found it to really be the most important part of movin' to a new life, and I want you to have it, too."

"I do want it," Eunice replied. "But how do I do that?"

"Let me give you a short explanation," Gino replied as he began sharing Christ with her. "Back in the very beginning, God created mankind, and he did it for a purpose. Even though He didn't have a personal, emotional need to create human beings, He wanted to be able to express His love beyond Himself. So, He created the earth as a place for mankind to live, and a special garden for their home. He then created Adam and Eve, the first man and woman, 'in his image' – that just means that He created 'em to be creatures He could love and could love Him back. When He did that, He came in a form on earth where He could enjoy a personal relationship with His new creation."

"Everything was great at first, but there came a time when the relationship fell apart. There was one thing God told 'em they couldn't do. Sadly, Adam and Eve disobeyed God on that one thing, and that sin destroyed the personal relationship they had with Him."

"From that time on, humanity has had to live with the consequences of that sin – we are separated from God, and the nature of our earthly existence makes it difficult to live daily life. Even your own circumstances with your mom and dad's divorce, your homelessness, your mother's death, your dad not wantin' anything to do with you, you have given up your personal dreams – all of that's a result of the sin that's in the world."

"Wow, you make it sound pretty hopeless," Eunice replied. "I thought you said it could be different."

Gino picked back up. "Well, so far, I've only explained to you the problem. I'm just now gettin' to the solution to the problem. You see, God didn't give up on man, and He created a way to fix the sin problem. In reality, we all should have to pay the penalty for our own sin. Since we've rejected God, we should have to be separated from Him. And because human beings, in general, have rejected God, we have to live in a world where there's a lotta evil. But God has a law that says while the penalty for sin has to be paid, it's possible for someone else to pay it. The only condition is that the person who pays the penalty has to be worthy – that means they have to be perfect – without any sin at all in their life.

"Eunice, as you just sorta pointed out, it's pretty obvious that it's impossible for any human being to do that. So, God decided He would, Himself, come to earth in the form of a human, live that perfect life, then die as a sacrifice in order to pay the sin penalty for all those who could not pay it for themselves. So, God took the form of a human in the man Jesus Christ, lived a perfect life to make Himself worthy of being the sin sacrifice, then died on the cross as the sacrifice. With that, He substituted Himself in our place and paid our sin penalty."

"Okay," Eunice interrupted to clarify something she wasn't quite understanding, "If Jesus paid the sin penalty, then why hasn't all of the bad stuff gone away? Why am I, and others, still sufferin' problems?"

"That's just the right question, Eunice. You see, the simple fact that Christ did what he did doesn't mean everyone automatically has their sins forgiven. It's possible for everyone, but each person has to engage God personally for the forgiveness to happen. Each individual has to accept what God has offered by personally recognizing that we're sinners, and that we should have to pay the penalty for sin ourselves. Then, once we admit to our sin before Him, we havta individually ask God's forgiveness and for Him to apply Christ's sacrifice to our lives. "Doin' that, though, is where the amazing wonder comes in. This is the place where God changes people's lives.

"You see, even though we're physical beings as we live life on earth, our physical part isn't all there is to us. We are also eternal spiritual beings. Our spirit is the part of us that makes us more than just some physical animal. If you think about it, there's a very big difference between human beings and other animal creatures. The difference is that we're spiritual beings. And since God is also a spiritual being, His Spirit is able to connect with our spirit."

"So when we ask God's forgiveness, we then ask Christ to enter our life. And when we do that, His very Spirit enters us and establishes a personal relationship with us – a personal connection to our own spirit. In fact, He actually adopts us into His family, and we become a child of God. Also, when He does that, He creates a new nature inside us so we can experience the changed life I've been talkin' about."

"So how about it, Eunice, would you like to invite Christ into your life right now?"

Listening to Gino share about God's love for her moved her more deeply than anything she had ever before experienced in her life. Eunice stood there already weeping and said, "Gino, I do. I want this for my life."

"Then Eunice, "Gino explained, "all you havta do is talk to God and tell Him what I explained to you. Admit to Him your sin, ask His forgiveness, then ask Him to come into your life. Can you do that?"

Eunice paused for a moment, then spoke out loud, "God, I don't know if I'm doin' this right, but I've really lived a messed-up life and wanna have a change. Would you please forgive me and come into my life and change me?"

Where she had been gently weeping before, suddenly, Eunice broke down into nearly uncontrollable sobbing. "Gino," she said through her sobs, "I don't understand it, but He did it. God has really come into my life. I can't even describe the inner peace and sense of joy I feel. God really accepted me."

"Yes he did," Gino responded, tears rolling down his cheeks, as well. "And from here He'll never let you go. But what about where you are here – right now? Do you wanna leave the gang and enter into a new lifestyle, as well?"

"I do, Gino," Eunice responded with a confidence he had not heard in her voice before. "Can you really make it happen?"

"Just as I promised, there are people just waitin' to help you. In fact, if you come with me right now, we'll get it goin'. You'll have a new place to sleep even tonight."

"Tonight? Even this quickly? Well, yes, I'm ready! Just a second while I give these drugs to Marshal."

Marshal had been watching what was going on across the street the entire time, and saw Eunice give her life to Christ. Now, as he watched her walking across the street toward him, he wasn't quite sure what was about to happen, so he braced himself for what she might say. When she got to him, she reached into her pocket, pulled out the drug supply she had, and handed it to him. "Marshal," Eunice instructed, "Take these back to George and tell him I got religion and am leavin' the gang. I'm gettin' a new life for myself." George was the leader of the Checkers. She then turned around, walked back to Gino, and said, "Let's go. I'm ready."

The two of them then turned and walked back toward the dojo. As they walked, Gino pulled out his cell and called Chris. When Chris picked up, Gino said, "Chris, I have a young lady here with me that we need to fix up. Can you get the wheels turnin'?"

"Absolutely, Gino," Chris responded. Where you now?"

"We'll be at the dojo in about five minutes. Can you pick us up?"

"I'll be right there," Chris replied.

A plan for helping people who left the gangs had already been put in place. So, Chris called Sybil to let her know of the need, and she instructed him to take Eunice to the housing complex where a room would be ready for her.

Gino himself was beyond delirious to see how God had worked through him. It made him even more determined to reach as many people in the gangs as he could, and it turned out this was only the beginning.

Meanwhile, Marshal quickly ran back to gang headquarters to tell George what had happened. He had been close enough to see and hear everything, and he explained the entire scene.

After hearing the story, George was hopping mad and screamed out. "Who's this guy think he is?!" At the same time, he was very conflicted. Gino was hurting his business, but he was not competing for money. And he didn't really know what to do with this religion thing. He wouldn't do anything rash right now but was determined to keep an eye on what was happening.

CHAPTER 40

DELTA'S PREGNANT

"That was a beautiful wedding the other week, wasn't it?" Colleen commented to Sybil as they ate lunch together at the taco restaurant. "It was so much fun to watch. It was so far beyond anything either of 'em imagined would happen. It was totally magical."

Sybil smiled as the image of the wedding once again flooded her mind. "Oh yeah, and the glow on Delta's face totally lit up the room. I think that'll always be a fantastic memory for me. Oh, and did you know? Delta's pregnant."

With that comment, Colleen was caught totally by surprise. "No! Seriously? I had no idea. How do you know that?" Colleen was immediately intent on knowing more.

"I overheard her and Gunner talkin' about it with Chris and Levi the other day when I was helpin' one of Gino's new gang dropouts get into an apartment," Sybil responded. "I don't think it's a secret or anything. In fact, I think that's one of the reasons they went ahead and got married."

Colleen pondered the thought for a moment, then said, "But both of 'em are just beginnin' school and startin' a new job, right? That's gotta be a really difficult thing by itself ... but to have a kid comin' on top of that? I think it's too much. We need to go over and have a talk with 'em."

"I don't know," Sybil responded. "I'm not sure that's any of our business right now."

"Don't be foolish," Colleen barked back, obviously feeling a certain amount of passion about the situation. "We need to give 'em some serious counseling about that."

As a member of her church's social service ministry, Colleen had been fully trained by Planned Parenthood to counsel young women in Delta's situation. In fact, she even volunteered at the Planned Parenthood clinic once a week and found a lot of personal satisfaction helping young women in trouble deal with their struggles when they found themselves with an unwanted pregnancy.

Sybil wasn't really comfortable doing that kind of thing, but Colleen insisted it was necessary in order to help Delta and Gunner, so she talked Sybil into going with her to do it. As soon as they finished their tacos, they got into Colleen's car and drove over to see Delta.

When they got there, Gunner wasn't home, and Delta was just relaxing in front of the TV. Colleen and Sybil walked up to the front door and knocked.

When Delta saw who it was, she was very excited. They had been so instrumental in creating her dream wedding. "Colleen, Sybil, what a surprise. It's so wonderful to see you," she said as she gave them both a big hug. "Can you come in for a bit?"

"Absolutely!" Colleen replied as she took control of the situation. "We were just talkin' about you and wanted to see how everything's goin', so we decided to come by."

"I'm so glad you did. Can I get you a cup of coffee or somethin'?"

Colleen was too anxious to get down to the issue of pregnancy with Delta to take time for coffee. "No, I don't think so right now. Thanks, though."

"Well, you guys come in and have a seat," Delta said as she led them into the living room. "I'm so glad you came."

They all sat down, and Colleen immediately got to the point. "Delta, I just heard you're pregnant. Is that true?"

Delta blushed. "Yeah, it's definitely true. We're not yet very far along, but we do know for sure I'm pregnant."

"Well Delta," Colleen quizzed, "I know both you and Gunner are about to begin school and are also about to begin new jobs. Do you think you're really ready to also have a child in the mix?"

Delta was a bit taken back by the question. "Well," she responded, "that's all true, but we'll somehow make it work."

Colleen pressed, "You know, I think you oughtta consider that question more deeply. With so little money, and with all the pressures of school and work, not to mention the stresses that go along with bein' newlyweds, you might wanna think about delaying havin' a child."

"Uh, what are you gettin' at, Colleen?" Delta inquired. "I mean, I'm pregnant. We'll just havta deal with it."

"Actually you don't," Colleen responded. "I have connections where we can get you an abortion and you can delay startin' a family until you guys are a little more settled."

"An abortion?" Delta responded with obvious surprise in her voice. "That thought never crossed my mind."

"Well, you should consider it," Colleen replied. "Being responsible for a child at your young age and with all you're going through'll be really hard. And like I said, I have connections to help with that – and it won't cost you anything."

"But what about the morality of having an abortion?" Delta asked. "I've heard that Christians don't allow abortions."

Colleen then began a more in-depth explanation. "Delta, think about this, I'm a Christian and I don't think it's wrong. And beyond that, our church even has a social services ministry to help young ladies in your situation get an abortion if it is called for. I'd never ask you to do anything immoral."

"So how does that work, Colleen?" Delta questioned further.

"What you need to realize, Delta, is that a fetus is not yet a real person. It doesn't become a person until after it's born – some even say 'til it's able to have conscious awareness. Until then, it is simply a mass of tissue that can be removed without feelin' bad about it at all."

Hearing that, Delta was totally confused. She had no idea how to respond. On the one hand, she knew Colleen was right – that it would be very difficult to raise a child while both she and Gunner were studying and working. On the other hand, she wanted to have the baby. Not knowing what to say, she just sat there for a moment with a blank stare on her face.

Colleen could see Delta was really struggling with the thought and broke the silence. "Delta, you don't have to make a decision right this minute. Think about it then gimme a call." She then reached into her purse and pulled out a business card and handed it to Delta. "This is the church's social services ministry business card with my name and phone number on it. Call me when you're ready."

Colleen and Sybil then got up and headed toward the front door. "Remember, Delta," Colleen reminded her, "we're here for you any time night or day. I'll wait to hear from you."

Delta walked in front of them and opened the front door. "Thank you, guys, for caring about me," Delta commented. "You were so kind to come by."

"It was our pleasure," Colleen responded. "You just call me when you're ready." Colleen and Sybil then walked to their car, got in, and drove away.

That whole conversation really got Delta upset. What Colleen had said to her seemed very logical in some ways. *Maybe we shouldn't have a baby right now*, Delta thought to herself. *I don't know what to think. I need to talk to Chris.*

Right then, she picked up the phone and gave Chris a call. She needed some advice from someone she trusted right now.

When he got the call, Chris was sitting on the couch watching the Golf Channel with Levi and Gino. "Chris, I need some advice," he heard Delta's voice pleading from the other end. "I'm totally confused and don't know what to do."

"Delta, what's goin' on?" Chris asked, picking up on the concern in her voice.

Hearing Delta's name, both Gino and Levi looked over in Chris' direction.

"Well, Colleen and Sybil just came over and I had a talk with 'em," Delta explained. "I know they were just tryin' to help, but now my mind's in total turmoil."

"So, what'd they say that's caused you this kinda confusion?" Chris asked.

"Really, it was pretty much Colleen who was doin' all the talkin'. She thinks I should get an abortion."

Hearing that, Chris was totally shocked. He never expected to have to deal with something like that. "Delta," he responded, "what does Gunner think?"

"Oh, Gunner's not here right now. He is out meetin' with the people from the new company he'll be workin' for. I don't expect him home for a couple more hours."

"I see," Chris replied. "I'll tell you what. When Gunner gets home, tell him what's happened, and that you called me to let me know about it. After he knows everything, give me a call back and I'll come over with Levi and Gino and we can talk this through. How's that sound?"

"Oh yes," Delta replied with a sense of relief in her voice, "that'd be great! Thanks so much for helping us sort this out."

"Listen Delta, you know you can call on me any time," Chris answered. "I wanna help you guys any way I can."

After Chris hung up the phone, he shared the conversation with Levi and Gino. Chris also shared some of his thoughts about what was happening. "You know, I wasn't expectin' this to happen, but in one way I'm not surprised. The Universalist Church, where Colleen and Sybil attend, has a ministry to help young girls that get pregnant, and Colleen's heavily involved in it. But it's affiliated with Planned Parenthood – the largest abortion provider in America. I'm guessin' that somehow Colleen heard about Delta's pregnancy and felt the best way she could assist was to help her get an abortion. There are elements of that church's theology that don't really align with biblical teachings. I can see this is an area we're gonna have to be aware of so we can keep that kinda influence from leading our people down a wrong path."

"Sounds like you're prob'ly right about that," Levi echoed.

"But there could be a positive side to this, as well," Chris went on. "While this could become a bit uncomfortable, it'll also be a great opportunity to share with Delta and Gunner some very important principles about livin' out a Christian life."

A couple of hours later, Chris' phone rang again. It was Delta. "Chris," she said somewhat nervously, "Gunner's here and I just shared with him about Colleen's advice. He's not too happy right now. Would it be a good time for you to come over?"

"Absolutely," Chris responded, "we were just waitin' for your call. We'll be over in about 10 minutes."

Since they were expecting the call, the three guys were all ready when it came, and immediately piled into Gino's car and drove over to Gunner's and Delta's place. They pulled up in front of the cabin, got out of the car, and walked up to the front door.

Before they could even knock, Gunner opened the door and invited them in. "Thanks for comin' over, guys," he said to the group. "Come on in and have a seat in the livin' room."

After they were seated, Chris asked Delta to tell them in detail what had gone on, and Delta obliged. When she finished, Chris spoke up. "First, you guys, don't be upset at Colleen and Sybil. You havta realize that they were just tryin' to help. They didn't mean anything malicious by comin' over. But there's somethin' else you need to be aware of, as well. I could tell from your voices that the suggestion of an abortion has upset you guys on an emotional level. The fact is, there's more to consider than just that. This whole thing actually has a connection with your new Christian life, as well."

"Chris," Delta chimed in, "I'm not upset at Colleen and Sybil. I could tell that they meant well. But Gunner and I've talked about this, and we really wanna keep the baby."

"I think that's very good," Chris replied, "but we wanna go into this a little more deeply with you so you'll have even more of a reason than simply 'wantin' to keep the baby.' Colleen was right about one thing: it'll be tough for you guys to both be studyin' and workin', while also takin' on parenting responsibilities. But that's not a reason for havin' an abortion. If you don't mind, I am gonna let Levi take over from here as this is more his specialty. I could explain it, but he can do it better."

With that, Chris glanced over at Levi and turned the lead over to him.

"Gunner and Delta," Levi began, "one of the most basic values taught in the Bible has to do with the sacredness of human life. When God created Adam and Eve, he did somethin' very special – He created them 'in His image.' That doesn't mean he created 'em to physically look like Him, but that they had certain characteristics He also had."

Gunner jumped in, "Do you mean we're also gods?"

Levi smiled, "No, nothin' like that. God's the only God. But when He made man, He put in us the characteristics of personhood – things like self-awareness, free will, creativity, analytical ability, a moral sense, and the like. These are characteristics unique to human beings. No other creature on earth has 'em. These special characteristics make it possible for us to have a self-conscious personal relationship with God.

"To put it as directly and simply as I can, God made us special this way. And the Bible teaches us there was a particular reason he did it. He did it because he wanted us to be able to have a relationship with Him. Since human beings are God's special creation, human life is sacred. The Bible teaches that taking the life of an innocent human being's a sin – and an unborn baby is an innocent human life."

Upon hearing this, Delta's eyes grew big. "Wait!" she blurted out. "What you're sayin' is that it's not like Colleen explained. She said before a baby's born, it's not a real person – it's just a mass of tissue. She also said she's a Christian and her whole church supported doin' it."

"Delta, I'm so sorry she told you that," Levi said sadly. "It's true that there are people who say they're Christians who are okay with abortion. But that's simply not what the Bible teaches. When a child is conceived, at that very moment it's an actual, living human being.

"But it is not just the Bible that teaches that. Science affirms it, too. Think about this. When a child is conceived in a woman's womb, is it human?"

"Well, I guess it must be," Delta responded. "I mean, it's not some other kind of creature. So yeah, it's human."

Levi went on, "And is it a separate human being – different from its mother and father?"

"I don't know." Delta answered tentatively. "Is it?"

"Think about it this way." Levi explained, "The mom and dad both have their own unique DNA, right? I mean, every person in existence does."

"Yeah, that's true," Delta answered, "but the baby's actually connected to the mother."

"Connected," Levi responded, "but not the same. The baby has its own unique DNA, as well. It's a completely separate person."

"Wow, that's interesting," Delta replied.

"But that's not all." Levi continued, "Even though the baby at that stage of development is dependent on the mother for keepin' it alive, it is itself alive. It's a living soul – a unique, living, human being. And as a living human being, it has value in God's eyes. It's an innocent person, and killing it constitutes murder."

"Murder?!" Delta blurted out. "Isn't that kinda harsh? I mean, it's not against the law."

"Well, this is where you havta realize that not everything that's immoral is against the law. Can you think of any other actions you consider immoral that fit into that category?"

Delta thought a second, "Well yeah, when you put it that way, I guess I can think of a lotta things. But murder's really bad – worse than other things I can think of."

"In some ways that may be true," Levi answered, "but remember, most people who believe abortion's okay don't consider a preborn baby to be an actual human being."

"Oh wow, you're right," Delta exclaimed. "I get it. I really get it. I didn't wanna give up my baby anyway, but now I could never do it. I need to let Colleen know."

CHAPTER 41

THE CONFRONTATION

"You've decided what?!" Colleen exclaimed in disbelief as she talked to Delta on the phone. "You don't wanna have the abortion? But havin' a baby now could really mess up your future."

"I really don't think so," Delta responded with a sense of deep conviction in her voice. "I believe we'll be just fine."

"Well just hang on to that thought," Colleen shot back. "I'll be over in a few minutes so we can talk this over some more." Then, before Delta could object, Colleen hung up. She immediately called Sybil and said, "Sybil, I'm comin' to pick you up right now. Be ready. I'll explain when I get there. She then immediately ran and jumped into her car.

Colleen had bought in – 100 percent – to the Planned Parenthood mindset that young people in Gunner's and Delta's situation should not be having children. She was convinced they needed to get their lives fully established before taking on the responsibilities of parenthood.

It only took a few minutes for her to pick up Sybil then get over to Delta's house, and when she arrived, she quickly parked, hurried up to the front door, and knocked. Sybil, not so enthusiastic about this visit, lagged behind.

Hearing the knock, Delta warmly opened the door and invited the ladies in. She then guided them into the living room where they all sat down. Gunner was already there sitting in his favorite easy chair. From then on, Colleen did all the talking.

"Delta." Colleen started, basically ignoring the fact Gunner was there. "I thought we'd decided that you'd go ahead and have an abortion. Why have you changed your mind?"

"Huh?" Delta responded. "I never decided that. My first thought was always to keep the baby. I told you that. But when I listened to what you told me, it did make a certain sense and caused me to think more deeply about my options – and I talked it over with Gunner. But we needed more understanding, so Chris and Levi came over and shared with us what was in the Bible, and we decided for sure to keep the baby."

"So, you talked to Chris and Levi? And you let them talk you out of it?" Colleen exclaimed indignantly with her voice rising. "You know they're men, right? You know they don't understand the real needs women have, nor the oppression they impose on us by makin' us carry a baby to term when it's not in our best interest, right? You shouldn't have let them talk you out of it."

Now Delta was becoming confused again. She didn't really get what Colleen meant about 'oppression of women' or 'imposing a baby on her.' All the while, Gunner just sat there dumbfounded. He couldn't believe what he was hearing.

"That doesn't really make sense to me, Colleen," Delta replied. "I don't feel oppressed, and no one's makin' me do anything. I wanna have the baby."

"You really don't understand what's goin' on, Delta," Colleen responded with a bit of exasperation in her voice. "Listen, I'm gonna go over and talk to Chris and Levi right now. What they're doin's just wrong!"

With that, Colleen got up and strode to the front door to leave, with Sybil and Delta straggling along behind. Colleen was really upset with Chris and Levi, and Delta was increasingly confused.

"Listen, Delta," Colleen exclaimed as she headed out the door and toward her car with Sybil in tow, "I'm gonna try to talk some sense into their heads. I hope we can talk about this some more later." The ladies then got into the car and drove over to Chris' apartment.

When they got there, they went straight to the door and Colleen started banging. Since it was already a bit late, and the guys weren't expecting anyone, no one inside could imagine who it could be. Gino was closest to the door, so he walked over, looked through the door window, and saw who it was. "Hey," he called out to the others, "it's Colleen and Sybil." Gino then began to open the door. But before he could get it fully open, Colleen pushed her way in and demanded to see Chris and Levi. Sybil nervously slipped in behind her and gently closed the door.

Chris and Levi both heard Colleen's demand and immediately walked into the living room where she stood. When she saw them, she hissed, "Chris, you and Levi, what do you think you're doin' fillin' Delta's head with all that garbage!?"

"Well hello, Colleen ... Sybil" Chris responded with a great deal of confusion at having been barged in on like that. "What's up?"

"Don't you 'hello Colleen' me," she bellowed. "You've done an awful disservice to Delta, and you need to go over and fix it right now!"

"Sorry Colleen," Chris replied back, "I have no idea what you're talkin' about. You guys have a seat and tell me what's goin' on."

"I don't wanna sit down! I want you to go straighten out the mess you've caused with Delta – RIGHT NOW!"

"Colleen, seriously, what are you talkin' about. What's goin' on with Delta?" Chris replied more confused than ever.

"She told me you and Levi talked her outta havin' an abortion. You were pigheaded MEN to do that to her," Colleen responded as she continued yelling.

"Oh, so that's what this tirade's all about?" Chris responded with a bit more resoluteness in his voice. "You want her to get an abortion, and since she's decided not to, you're mad at us. Is that the deal?"

"You had no right to do that," Colleen snapped back with fire in her eyes.

Chris listened to Colleen's continued vitriol and replied back, "And why did we not have the right to give her a different perspective? What is it about your advice that makes it right for her?"

Colleen fired back, "Do you not realize that you've now put her in a position where she's gonna be tied down to a baby and not be able to live her life free of those chains? Only male chauvinist pigs would do somethin' like that to an innocent young girl."

"Okay Colleen," Chris snapped back, "you've crossed a line here. You're assuming a number of things based on your own personal attachment to a particular point of view, with absolutely no knowledge of why we advised her the way we did, and no understanding of our actual motivations. Now, if you honestly wanna talk about this, which apparently you do since you came over here and just barged in, come over here and sit down, and let's have a civil conversation."

With that, Colleen glared at Chris for a moment, then strode over to the couch and plopped herself down. Sybil timidly followed. She was quite uncomfortable with what was going on and was determined not to get in the middle of it.

"Okay Colleen," Chris said calmly, "here's the way this is gonna work. We're gonna sit here and listen to your entire reasoning as to what you wanna happen and why. Then, when you finish, you're gonna listen to us give our point of view. After that, we can discuss how to move forward. So, tell us your reasoning."

Colleen took a deep breath, calmed down a bit, then began her explanation. "Listen, I've come to care a great deal about Delta. She's comin' out of a really difficult situation and wants to turn her life around. She's going to school AND has gotten a job to make that happen. On top of that, she just got married and is settin' up house. All of this is new for her, and all together it's a LOT for a young lady to process all at once. And now, another factor's thrown into the equation – she's pregnant. I've seen it too many times; a young woman gets pregnant, has a baby, and her entire future's derailed. From that moment on she becomes dependent on a man or the government just to survive. It's just wrong, and she should be encouraged to terminate the pregnancy."

After Colleen had finished saying her piece, Chris began to respond to her concerns. "Okay Colleen, I've made a mental note of the concerns you've expressed, so let me address 'em one by one. First, I think it's absolutely wonderful that you care about Delta the way you do. Indeed, she is comin' out of a difficult situation, and the care you've shown her means a lot. She needs that kind of friendship. So, I wanna commend you for that, and I hope you'll continue your friendship with her. You're a true princess to stick up for her that way. But I'm not sure all of your concerns are completely valid. Let me ask you this, 'Have you ever seen situations where a young woman decided to keep the baby, and the woman and the child both thrived?'"

Colleen thought a second, "Well yes, I've seen that a few times. But it's the exception rather than the rule."

"Well let me ask you a follow up question. Of the ones who didn't succeed well, how many of 'em were married and had a strong support group surroundin' 'em?"

"Almost none of 'em," Colleen answered, "but that's irrelevant. The statistics are there."

"No, it's not irrelevant!" Chris interjected. "Delta's married, and she has a very strong network of friends surroundin' her who'll help her face the difficulties that come up. She won't havta become dependent on the government."

He continued, "But there's another thing that I deeply object to that you've thrown into your accusations. What are you talkin' about that she'll be 'dependent on a man?' You've totally mischaracterized the nature of a marriage relationship. A husband and wife are dependent on each other – by definition. It's not just the woman dependent on the man, but both dependent on one another. That is exactly the biblical ideal."

"Whoa, just wait a minute," Colleen snapped back as she raised her voice again. "Now we're gettin' down to cases. One of the things you obviously did to try to convince her not to have an abortion was to scare her by tellin' her God would be mad at her if she did it. I despise you Bible thumpers for doin' that! It's evil and manipulative."

"Whoa! Now you just wait a minute, Colleen," Levi jumped into the conversation. "First of all, no one told her God would get mad at her for doin' it. That's just false. But beyond that, what foundational principles are you basing your opinion on? If you don't base your beliefs on the teachings of the Bible, what do you base 'em on?"

"I do base my beliefs on the Bible," Colleen fired back. "You're just interpreting it wrong!"

"So, are you saying that getting married and having children is not a biblical ideal?" Levi asked. "And are you sayin' it's okay to murder an innocent preborn baby?"

"Of course there's nothin' wrong with marriage. I helped Gunner and Delta get married, remember?" Colleen fired back, her anger level increasing once again. "But the idea that abortion is murder is a bunch of hooey! A fetus is not a sentient human being and terminating it's not a sin!"

Levi had already been over this with Delta, but it seemed Colleen had no understanding of either the actual teachings of the Bible, nor of the scientific rationale for recognizing a preborn baby as an independent human being. It seemed prudent, at this moment, to explain that to her.

"Okay Colleen," Levi began, "let's start with the biblical view of human life. According to the Bible, one of the most basic values revealed by God has to do with the sacredness of human life. When God created Adam and Eve, he created 'em 'in His image.' What that means is that they had certain characteristics that He also had. That would include characteristics such as self-awareness, free will, creativity, analytical ability, a moral sense, and the like. These are personhood characteristics, and of all the creatures on earth, only humans have 'em. They are the characteristics that make it possible for us to have a self-conscious personal relationship with Him. In fact, God made us this way for that very purpose – to have a relationship with Him. Because of that, He's revealed that it's a sin to take an innocent person's life – and a preborn baby is an innocent human life."

"Wait!" Colleen jumped in. "A fetus is not yet a human life. What you've said does not apply to an unborn child!"

"Colleen, that's simply not true," Levi continued. "When a child is conceived, at that very moment it's an actual, living human being. Answer me this, 'When a child is conceived in a woman's womb, is it human?'"

"I just told you it's not," Colleen snapped back.

"So what is it then?" Levi countered. "Is it a horse? Is it a mouse? If it's not human, what is it?"

"Well, in that sense it's human," Colleen conceded, "but it is not a viable person."

"Not viable?" Levi remarked? "What do you mean by viable? Do you mean it's not alive?"

"No, not that," Colleen fired back. "But it can't survive on its own."

Levi responded again, "But what does that have to do with whether or not it is a living human being? Do you also feel it's okay to just up and kill someone who, for instance, is on a respirator? By your definition, that would seem to be okay."

"Quit twistin' my meaning," Colleen practically yelled back. "You know what I mean!"

"No, I actually don't know what you mean. You seem to now be contradicting yourself. But let me ask you one more question," Levi went on. "Is a preborn baby a separate creature from its mother and father?"

"And the answer's 'NO!'" Colleen snapped. "It's a part of the mother's body – which is another reason abortion's fine. No one should be able to tell a woman what to do with her own body."

"But is that actually true?" Levi responded. "We know that the mother and father both have their own unique DNA, right?"

"Yeah, so?" Colleen replied sarcastically.

"Well, what about the child?" Levi continued. "Is it the same as that of its mother or father, or is it unique to the child?"

Colleen was definitely not expecting that question. She'd never heard any-one talk about that before. "Uh, I don't know," she replied with a bit of doubt in her voice." But then came back strong, "But it doesn't even matter! It's part of the woman's body."

Levi continued his explanation, "Well, it is true that the baby, at that stage of development, is totally dependent on the mother for keepin' it alive. But it's not a part of the mother. The baby has its own unique DNA. It's a completely separate person. And as far as its spiritual existence – it's a living soul. And as a living human being, it has value in God's eyes. It's an innocent person, and killin' it constitutes murder. So you see, Colleen, the encouragement we gave to Delta to keep the child is not simply a matter of what's convenient on a temporal level, it truly is an expression of the way God created reality to exist. It actually is immoral to abort a baby."

That last argument was all Colleen could stand. "You guys are nothin' more than religious fanatics!" Colleen screamed out as she jumped to her feet and stormed toward the door. "You think you're so pious and holy, and that you can just get away with accusing people of murder for trying to help 'em. I don't ever want to see you again!"

With that, Colleen opened the door and stormed out. She didn't even look back. Sybil was mortified at all that had taken place. As she ran to catch up to Colleen, she looked over her shoulder at Chris, Levi, and Gino, with a gri-mace on her face, and shrugged her shoulders to signal to them that she had no idea what was going on with Colleen. Then they got in her car and left.

CHAPTER 42

TOURNAMENT PREP

"**H**arder, Chris! Go harder! Now, throw those punches faster! Faster still! Still faster! Now, three consecutive roundhouse kicks – low, middle, high. Do it faster! Even faster! Okay. Great work. Now take a short break and catch your breath."

Sensei Lance had come over to Skeptopolis a week prior to work with Chris as he prepared for the regional tournament in St. Louis. He would normally have stayed with Chris, but since his place was full, CJ invited him to use one of the apartments in his dojo. It was a win-win for both Lance and CJ. They knew each other from prior tournaments but had never spent any time together, and this gave them a chance to get to know each other better and compare notes on running a karate dojo.

While in Skeptopolis, Chris had mostly been working out on his own while training for the tournament, with CJ coming in sometimes to also do a little coaching. But he wanted one last push to get him into peak shape in preparation for regionals. Since Sensei Lance had actually participated in the regional tournament before, Chris thought his insights would be helpful, and invited him to come over for a week – which he gladly accepted.

While taking a break, the three went over to the break room where Chris got a bottle of water and they all sat down at the table. "Sensei Lance," CJ broke the silence, "you've been so fortunate to have a student like Chris to teach all these years."

"Yeah, he's definitely a special talent. And it's not only his skills, but his attitude, as well. I've had a lotta students who had such great potential, but never lived up to it because they didn't have the mental toughness or stick-to-itiveness necessary to excel. To really be elite, you havta have the whole package."

"Yeah, you've got that right," CJ responded. "I've experienced the same thing."

"Hey guys," Chris interrupted, "I'm right here, you know. You're embar-rassin' me."

"Humble too, isn't he?" Lance quipped. And they all cracked up laughing.

"Seriously, though, you're right. It really does take the whole package." CJ noted thoughtfully. "I wish there was some training secret to inject the atti-tude part into people."

Lance thought about that for a second then put in his two cents worth. "You know, so much of the attitude part comes not just from the athlete him-self, but also from the family environment he was raised in and the underlying beliefs of that environment. Some environments simply don't encourage that kinda attitude."

CJ's brow wrinkled and he looked inquisitively at Lance. "Hmm. That's an interesting thought. Would you care to elaborate?"

"Well," Lance answered back, "just for instance ... If a kid grows up in a home where he's not encouraged to achieve, or doesn't have a good role mod-el for perseverance, he'll probably not get those attitudes implanted in his own life. By the same token, a person's actual belief structure also makes a differ-ence. I know it hasn't escaped you that a massive part of Chris' motivation for always doin' his best comes from his faith in Jesus Christ."

CJ chuckled. "Yeah, Chris talks about that all the time. You know, right, that he's become pretty famous all over town for bein' a Christian?"

Lance smiled back, "Yeah, I keep hearin' that. But it's true. I've known Chris for years, and, in fact, we go to the same church. So I see how his faith's been shaped and how it plays out beyond just at the dojo. I know for a fact he's deeply devoted to Christ, and his desire to excel is not just to be good in karate. He wants to please Christ, as well. I'm sure you must've sensed that, just watchin' him work."

"Well, more than just sensed it, actually. We've had some long talks about that very thing. It's been pretty amazing watching how his faith plays out – not just in karate, but in dealin' with opposition, and even helpin' people out. Are you aware that two of the gang members that he helped influence to get out of the gang actually live in a couple of the apartments beside you? Somehow Chris wrangled that, too," CJ noted with a chuckle in his voice.

Lance nodded. "Actually, I am aware of that. I've even had a couple of chances to talk with Zander and Axel. Pretty amazing stories, they have. In any case, you can see a lot of where Chris' attitude and work ethic come from.

"So what about you, CJ?" Lance continued. "Have you thought about the possibility of entering into a relationship with Christ yourself?"

CJ shifted a little nervously, then looked right at Lance. "Well, like I said, Chris and I've had that conversation several times, and right now I'm just not ready to make a move like that. I mean, I love Chris like a brother, and there's a lot that's very attractive about what he says and does. And I have nothing but the utmost respect for him and his beliefs. But at this point, I just don't see it for me."

Lance nodded in a way that indicated he understood what CJ was saying. "Well, I hope you'll keep thinkin' about it. But you're right not to take a decision like that lightly. Still, I want you to know that Chris and all his friends are here for you no matter what."

With that, Lance paused a second, then changed the subject. "Well, I hate to break this party up, but I think Chris has already had too much time to goof off. Let's get back out there and put him through his paces."

Lance and CJ smiled, but Chris busted out laughing. "Oh, so I get to get out there and work my bottom off while you guys just scream at me to work harder? I know how that works."

CJ and Lance continued smiling and nodding their heads as they headed back into the gym.

CHAPTER 43

REGIONALS

There are 10 regional tournaments in all, and each covers five states. Chris would be competing in St. Louis, Missouri. His region includes Missouri, Tennessee, Kentucky, Indiana, and Illinois. Of course, the tournament in Skeptopolis was no walk in the park, but since every one of the people in this upcoming tournament were state champions, the competition level would certainly be a notch higher.

Chris wanted to give himself plenty of lead time to get settled in and rested up before the tournament, so he left about a week early to drive the 250 or so miles to St. Louis. That gave him time to get oriented and prep for the tournament. He had taken up Butch Grissom on his offer of sponsorship, so he had some extra funds for travel, lodging, and various miscellaneous expenses for the trip. He also carried a "Butch Grissom Construction Company" gym bag that he used to advertise for Butch as a condition of the sponsorship.

The Regionals would be held at the Chaifetz Arena on the Saint Louis University campus. The North American Martial Arts Association (NAM-MA) had rented the facility for the entire week before the tournament so contestants who came early could continue to prepare. Chris took advantage of that opportunity to get in some extra training, and both CJ and Lance came up two days before the tournament to encourage him and help with his final preparations.

Since five states were competing, each division would have five people competing. They set up the tournament so that, in the first round, each competitor would face each of the other four in their division. The top two would then fight for the championship. This tournament had only one ring, so each division had to wait its turn. All the divisions would complete their first round before the second would begin. This gave the finalists time to rest before the championship round.

On the day of the tournament, the arena pulsed with energy and excitement. The day kicked off at 9:00 AM with an opening ceremony, then the matches began to unfold in the order printed on the program.

When the time for Chris' division came up, he got into a groove very quickly. He dispatched his first two opponents without any problem at all. However, his third opponent defeated him three points to one. After that one stinging defeat, Chris took out his last opponent and ended the first round with one loss. That was good enough to get him into the finals, but his opponent would be Damon, the one who defeated him in the first round. Damon made it through without any defeats.

After his round, Chris went into the stands and sat with Lance and CJ to await his turn in the final round. As they talked, Chris wanted to pick their brains to see if they noticed anything that would be helpful as he took Damon on in the finals.

CJ leaned over and whispered to Chris so that only he and Lance would be able to hear. Lance leaned in as well so they could both consult with him. "Actually, we did see somethin'. Lance and I were just talkin' about it."

"I'm glad to hear that," Chris responded. "That guy was really confusing and difficult to figure out. It was like his kicks came outta nowhere.

"Well, here's what we noticed," CJ continued. "Two of the times he tagged you, he tapped your leg with his right foot, then faked comin' up with a roundhouse. But in mid kick, he shifted his body and came up the other side with a reverse. When he did it, you were already leaning in to block the roundhouse and were just enough off balance for him to slide his foot through and tag you in the side. In watchin' him fight his other opponents, he was foolin' everyone with that same move. He's really good at it."

"Okay, hearin' you describe it, I see exactly what you're sayin'," Chris replied rather hesitantly. "He really did have me thinkin' he was coming up the one way, but then came up the other. The only problem is, he actually could've thrown the roundhouse if he'd wanted to. And if I'd shifted to block his reverse, he prob'ly would've thrown it and tagged me with that one. What do you guys see as a way to handle that?"

Lance then offered a thought. "What you need to do is put him in a position where he can't throw any of 'em. While you weren't able to easily detect which way he wanted to go, you did notice *when* he was about to kick. So when he gives you that first tap on the leg, immediately step forward inside his kick. Then, at the same time, throw a straight double punch to his chin. He won't have anywhere to go with his kick, and with both your arms stretched out, he won't be able to get anything inside your punch to counter. He thinks he owns you with that move, so he's bound to try it at least twice. You should be able to get at least two points from that alone. And you were able to tag him when he tried other things, so I think you can easily get one other point."

"Yeah, I see what you're sayin'. I think that might actually work. Thanks for those insights. Hopefully that'll do the trick."

Chris continued to sit with CJ and Lance until it was time for him to make his way back to the ring. When that time arrived, he went back down to the arena floor and stepped into the "on deck" area to wait his turn. As he waited, an official came over and placed the red armband on his arm.

When he was called, Chris once again walked into the ring to take his place. Facing him was Damon, and the referee stepped in from the side. When the ref stepped in, both he and Damon turned to bow, then once again faced each other and bowed. As was usual, the referee stepped between them and give his final instructions, then stepped back, stuck out his right arm, and yelled, "Hajime!"

With that, the two fighters moved in and started circling the ring looking for an opening. Both threw a couple of feints, then, right on cue, Damon threw out his right leg and tapped low on Chris' left leg. Then, just as he was cocking his leg as if to throw a roundhouse, Chris stepped inside and threw a double punch to his chin. Damon had no idea what had just happened. "Point, red!" the referee yelled out.

As the two fighters moved back to their starting positions, Damon was shaking his head and cursing under his breath. When they were ready, the referee once again reached out his arm and shouted, "Hajime!"

Just as before Chris and Damon began circling the ring. Damon was sure the last point was a fluke. He had crushed Chris with that move before and absolutely knew he could do it again. So as soon as he was in a position to try it, he once again tapped Chris' leg with his foot ... and once again, before he could get the roundhouse up, Chris stepped inside and threw the same double punch. "Point, red!" the ref shouted again.

At that point, Damon was totally flustered. That move had worked so well for him for so long. It was the one that got him to the regional tournament in the first place. Now, however, it wasn't working, and he began to doubt himself and didn't know what to do.

As the two faced each other again, Chris could sense Damon's hesitancy. It was at this point that all his training with Sensei Lance and CJ would pay off. They were always pushing him to go faster. This was the time to do that.

When the referee started the round, Chris flew in like a bullet and threw a front kick right in Damon's chest. He was expecting Chris to circle like he had done every time before and was caught totally flatfooted. "Point, red. Match!" the referee shouted as he lifted his hand high toward Chris indicating he had taken the match. Chris had won again.

After the medal ceremony, the winners were instructed to go over to the press area and do interviews. Just as Chris was finishing up, one of the reporters walked up holding a phone to his ear. "Congratulations, Chris," he said with a smile. "Great job." Then, without pausing, he said, "Don't leave yet. "You have one more interview. Connie Baker's on a Zoom call for you.

Chris smiled, took the phone and said, "Well hello Connie. Why am I not surprised?"

They both chuckled and Connie explained. "The guy that just gave you the phone's a reporter friend of mine who lives in St. Louis. I worked this out with him last week. I knew you'd win."

"Well, Connie, I appreciate the confidence. It was a tough tournament, and I didn't come through this one unscathed like the last one. But ultimately, I did pull it off. It was a very satisfying win." Chris then took the next 20 minutes to answer Connie's questions so she could write her article for the next day's paper.

After the interview, Chris went back to the hotel and cleaned up, then the three guys went out to eat. It was a great celebration. The next morning, Chris drove back to Skeptopolis.

CHAPTER 44

HAIL TO THE CHAMP

When Chris got back home, a copy of the *Skeptopolis Times* was waiting for him.

𝖲keptopolis 𝕿imes

July 7   *Always There for You*   SkeptopolisTimes.com

Chris Bel Wins Regionals

By Connie Granger

By now, no one will find it surprising that Chris Bel has won the regional karate tournament in St. Louis and will be heading to nationals. After completely destroying the field at the state tournament, it became obvious he is a top-flight talent. He has proven it again in the regional tournament.

Each regional tournament hosts the five state winners, so Chris faced up with four other state tournament winners. The regional tournament has fewer competitors, so the format was slightly different. In this one, the state champions in each division faced all the people in their division. The top two then moved on to the final round.

Chris came in second in the first round with one loss, but he scored high enough to qualify for the championship round. In the championship round, he faced the only opponent who had defeated him in the first round. That opponent was undefeated.

In the championship fight, Chris showed the form we saw at state. He won that match 3-0.

I had the opportunity to talk to Chris on a Zoom call after the tournament. Here is that interview.

Chris, first, congratulations on another extraordinary win.

Thank you, Connie. I can tell you; the competition was definitely a level up from state. I feel very fortunate to have come out on top.

So, what were you thinking when you lost a match in the first round?

Actually, that was quite nerve wracking. I knew I couldn't lose a second one or it'd be all over for me. I had to really focus and draw on all the training I've done, and the lessons I've learned, in order to pull it off. And those other opponents, all of 'em, were very good.

When you got into the championship round, you had to face the person who had defeated you in the first round. What did you do to prepare yourself for that?

Well, first let me say that my opponent was probably the best fighter I've ever faced. He was lightning fast, and he had one particular technique that was completely foolin' me. He beat me 3-1 in that first round, and two of his points were off that single technique. He was usin' it to defeat the other people in our division, as well.

But at that point I was very fortunate. I actually had a secret weapon with me. CJ, the dojo owner in Skeptopolis, and Sensei Lance, my instructor from Templeton, both came to support me and were watchin' what was goin' on. They spotted a weakness in his technique they were able to point out to me. We strategized about how to defeat it, and it worked. When he tried it on me in the finals, I was totally prepared and quickly got up on him two-zip. With that, I think I had him disheartened a little and pounced for the third point.

So, Chris, what do you plan to do now? I assume you'll begin to prepare for the national tournament.

Absolutely! That tournament'll be in Washington, DC in about three months. I'm very excited about the opportunity.

And will you now return to Templeton to train for that?

Oh no. Skeptopolis is now my second home, and I definitely plan to continue there. CJ's been a fantastic host– givin' me not only a place to train, but also helpin' me train. I couldn't ask for a better situation in that regard.

Besides, I've made so many friends and have been welcomed by so many people in Skeptopolis, I'm just not ready to give that up.

You do realize though, don't you, that not everyone in Skeptopolis is excited about you being around?

I definitely wish that weren't so. You know, when I first came, I told you I wanted to be a bridge between the people of Templeton and Skeptopolis to better our relations. I still have that vision and hope it'll one day become a reality. I really have come to love Skeptopolis.

One Last Observation

When Chris went to the regional tournament, he went as the representative of our state. That means he was our representative – and he represented us well. Regardless of what anyone thinks of his religion or the work he is doing among the gangs, we can all be proud of the fact that he is our champion. Congratulations Chris!

CHAPTER 45

NEW OBSTACLES

Soon after Levi arrived in Skeptopolis, he began looking for a location to start a new church. Gino and the other former gang members were to be the core of this new effort. The entire process had begun so quickly, that initially, Chris' and Levi's church in Templeton was not able to commit to funding the start-up. The approval had to go through the church's committee process, then be approved by the church as a whole. A wealthy church member, though, had told Levi to go ahead and move forward, and that if the church decided not to approve, he would fund it himself for a year.

As it turned out, that did not become necessary. When Chris' and Levi's church found out about the opportunity, and about what was happening through Chris' influence and Levi's efforts, they enthusiastically got behind it. All that was needed now was to find an appropriate location.

With Levi ready to begin that process, Chris decided to call Denise Norton, the realtor he had met at the Chamber meeting. She had been keeping up with Chris' exploits in the newspaper and was intrigued by all he'd been doing. She had even gone to watch Chris at the roundtable held at the college, along with a few others from the business community.

"Denise, this is Chris Bel. How you doin' today?" Chris asked as he got her on the phone.

"Chris," Denise replied, "how delightful to hear from you. I want you to know it was a great pleasure to meet you at the Chamber meeting, and I've been followin' your exploits as much as I possibly can in the paper. To what do I owe the honor of this call?"

"Well," Chris replied, "we've actually pulled together a group of people who are interested in starting a church and we need to come up with a meeting location. I thought having a realtor who knows the lay of the land would be a prudent thing, and I thought of you. Might you be able to help us locate somethin'? Our thought is that, in the beginning, we'd lease a storefront location. Hopefully it'll eventually grow enough to where we need to find a larger place, but we havta start somewhere. Do you think you could help us out?"

"Chris, I'd be honored. Gimme a little more detail about what you're lookin' for, and I'll come up with some possibilities for you." With that, Chris laid out the approximate size needs, along with the budget they had to work with.

A couple of days later, Denise called Chris back with a list of six different locations that fit the specs he had given her. She then drove Chris and Levi around to all six and helped them evaluate the suitability of each one. As it turned out, any of them would've worked, but they prioritized the locations based on what seemed to be the best value for the money.

When Denise approached the owner of the property at the top of the list, she was excited to receive a proposal. Her location had been sitting vacant for over a year already, and she was thrilled at the prospect of the land supporting itself again with a tenant. Denise and the owner went through the entire process of getting the paperwork prepared, and everything seemed to be right on track. That didn't take long because the owner already had a contract ready that only needed names, dates, and signatures

But then, just a day before signing the contract, the owner called Denise and backed out of the deal. She said there was someone else who wanted to look at it who was willing to pay considerably more than the church.

Obviously, Chris and Levi were disappointed with the setback, but there wasn't much they could do. So, Denise moved on to contact the owner of the second property on the list. He, too, was excited at the prospect of getting a new tenant. This property had been vacant for about a year and a half. So again, they went through the process of drawing up all the paperwork and set a day for signing the papers. However, once again, the day before the signing, this owner also contacted Denise and said he was pulling the property off the market. Strangely, he would not give her a reason.

This was even more frustrating, but again there was nothing to do but move on to the third property. They reasoned that God must be working to guide them to something better. The third property was a little older, so would need a little more work to get it in shape. But it was also a little larger, and the price was very good. So once again, they made all the necessary preparations. But just like before, the day before signing the contract, the owner contacted Denise and told her they could not rent the property.

Having the same problem occur once, or even twice, could be just bad luck. But having the exact same thing happen three times in a row could not be a mere coincidence. At that point, Denise went to meet the owner in person and explained to him what had been happening. She then asked him point blank, "What's goin' on?"

This owner was, himself, quite ticked off at the situation and was even willing to give her an honest answer. He confessed that representatives of the mayor's office had contacted him and told him that if he rented to a church, there would be "unspecified repercussions" to his business. He also mentioned he had heard scuttlebutt from people in the mayor's office that this was a directive directly from the mayor herself, and that anyone who tried to do business with the church would get the same threat. At this point, the church, and any property owner who wanted to do business with them, was in a no-win situation.

CHAPTER 46

THE WORKAROUND

Denise found the heavy-handed government interference in the affairs of private businesses downright disgusting and tried to figure out a way to get around it. But not having any ideas, she called Chris the next morning to talk the situation over. "Chris, at this point I'm out of ideas. I can't imagine what's going on is legal, but I'm not sure what to do about it. How'd you like to proceed?"

"Denise, I'm not sure what to do at this point. This matter's completely beyond my area of expertise. But I know some people who might have some ideas. Let me get in touch with 'em and I'll get back to you when I have somethin.'"

When Chris hung up with Denise, he went into the living room to talk it over with Levi. "Well, Denise is pretty much outta options at this point. I think we're gonna have to consult with some people who know this kinda stuff and see what we can come up with. Who do you think we should talk to?"

Levi thought for a second then proposed an idea. "I think the first person we should call is Pastor Trumann and get him to talk with Jim Scott, his elder chairman. What do you think?"

"Yeah, that's a great idea. I'm sure they'll at least be able to point us in the right direction."

So, Levi called Pastor Trumann, explained the situation, and asked him if he, along with Jim Scott, could participate in a conference call that evening at 7:00 pm. Pastor Trumann agreed that was a good first move and scheduled the meeting.

So, at 7:00, Pastor Trumann called Levi's phone. Levi put it on speaker so he and Chris could be on the call together. Pastor Trumann had Jim with him in his office, and they had theirs on speaker, as well.

Levi chimed in first, "Great to speak to you guys. I really miss seein' you every week at church."

"The feelin's mutual here," Pastor Trumann responded. "But you can't imagine how excited people are about what you guys are doin'. And I have Jim here on the phone with me."

"Hello, gentlemen," Jim chimed in. "Pastor Trumann's absolutely right. There's tremendous enthusiasm here for the work you guys are doin'. So, what seems to be the problem?"

"Well," Levi began to explain, "it seems we have some opposition to us starting a new church. We found several adequate properties to rent, and actually started goin' through the process of getting' three different ones under contract. Then, for all three of 'em, right at the last minute, the owners pulled 'em. After the last one, we were able to find out that those property owners were getting' threats from the mayor's office to not rent to us. So now we're at a roadblock and wanted to consult with you guys about how you think we outta proceed from here."

Jim was a very accomplished businessman and had seen it all in his days of running his own large manufacturing company. He had plenty of experience dealing with political shenanigans and immediately knew what to do. "Okay, guys, looks like those people wanna play hard ball. Well, we can do that, too. Pastor Trumann, with your permission, I'm gonna suggest a plan of action for the next step."

"Jim, this is your area of expertise," Pastor Trumann replied. "I feel very confident that you'll know exactly what to do."

With permission granted, Jim proposed a solution. "Gentlemen, here's what we're gonna do. Levi, go back to your realtor and tell her to come up with some properties you can buy. The church has already voted to support you, and we can use that money to take care of the day-to-day operations of your new church. What I'm gonna do is take the money I was gonna to use to support the church start, if it had been necessary, and buy the property. Then I'm gonna donate it to your church. You find the right place, get back with me, and I'll take care of gettin' it bought. They might can get away with refusin' to rent to you, but it'd be discrimination for 'em to not be willin' to sell. They'd get in trouble with the law."

"Are you sure, Jim?" Levi responded in amazement. "That's an amazing offer."

"Oh, I'm sure alright," Jim replied. "This is all God's money anyhow, and I count it a great privilege to be a part of what He's doin' through you guys. Gimme a call when you get somethin' and I'll make it happen."

After some small talk and a report of happenings in Skeptopolis, they all hung up the phone. Chris and Levi were totally amazed at how God was working. No doubt, anything they could buy would end up being way better than whatever they would've leased.

The next day, Chris and Levi got in touch with Denise and told her the new plan. She was very excited for the opportunity and got busy locating properties that would be appropriate for what was needed.

CHAPTER 47

JUST THE RIGHT SPOT

It didn't take Denise long to find something since they had already been consulting about the kind of place that was needed. However, since this was going to be a more permanent situation, they began exploring properties with potential for growth and expansion.

It only took Denise a day to locate several possibilities. Then, when she pulled that information together, she began touring Chris and Levi around to each one to assess their potential.

After looking at 10 properties, over a four-day period, Chris and Levi decided on one that would be ideal. It was formerly a warehouse used for manufacturing. It would require some clean-up and build-out, but not only was it in a great location, it would be large enough for future growth, as well. And even better, it sat on twenty acres of land that would allow for even more expansion if God really began doing a work there.

From here on out, since Levi would be the church pastor, Chris told him to take the lead in dealing with Denise and Jim. So, after deciding on the property, Levi called Jim back and told him all about it. Then, after doing his own due diligence, Jim got back with Levi and agreed it was a perfect fit. "Levi," Jim said approvingly, "you've done a masterful job at finding this. If you weren't called to do what you do, I'd want you to work for me. Give me a couple of weeks and we should be able to get this done. It should go quickly because I'll pay cash for it."

CHAPTER 48

DONE DEAL

Another obvious miracle to celebrate: the financial transaction and all the paperwork went through in record time, and they had the deed for the property in hand. The only thing left now would be renovating the building for use as a church. A few places in the new building were already usable for meetings, and the building became available none too soon.

The Bible study that had begun in the five-room cottage was bursting at the seams, as new people were coming every week. Some were friends of people who came to previous meetings and were just curious. Some were parents of a few high school students at the dojo who wanted to see what their kids were getting into. Then several college students – mostly from Steve's class – had become intrigued with Chris and wanted to learn more. But the largest number by far, were more gang members coming to Christ because of Gino's efforts.

Within two weeks of purchasing the building, they moved the Bible study meeting to the new church. At that point they were averaging about 50 people per week.

The usable space they had now would work for a Bible study, but not much more. They would need to get moving on the build out to actually use it as a church.

"Butch, this is Chris Bel." Since Chris already had a relationship with Butch Grissom, and he also had the reputation for being the best contractor in town, it seemed like a no-brainer to hire him to do the build out on the church. Chris had hoped something could get going rather quickly, though he felt iffy about that possibility because of how busy Butch had been with several other building projects.

"Chris, how great to hear from you. I hope the sponsorship's worked out good. I know the publicity I've gotten from it's already landed me a couple of new clients. And the fact that you took regionals and are now headed to the national championship round has put you in the spotlight even more. I think I made a good investment in you."

"Well thanks, Butch," Chris responded with a chuckle in his voice at the idea that he was somehow an investment. "It was really helpful for me, too. I used the funds to pay my expenses for the regional trip."

Chris then transitioned to what he wanted to talk about. "I actually have a business matter I wanted to talk to you about today. Ya got a second?"

"For you? Absolutely! What's happenin'?"

"Well, I need a contractor," Chris shared as he began to tell Butch what was going on. "We have a situation where we have a building that needs to be renovated for a specific purpose. But we can't really do a whole lot with it until at least part of the work gets done. I wanted to ask if you'd take the job."

"Well, I am certainly not one to turn down work, Chris," Butch replied as he took in what Chris was saying, "but I don't know how soon we could get to it. We're pretty slammed right now."

"I was afraid of that," Chris groaned as he tried not to let Butch hear too much disappointment in his voice. "You see, we have a situation. We were gonna rent a storefront to use to start a new church for the former gang members who are gettin' their lives straightened out. But we ran into a roadblock.

"As it turns out, the mayor's office started threatenin' those we planned to lease from, and three different locations backed out at the last minute because of the threats. So, we decided to go in a different direction and actually buy some property. You know that empty warehouse over near the river? We've bought that. We can already use sections of it, but it needs some work for us to turn it into a fully usable facility. All the work doesn't have to be done at once, we just need to build it out enough to start usin' it as soon as we can."

When he heard Chris' explanation, Butch got hopping mad. "That mayor! Those folks at city hall are always pullin' stunts like that. It really ticks me off! They can be so dadgum dishonest and spiteful. Chris, here's what I'm gonna do. I'll take the job, and if, like you said, we can do it in stages, I'll help you get the initial part done immediately so you can at least start meetin' there. Are you over there now? I can be there in about 30 minutes, and we can talk about what's needed and get the ball rollin'."

"Oh wow! I'm not there right now, but I can meet you in 30 minutes. I'll see you in just a few."

When Chris got off the phone, he yelled out, "Levi! Let's go! We have to get over to the church building to meet the contractor."

"What?" Levi called back. "What's happenin'?"

"I'll tell you on the way. Butch Grissom, the contractor I was tellin' you about, is gonna meet us there in 30 minutes."

As Chris and Levi drove over to the new church, Chris explained what was going on and how Butch was going to help them get the project underway.

"Wow!" Levi let out a shout of joy. "You realize, don't you, that God just performed another miracle for us? The more I see, the more clearly I realize God's at work in this place. I know as we keep movin' forward, not everything's gonna be easy, but when He wants to make somethin' happen, he eliminates all the obstacles. This is exciting!"

Chris and Levi got to the church five minutes before Butch, so they got out of the car and stood by the front door while they waited. When Butch arrived, he got out of his truck, walked over to where they were standing, and they all shook hands. "Butch, this is my friend, Levi Berger. He's the one who'll actually become the pastor of this church, so he's the one you'll mostly be dealin' with as you determine all that needs to happen."

"Levi, it's great to meet you," Butch said enthusiastically. "Any friend of Chris is a friend of mine."

Levi laughed, "You know, if I've heard that once, I've heard it a hundred times. I've known Chris since childhood, and he never seemed that special to me."

All three of them laughed out loud at that comment. "Well, I don't know about that," Butch retorted, "but somehow he's made a pretty good impression around here.

Butch then got down to business. "So, you guys actually bought this place, huh?" Butch inquired as he looked it over. "You probably don't realize it, but my company built it. We actually have the plans for it on file, so making any renovations should be pretty easy. So how in the world did you guys get the money to buy this place?"

For the next 15 minutes, Chris went through the entire story that led up to purchasing the warehouse, how they had already begun using it for the Bible study, and what they wanted to do with the renovation. When he finished telling the back story, Chris asked, "So what do you think? What can you do for us?"

"That's one of the most amazing stories I've ever heard. So your friend just up and bought it and gave it to you? And your church in Templeton's payin' for the renovation? Incredible!

"Okay, here's what we can do. I can send a crew over here beginnin' tomorrow, and in two weeks we can put up walls in the dimensions you've described so you can have the areas you need to do your thing for an auditorium and some classrooms. You said the warehouse office space'll work for you as is for now for an office area, so we don't need to do anything special with that immediately. It won't be finished out, of course. We'll have to work on a timeline for that. But I think we can have you in the buildin' in two weeks – three at most if we hit a snag."

"Butch, that would be amazing!" Chris gushed. "Let's do it."

"Alright. Can one of you come over to our office this afternoon at four to sign all the papers to get this ball rollin'?" Butch asked.

"Four o'clock it is," Levi responded as he reached out again to shake Butch's hand. "Look forward to seein' you then."

CHAPTER 49

SYBIL

The Bible study continued to meet weekly at the church location while the initial renovation on the building kept moving forward. With more space to meet, Chris and Levi's excitement grew as they saw how the group continued to bring in new people from the community. They now had up to 70 or more people attending each week. In addition, they also had new people coming every week, many who prayed to accept Christ. And those who came began telling their friends – not only about the new group – but they were getting better and better at actually sharing their faith, as well.

During the renovation, Chris also took the opportunity to invite both Butch and Denise to the Bible study. Butch thanked him and pretty much brushed it off saying he really didn't have time at the moment to do something like that. But Denise expressed some interest. She wasn't ready, yet, to actually start attending, but told Chris to keep in touch, and at some point, she might.

In the meantime, Sybil continued attending – but without Colleen, of course. The whole time, though, she experienced a deep and increasing inner struggle. She felt *almost* compelled to listen to Levi's teaching, but at the same time couldn't seem to break free from what she'd been taught at the Universalist Church. As she heard the message of the gospel over and over again and listened to the testimonies of new people giving their lives to Christ, she knew – in her heart of hearts –it was true. But what about her friends at the other church? What would they think? Would she be betraying them if she changed churches? It was almost more than she could bear.

During the last week, before the church was about to open, she couldn't hold it in any longer. So, at their Wednesday meeting, she went over to Chris and asked if they could talk. "Chris, I'm really agonizing right now. The message of Christ you guys keep sharing seems so real and right, but I don't know what to do. If I accept it in my heart, I'm afraid of what that might mean with my friends and the people at my church. I don't know what to do."

Chris looked at Sybil and his eyes began to tear up seeing the spiritual struggle she was experiencing. "Sybil, there are a couple of things you need to think about. First, do you believe the gospel is the truth? If you do and refuse to follow it, what are you doin'? You're rejecting the truth for a lie. But also, are the friends you're concerned about really friends? If they are, they care about you more than about what decision you make about Christ. True friends won't abandon you no matter what. Any who do are not really friends, are they?"

Sybil thought about that for a moment, not saying anything, then replied, "Chris, you're right. And I do believe. I want to invite Christ into my life."

At that moment, Chris led her to make her decision for Christ. When she had finished praying to ask Christ into her life, Chris called out to the group, "Everyone, Sybil just accepted Christ."

There was a moment of stunned silence, then the room erupted with clapping and cheering that lasted a full 45 seconds. Then Chris quieted them down and allowed Sybil to share her journey to Christ. When she finished, there was not a dry eye in the place.

In the meantime, the renovation work on the church got underway. With Butch eagerly on board, they completed stage one in two weeks – no snags – just as he had promised. And while they'd been working, Levi ordered the tables, chairs, equipment and other things to turn the warehouse into a proper church building. As things hummed along, they planned to have their first church service in the building on August 29. Everything was ready to go.

However, the mayor's office inevitably got wind of the progress and, on the day before opening, a courier brought a notice from city hall to cease and desist. The notice read:

THIS PROPERTY IS NOT ZONED FOR USE AS A CHURCH.
YOU MUST CEASE WORSHIPING AT THIS LOCATION
IMMEDIATELY UNDER PENALTY OF LAW.

CHAPTER 50

A MEETING WITH THE MAYOR

The sign on the door read: Jill Gadsden, Mayor.

As Chris sat in the waiting room of the mayor's office, he watched as several people went into the office before him – one at a time. His appointment to meet her was scheduled for 8:30 a.m. His name was finally called about two and a half hours later. He definitely didn't appreciate the way he was being treated, but he really did need to talk to her and felt he couldn't leave before he did.

Chris was determined to make as good an impression as possible. No one could deny the obvious … that political shenanigans had something to do with the "Cease and Desist" order, and he wanted to get to the bottom of it. Back when he had won the state karate tournament, Jill eagerly maneuvered to get a photo op with him – and later there was that awkward incident in his hotel room. Then, of course, she showed up at the roundtable playing nice. He hoped that at least some "good will" might result from those incidents that would carry over to this meeting.

Alas, he was about to be very disappointed. Her vitriol had been slowly reaching a boiling point and had built up enough steam to now explode in his face. But she wanted to do it in a way that would cut him as deeply as possible.

As he walked through the door into the mayor's office, Jill got up from behind her desk, smiled broadly, then walked over to where he was to give him a big hug. As she approached, she gave him a flirty sideways glance and said, "Chris, how wonderful to see you again. She then pointed to a chair at a small table in the corner and said, "Please have a seat." As he took his seat, she sat down across the table from him. "I'm truly sorry we're runnin' so behind on our appointments this mornin'," she said apologetically. "Things have been a bit crazy today. I hope you didn't have to wait too long."

"I completely understand, Jill," Chris responded. "I know you have so many responsibilities and are always really busy."

"So, to what do I owe this pleasure today? What can I do for you?" Jill inquired … as if she didn't already know.

"Well, first I want to thank you for takin' the time to see me. The reason I dropped by is that we seem to be havin' a bit of difficulty getting the new church going. I'm sure you're aware that we've been making attempts to do that, but we keep runnin' into roadblocks from city staff. I was hopin' you might be able to help remove some of those."

As soon as those words left his mouth, her demeanor shifted so dramatically that Chris was completely taken aback. Her smile turned to a scowl and her eyes morphed into a cutting glare. "Ohhh," she seemed to almost hiss, "I didn't realize you had anything to do with that," Jill lied, trying to make the cut a little deeper. "However, the city government feels that this is NOT a project that's good for Skeptopolis."

"So, what's the problem with it?" Chris inquired, "There are other churches in town, and they seem to have favor here."

"Those churches have been around for a long time and are part of the local establishment," she said with some venom. "Besides, we believe there's already more than enough churches here. We just don't need any more."

"Actually, there are only five churches in this city of over 100,000 people," Chris replied. "The city could actually use a lot more."

"Chris, you're barkin' up the wrong tree here. This is Skeptopolis! We don't want the influence of Christians polluting the atmosphere of our town. As you well know, I've been keepin' up with your exploits, and you've managed to create enough of a stir as it is. As one person, you can only cause so much damage. But what you're doin's gonna spread your poison even further. We simply don't want your kinda belief gettin' too much of a foothold here. That's not a threat, of course, but you really should leave well enough alone."

"I'm not sure I understand the issue here, Jill," Chris rebutted. "This is not a matter of politics, so why would you have such an objection to us beginning somethin' that'll be a fundamental help to the community. Please explain why you have such a fierce objection to this."

"Look Chris," Jill replied argumentatively, "We all know that the beliefs your church espouses are not compatible with the values of this community. We hold very liberal values here, and we simply don't want your poisonous hate speech to be part of our community discourse."

At this, Chris was genuinely shocked and replied with total disbelief, "What in the world are you talkin' about, Jill? We genuinely do care about people and have a long track record of helping those who are down and out. Can you give me somethin' concrete to help me understand your objection?"

"Well," Jill replied in a voice dripping with sarcasm, "Let's begin with your views on abortion. I know for a fact you're against a woman's right to choose. Then we can move on to your homophobia. You guys are anti-gay to the core. Beyond that, your negative views concerning transgender rights are right outta the dark ages. And we could go on listing things like your racist views about people of color, your anti-immigrant stance, your pro-gun views, your climate change denial, your opposition to universal health care .... Do you get the idea, or should I go on?"

"Jill, seriously?" Chris countered. "To begin with, you've totally mischaracterized our point of view on virtually everything you listed. If you wanna have a conversation on each of those issues, we can do that. But at the very least your accusations are misguided. Beyond that, you've conflated political issues with faith issues in a way that does not represent reality. Our faith compels us to help all people."

"Let me see if I can be a little more specific, then, Chris," Jill retorted. "When it comes to the matters I listed, EVERYTHING is political. There is no distinction between politics and religion. Even if your religious beliefs don't deal directly with these issues, the values of your faith intersect with 'em in a way that opposes our town's liberal values. If we let you operate here, you'll be promoting values we totally object to, and we're not gonna let that happen. We don't want more of your kind here. There, is that clear enough?"

Chris paused a moment to take in more fully this ridiculous scenario, then replied with a tone of deep disappointment in his voice, "Jill, in spite of our different views, I thought we were at least friendly. I truly am deeply disappointed that you've made these personal attacks on me this way."

Hearing Chris say that brought Jill a deep sense of satisfaction. That's exactly what she was hoping for – to dig deep enough to make him feel some pain – like she felt he'd done to her.

Chris continued, "You've definitely made your position clear. I do find your level of intolerance for other points of view to be very sad, but I absolutely do understand your position."

That comment really ticked Jill off. "We're not the ones that are intolerant!" Jill shouted back. "That would be you!"

Chris just ignored that last outburst and went on, "And Jill, I sincerely do want you to know that I came to Skeptopolis for the purpose of making a positive contribution to this community – and I think I've already done that in some very meaningful ways. And in spite of the fact that you're tryin' to push me away, I plan to continue doin' that. In the process, I'd genuinely like to be your friend. I'm not sure at this point that you're gonna allow that to happen, but I want you to know that I'm always open to you in that respect."

Not seeing anything further to be gained, Chris stood up to prepare to leave. Jill looked up and stared coldly into his eyes, "Oh, don't leave just yet. There's some people who'd like to speak to you."

CHAPTER 51

THE CITY FATHERS

Chris didn't realize it, but while he was sitting outside Jill's office waiting to speak to her, she was well aware of the fact he was there and had used the time to hatch a larger plan.

In her effort to really "put the fear of God in him," she arranged for the city fathers who supported her to come in and pile on after she delivered the initial bad news. "Chris, I was deadly serious when I told you to LEAVE WELL ENOUGH ALONE. There's a whole lot of very powerful people in town who are allied against you in this. You can't win."

Right then, Jill's office door opened and in walked Warren Hamilton and Julia Cromwell. These were probably the two richest people in town, and basically ran Skeptopolis behind the scenes. "Chris, I'd like you to meet Warren Hamilton and Julia Cromwell. Their ancestors were primarily responsible for founding Skeptopolis, and, pretty much, their word is law in this town."

As per Jill's plan, Chris was quite stunned to be ambushed like this. He turned around to face the two, and as they walked up to where he was, he reached out to shake hands. "Mr. Hamilton, it's a pleasure to meet you," Chris said as he shook his hand.

"Please call me Warren. And may I call you Chris?"

"Of course. Please do," Chris replied.

Chris then turned to Julia, "Ms. Cromwell, it's a pleasure to meet you, as well."

Julia basically ignored Chris' overture as she brushed past him and said gruffly, "Chris, please have a seat. We'd like to have a word with you."

At that, the four sat down around the table and Warren began. Being the more diplomatic of the two, they decided he should be the one to do the talking. He took a deep breath and began in his slow southern drawl, "Chris, first let me tell you that I've been admirin' your karate performances. I took karate many years ago when I was a kid but didn't stick with it. Kinda wish I had now, watching you work."

"Well, thank you, Warren, for the kind complement. I hope I represented Skeptopolis well at regionals, as well."

"Indeed. From the description in the paper, I wish I could've seen it in person. But, of course, that's not why we're here. We wanna talk to you about what you're doin' here in Skeptopolis."

"Well, I gathered that," Chris replied. "What can I clear up for you?"

"Chris, it's come to our attention that you're tryin' to start a church here in our fair city, and frankly we'd rather you not do that. It, shall we say, doesn't put off a good vibe for us. Do you get my drift?"

"Warren," Chris replied, "I appreciate the fact that you're tryin' to be diplomatic, but no, I really don't get your drift – other than understanding that you don't have much use for Christians. You really don't have to pussyfoot around me. I'm a big boy. What exactly are you tryin' to say?"

Warren smiled and nodded his head. "Direct and to the point. I like that. Okay Chris, this is how it goes. You will not put a church in this town. We have our ways and will make it, shall we say, very uncomfortable for you and your friends if you don't just back off and return to your little religious enclave in Templeton. If you don't, you'll find the weight of the entire town bureaucracy comin' down on your head."

Chris heard him out, then asked, "Warren, I'm havin' a difficult time understanding why it is that what we're doing is such a problem for you. You know how this all got goin', right? About the former gang members who've left gang life to become productive members of society? I'd think you'd consider that to be a positive thing for Skeptopolis."

"Of course that's a positive thing," Warren replied, continuing with his diplomatic initiative. "But you don't havta start a church for that to happen. Besides, as I understand it, the Universalist Church is takin' care of that."

"Well, they're certainly helpin' with a lot of the logistics, but they aren't the catalyst for the change taking place in these people's lives. Their very souls have been touched by Jesus Christ, and he's changed their entire motivation for living. What is it about that you don't like?"

"Like I said, it's not that we aren't glad that some of the 'shadier' folks in our town are findin' help. It's just that we don't believe it requires more religion."

"Warren, what I hear you sayin' is you don't like the religious competition – that you want your atheistic religion to be the exclusive faith system in Skeptopolis."

That comment caught Warren totally off guard. "What? I'm an Atheist. I don't have a religion."

"Of course you do," Chris responded going on the offensive. "Your atheistic faith is just as much a religious point of view as my Christian faith."

"That's preposterous," Warren replied with his voice rising. "I'm anything but religious."

"I think your problem in understanding, Warren, has to do with your definition of religion. If you're like so many other Atheists I've met, you think of religion as some kinda system that involves belief in some god, and meetings with rites and ceremonies. Am I right?"

"Well, what else could it be?"

Chris went on to explain, "Actually, for somethin' to be a religion, all it has to be is a faith system – and Atheism is definitely a faith system."

"That's crazy!" Warren fumed. "I don't have faith at all! Atheism is, in fact, the very opposite. It's the absence of faith!"

"Oh really? Chris countered. "So let me see if I can lay out what you believe. What you seem to be tellin' me is that you believe that the natural universe operating by natural laws is all that exists, and that ultimately, with the advance of science and technology, humanity'll be able to completely understand everything about all of reality. Does that sum it up?"

"Well," Warren nodded his head, "that's actually a pretty good definition. Your beliefs are based on faith, and my beliefs are based on science."

Chris then looked Warren in the eye. "Okay, then, where did the matter and energy that formed the natural universe come from?"

Rather shocked that Chris was putting him on the defensive, Warren replied. "Well, it came from the Big Bang."

"But that didn't answer my question. Where did the matter and energy come from that made up the Big Bang?"

"Well, Chris, science is still workin' on that one, but we're advancin' in knowledge more and more each day. We'll soon know."

"Well, here is another question for you. What is the origin of life? How did life emerge out of non-life?"

Warren squinted his eyes at Chris as if to stare a hole in him. "Science is makin' great progress on that front, as well. We know more about the nature of life now than at any time in human history – and we're very close to solving that puzzle.

"Well try this one." Chris asked a third question. "How did this world come to have the vast variety of life forms that currently exist here?"

"Everyone knows that one, Chris. It happened by naturalistic evolution."

"You say that," Chris responded, "but that really didn't answer my question. What is the biological mechanism that caused the variety of life forms that now exist on earth to come into being?"

"Why natural selection, of course," Warren replied. "Everybody knows that."

"But natural selection only works at the micro level – with creatures that are basically the same kind. There's a point beyond which natural selection quits workin'. But for naturalistic evolution to be true, it has to work in a way that causes less complex life forms to evolve to more complex forms. What science can you point me to that demonstrates that to be biologically possible?"

"Well, scientists think it happens based on mutations. But these things take tens of thousands of years. It can't be duplicated in a lab."

Chris nodded his head and moved on. "Okay, I have one more question. What's the origin of consciousness, or how did consciousness emerge out of non-consciousness?"

"Listen Chris," Warren replied beginning to show signs of exasperation, "Evolutionary scientists have made massive progress in understandin' the function of the brain. The answer to that question is, literally, right around the corner. ... But hey, you've played your little game of distraction long enough. What does this even have to do with what we're talkin' about?"

"Well," Chris responded, "You claimed that your beliefs are based on science, thus were not religious. I've laid out for you the most elemental aspects of our existence in the natural universe and asked you to share with me the science behind 'em. Do you realize that you did not give me even one bit of actual science in answer to any of the four questions? All you gave me were statements about *what you 'believe'* based on your belief in naturalistic philosophy. EVERYTHING you told me was based on your faith in that philosophy. There was not a shred of science anywhere to be found. What you've shared with me is your religious beliefs. Like I said, your atheistic beliefs are as much a religious point of view as my Christian faith. It still seems to me that what you're really against is the religious competition."

"Chris," Warren's voice thundered, "you've been warned. You either quit what you're doin' or you'll pay a price. Have I made myself clear!"

Chris calmly nodded his head and replied slowly and deliberately. "Yeah, I'd say you've made yourself abundantly clear."

Chris then turned to Jill. "Jill is there anything else you wanted?"

Jill glared, then slowly shook her head. "Well, then," Chris continued, I guess there's not really anything else to do here. Warren, Julia, it was a pleasure to make your acquaintance. Jill, it was good to see you again. I believe I can show myself out. Thank you for a very enlightening morning.

Chris stood up, then turned and headed toward the door of Jill's office. When he got outside the door and through the outer office, he walked down the stairs to leave the city hall complex, then went and got his car. Once there, he called Levi on his cell and explained how the conversation went.

CHAPTER 52

PLAN B

When Chris had finished his explanation, he said to Levi, "Well, it looks like the powers that be have made this a game of hardball, Levi. I believe it's time to move to plan B. I'll pick you up in about 10 minutes."

Chris arrived at the house to find Levi already waiting out front. He got into the car, and they drove straight to the law office of Mark Johnson. Mark was another person from the local business community whom Chris had met at the Chamber of Commerce meeting he attended with CJ. Since they had sat at the same table, Chris got to know him a bit and it turned out they had certain interests in common. He hoped Mark would be willing to help out with this situation.

Mark actually had no interest in religion at all and was not particularly interested in helping Chris accomplish his objectives of starting a new church in Skeptopolis. However, he did have political ambitions and saw Jill Gadsden as a hindrance to his goals. Because he was often at odds with her politically, and because he wanted to defeat her whenever he could, he never shied away from an opportunity to upstage her.

As the chief representative in Skeptopolis for the American Civil Liberties Union – better known as the ACLU – he often took on controversial cases. For Mark, taking these types of cases served two purposes: sometimes it gave him a platform to oppose Jill, but just as importantly, it kept him in the news.

After his meeting with Jill, Chris knew he needed a local advocate who had influence in the community. Jill's recent hardball tactics certainly came across as unethical, and even more than that, illegal – but he needed someone who would be willing to take up the case.

Chris and Levi didn't have an appointment but took a chance to see if Mark would meet with them anyway. When they arrived at his law office, they parked, then walked inside. As they stepped through the front door, Mark's receptionist, Katie, greeted them immediately and asked how she could help.

Since he had met Mark before, Chris took the lead in introducing themselves. "My name's Chris Bel and this is my friend Levi Burger. I met Mr. Johnson a few weeks ago at a Chamber of Commerce meeting. I was wonderin' if he might have a couple of minutes to talk."

"I know who you are," Katie exclaimed, quite surprised to see him there. "I've been reading all about you in the paper over the last few months. Wait here just a moment and let me check."

About 30 seconds later, Mark strode through the door with Katie tagging along behind, walked up to Chris, stuck out his hand in greeting, and they shook hands. "Chris, great to see you again. It's been a while. I've been keepin' up with you in the paper, though. Seems you've been stirrin' things up around town."

Chris smiled, "Well, that hasn't really been my intention, but I think it's turned out that way. Let me introduce you to my friend Levi Burger."

Mark shook hands with Levi and said, "Levi, great to meet you. Any friend of Chris' is a friend of mine. You guys come on into my office."

When they got inside, Mark offered them a seat around a small conference table and the three sat down. "Can I offer you anything to drink?" Mark asked.

"Thank you for your kindness, Mark, but I think we're fine," Chris responded.

"Well then gentlemen, what can I do for you?"

"Mark," Chris began, "we seem to have found ourselves strugglin' with some political and legal problems and need some assistance to deal with 'em. I wanted to see if you might be able to help."

When Chris mentioned political problems, Mark's ears perked up. "Really? What kinda political problems are you facing?" Since Chris and Levi were not permanent residents of Skeptopolis, Mark couldn't imagine what that might be about.

Chris felt he was taking a chance talking with Mark and was concerned that when he shared that his problem had to do with starting a church, Mark might balk. Having decided he had nothing to lose, he began his explanation. "Mark, we've been able to help a group of gang members get out of a gang here in Skeptopolis. It's happened through a spiritual experience for them. To continue helping 'em, we thought it'd be good to start a church to give 'em a place to grow. But we've been runnin' into some problems. First, we tried to rent a storefront, but after three different property owners offered us a contract, all three backed out at the last minute. Because of the strange nature of those events, we suspected there was somethin' nefarious goin' on, and later found that pressure'd been put on 'em by people in the mayor's office."

Hearing that, Mark's ears perked up even more. If he hadn't been interested in Chris' plight up until that point, his curiosity just took a giant leap forward.

Chris continued, "So we decided to buy a property we could use. We bought it and actually began having meetings there. But suddenly, we got a notice by special courier from the mayor's office to cease and desist. It claimed we were violating the city's zoning regulations.

"I checked to see if that was really true, and it appears to me that zoning in that location shouldn't be a problem. So, this morning I went to talk to the mayor in person. At first, she was quite warm and gracious, but when she found out I was there to ask about the church, she went ballistic. She obviously knew about the church and made it quite clear she was behind the 'cease and desist' order – and even the deals that had fallen through. She pretty much told me flat out that she, and other 'heavy hitters' in the city, didn't want 'our kind' having any kinda presence here. She even called in Warren Hamilton and Julia Cromwell to reemphasize her position. By that point I felt I was being bullied. So, we're now in a position where we either push back or walk away. We don't want to walk away. Can you help us?"

Mark hardly batted an eye. "Are you serious? She brought in Hamilton and Cromwell? Guys, you have a lawyer – and I'm gonna do this pro bono. But there is somethin' you need to know goin' into this."

Chris was a little concerned he might ask for some kind of compromise they would not be willing to make and asked, "Yeah? What's that?"

"You're prob'ly not aware of this," Mark explained, "because you guys aren't from here. But Mayor Gadsden and I are longtime political rivals. I'm willin' to help you get what you want, but my motivation's not really to help you.

No offense, but I really don't have any interest in whether you start a church or not. My interest is to do some political damage to Gadsden. Are you okay with that?"

Chris replied, "Well, that depends. Do you plan on doin' anything that'll be unethical or reflect badly on us and the church? That'd be a deal breaker."

Mark chuckled and answered. "No, nothin' like that. Everything'll be completely on the up and up in that respect. I'm just bein' up front about my own motivations. But this could be a win-win. I mean, it looks like your goals and mine intersect in a pretty significant way. I just see this as a way to embarrass the mayor and make her look like the hater she is. So how 'bout it? Shall we go forward?"

Chris and Levi looked at one another. "Levi, what do you think?" Chris asked.

"Well, as long as this stays in the arena of what's ethical and outwardly civil, I'm good with it."

"Mark," Chris affirmed, "you've got a deal."

"Well," Mark suggested "let's begin right now. I'm gonna give the mayor a quick call and ask her to cease and desist. She's not gonna do it, of course, but it'll get the ball rollin' and we'll have her hooked. To be honest, guys, she's 100 percent in the wrong, and she will lose this!"

Mark picked up the phone and dialed the mayor's office. When the mayor's secretary answered, he got straight to the point, "Hello, this is Mark Johnson. I'd like to speak to Jill if I may. This is rather urgent."

"Hold on, Mr. Johnson," the secretary replied, "let me see if she's available."

After a couple of minutes, Jill came on the line, "Hello Mark, this is Jill, what can I do for you?"

"Jill," Mark replied, "I have a little problem I need you to solve for me."

Jill was never inclined to help Mark with anything, but because of her position, and his influence in the city, she had to keep up appearances. "So Mark," she answered, "how can I help?"

"Well, I have a new client that's havin' some problems with city hall, and I need you to cut through some red tape for me. Can you do that?"

"What is it this time, Mark?" she inquired sarcastically. "Has someone complained again about gettin' a parkin' ticket?"

"No," Mark replied matter-of-factly, "nothing like that. This has to do with a zoning issue. I have a couple of young men in my office who say they're bein' harassed by city hall and are bein' told they can't have a church in a place that's clearly a legal place to do it. I'd like for you to call off the dogs."

At that, Jill went ballistic. "Mark, you can't be serious about representin' those outsiders in this case," Jill screamed into the phone. When she started yelling, Mark held the phone about arm's length from his head, and Chris and Levi could even hear it. "You know very well there's a lotta very powerful people in this town who are adamantly opposed to that. If you take their case, you're gonna make some very muscular enemies. I'm warnin' you, Mark, don't do it."

Mark started laughing. "Jill, Jill. "You know very well that the enemies you're talkin' about already hate me. Nothing'll change. But that's really not the point. What you're doin' is illegal, and you'll lose this case. Seriously, you need to call off the dogs."

"Never!" Jill yelled back. "We'll see you in court!" And with that, she slammed down the phone.

Mark smiled at Chris and Levi. "Well gentlemen, we have our hooks in her."

CHAPTER 53

IN THE NEWS

Mark knew how to play this game, and he knew he needed to draw first blood. Shortly after Chris and Levi left his office, he picked up the phone and called Connie at the *Skeptopolis Times*. He knew she had been writing about Chris and would be hugely interested in this story.

"Connie, this is Mark Johnson." Mark and Connie knew each other because of various stories she'd written in the past. She had even used him occasionally as a subject matter expert, but had also interviewed him on various cases, and chronicled many of the run-ins he had engaged with the mayor. "I have a story I think you might be interested in. Ya have a few minutes?"

"Sure," Connie responded. Knowing Mark, she was pretty sure that if he called her with that kind of intro, there was probably something worth hearing. "What's happenin'?"

"Well," Mark continued, "this has to do with your friend Chris Bel."

When she heard Chris' name, Connie's ears perked up. "You have my attention," she replied, providing Mark the opening to continue.

"Well, it seems that Chris and Mayor Gadsden are buttin' heads a bit, and the mayor's improperly using political influence against him." He paused just a moment to let that sink in and draw Connie in even more. "I believe you know how Chris has had a positive influence on certain gang members and is tryin' to help 'em leave gang life. You know about that, right?"

"Yes," Connie replied, "I do know about some of the efforts he's made in that area."

"Well, it seems that his spiritual influence on 'em is one of the primary things that's led 'em to go in their new direction," Mark continued. "So, to continue that work, Chris and his friend Levi are tryin' to start a church. They initially attempted to rent some storefront property for that effort, but after agreein' with a property owner to sign a contract, she backed out at the last minute. In fact, that happened three different times. They later found out that the mayor's office exerted influence on those property owners to not rent to 'em.

"So then they decided to buy a property. After buyin' it and getting' it ready to use, they were just about to begin having services and received notice from the mayor's office that they couldn't have a church there because of zoning regulations. This, of course, is a complete lie, but they did it anyway. Chris even went up to the mayor's office and had a face-to-face to try to resolve the problem. But guess what? She not only badgered him herself but called in some of the "town fathers" to pile on. She then basically just threw him out. I spoke to the mayor about this and asked her to reverse her objection, and she adamantly refused. It looks like this is gonna go to court, and she's gonna lose badly – costin' the taxpayers a lotta money. I just wanted to let you know this is coming."

"Wow," Connie replied rather dumbfounded. "If this is true, it's a pretty big story. I'll definitely check it out further. Of course, you know I can't just go with what you've told me without getting' the mayor's side, as well."

"Of course, Connie," Mark replied. "And I definitely believe you'll get some major spin from her. But if you're willin' to probe a little, you'll see I'm right. I'll be filin' the lawsuit within the next couple of days. You might wanna keep your eye on the court filings."

"Well Mark, I want to thank you for the exclusive tip on this one. I'll definitely get right on it."

"My pleasure, Connie," Mark responded. "We'll talk again soon, I'm sure."

As soon as she hung up, Connie dialed the mayor's office. When the receptionist answered, Connie jumped in, "Hello, this is Connie Granger with the *Times*. I'm workin' on a story with a deadline that involves the mayor and wonder if she might have a few minutes to comment. If possible, I'd like to come to her office this afternoon. Might she be available?"

"Well, can you tell me what it's about?" the receptionist replied.

Connie didn't want to give away the surprise factor, so she responded, "Only that it's a story involving the mayor and the office."

"Okay, if you'll please hold for a moment, I'll check with the mayor and see what she says."

"Absolutely," Connie answered, "glad to hold."

The receptionist put Connie on hold, went into the mayor's office, and told her what Connie had said. "Well, did she say what it was about?"

"No. I asked, but she wouldn't tell me – only that it had to do with you and the mayor's office. Would you like to see her?"

At that point, Jill was not only curious, but a little concerned, as well. She thought to herself, Why in the world would a reporter wanna meet me to get a reaction to somethin', but not be willin' to let me know in advance what it was about? If there's somethin' out there, I need to get out in front of it.

"Okay," Jill responded, "tell her I can see her at 4:30 this afternoon."

The receptionist then went back to her desk and picked up the phone. "Ms. Granger, the mayor said she could see you at 4:30 this afternoon. Will that work?"

"That'll be perfect," Connie replied. "I'll see you then."

Connie left her desk at 4:00 to be sure she was at the mayor's office in plenty of time and arrived about 15 minutes early. When she walked in, the receptionist informed the mayor and told Connie to have a seat in the waiting area, and that the mayor would be with her shortly.

At 4:30 sharp, Jill opened her door, walked over to Connie and shook her hand. "Connie, great to see you again. Please come into my office and let's chat." Once inside, Jill pointed to a chair at the small table in the corner and the two sat down.

"Now, what can I do for you, Connie?" Jill asked.

"Well, I got a call a little while ago about a lawsuit that's about to be filed against the mayor's office, and I wanted to get your side of the story before we go to print with this."

"A lawsuit?" Jill inquired. "What kinda lawsuit?"

"I just got off the phone with Mark Johnson," Connie responded, "and he claims that the mayor's office is using illegal influence to stop a church from being started in Skeptopolis. Is there any truth to that?"

Hearing Connie's explanation, Jill's face immediately turned crimson. She tried desperately to control her anger but had a difficult time covering it up.

"That sorry jerk ..." Jill caught herself before she said more. "So, he really is gonna file suit to help those people?" Jill inquired.

"That's what he told me," Connie replied. "He actually made two accusations. First, that people in your office exerted influence to prevent certain property owners from renting to Chris' group, then notified 'em that a property they had bought could not be used for a church – property that's clearly zoned in a way that allows for it to be used that way. What do you have to say?"

"Well, the first thing I have to say," Jill retorted, "is that Skeptopolis does not need any more churches. Everyone knows this is not a religious town, and we already have enough churches to accommodate those who have religious inclinations."

Connie interrupted, "Well, madam mayor, that may or may not be true, but the accusation relates to points of law, not to anyone's feelings about whether or not another church is needed."

Jill immediately jumped back in, "As far as the law, this office has done nothin' wrong. We've consulted with the city attorney, and a church cannot go in that spot according to the way we read the zoning law. We'll definitely fight this in court."

"And what about the other accusation – that you used the influence of the mayor's office to intimidate people not to rent to them?"

"I don't know anything about that," Jill responded angrily. "I think that accusation's just a ploy to try to make a case where there is none."

"Well, madam mayor," Connie asked as she prepared to wrap up the interview, "I think I've asked all of the questions I came to ask. Is there anything else you'd like to add?"

Jill couldn't help herself, "Connie, everyone knows Mark Johnson's a shameless self-promoter, and that he has his eyes on this office. I think this is just a huge publicity stunt, and he's ultimately gonna fail if he tries to push this."

"Well," Connie wrapped things up, "I wanna thank you for your time, madam mayor. I look forward to seein' how this all plays out."

The two of them stood, said their last goodbyes, and Connie left to go back to her office.

CHAPTER 54

SCANDAL

The next morning, a blockbuster headline greeted the *Times* subscribers.

————— ◆ —————

𝕾𝖐𝖊𝖕𝖙𝖔𝖕𝖔𝖑𝖎𝖘 𝕿𝖎𝖒𝖊𝖘

| August 31 | *Always There for You* | SkeptopolisTimes.com |

Potential Scandal in the Mayor's Office

By Connie Granger

After receiving a call from Skeptopolis lawyer, Mark Johnson, it was alleged that the mayor's office exerted improper influence in a zoning dispute. The story goes that a group connected with karate champion, Chris Bel, was attempting to start a new church in the city to serve a group of ex-gang members who decided to walk away from gang life (see associated story below). Johnson alleges that the mayor's office put pressure on property owners in the city not to rent property to this religious group. When the church tried to circumvent this power play and purchased a property for their church, the mayor's office sent a "cease and desist" notice, stating the property could not be used as a church because of zoning restrictions.

We contacted the mayor's office about the allegations, and they denied the accusations. Mayor Jill Gadsden specifically said she did not know about any attempts to influence property owners, and that the city attorney had looked into the zoning allegation and indeed, a church is not allowed in that location.

Mr. Johnson indicated that the lawsuit would be filed in the next few days. The mayor's office said they are ready to go to court. We will update this story as things develop.

◆

Gang Break-up

By Connie Granger

For full disclosure, following is a story this reporter has been sitting on for a while to protect those who might have been endangered had it come out sooner. The lawsuit against the city (see associated story above), however, has exposed the story so it can now be told.

Shortly after Chris Bel, the now well-known karate champion, came to Skeptopolis, he had an encounter with lead members of the Red Flag Pack – a gang headquartered on Straight Street. After a seemingly rocky start, Chris became friends with Gino Chrysler, its leader. Over time, Chris influenced Gino, with his religious teaching, to leave the gang. It seems that nine others left with him. In the process, Chris teamed up with the Universalist Church in town to help the former gang members find housing and jobs and got them in school.

In order to help these former gang members on their spiritual journey, Chris called on his friend Levi Burger, himself a pastor, who agreed to come to Skeptopolis and help with this project. Part of this help involves starting a church for the gang members and others. As of now, all of these former gang members have jobs and are in school. Two of them even recently married and are expecting a child.

Their attempt to begin a church, however, allegedly drew opposition from the mayor's office. As of now, the matter is unresolved, but all of the former Red Flag Pack members, plus a number of additional gang members who have subsequently left other gangs, are demonstrating an amazing turnaround in their lives. Chris suggested that anyone who would like to contribute to help these young people on their new journey, may contact the Universalist Church, which will be able to receive their contributions.

CHAPTER 55

COOPERATION CONTINUED

"Chris, this is Dr. Albritton at the Universalist Church. Do you have a minute?"

"Of course, Dr. Albritton, I always have time for you. How can I help?"

"I'd like to have a discussion with you if you're able," Dr. Albritton continued. "I saw the article in the *Times* about the ministry with the gang members and wanted to interact about that a little."

"Absolutely," Chris replied. "Just tell me when and where and I'll be there."

"Well, how about this afternoon at my office at the church? Say 2:00? Would that work?"

"Two o'clock it is," Chris replied. "Look forward to seein' you then."

Chris really didn't know what to think about Dr. Albritton's call. The two of them had seemingly gotten along fine since they first met, and there didn't appear to be any tension between them that he could recognize.

At 2:00 Chris walked up to the Universalist Church office where Dr. Albritton's secretary, Dee, greeted him warmly. "Chris, great to see you," she offered. "Dr. Albritton's in his office and is expecting you. Please come this way."

Chris followed her around a corner and down a short corridor until they came to a door on the right. Dee knocked, and after hearing permission to enter, opened it and said, "Dr. Albritton, Chris is here."

Dr. Albritton got up from his desk, walked across the room, and reached out to shake hands. "Chris, welcome. Please come in." Then, to dismiss her back to her work, he said, "Thank you, Dee. Please hold any calls until after we're done here. Thanks." Dee nodded, then closed the door and went back to her desk.

There was a small conference table on the opposite side of the room from his desk, and Dr. Albritton pointed to it. "Let's sit over there at the table. I think it'll be more comfortable." So they walked over and took a seat. "Can I offer you some water or coffee?" he asked.

"Thank you, Dr. Albritton. Some water would be nice."

Dr. Albritton walked over to the mini fridge in the corner and got two bottles of water, then brought them over to the table and handed one to Chris. After sitting back down he got right to the point. "Chris, I wanted us to have a little discussion because it appears the two of us are tied together in some interesting ways, and I just wanna make sure, going forward, everything continues in a good way."

"Thank you, Dr. Albritton," Chris replied warmly. "I absolutely feel the same way. So what's your concern?"

"Well first," Dr. Albritton began, "let me fill you in on something pretty amazing that's happened. Ever since you made the appeal in the *Times* about helpin' the former gang members, contributions to the church's ministries have gone through the roof. The phone's been ringin' off the wall. As of this mornin' we've already had over 500 separate donations for a total of over $12,000.00. We haven't seen that kinda support in such short time since the beginning of the ministry – and I believe it's all because of you."

"Wow!" Chris gushed, "That's fantastic! We can definitely praise the Lord for that."

"But this brings me to another matter," Dr. Albritton continued. "You realize, don't you, that our views on theology are very different? I'm wondering if those differences will ultimately drive a wedge between us. I have just a little bit of concern there."

"Well," Chris responded, "I can see the potential for that to happen, but it doesn't have to – as far as I'm concerned. Perhaps you can share with me your apprehension."

"Well Chris, the main thing has to do with our radically different theological positions. You, obviously, come from an evangelical point of view. We, on the other hand, embrace a view based on Postmodern Theology. I don't think we'll ever see eye-to-eye theologically."

"I definitely agree on that point," Chris concurred. "Theologically we're on polar opposite ends of the spectrum. Would you like to discuss those differences?"

"I was hopin' you'd wanna do that, Chris," Dr. Albritton responded. "I think just layin' everything out on the table'll be the best way forward for building a solid relationship."

Dr. Albritton was also hoping that, by laying out his theological case, he might help persuade Chris to come over to his way of thinking – at least a little bit. With his Ph.D. in religion and his practiced formula for explaining his point of view, honed by years of teaching at the university, he hoped there might be some chance of changing Chris' views.

Dr. Albritton continued, "To begin with, Postmodern Theology is quite suspicious of absolute truth claims. As human beings, we're confined to a temporal space where it's difficult for us to know much with absolute certainty – especially when it comes to understanding an infinite God. We can, of course, say a lot of reliable things about this world, but claimin' absolute truth has no place in Christianity."

"Dr. Albritton, I get what you're sayin'," Chris responded, "but I see a very serious problem with your point. You're asserting that there's no such thing as absolute truth, but in makin' that point, you are, yourself, making an absolute truth claim. You're claiming absolutely that we can't know truth absolutely."

"That's actually a very good point Chris, and a rather sophisticated one at that." Dr. Albritton replied. "But it doesn't change the fact that it's impossible for humans to know absolutely all there is to know about God."

"That's certainly true, Dr. Albritton," Chris conceded. "I completely agree with that. But I don't think that's somethin' evangelical Christians claim. There's a difference between the existence of absolute truth and the absolute knowledge of that truth. We certainly can't know everything there is to know about God because the fulness of His eternal existence is well beyond our ability to grasp – since we are finite creatures. But we don't have to know everything in order to have 'sufficient' knowledge of Him. We believe God's revelation of Himself in the Bible gives us enough knowledge to be absolutely confident that we know Him."

"The problem you run into, though," Dr. Albritton picked back up, "is that the Bible claims to be an overarching point of view that ignores the points of view of everyone who doesn't believe it. I believe everyone has their own personal point of view that's truth for them, and that their perspective is able to organize their lives in a meaningful way."

"Well," Chris responded, "there's a certain truth in that. But what you just said does exactly the same thing you criticized me for, just from a different perspective. You're sayin' that acknowledging the many 'personal points of view' is the right way to view life, while dismissing the evangelical view as an 'overarching' one. But by doin' that, you've actually turned the 'personal points of view' paradigm into the kind of overarching view you just dismissed."

"But that's the problem, isn't it Chris?" Dr. Albritton countered. "We have to either select the overarching approach or the personal approach. You can't have it both ways."

"Actually, I don't think that characterization's quite accurate," Chris replied. "You're not contrasting an overarching approach with a personal approach. You're contrasting two different overarching approaches. The biblical approach sees God's revelation as the basis of ultimate truth, and the teachings of the Bible as the expression of that truth. Your postmodern approach sees human perception as the basis for ultimate truth, and the many different personal approaches people have on earth are viewed as the expression of that truth. What we have to sort out, then, is which of those two overarching approaches reflects what is actually real."

"I must say, Chris, you're not only very perceptive, but also quite articulate," Dr. Albritton replied. "I can see why so many people like you. But the problem we run up against with this is the problem of knowing for sure. Since God doesn't present Himself to us in a physical way, it's impossible for us to actually know what you're claiming to know regarding Truth. We have to make it up for ourselves."

"Well thank you for the kind complement, Dr. Albritton," Chris replied. "I must say, that even though we are disagreeing, I'm also enjoyin' having this discussion. I haven't found too many people who disagree with me that are willin' to be respectful like that."

"Well honestly, Dr. Albritton responded with a chuckle in his voice, "There are probably not too many people who'd even understand what we're talkin' about. This is really more the level of what my Ph.D. students might be discussing."

"But back to your last statement," Chris picked back up, "what you said is only true if the natural universe, operating by natural laws, is all that exists. If, though, as the Bible teaches, God is a spiritual being who exists in eternity as described in the Bible, and if He did create the natural universe, and if He actually did create man with a spiritual part capable of interacting with Him spirit to Spirit, and if He has, indeed, revealed Himself in language that human beings can understand, then the biblical approach to knowin' God is not in the least unreasonable."

"But there's no way for you to prove what you're saying is true," Dr. Albritton countered.

"Of course there is," Chris countered. "But if you're gonna insist that the only kinda evidence that's valid is empirical evidence, then to be consistent, you're gonna havta use that same standard to prove *your* point of view. But of course, that can't be done either.

"Here's what I perceive from your argument," Chris continued, "What you really object to is that my biblical position creates a situation where a majority of people in the world will ultimately end up in an eternity separated from God, while your universalist beliefs hold that ultimately a God of love'll bring everyone into heaven."

"Again, that's very perceptive, Chris," Dr. Albritton conceded as he recognized the logic of Chris' argument. "So how do you account for God sending people to Hell if He truly is a God of love?"

With that invitation, Chris brought his argument home. "Dr. Albritton, God demonstrated his love for us in that Christ died for us as an atoning sacrifice. Because we are sinners, we're the ones who deserve to pay the penalty for our sins – spiritual death, or eternity separated from God. But as a person undeserving of death who offered Himself in death as a sacrifice for our sins, Christ gave Himself as a substitute for us. All that remains is for each of us, as individuals, to acknowledge our sinfulness before Him, repent of our sin, and willingly receive His grace gift of eternal salvation by an intentional decision. God doesn't send anyone away from Himself to Hell. Every individual makes that choice for themselves. God doesn't force people who don't want to receive Him to do so. That's how love works based on a biblical perspective."

"Well Chris, I think we could go on with this discussion for hours," Dr. Albritton noted as he reluctantly brought the theological discussion to a close.

"I've actually very much enjoyed it. I hope you have, too. I'd love to have these little discussions periodically."

"I'd like that," Chris agreed.

"There's one more thing we need to hash out, though," Dr. Albritton went on, "about how we continue working together with the former gang members. Since you're gonna be attemptin' to start a church for 'em, how's that gonna work between us?"

"Dr. Albritton," Chris replied, "I want you to know that even though we have very divergent theological positions, I have a great deal of respect for the helping ministries your church has created. You've developed both the resource base and the networks to help these guys. I'm perfectly willin' to work together on that front. We may have differing beliefs and priorities regarding spiritual things, but we both obviously want to help people get their lives turned around. I don't see why we can't work together to do that based on our own priorities. In fact, I can actually envision somethin' even more long term. I'm hopin' and prayin' that these aren't the only ones we can help out of the gangs. I envision a need for even more cooperation in the future, and even among a wider group of people. I'm truly all for us collaborating where we can if you are."

"Perfect! Our discussion today was dramatically beyond anything I dared hope for," Dr. Albritton remarked enthusiastically. "I'll admit I was concerned, and there's still some of our ministry team people who are a little wary of this kinda cooperation. But based on our discussion today, I believe I can ease their minds."

"Well Dr. Albritton, I wanna thank you for inviting me over today, and for your transparency in dealin' with our relationship. It really does make things a lot easier when we don't have to play games and tippy toe around each other. There's several places now where I *am* havin' to play footsies with people who can't just be honest, and it definitely makes communication and relationships much more difficult."

"I feel exactly the same way, Chris," Dr. Albritton responded as he walked Chris to the door. "I look forward to seein' you again soon."

"Me, too," Chris replied. With that, he headed back to his car and returned home.

CHAPTER 56

THE TRIAL

"All rise," the bailiff called out as the judge entered the chamber. "The Court of the City of Skeptopolis is now in session. The Honorable Judge Wright presiding." After the judge entered the room and took his seat behind the bench, the bailiff called out once again. "Please be seated."

After everyone was seated, the judge announced, "Well, it looks like our case today is Skeptopolis Community Church vs. the City of Skeptopolis. Mr. Johnson, I see you're representing the church, and City Attorney Opperman, you're representing the city. Gentlemen, you have both chosen for this to be a bench trial to be decided only by a judge, so there'll be no jury seated. And since the matter in question has immediate repercussions on the aggrieved party, we've scheduled this hearing very quickly. As I read the complaint submitted by the church, and the rebuttal by the city, it appears to me that this has to do with a dispute about zoning. We'll begin with opening arguments. Mr. Johnson, you may proceed."

Mark Johnson had seen these kinds of political shenanigans before. Politics in Skeptopolis had always been a bit shady, with those in power frequently pulling dirty tricks to promote their favorite political policies. About 80 percent of the time no one challenged the power plays, so politicians were more likely than not to get away with them. In fact, even when challenged, the incumbent politicians usually found some random loophole that allowed them to get their way. It was actually rare for someone to go up against the political establishment and beat them at their game, and that pretty much happened only when the general public could see through their shenanigans as particularly blatant and egregious. Mark felt quite sure this would be one of those cases, and they would easily win.

When the judge called on Mark for his opening statement, he walked from behind his table and stood before the judge. "Your honor, what we have here is a situation where the City of Skeptopolis has used unethical, and even illegal, means to deny an entity's actual existence in the city. Here's the story.

"Chris Bel came into the city to participate in the state karate tournament that was held in our fair city. As pretty much everyone knows, he won in quite dramatic fashion and has subsequently become somewhat of a celebrity. Afterwards, he decided to stay for a while and has actually participated in a number of public functions, including putting on a karate workshop for the city's karate community.

"One day he had a chance encounter with the leader of one of our local gangs that ultimately led to them forming a friendship. Through that friendship, he convinced this gang leader, along with nine of his associates, to quit the gang. It should be noted that central to all this was Chris' religious message.

"After working with a local church in town to set these former gang members up with housing, food, and clothing, they also worked to find jobs for each of them, and even got them enrolled in various kinds of classes to further their education – everything from GED, trade school, and even college.

"Since religion was a central part of the whole picture, they also wanted to start a church to help these people religiously. They initially tried to rent a storefront for that purpose, and actually had a contract with a property owner ready to sign. But the day before the signing was to take place, the property owner pulled the offer. Chris and his colleagues went through the same process with two other property owners with the exact same result. It was later discovered that the pulling of the contract offers happened as a result of threats by officials in city hall. As a side note, I have all three of these property owners ready to testify to that effect if it becomes necessary.

"After failing in their attempt to rent a location for their church, they decided to buy a property instead. They found an abandoned and unused warehouse that was suitable to convert into a church building, bought the property, and began renovation work. However, just as they were to begin holding services, they received a cease-and-desist notice from the mayor's office saying they could not have a church at that location because of zoning regulations. This notice demanded that they not hold services under threat of legal action.

"Your honor, after separate personal and unsuccessful attempts, both by Mr. Bel and myself, to ask the city to reverse their decision, I felt we had no recourse but to bring this before the court. It's my contention that the interpretation of the zoning regulations by the city is erroneous, AND that the attempt to deny this church the opportunity to exist is malicious. We'd like to ask the court to repeal the city's declaration – that having a church in that location is a violation of city zoning ordinances. With that, I close my opening remarks. Thank you, your honor."

With that, Mark went back and sat down at his table. Once he was seated, the city attorney stood up, walked from behind his table, and took his place before the judge.

Bill Opperman had been the city attorney for nearly 20 years. He was very much accustomed to the rough and tumble of Skeptopolis politics. In fact, he had personally masterminded most of the loopholes used by politicians over the years to enact their pet policies. He considered himself to be the ultimate pragmatist and had no problem operating in gray areas of the law in order to win his cases. In fact, he even had no problem lying – if he thought he could get away with it. With this case, though, he was rather nervous that he stood on shaky legal ground. But as a loyal foot soldier for the city, he was determined to do his best to implement the mayor's priorities.

"Your honor," Bill began, "what we have here is a very clear violation of the city's zoning laws. City statute zones this property, that the church wishes to use as a church building, to be commercial and industrial. Obviously, a church is neither of those. Thus, it is not appropriate for a church to be in that area. It's the city's position, and recommendation, that this church should not be allowed. Thank you, your honor."

With that, the city attorney went back to his chair and sat down. He fully expected that he would be able to call some witnesses to bolster his case.

But when he took his seat, the judge began asking him questions. "Mr. Opperman, is it true that some people in city hall threatened certain Skeptopolis businesses in an attempt to keep them from renting property to the church?"

Bill replied, "Your honor, I'm ashamed to say there was a person who became a little overzealous in attempting to enforce our zoning regulations and applied inappropriate pressure in that regard. When we found out about it, we addressed the issue in house and appropriately disciplined that individual."

"So, were the properties the church was attempting to rent also zoned commercial and industrial?" the judge asked in a follow-up question.

Bill replied, "That's correct, your honor."

"Mr. Opperman," the judge went on, "there are several churches that do exist in town. Is there a zoning designation specifically for churches?"

"No, there's not, your honor," Bill replied.

"So," the judge continued, "what is the zoning category of the properties of those other churches?"

"That's rather complicated, your honor," Bill answered. "Some of 'em are in areas zoned residential, and a couple are in areas zoned commercial. The reason for this is that those churches have been here for many years and were grandfathered in when the city's zoning regulations were established."

"So," the judge queried, "for a church to be approved, what zoning category would it have to exist in?"

"Your honor," Bill responded, "Skeptopolis has not had a need for a church category in over 75 years. We simply do not have a category for that."

At that point, the judge was getting a little indignant. "So are you telling me that since there is not a zoning category for a church, that it's impermissible for one to be established here?"

Bill replied, "Your honor, as strange as it may seem, that is correct."

"Thank you, Mr. Opperman, I think I've heard enough," the judge said as he shook his head. "Mr. Johnson, do you have anything more you'd like to say? I actually think I've heard enough to render a decision."

Although Mark had prepared a very vigorous case, he quickly recognized the turn of events, and that Judge Wright was about to rule in his favor. "Your honor," he said, "I'm certainly willing to defer to you at this time."

The judge took very little time to render his decision. "I'm very sorry to say that this is one of the most disgusting displays I've ever witnessed by the city of Skeptopolis. I'm not able to speak to the motivations of the city officials, but the case, as it's been presented here, is nothing short of unethical, and has been an attempt to promote an agenda that has no place in a modern democratic republic.

"So here's my ruling," he continued. "As there is no zoning category under which a church can be established, I'm ruling that the same provision that was applied for the grandfathering in of the other churches in town, also applies to this one. Furthermore, should the city in the future decide to create a zoning category for churches, Skeptopolis Community Church will not be affected. I now deem this case closed."

With that, the judge rapped his gavel on the bench. The bailiff then shouted out, "All rise!" and everyone stood as the judge exited the courtroom.

Once the judge had left the courtroom, a massive buzz arose throughout the room – with all in total disbelief at what had just happened. As it was already late in the afternoon, Connie, who was there covering the story for the *Times*, immediately jumped up to head for her office without speaking to anyone. She had just enough time to get the story in before the deadline for the next morning's paper.

CHAPTER 57

EVERYONE KNOWS

The next morning when Jill looked at the *Times* headline, she saw her worst nightmare.

———————◆◆———————

𝖘𝖐𝖊𝖕𝖙𝖔𝖕𝖔𝖑𝖎𝖘 𝕿𝖎𝖒𝖊𝖘

September 10   *Always There for You*   SkeptopolisTimes.com

Chris Bel Wins Again

Mayor's Office Goes Down

By Connie Granger

In a stunning development, Judge Wright of the City's Municipal Court issued a summary judgement in record time exposing serious political corruption in Mayor Jill Gadsden's office. As we have been reporting, the mayor's office was accused of corruption with regard to zoning regulations. In response to the *Times* inquiry, the mayor's office had insisted that the accusations were not true, and they were determined to fight them in court.

In trying to help former gang members who had given up their gang membership, Chris Bel has been working together with the Skeptopolis Universalist Church over several months to provide these individuals with housing and food while also helping them find jobs and get enrolled in school. Additionally, to provide for their spiritual well-being, Bel and his pastor, Levi Burger, had established a new church, Skeptopolis Community Church, and purchased a building.

For the purpose of preventing the new church from getting off the ground, it appears that the mayor's office did, indeed, apply unethical and illegal tactics in attempting to use the city's zoning laws to squash the new church. Judge Wright ruled that the city's interpretation of the zoning laws was incorrect, and that the city had no legitimate basis to prevent the church from forming and meeting in their newly purchased property. The hearing lasted no more than 20 minutes as the judge determined that the city acted in bad faith.

We will update this story with more details as they become available.

CHAPTER 58

HEART TO HEART WITH MARK

"Hello Chris, this is Mark Johnson. I need you to come by my office to sign a few papers to wrap up the trial paperwork. Could you come by around 3:00 this afternoon?"

"Sure," Chris replied. "That won't be a problem at all. And thanks again for your willingness to go to bat for us. We're really pleased with the outcome."

"Not at all, Chris," Mark replied. "I can assure you that I got as much out of it as you did! Look forward to seein' you this afternoon."

Mark's office was not too far from Chris' apartment, so about 2:45, he and Levi got in his car and headed over. As the one signing all the church's official paperwork, Levi needed to be present. When they walked in the door, the receptionist, Katie, jumped up from her chair to greet them. "Oh, hello Chris, Levi. Mr. Johnson's expecting you. Please come this way."

She led them to Mark's office, cracked the door open and stuck her head in. "Mr. Johnson, Chris and Levi are here to see you."

"Great! Send 'em on in," Mark called back. With that, Katie opened the door wide and allowed the two to enter.

Mark immediately got up from behind his desk and walked across the room. As he extended his arm to shake hands, he said, "Chris, Levi, wonderful to see you again. That was a great victory yesterday. We definitely have something to celebrate."

Mark then led them to the conference table on the other side of the room, "Come over here and have a seat. Just a few papers we need to get signed to wrap this all up." Levi sat down where the papers had been set out, and Chris sat down beside him. Mark pulled up a chair on the other side of the table. "There are just three papers to sign," he instructed. "Just put your old John Hancock on the lines we've highlighted in yellow."

Levi signed all the documents, then handed them over to Mark. He took just a moment to glance at each one to make sure all was in order, then smiled and nodded his head in approval. "That should do it. I appreciate you comin' so quickly to get this wrapped up. Since we won, the city's gonna have to pay the court costs – which includes a nice little fee for me. I need to turn these in to get paid."

"Our pleasure," Chris replied. "Now we can officially get the church goin' without anything hangin' over our heads. I hope we'll see you pop your head in once in a while, Mark."

Mark chuckled at the thought. "No, I don't think you'll see me in church. That's definitely *not* my cup of tea."

"So what exactly is next for you, Mark?" Chris inquired. "Got any more big cases comin' up?"

"Well," he replied, "I will say that the publicity from this case has provided some excellent notoriety for the law firm, and we've already set up a few extra appointments because of it. We'll see how it all turns out, but the big thing for me now is to take advantage of the win and announce that I'm gonna run for mayor next year to try to unseat Jill. I've caught her in a weakened political position right now and plan to 'strike while the iron's hot.'"

"Oh," Chris replied, "I remember you told us before that you guys are political rivals."

"Absolutely, we are," Mark answered back. "We have been for a number of years now. So far, I haven't been able to put a chink in her armor, but this case has put me in a pretty strong position."

"So do you guys have different policy agendas?" Chris asked.

"Actually, not so much," Mark replied. "Are you aware that Jill's father was also an ACLU lawyer?"

"Actually, I was aware of that," Chris replied.

"In fact," Mark continued, "he's the person who influenced me to join in with 'em. The truth is, Jill and I pretty much have the same political philosophy and policy priorities. That's one of the reasons it's been so hard to make a dent in her political armor. I needed somethin' to distinguish us."

"So you share her socialist values?" Levi chimed in.

"Indeed, I do," Mark replied confidently and proudly. "I think that's definitely the way to go."

"Hmmm, that's interesting," Chris remarked. "That seems to be the exact opposite of the values that the Chamber of Commerce promotes, yet you're a part of their group, and you side with 'em on a lotta things."

"Well again," Mark replied, "sometimes you do things out of political expediency, and I'm a pragmatist when it comes to things like that. Like I said, I've had to do some things to distinguish myself from Jill, and that's been one way to do it. But it's not really as big a deal as that. While my political philosophy's pretty much the same as hers, I do have a stronger desire to protect civil liberties than she does. Sometimes she just steps over the line – like she did with your church. I can help businesses in that arena without compromising my political values, and it gives me a way to attack her credibility without attacking her political philosophy."

"So exactly what do you agree with her about?" Chris inquired. These kinds of nuances had Chris intrigued.

"Well," Mark replied, "we're both pretty strong advocates of providing universal housing and health care. We also agree when it comes to having the city provide supplemental income for those in need. And we believe that businesses should pay their fair share to keep the city running smoothly."

"So by that," Chris interrupted, "you mean you believe local businesses should pay higher taxes."

"Well, obviously, the money to do all the needed social programs has to come from somewhere," Mark responded, "and those entities that make more should pay more."

"Does that include law firms?" Chris asked.

Mark smiled and went on without answering. "So to answer your previous question, I do see the need to use a modified collectivist approach to make the city a better place."

"Well, that, indeed, is quite different from a Christian point of view," Chris remarked.

"So how do you see it then, Chris?" Mark asked. "I thought you guys were all about helpin' those in need."

"Oh absolutely," Chris responded. "Just look what we're doing with the gangs. That said, helping people with their social needs is not our top priority. Our main goal is to help 'em with their eternal spiritual situation."

"Well, I don't see how that's of utmost benefit for society," Mark responded.

"Actually, it's not that hard to understand," Chris explained. "While Socialism puts a priority on the collective, Christianity puts the priority on the individual. It's as individuals that people must make their decisions about what they'll do concerning God, and God has revealed in the Bible that individuals are responsible to Him for stewarding, or managing, the world. When you have a collectivist approach, individuals are pushed aside and forced to abide by the dictates and values of a political elite. We feel the best help is given directly based on our Christian values, rather than through government funding based on the values of politicians and bureaucrats.

"Well, the world has to be managed in some way, and it's the elected politicians who have the ability to see where the needs are and act on 'em," Mark responded.

"Well, to really get at this issue, we actually havta take a step back," Chris replied. "Otherwise, we get stuck in round after round of everyone just throwin' out their personal opinions. You asked about the priorities of Christians. To really grasp that, it's necessary to look at what the Christian faith believes about God and the nature of human individuals. Christians believe God is an objectively real person who has revealed Himself and His ways to mankind. That includes knowledge of His values and His purpose for mankind. This revelation can be found in the Bible.

"With that as a starting point, it emerges that God's purpose is for every human being to decide individually to enter into a personal relationship with Him, then live life based on the values He's revealed in Scripture. So as Christians, we do seek out opportunities to do good deeds and help people, but not as an end in itself. Rather, it's because we know and love God and wanna please Him. Our good deeds are the result of us fulfilling our purpose before God, not the means for it."

"But that still doesn't take away the need to guide society down the right path. You need people to do that, and politicians are the ones who get that job," Mark countered.

"Of course, Mark," Chris replied. "But you're still missin' the point. We're not talkin' here about the fact that leadership is needed in a community. We're talkin' about the values that guide the leaders. How, exactly, do you decide what political policies to pursue?"

"Well, we look at where the needs are, decide how we can help the people who are in need, then make decisions we believe will solve the needs," Mark replied. "What's wrong with that?"

"But what if the policies you make help one group but hurt another?" Chris answered back. "How do you decide what's the right thing to do?"

"We just have to decide. You can't always please everybody," Mark answered.

"But how could you know if you are makin' the *right* decisions?" Chris asked again.

"Actually, that's kind of a weird question," Mark replied not really seeing where Chris was going with that.

"So why do you think it's weird? It's actually very important."

"It's weird because there's no such thing as a moral value being objectively true or right. We all just havta do the best we can to help promote the best for the most people," Mark answered.

"So there you have it," Chris replied. "You've just articulated the difference between your socialist values and Christian values. You, for your part, don't believe there's any such thing as objective morality or values, so you havta make it up as you go along. And if there are disagreements, then decisions are not made based on any kind of objective moral framework, it becomes a power play. The ones with the most power get to decide for themselves what'll happen based on their own personal preferences. As Christians, we *do* believe there's such a thing as moral right and wrong. Then, based on that set of values, we believe decisions that affect society should be based on those particular moral values. Are you interested in knowing the ultimate root of those two competing approaches to morality?"

"Okay, I'll bite. What do you think's the root of the differences?" Mark asked.

"The root lies in the fact that the two value systems come from entirely different worldview belief sets," Chris responded. "They're the result of two entirely different ways people understand how reality's structured."

"Hmm, that sounds pretty philosophical. I don't see how what you said has any relationship to how we live real life," Mark objected.

"Oh, but it does," Chris responded. "Socialism's an expression of a naturalistic worldview – the belief that the natural universe, operating by natural laws, is all that exists. If that's true, then there is no God and no basis for any objective moral beliefs. And also if that's true, man must make up moral values for himself, as there's no other possibility."

"Okay, I can see that," Mark replied as he nodded his agreement. "That actually does represent what I believe."

"Christianity, on the other hand," Chris continued, "is an expression of a theistic worldview – the belief that a creator God does exist. We also believe He created the natural universe for a particular purpose and caused it to operate the way it functions. And we believe He's revealed the nature of that reality to man in the Bible. If that's true, then there *is* a basis for objective moral beliefs – God's revelation of Himself and His ways in the Bible.

"Based on those two worldview approaches, it should be pretty easy to see not only the differences between your beliefs and mine, but also *why* those differences exist. You should also be able to see that if your beliefs are true, then my objections to your approach don't really matter. But if my beliefs are true, you're actually living based on an understanding of reality that's not only false but opposes the very Creator of the universe."

"Well, Chris, I must say this is all very interesting. I definitely see why people enjoy discussing things like this with you. But I honestly don't believe in God. I actually do believe we have to make it on our own; and frankly, that my approach to political policy is best for the survival, and even the thrival, of mankind. Of course, I'm not responsible for the entirety of mankind, but I do believe that the same principle applies to our local society. When I become mayor, and I believe one day it'll happen, I'll use my best judgment to implement policies I believe'll help our local community the most."

At that point, Chris could see that Mark was shutting down the conversation. He was no longer interested in hearing a point of view that contradicted his own. Perceiving that, Chris moved to finish up their talk. "Well Mark, this has certainly been an interesting conversation. I hope I haven't taken up too much of your time."

"Not at all, Chris. I also found it rather stimulating, and I must say, rather insightful. You've given me some insight into the thinking of a certain segment of people I believe'll help me govern better when I get that opportunity,"

Mark replied in a way to make Chris feel complemented. "Beyond that, I think you've been instrumental in helpin' me move my political ambitions forward, and I'm grateful for that."

With that, the three men stood up, shook hands, and Mark guided them to the door. "Listen," Mark said as they headed out, "you guys let me know anytime I can be of service to you. I'm always here to help."

As Chris and Levi headed out, Chris stopped, turned his head back, and looked at Mark again. "Thank you again, Mark, for all your help. I look forward to future opportunities, as well." They then walked out the front door, got in Chris' car, and drove back home.

CHAPTER 59

FIRST DAY OF CHURCH

The day for the first public service in the new church building had arrived. Already, Levi and Chris had been using the building as a worship and training location for Gino and his former gang members, along with the others who had taken notice of the opportunity and wanted to learn more. But because of the legal issues, the church had not officially opened to the public for worship services. Now that the legal challenge was resolved, they could move forward.

Activities for the first service were slated to begin at 9:00 a.m., but Levi and Chris arrived at 7:00 am to prepare everything for the big day. Because of all of the trial publicity in the newspaper, and the special efforts of Chris, Levi, and the others to invite people, they anticipated a lot of people attending on what should be a very special day. The publicity from the mayor added another reason to expect a large crowd. Some curious members of the community might show up hoping to see some kind of spectacle. And of course, Connie would no doubt show up to cover the event for the newspaper.

They were not naïve to the fact that the recent publicity had also created potential for problems. The mayor, for one, didn't take kindly to having lost face – and the court case. The very fact of the church's existence infuriated her. And, while there was nothing she could legally do about it, she was determined to make it as difficult on the church as she possibly could.

In fact, for this first service, she had called for a huge protest to coincide with the opening. She had even put an ad in the *Times* calling for as many people as would come to join her in protesting at the church. She was hoping to have in excess of 100 people there.

Knowing this in advance, Levi and Chris decided to pull a surprise of their own. First, they decided to hold the service outdoors so everyone could have a full view of the skirmish about to take place. They set up a platform and speakers in a way that could accommodate a large crowd. And they also brought the chairs from the auditorium outside and arranged them to face the platform so people could sit down and be comfortable.

To properly accommodate their "surprise," Chris and Levi designed an agenda that would allow them to blunt the effect of the protest, but also be able to hold a true worship service. They already knew the protesters would gather at a park down the road at 9:00, then march to the church to arrive at 9:30. Jill planned it that way to maximize the disruption factor.

People began arriving at the church around 8:40. As they arrived, Chris and Levi mingled among them and directed them to find a place to sit. By the 9:00 starting time, about 300 people had arrived – many were just regular people who had somehow been impacted by Chris, and others who were just curious. And then there were those who didn't want to participate in the protest but did want to support Jill's crusade.

Right at 9:00, Levi came to the platform and began the service with prayer, then led the crowd in a couple of songs with his guitar. He picked a handful of choruses that weekly attenders to his Wednesday meetings would already know, and that others could pick up on easily. He then began by thanking those in attendance for showing up. He also shared the story about how the church came to exist. In particular, he shared about Chris' arrival in Skeptopolis and the events surrounding that, along with how the former gang members became the catalyst for actually starting something. He then conveyed how that small core group had been sharing Christ with their friends to increase the number of believers. In his explanation, Levi even shared a brief account of what it meant to be a Christian, and how a person could invite Christ into their life. This was all timed to be completed right at 9:30 when the protesters were expected to arrive.

And they were not disappointed. Right at 9:30, a group of about 80 people could be seen halfway down the block. Soon after that, they could be heard as well, chanting, "Hey, Hey, Ho, Ho, Bigoted Christians got to go! Hey, Hey,

Ho, Ho, Bigoted Christians got to go!" As the protesters got closer, and louder, everyone could see that Mayor Gadsden was leading the mob. Then when they got directly in front of the church building, they gathered behind all of the chairs where people were sitting and continued their chant.

When they had all settled into place behind the church congregation, Chris walked up to the microphone. Since he had actually met and talked with the mayor, he and Levi felt it would be best for him to take over at this point. "Mayor Gadsden, what a pleasure to have you and your friends join us for the opening service of our new church. We're delighted that you've come to be here with us."

When Chris addressed the mayor directly, everyone was rather shocked, and a strange silence came over the group. He continued, "Most of you prob'ly don't know this, but Mayor Gadsden and I actually know each other a little bit. Shortly after we made a decision to start this church, I went to her office, and we had a little chat. Now it's rather obvious she's not too happy about us bein' here, and it's true that she has a very different set of beliefs than we do. But we did take that opportunity to hear each other out about our differences.

"We really didn't have much time that day, though, to get into any kind of detailed discussion. But she did identify several areas where she said she disagreed with me. In her list she included abortion, homosexual marriage, transgender rights, race, immigration, gun rights, climate change, and healthcare. Since we didn't have time to have that discussion then, and since she cares enough about these topics to have come here today, I thought it'd be a meaningful gesture to invite her up on stage so we could cordially discuss the topics. How 'bout it mayor, will you join me up here on stage?"

When Chris did that, Jill was totally stunned. This was *not* on her radar. She had a sinking feeling this would not end well for her. But she also knew she couldn't back down without coming across as a complete fool. For about 30 seconds she glared at Chris with fire in her eyes as she contemplated how to respond, then suddenly strode toward the stage. When she got there, she walked up the three steps onto the stage and marched over to where Chris was standing.

"Again, thank you for coming, madam mayor," Chris said as he reached out his hand to shake hers. She was really in no mood to make nice, but in order to not lose face, she also reached out to shake his hand. As they shook hands, Levi walked up and handed her a microphone.

"Mayor Gadsden," Chris began, did the list I mentioned cover most of the things you believe you disagree with us about? Is there anything you'd like to add to that list?"

Jill responded coolly, "I'm sure there's other things, but that was a pretty good list, I think."

"Very good," Chris replied. "Well, where would you like to begin?"

At that point, Jill knew she had to go all in, so she decided not to hold anything back. "Well, the first thing you mentioned was abortion, so let's begin there."

"Okay, let's begin there," Chris replied. "Tell me your position about abortion and why you believe a Christian view is wrong."

Jill immediately jumped in using the talking points she always used when discussing this subject. "Please don't be offended, Chris, but I'm just gonna tell it like it is. Christians are bigots when it comes to their view of women. You guys try to control women by controlling their bodies. No one has a right to tell a woman what she can or can't do with her body. Your anti-abortion point of view is tyranny."

"Okay, Ms. Gadsden, I believe you've made your point rather clear and direct." Chris replied. "But are you trying to tell me you believe it's okay to murder innocent human beings? Because that's what abortion is – the killing of an innocent human being."

"No it's not!" Jill bellowed. "That's an argument you people use, but it's simply not true. Before a child's born, it's nothin' more than a mass of tissue – like a tumor."

"Oh really?" Chris retorted. "So are you sayin' it's not human?"

"No, it is not yet human! Jill barked back.

"Well let's look at that for a second," Chris replied. "If it isn't human, then what is it? Is it some other animal? I mean, it received its DNA from a human mother and father. I think it must be human."

"You're twistin' my meaning," Jill responded. "Of course it's human in that sense, but it hasn't yet developed into a viable human being."

"Well, let's examine that for a second," Chris responded again. "Are you sayin' it's not a living thing before it's born?"

"Exactly right!" Jill scoffed at Chris' suggestion. "It's merely a part of the mother's body – which, by the way, she has a right to control."

"Well, it certainly is getting its nutrients and is being protected by its mother at that point, but medically speaking, it *is* a living being. But that's not what you mean, is it?"

"Of course not! It's just not a *viable* human being at that point," Jill barked back.

"Okay. Then based on what you've said so far, we've established that a pre-born baby is a human being and it's alive. What you seem to be saying now is that what determines whether or not it's eligible to be killed has to do with its stage of development or its physical location. You know, of course, from the moment of conception, every human being begins a journey of growth, and is in a continual state of change until the moment he or she dies. Why do you think it's okay to kill a human at one stage of development rather than another? I mean, do you think it's okay to kill old people?"

"Alright, Chris, quit twistin' my words," Jill growled back sharply. "A fetus is simply not yet a conscious human being. It's not able to do things that already born humans can do. It's as simple as that. And until they can, they're not *viable* human beings."

Chris responded, "Are you sayin', then, that consciousness is the criteria? Well, what about people who are in a coma – or even are asleep. At that point they're not conscious. Is it okay to kill them?'

With every suggestion Chris gave, Jill became increasingly unglued. She herself had a child who was in a coma. Chris didn't know that about her situation, but for her, equating a preborn fetus to a living human being was outrageous. "Of course not!" Jill screamed back. "You're completely missin' the point."

"Listen, I think we need to take this discussion back a step to really get at the most basic core issue," Chris responded. "It really all comes down to a person's view of a human being. Based on your beliefs, what is a human being?"

"Chris," Jill scolded, "you Christians have some lofty view of human beings as if they are some kinda spiritual creature with a magical connection to a supernatural god. That's simply not the case! Human beings are nothin' more than one particular species of animal among many. We're born, we live, we die – just like every other animal. There's no soul, no afterlife, and there's no God. As such, the moral beliefs you have about humanity, and about abortion in particular, are simply beliefs that are designed to keep women in subjugation. That's it!"

"Madam mayor," Chris responded, "I believe you've made your argument as clearly as anyone I've ever heard. And if you're right in your assessment about the nature of humanity, then I'd have to say your conclusion's also right. The question is, 'How do you know that what you are sayin' is true?' Science can't tell you that. In fact, science can't even deal with this topic. What you've explained is merely the implications of your personal belief system. You believe it ... well, just because you believe it.

"But I'm here to tell you that there's an element of reality that you don't know. God is real, and He's actually revealed Himself to mankind. And it's not merely a revelation that's private to individuals, but one He's revealed to all mankind.

"But we all have a choice to make as to whether or not we'll open up our lives and allow Him to reveal Himself to us individually. Literally billions of people across time and around the globe will affirm this.

"But let's not get stuck on this one topic," Chris continued as he moved to refocus the conversation. "What subject would you like to tackle next? What else do you believe Christians get wrong?"

In truth, Jill was kind of glad to get off that subject. She didn't like it that Chris had provided some very rational responses that opened the possibility he was right, but she had given her best argument and was satisfied it was a good one. "Well for another thing, you Christians are homophobes!" Jill chided. "You hate gay people and go outta your way to berate 'em."

"But madam mayor, "Chris responded, rejecting her accusation, "that's simply not true. As Christians, we don't hate anyone. In fact, we love everyone, and do our best to share how they, too, can know God and have their life changed."

"See, there you go!" Jill scoffed. "You don't seem to be able to accept 'em as they are. You feel you have to change 'em."

"Wait, mayor." Chris replied, "You seem to completely misunderstand the issues involved. When I talk about people havin' their lives changed, I'm not directing that specifically toward people who are gay. Every single person in the world is separated from God because of sin in their lives. But when they come to know God in a personal relationship, he changes 'em and gives 'em a new heart with new motivations – motivations that cause 'em to WANT to live a life guided by the principles of His very character."

"But you do want gays to change – to give up their gay identity!" Jill hissed. "You guys are just homophobes."

"First let's clean up a little terminology," Chris redirected the conversation for a moment. "The suffix 'phobe' means someone has a fear of something. Christians don't fear people who are homosexual. In truth though, you've taken a word that means one thing and are using it to mean somethin' entirely different – that Christians hate people who are gay. That's simply not true. Would you think it proper for me to go around calling you a Christophobe? I don't think so.

"But now to your point," Chris continued. "The Christian view of sexuality is not focused on homosexuality. When God created human beings, He created two complementary sexes – male and female. They're not only complementary physically, but spiritually, as well. And when He created man and woman, He also revealed how they were to interact – including sexually. He revealed that they're to form a family unit comprised of a man and a woman who should be exclusive to one another until death. Thus, ANY sexual relations outside that model is understood to be contrary to the ideal God has revealed for humanity. We have the same point of view as it relates to adultery, fornication, polygamy, polyandry, and any other philosophy of sexual relations, that we have for homosexuality. Now it's obvious that you don't agree with that either, but your accusation about how we think of homosexuals is simply wrong."

"You've got that right," Jill interrupted. That prudish view of sex is one of the reasons I despise Christians."

Instead of getting sidetracked by Jill's comment, Chris continued, "Now I don't know whether you've realized this yet or not, but the difference between your view of sexuality and mine has the same root as what we talked about before – the different understandings we have about the very nature of man. What you described before was that human beings are nothing more than natural animals – like any other animal. And, once again, my beliefs come from an understanding that God is real, that He has revealed Himself and His ways to mankind, and that we can actually know Him in a personal relationship. If your belief is true, then you'd be perfectly right to criticize my point of view. But you can't demonstrate your view to be true. You believe it, but merely believing somethin' doesn't make it true."

At that point, Chris thought it was time to bring this subject to a close and asked Jill, "Madam mayor, I think prob'ly both of us have pretty much expressed our point of view on this subject. Is there anything else you wanna say about this before we move on to another subject?"

"Chris, this has been fun," Jill responded with heavy sarcasm dripping from her voice, "but I do have other things to do. I really don't have any more time to play your little game."

"But this isn't a game," Chris replied. "This is real life. You see, the topics we discussed, and every other one that we didn't get to, are not mere political policies. Based on your naturalistic worldview beliefs, there *is* nothing else, so you think of these topics that way. But they're really, at their core, moral expressions based on what we believe is real and what is not real. With a view that man's nothin' more than an animal creature, there's no such thing as objective moral right and wrong, so you have to make it up for yourself. With my belief that God exists, and that human beings are persons created in the image of God, we have a loving heavenly Father whom we can know, and an objective standard of morality we can lovingly follow."

"Well, enjoy your fantasy!" Jill barked back. She then reached over and handed Chris her microphone, turned around, and strode off the stage and back to her group. When she reached the other protesters, she started up the cheer again, "Hey, Hey, Ho, Ho, Bigoted Christians got to go! Hey, Hey, Ho, Ho, Bigoted Christians got to go! ..." as they marched back to their staging point.

CHAPTER 60

AND SO IT BEGAN

After the protesters left, Levi came back to the front of the stage and addressed the audience. "My friends," he began, "in one way I'm very sorry you had to experience that. It's such a sad thing that those people felt the need to try and destroy somethin' they don't agree with – and do it in a way that shows such disrespect for God and for you. At the same time, I think we can take away some positive things from this experience.

"If you were to ask those who disrupted us about their religious faith, I feel pretty certain most of 'em would claim to be 'non-religious.' The truth is though, they're very religious. In fact, the underlying reason they felt the need to challenge our meeting in this way is that they believe our religious faith is a direct challenge to theirs. That may seem a little odd to some of you, so let me explain.

"Most people believe that in order for somethin' to be categorized as religious, it has to be connected to a group or organization that engages in some type of ceremony or ritual. As it relates to Christians, they'd see a church having worship services as proof that Christianity's a religion. By the same token, most Atheists believe they are *not* religious because they don't believe in God, and don't participate in formal religious rituals.

"The truth is, however, that most religions actually *do* have these elements – but not all. The confusion occurs in the very *definition* of **religion** itself. If you define it the way most people do, associating it with ceremony and ritual, then Atheists can legitimately say they're not religious. But that's factually false. The truth is: **a religion is comprised of any belief that one must accept by faith** – whether rituals and ceremonies are involved or not.

"As Christians, we certainly do believe, by faith, that God exists, and that entering into a personal relationship with Him is done by an expression of that faith. But the beliefs of Atheists are also held by faith. Their most fundamental belief is that the natural universe, operating by natural laws, is all that exists. With that as a **foundational belief**, they're convinced that ultimately, when knowledge and technology advance far enough, everything, in every part of reality, will be able to be understood using empirical science.

"But think about that notion for a moment. They assert as a fact that the natural universe, operating by natural laws, is all that exists. Yet where does that belief come from? Is it a statement of fact derived from scientific research, or is it an **article of faith**? Well, there's certainly no science to back it up. It's purely a **faith assumption**. You see, their belief is based on faith – making it a religious belief.

"How do they know God doesn't exist outside the natural universe? How do they know God hasn't revealed Himself to mankind in a way that allows us to know about Him? How do they know human beings weren't created as spiritual creatures with the capacity to connect and communicate with God? How do they know God can't reach into the material environment He created and interact with it in ways that defy the laws of nature?

"The truth is, they don't *know* any of these things. They only *believe* them. And the basis of their belief lies in their faith in the assumption that the natural universe, operating by natural laws, is all that exists. The people who showed up to protest here today actually came to advocate for their own religion as they pushed against ours.

"I actually have a few more things I wanna share before we finish up today, but before I continue, I'd like for us to have a word of prayer for those who protested against us. I wanna pray for them – that God would somehow touch their lives and reveal Himself to them. Let's pray.

"Father, we come before you at this time because we love and care about those who came here today to speak against You and Your church. In some ways, we fully understand why they have such strong feelings against us. But we also recognize that they simply don't know You or what You're doing in the world, and in the lives of those who do know You. We wanna pray for them right now, that as they reflect on what they've done today, and as they hear the message of Your love in the future, that You'll open their hearts that they may come to know You in a genuine personal relationship. I pray this in the name of our Lord Jesus Christ. Amen."

Following his prayer, Levi took the opportunity to explain a little more about the church. "Before we conclude today, I wanna share with you a little more about who we are and what we do. There are a number of you who've already been meeting with us and participating in Bible study, Christian growth training, and worship. But I also recognize there are likely many of you who have not, and this might possibly be your first time to ever come to a church. In fact, since the protest was so highly publicized, some of you may have even come just to see the drama. Since today's activities are so unusual, let me share with you for a moment what our normal practice actually looks like.

"Obviously, what happened today has been quite unusual. We won't normally meet outdoors, and we won't normally have protesters coming to interrupt what we're doin'. Usually, we'll simply conduct a worship service where we give praise and honor to God and provide Bible study and Christian growth training for those who want to participate. Here's how it'll break down.

"Every Sunday morning, our activities will consist of three parts. The first part'll be a Bible study. Many of you don't know much about the Bible, so we'll work our way through it a little each week to teach you how to become familiar with the Bible. The second part will consist of Christian growth training. We want you to not only know the Bible, but also how to effectively use its principles and teachings in your everyday life.

"Many people believe that preachers or professional religious workers are most central to the Christian faith. While that's true in many religions, it's not true in Christianity. In the Christian faith, ordinary, everyday Christians are most central to the activity and spread of the Christian faith. Pastors and professional ministers help to equip everyday Christians for the task of living out their faith in their community and the world.

"Most of you know, or at least are familiar with, Chris Bel. Chris is not a professional Christian minister. You know him because he came here to participate in a karate tournament. Yet he's expressed his faith in some very dramatic ways at the university, in public forums, to business people, to politicians, to those who are generally looked down upon in society, to the media, and in many other places. I, as a professional Christian minister, went to school to learn to pastor a church and do work in a church context. Chris has learned everything he knows through Christian growth training in his church back home. We want those of you who come to know Christ to get that same kinda training so you can also be effective in sharing the love of God in your world. That's why we'll have Christian growth training as a part of what we do.

"The third part of our Sunday activities will consist of a worship service. We, as Christians, believe God is a real person we can know in a real personal relationship. And we believe every person who enters a relationship with God becomes a member of His spiritual family. That makes every believer in Christ a brother or sister to every other believer. Our worship services, then, are spiritual family gatherings where we share fellowship with one another and express praise and honor to God for loving us the way he does. It's our hope and prayer that you'll come, grow, and fellowship with us right here. We'll begin each week at 9:00 a.m.

"Before we wrap up, I'd be remiss if I didn't make you one more offer. I'm certain a number of you came here today not knowing anything about Christ or a Christian church. Maybe you had some preconceived ideas about Christianity, but after witnessing what you've seen today, and hearing what you've heard, want to know more. After the service is over, please come talk with Chris and me at the tent to my right! We want to answer your questions and share more about Christ for any of you who might be interested."

After Levi finished sharing these words with the attendees, he closed in prayer and dismissed the crowd.

As people started to get up from their seats, Chris and Levi both made their way to the Welcome Tent, which had been set up to meet with visitors. They didn't know what to expect following the service, but fifteen people made their way over to take Levi up on his invitation. Over the next 20 minutes, Levi and Chris answered questions, then shared with the group how each of them could personally enter into a personal relationship with Jesus Christ. When Levi asked who would actually want to follow Christ, 10 people raised their hands. With that, he invited them to ask Christ into their lives, and they did. The other five were still interested but said they wanted more time to think about it. Levi gave each of them material to read that would help them think more deeply about the meaning of faith in Christ. He also gave them his personal contact information so they could connect with him individually if they had more questions.

After the last person drove away from the church and they locked up the building, Chris and Levi went to lunch and unpacked the morning's events over a steak and salad. What started as a potentially tumultuous event had become an unbelievably fantastic start for their new church.

CHAPTER 61

THE CHURCH REPORT

On Monday morning after their opening day, Chris once again blazed the headlines. He was personally mortified to see the way that Connie and the *Times* had characterized the protest and his church, but there was not much he could do about it. They were trying to sell newspapers, and often used sensational headlines to pique people's interest – sometimes even using deceptive wording.

In this case, it was not, perhaps, actually deceptive, but Chris' would never have desired to embarrass anyone, even a person like Jill who seemed to take every opportunity she could to thwart his efforts as a Christian. Even with someone like Jill, he always held out hope that she would one day have a change of heart.

𝕾keptopolis 𝕿imes

September 20   *Always There for You*   SkeptopolisTimes.com

Mayor Embarrasses Herself Again in Public as New Church Opens

By Connie Granger

It seems that Templeton's Chuck Norris, Chris Bel, has once again demonstrated his ability to counter the moves of those in Skeptopolis who are working against his interests. Over the last couple of weeks, after losing her zoning case against his church, Mayor Jill Gadsden has been organizing a protest of the new church that Chris and his pastor, Levi Burger, have been working to start. She went all out in her latest effort, even going so far as to advertise in this newspaper, to promote her planned protest at the church during its grand opening. Based on my interviews with her before the event, her intention was to enter the building after their church service had started and march up and down the aisles in order to disrupt their meeting.

When the group arrived at the church location, however, they found that the activities had been moved outdoors. The church had set up a stage and sound system on the front lawn and had even set up chairs to accommodate those attending.

It was quite a surprise to see the large crowd of about 300 people in attendance. It is difficult to know how many came to truly participate in the church service, or how many wanted to see the protest. But the large crowd, at the very least, indicated quite an interest in what Chris and the people in his church are doing.

The church's activities began at 9:00 a.m. with a prayer, some singing, and a brief introduction and explanation by pastor Levi about the church. Everyone knew that the protesters planned to arrive at 9:30, and it appeared that the church had timed their event to accommodate their arrival.

As 9:30 approached, the audience could hear the demonstrators marching toward the church and chanting, "Hey, Hey, Ho, Ho, Bigoted Christians got to go! Hey, Hey, Ho, Ho, Bigoted Christians got to go! ...." When they arrived at the church location, they marched up and planted themselves behind the rows of chairs facing the platform.

At that point, Chris took the microphone, welcomed the mayor by name, and indicated how glad they were to welcome the group's attendance. That seemed to catch the protesters completely off guard and their chants fell totally silent. Chris then invited the mayor to come up on stage and discuss her specific grievances against the church and the reason for her protest. The mayor took him up on his offer and the two of them dialogued back and forth sharing their points of view. During the discussion, Chris obviously got the better of the exchange.

In spite of that, Chris did not go out of his way to embarrass the mayor. The embarrassment was based purely on the fact that he skillfully presented his point of view in a way that clearly contrasted his view with hers, and that she was not able to make him look foolish. After the exchange from the platform, the mayor rejoined her group and they marched away as they had come, chanting the same slogan.

Once the protesters had disappeared, Pastor Levi took over and shared about the beliefs of the Christian faith, also explaining what a more typical weekly service would look like. He then invited the audience to come back next week at 9:00 a.m. when they would begin their regularly scheduled activities. At the end, he also invited anyone with questions to meet him and Chris at the welcome tent to talk further.

I must say that this reporter continues to be amazed at the acumen of Chris and his colleagues to stay one step ahead of the opposition in the community. Even for those not particularly interested in the content of the Christian faith, it is worthwhile to observe how these people operate so effectively in a relatively hostile environment.

For those interested in contacting the church, you can call or text 101-462-3375.

———————— ◆◆◆ ————————

After the article hit the streets, the church received dozens of calls. Levi stayed very busy following up on the calls, whether they were a few crackpots who just wanted to harass, or the majority of people interested in what they had seen and who wanted to learn more.

CHAPTER 62

GETTING IT RIGHT

When Chris saw the newspaper, he was mortified at the tone of the article – particularly the way it characterized Jill. While he opposed her beliefs, he was not out to put her down, but to help her see the truth of the gospel message.

In an attempt to calm things down, he tried several times to contact her, but she apparently was not willing to take his calls. So, he decided to write her a letter and deliver it to her office personally in hopes she would at least read it. The letter read:

Dear Jill,

First, I want to thank you for attending our church opening last Sunday. I realize your intent was to protest, so I don't want you to think I am writing this letter to be patronizing in any way. I sincerely mean what I write to you today. I also want to thank you for your willingness to engage in the dialog we had. While the church service yesterday was very atypical, I truly believe it is important for people who disagree to have honest and open dialog and to respect one another in the exchange.

The main reason for this letter, though, is that I want to express to you my complete disappointment with the article that appeared today in the Times. I believe the way they characterized you and your group was totally out of line, and that you certainly deserved better. If my statement here has the potential to help your situation in any way, you may feel free quote me.

In any case, I do hope in the future it becomes possible for us to have the kind of relationship that allows for further dialog on topics important to us both.

Please feel free to contact me anytime.

Sincerely,

Chris Bel

When Jill received the letter, she was completely taken aback. Not only was Chris conciliatory, but he had also expressed the exact kind of attitude he claimed to believe. From her perspective, it seemed very hard to imagine he was truly sincere, because literally no one she had ever known was like that. In the rough and tumble of politics in Skeptopolis, it was dog-eat-dog, and no one in that arena could trust anyone else.

Jill was actually moved by Chris' conciliatory gesture and decided to write back to him. She was not about to show any weakness by actually extending a hand of friendship, but she did feel stirred to at least acknowledge his seemingly kind outreach and sent it to his house by courier. She wrote:

Dear Chris,

I just wanted to thank you for your kind outreach and show of support following the hit piece in the *Times*. Their tactic to attack that way is not unusual for them, as they try to sensationalize headlines to sell more papers – as disgusting and demeaning as it is.

Please feel free to contact me anytime there is anything I can do for you.

Sincerely,

Jill

Chris didn't want to let it rest there, either. After dropping off his letter to Jill, he went over to the newspaper office and asked to speak to Connie. The receptionist took his information and walked back to her office to deliver it.

When Connie received the note, she thanked the receptionist, then went immediately to the lobby to greet Chris. "Chris, what a pleasant surprise. What can I do for you?"

Chris responded, "Hi, Connie. Have you got a few minutes to talk?"

"For you, anytime," Connie replied enthusiastically. "Come on back to my office where we can have a little privacy."

Connie led Chris through the door that went back into the paper's business complex and led him to her office. When he came through her door, she offered him a seat and closed the door behind them. "So, what can I do for you, Chris?"

"Connie," Chris began, "I just wanted to let you know I was very disappointed with the article you wrote about what went on at the church yesterday. I really wish you hadn't gone out of your way to embarrass Jill the way you did."

Connie was completely taken back. "Really?" she exclaimed. "I honestly thought you'd love it. After all, she deliberately tried to crush you and all that you're doin'. You realize that, right?"

"Yeah, I know," Chris responded, "but you should know by now it's not my style to treat people badly like that – even people who set themselves against me as enemies. I always hold out hope that somehow, it'll become possible in the future to win 'em over – or at least create an opportunity for constructive dialog. I wonder if you noticed the way I interacted with her when she attacked me was not to try to embarrass her, but to turn our discussion into an honest dialog. If you remember, I did the same thing when I spoke to Dr. Craven's class, and at the roundtable with the other professors. I really do believe my point of view represents the truth, and that in an honest and open sharing of ideas, the truth'll win out."

After listening to Chris' explanation, Connie responded, "Well, Chris, I really appreciate you comin' and talkin' to me in person. It does show, quite powerfully, that you're a man of integrity. And I honestly do respect your point of view. But you also havta realize I have a job to do with the paper, and sometimes I just havta call it like I see it. Your Christian beliefs really do represent a beautiful ideal. But the fact is, we don't live in an ideal world. The power struggles that go on in this town really do represent its beating heart, and the newspaper represents one part of that system. I've honestly tried to be sensitive to you, and I really believe I've covered you in a very favorable way. I hope that at least counts for somethin'."

"Oh, it's not that," Chris replied. "You've been very kind, and extremely fair in the way you've covered me, just like you promised – and I want you to know I really appreciate it. I guess I'm still strugglin' to understand why there's so much vitriol against me in so many arenas. I still don't understand the root of Jill's anger."

"Oh, that's easy," Connie responded. "To get that, you need to understand the kind of pressure cooker she lives in. You know some of it, but you don't really know the half of it."

"What are you talkin' about?" Chris inquired.

"Well, did you know that she has a six-year-old child that's in a coma?" Connie offered. "I think when you gave your illustration yesterday about people bein' in a coma, it really shook her."

"What?" Chris exclaimed. "How'd that happen?"

"Well, it seems about three years ago, when her child, Tonya, was three, she caught some kinda virus that put her in a vegetative state. She's been on a ventilator ever since. The doctors've tried everything they know to do but haven't been able to solve the problem. Jill really loves that little girl, and she goes up to the hospital every evening and spends the night with her.

"I've known Jill for a long time. She didn't used to have the kind of bitterness and anger in her that she has now. But over the last three years it's really taken a toll on her. It actually destroyed her marriage. Her husband finally couldn't take it anymore and left."

"Ooh, that's horrible!" Chris responded with his mouth gaping wide open.

"But that's not even the worst part," Connie continued. "Keepin' the child on the ventilator is costin' the hospital an arm and a leg. They've told her they'll be takin' her off life support day after tomorrow. It's amazing Jill's held out this long. She's fought the hospital in court for the last two years to keep 'em from doin' it. The closer the time comes, the angrier she grows, and the deader she seems on the inside."

"Connie," Chris replied, "that's devastating. I'm totally brokenhearted to hear her story. Thanks for sharin' it with me."

"Not at all Chris. And I hope you aren't too mad at me for doin' my job," Connie said apologetically.

"Oh, I'm not mad, Connie," Chris responded. "I know you're doin' your job. But I do hope that talkin' to me today's given you some insights into my thinking that'll perhaps influence future articles."

Connie smiled and nodded. "No promises," She replied, "but I'll try."

With that, Connie escorted Chris back to the lobby and said her good-byes. As he left, she added, "Again, thanks for comin' by Chris. I want you to know you're welcome anytime."

CHAPTER 63

A PROFOUND MIRACLE

After leaving Connie's office, Chris drove immediately home to find Levi. When he walked in the front door, Levi was sitting on the couch with his shoes off watching TV. "Levi," Chris called out. "Turn the TV off. We gotta talk."

"Sounds kinda serious," Levi responded as he gave Chris an inquisitive look. He turned the TV off, sat up straight, and gave Chris his full attention.

Chris sat down and began explaining. "I went up to the *Times* today to talk to Connie about the unpleasant tone of the article she wrote. In the conversation, she shared somethin' that shocked the fool outta me. I found out Jill has a six-year-old daughter that's in a coma, and's been on a ventilator for nearly three years. What's worse, Jill's been fightin' in court to keep her alive, but just lost her last appeal. The hospital will be unhookin' it the day after tomorrow. She spends every night at the hospital with her child. I think we should go up there and pray for her."

"Ya think she'll let us in?" Levi probed.

"I don't know," Chris responded, "but I really feel led to try."

"Then let's go," Levi replied as he stood up and stuck his feet in his loafers. So, the two of them left the house, got in the car, and drove to the hospital.

Once there, they went inside, walked to the front desk, and asked, "Could you tell us where we can find Tonya Gadsden?"

The receptionist looked up the room number. "She's in room 627, but I'm not sure they're takin' visitors."

"Well," Chris replied, "could you ring the room and tell the mayor that Chris Bel's here to visit, and ask if it's okay if we come up?"

The receptionist picked up the phone and rang the room. After three rings, Jill picked up the phone. "Hello?"

"This is the front desk, Ms. Gadsden. Chris Bel's here to see you and wanted to know if he could come up to the room for a few minutes."

After a short pause, Jill replied, "Yeah, go ahead and send him up." At that point she was in such despair she didn't care much about anything. She couldn't imagine why Chris would be coming to the hospital to see her and wasn't sure she even wanted to fool with him right now. But there was a nagging feeling inside that made her think his intentions were good – besides no one ever came up anymore. In fact, people had even quit talking to her about Tonya at all.

After a few minutes, Chris and Levi entered the room. Chris walked straight up to Jill, put his arms around her, and gave her a tight hug. The moment he put his arms around her, the tension and frustration she had bottled up inside exploded, and she began sobbing uncontrollably. Chris just stood there with his arms around her without saying a word and let her grieve.

After about three minutes, Jill gathered her composure, wiped her tears away and said, "Wow, I have no idea where that came from."

"I do," Chris replied. "You're in deep pain right now, and you're responding the way any loving mother would – seeing her child that way."

Jill didn't really know what else to say. Here Chris was treating her better than anyone else in town – and this after she'd been so mean to him.

"Jill, I think you've met Levi, but maybe not formally. He's my very good friend and is the pastor of the new church we're starting."

Jill reached over and shook his hand, "Nice to meet you, Levi."

"Jill," Chris spoke in a consoling voice, "I just learned about Tonya a couple hours ago. When I heard about what happened, it literally broke my heart. I had a very deep sense of sadness both for her and for you. I don't know what I can do, but I wanted to at least be here for you if that'd help you feel better."

At that, Jill broke down crying again. "You know, it's bad enough that my daughter's dying, but it's even worse that nobody seems to care. Even her dad quit comin' to see her about a year ago. I've just about given up on life. And when she dies, I don't know if I even wanna keep on livin' myself."

Hearing that, Chris took her hand and said, "Jill, this situation is sad beyond words, and I know you must feel totally heartbroken. There are times in life when there's just nothin' left to say verbally, and our spirit just reaches out to take hold of anything that'll bring peace. I know you don't believe in God, but I want you to know that in spite of that, He'll reach out and touch your spirit if you'll just release it and let Him in. Would you mind if I prayed for you right now?"

Normally, hearing someone be religious in her presence would've made her recoil in anger. But she sensed something in Chris and Levi that somehow went right past that. *What've I got to lose?* she thought. So she nodded for him to proceed.

Chris took her hand and began, "Father, right now Jill's deeply hurting. Her six-year-old daughter, Tonya's on death's door, and Jill's emotionally at the end of her rope. Life seems like it's just crashin' down on her. If there was ever a time when you should reveal yourself to her, now's the time. Would you let her experience the touch of your presence, and in spite of the dire circumstances of the day, put a peace in her heart that she's never experienced before, and confirm your presence in her. Thank you, Lord, for hearing my plea. It's in the name of Christ I pray. Amen."

When Chris finished praying, he sensed a persona that was much different from before. And when he looked up, tears continued streaming down Jill's cheeks. This time, though, her countenance was entirely different. She had a sense of inner peace and joy that seemed to radiate from her very being. "Jill," Chris exclaimed, "what's happened?"

Jill responded, "Chris, I don't know. But as you were prayin' for me to have inner peace, a peace did come over me – and in a way I've never experienced before. There's a presence – a personal presence. It feels like it has to be God. I can't explain it, but it's there. I don't know how to process this, but God really is here. All of a sudden, I believe in God. I don't know what to say or what to think. It doesn't make any logical sense, but I have a sense of peace like I've never experienced before in my life, just like you prayed – He's really real, isn't He?"

"Yes He is, Jill," Chris replied, "God loves you. He's always loved you. He's only been waitin' for you to open your life to Him."

Jill continued crying, stepped toward Chris and Levi and gave them both a warm, loving hug as she basked in the feeling of God's presence in her life.

After a moment, though, her countenance changed to one of deep sadness. "I still don't know how I'm gonna handle the next couple days, though, but somehow I believe everything's gonna be okay."

At that point, Levi spoke up, "Guys, I wanna pray for Tonya. Would that be okay?"

Jill looked at Levi, still having a difficult time understanding how he and Chris could express such love and compassion toward her – especially considering how she had tried to publicly humiliate them. But after a few seconds, and with a sense of deep gratitude, she replied, "Would you?"

"Of course," Levi responded. "Why don't we stand around her bed and hold hands. I'll pray."

When they linked hands around the bed, Levi began to pray, "Father, we've already witnessed a miracle in Jill's life today as she opened her heart to you. She's experienced the reality not only of your existence, but your very presence – and it's changing her life. But now we want to pray for Tonya. Lord, she's such a young life, and she's been in a coma for half of it. I don't know what your intention is for her, but we'd like to see you perform a miracle and open her eyes right now. And if it's your purpose to use her life for what you're doin' on earth, we ask that you raise her up right now. But if you have some other purpose for her, we commend her spirit to you. It's in the mighty name of Jesus I pray this prayer. Amen."

When the three of them opened their eyes from the prayer, looking up at them from her bed, with eyes wide open, was Tonya. Jill's jaw dropped wide open, and as she fell to her knees, she spontaneously let out a scream that could be heard all the way to the nurse's station.

Hearing the scream, a nurse rushed into the room to see what was happening. And when she saw the little girl looking at her, she rushed to the intercom and put out an emergency call for the doctor. The doctor on call was there in a flash, and when he entered the room, he, too, could not believe his eyes. He walked over to Tonya, took her hand and began speaking to her. "Tonya, can you hear me?" he asked.

She couldn't talk because of the tubes down her throat but nodded in response. The Dr. quickly began checking her vital signs and doing several neurological tests to see if she was actually awake. She was. He then proceeded to remove the ventilator to see if she could breathe on her own, and she did it just fine. "Nurse," the doctor ordered, "get on the phone, call her doctor, and get him up here *stat*."

The nurse immediately left the room to do as the doctor ordered.

"Jill," the doctor said, "I've never seen anything like this in my life. Your doctor'll have to run her through a battery of tests to see the full extent of what's goin' on, but I think she's gonna to make it. This is one of those unexplained medical miracles."

Jill began sobbing once again. "Doctor," she replied with her voice cracking with emotion, "it's a miracle alright, but not an unexplained one. God's been in this room and done miracles that you can't even imagine."

CHAPTER 64

MAKING A PLAN

In a relatively short period of time, Gino had exercised an oversized influence on gang members in the city's gang district. Word had spread widely that a former gang leader had ditched his gang life for religion. Most of those in gangs were relatively uneducated, and many a bit superstitious. In one way, they were not particularly interested in Gino's religion because it didn't line up with their beliefs. At the same time, a certain level of fear and intrigue had caught their attention. Overall, they didn't want to cross Gino for fear that God might do something bad to them. Because of that, Gino had enjoyed a sort of unspoken immunity from attack.

Word had spread not only about how he had personally changed and left his gang, but also about all those who were leaving with him. Beyond that, people could actually see the effects of this change in real life. For the most part, those who entered into gang life couldn't imagine any other possibility. But now they watched as real-life examples of youth successfully leaving gang life showed up all around them. Not everyone was attracted to that, but many were.

Gino recognized the interest his new faith had generated, and this window of immunity from attack that allowed him to operate without fear for the time being. Because of his newfound desire to help as many as possible, he began taking every opportunity to use his status to share his new faith.

Chris, Levi, and those at the Universalist church involved in helping Gino's group knew that he actively worked to help other gang members. They had let him know they had systems in place to help anyone who wanted to leave gang life. So, when gang members showed an interest, Gino stood ready to offer help.

At first, a small trickle from several different gangs began to open up to him. And as more people began seeing positive results, that trickle increased significantly.

At first, the various gang leaders tried to ignore Gino's growing movement. When it only touched a person here or there, they merely saw it as a nuisance, but it didn't yet interfere significantly with their ability to conduct business. However, as more gang members saw their friends leaving and getting away with it, interest grew. And, with Gino's increasing effectiveness, it started affecting the gangs' business operations until several gang leaders felt the need to do something about it.

For the most part, the various gangs were competitors, sometimes even clashing in deadly gun fights over territory, product, or even perceived insults. But in order to prevent all-out war, and maintain the order necessary to protect their enterprises, they did periodically hold a council meeting of all the gang leaders. These were typically held twice a year, but they could call a special meeting if something came up that needed immediate attention.

By now, Gino's increasing influence had emerged as a big-enough problem to warrant such a council meeting. In fact, it was Selena who made the call. Since Gino already had a relationship with the members of his former gang, and they all knew the ones who had left and could see the changes in their lives, Selena had grown especially concerned about her gang. Not only had the Red Flag Pack been affected, but the other gangs also felt enough concern that they wanted to talk about it.

When it came to the actual gang work on the streets, the rank-and-file members carried out most of the work and were not particularly concerned with the big picture. It was the leaders who had to keep track of profit and loss, make decisions about how to manage inventory, determine when to move into new lines of business, and decide personnel issues. As such, they had more at stake when problems like Gino's impact came up.

They wasted no time in setting a day for the gang council to come together, and Selena led the discussion – since she had called the meeting. "Alright, everyone, the operations of the Red Flag Pack are being severely affected by Gino's religious crusade. It's gettin' to where I don't have enough workers to move my product, and I'm really gettin' ticked off. Early on it was more of an annoyance, but now it's turned into a serious problem. It's obviously gettin' to be a problem for you, too, since you agreed to this meeting."

George, the leader of the Checkers, spoke up. "It's not as bad for me as it is for you at this point, but it's increasingly a problem for me, too. I'm seein' our sales down about ten percent compared to this quarter last year, but it's trending further downward. And if the current trend continues, it'll start hurtin'. Obviously, we have our ups and downs for any of a number of reasons. But the loss of members does mean less people on the street – which is responsible for our current downward trend. If this pace continues for another quarter, I see us bein' impacted like what Selena's described."

After George finished speaking, three other gang leaders expressed the same sentiment. A consensus was obviously building.

George spoke back up, "Well, it seems we're all recognizin' this as a problem. Now the question is, 'What are we gonna do about it?'"

Trey from the Black Lords spoke up. "Well, for one, I think we need to be really careful. This has been gettin' a LOTTA publicity lately, and if we do somethin' stupid, it could backfire and create even more problems."

The meeting went on for another hour as each person shared their thoughts on the pros and cons of various courses of action. In the end, they decided to begin slowly, with some warnings, and see if they could get Gino to back off. If he did, then problem solved. If not, they would need to consider more drastic measures. Since Selena had called the council, and since she knew Gino the best, everyone thought she should be the one to enforce their will.

CHAPTER 65

THE ULTIMATUM

"Gino, we need to talk. Meet me at the park in an hour," Selena growled into Gino's ear and quickly hung up. She figured the best way to give Gino the message was to have a face-to-face conversation.

When Gino saw Selena's name and answered the phone, her voice sounded unusually harsh – even for Selena. He had no idea what she might be planning but agreed to meet her.

When they got to the park, Selena glared at Gino and laid it out. "Gino, we had a gang council meetin' last night, and you were the topic of discussion."

"I hope everyone was expressing fond memories of me," Gino joked to try to get Selena to loosen up a little.

"This isn't funny, Gino," she barked back, trying to impress on him the seriousness of the situation. "It seems your religion talk among the gang community's startin' to cause problems for everybody, and they want you to stop. Out of respect for you and your former association, they wanted me to convey a warning to lay off. If you do, everything'll be cool."

"And if I don't ...?" Gino inquired.

"If you don't," Selena finished his sentence, "more drastic measures'll be taken."

"You don't seem to understand, Selena," Gino replied. "God is real, and He's in the life changin' business. He's changed my life. And if He chooses to work in the lives of other people, then that's *His* work. I'm only a messenger. You know, He loves you too, Selena. The opportunity to have a new life, both spiritually and in your daily life, is open if you wanna step into it. I can help you with that."

"SHUT UP, GINO!" Selena screamed back. "I don't think you're takin' me seriously. This could be a matter of life and death for you. You better heed my warning!!"

"Selena, I can't back off," he replied with total calm in his voice. "God's changed me, and I not only want to experience that for myself, but I want others to experience it, too. I can't help but share the love God's poured into my life."

"Have it your way, then," Selena bellowed, "but you're responsible for the consequences you bring on your own head." She then turned around and stormed off.

CHAPTER 66

POW!

When Gino got back to the apartment, he found Chris sitting on the couch listening to a podcast and taking some notes. He walked over and waved to get his attention, "Chris, I just had a pretty heavy talk with Selena, and I'd like to get your advice. Can we take a walk and talk for a few minutes?"

"Absolutely!" Chris responded. He paused the podcast, pulled off his headphones, and jumped up. "We can go right now."

As they walked, Gino told Chris about the meeting he'd just had with Selena. "I must be disruptin' the gang operations pretty badly if they called a council meeting just to get me to quit. They don't usually have special meetings like that unless some out-of-town gang is tryin' to infringe on their territory, or inter-gang skirmishes start to negatively affect business. I'm really taken back by this."

"Wow," Chris replied, "that's unbelievable. God's really workin' in your life to touch a lotta people. How many so far have left the gangs and are bein' helped by the churches?"

"Well, countin' our guys, there's 42 ... and that's just the tip of the iceberg. There's prob'ly another 40 who've expressed some degree of interest."

"Wow, no wonder they want you to stop," Chris blurted out in amazement. "I bet that's really puttin' a dent in their bottom line. How you holdin' up?"

Just as Gino was about to respond, they heard the sound of screeching tires behind them. Instinctively Gino knew what was happening. "Chris! Hit the ground!!" Gino screamed. He then pushed Chris to the ground and laid on top of him. Suddenly the sound of gunfire rang out. Six shots were fired from a speeding car that then sped away.

"Wow, that was scary!" Chris yelled out as he pushed Gino off him and jumped up. "What was that all about?"

When Gino didn't respond, Chris looked down and saw blood all over Gino's back. He then noticed blood all over his own shirt.

Chris immediately pulled out his cell and dialed 911. A voice from the other side responded, "911, what's your emergency?"

"I'm on the sidewalk about halfway down Straight Street. There's been a drive-by shooting and my friend's been shot. Send an ambulance right now."

"I'm sending an ambulance right now," the voice on the other side replied. "Are you still in danger?"

"No," Chris responded. "The car with the shooter sped off and's now outta sight."

The 911 operator replied back, "Emergency personnel are on the way. Please stay on the line until they arrive."

Chris kneeled back over Gino and said, "Hang in there, buddy. Help's on the way."

Gino's voice was faint, but he had something he wanted to say. He spoke in a very labored fashion, "Chris, I'm gonna be okay. Whoever that was, I forgive 'em. Help 'em find God."

At that point, Gino lost consciousness as blood still poured out of his left side. Chris pulled off his shirt and used it to apply pressure to Gino's wound.

From a couple blocks away, Chris began to hear sirens approaching. A police car pulled up within one minute of his call. An ambulance pulled up about 30 seconds later.

The police officer pulled Chris over to the side to make way for the EMTs, who flew out of the ambulance as soon as it came to a stop beside Gino. The first paramedic ran over to assess the situation. "I've got this, sir," as he took over from Chris applying pressure. "Let me take over."

The other EMT quickly checked Gino's vitals. "He's still breathin' and has a faint pulse, but he's lost a lotta blood. This is really bad. I'm gettin' the gurney."

When they had it in position, they lifted Gino onto it and put him in the back of the ambulance.

Chris then asked, "Can I ride with him?"

To that, the police officer responded, "It's better to stay outta their way. Hop in my car. We'll follow it to the hospital."

When Chris arrived at the hospital, the EMTs had already begun unloading Gino, and a team of doctors began leaning over him to tend the wound. They immediately wheeled him into the hospital and took him straight to surgery. Chris tried to follow, but a nurse ordered him, "You stay here! We'll let you know as soon as we know somethin'."

Since there was nothing left to do but wait, the police officer asked Chris if they could talk, and if Chris would share as much as he could about what happened. So the two of them walked over to quiet corner in surgical waiting and sat down. The officer pulled out his note pad and began to write as Chris shared details of the events.

"Officer," Chris began, "I can tell you the circumstances surroundin' what happened, but honestly, I didn't see a whole lot."

"First, tell me your name and the name of the victim," the officer requested.

"Yes sir," Chris replied, "my name's Chris Bel and that's Gino Chrysler."

"Wait," the officer interrupted, "Gino Chrysler the gang leader?"

"Former gang leader," Chris corrected him. "He's no longer in a gang."

"And you're that karate kid, aren't you?" the officer continued.

"Yes sir, that's right." Chris didn't really care to be referred to that way but had pretty much gotten used to it.

"Okay, now I get it," the officer replied. "I've seen your story in the paper over the last few months. So what happened?"

Chris continued, "Over the last couple months since he left the gang, Gino's been tryin' to help other people leave their gangs like he did. He must've been having an effect, because when he came home today, he was tellin' me he got a warning that if he didn't quit there'd be serious consequences. Apparently, there's some kinda inter-gang council, and they got Selena, the new leader of the Red Flag Pack, to deliver the message. He refused to quit and told her that directly. Gino and I were walkin' around the block, and he was sharin' that with me.

"Suddenly, we heard tires squealin', then Gino threw me to the ground and jumped on top of me. The next thing I knew, I heard gunshots. After that, the car sped off. I hardly saw it because Gino threw me down and my face was to the ground. The only thing I can tell you about the car is that it was one of those older model Cadillac lookin' cars, and it was gray. It happened so fast. When I got up, I saw Gino bleedin' badly. That's when I called 911."

"Well, that's not much to go on, but it's somethin'," the officer replied. "Let me call that in and I'll be back in a minute."

At that point, there was nothing to do but sit and wait for the doctors to come out ... and it didn't take long. When the door to the ER opened, one of the doctors, and the nurse Chris had spoken with earlier, came out with solemn looks on their faces. When they came up to him, the doctor said, "I'm so sorry, but we were unable to save your friend. Two bullets struck him – one caught part of his heart muscle."

Hearing that, Chris broke down crying. Gino's last act on this earth was to save his life.

It didn't take long for police to find the shooters. Selena had used her own car in the drive-by, and by having her name and the description of the car, the police found her pretty quickly. They also found the gun she used.

In her defense, Selena kept claiming she wasn't trying to kill Geno, only scare him. She was aiming for his leg, but when he pushed Chris down and fell on top of him, his body was down low where his leg should have been.

Chris knew he had to tell all the former gang members before they heard it somewhere else. So he called Levi, told him what had happened, and asked him to get everyone together at the church in an hour. He then called Sybil, told her what had happened, and offered for anyone from her group to come if they wanted.

Levi was able to get everyone there and had them seated in the auditorium just before Chris arrived, still wearing a blood soaked shirt. Sybil, Melanie, and Dr. Albritton also drove up right about the time Chris arrived and they all walked in together.

When Chris walked in and saw everyone was present, he told them the news, along with the entire story. There was not a dry eye in the place, and many expressed a great deal of anger. When he heard Chris' story, Zander jumped up and screamed, "I'm gonna kill 'em all!"

Chris walked over to Zander, put his arm around him and said, "Zander, we're all mad about this, but before makin' any moves, we need to talk this through. Whatever we do, it has to be the right thing."

They all knew Chris was right, and that he probably had a plan. So everyone calmed down to hear him out. "First of all," Chris began, "Selena was the one responsible for the shooting, and the police already have her in custody. The justice system'll take care of the vengeance portion of this, and we need to let 'em do it. But there's somethin' even more important we need to take responsibility for."

"Somethin' more important?" Gunner yelled out. "What could be more important than that?"

"Think about it," Chris continued. "Why were the gangs so upset at Gino that they were willin' to go after him that way? It was because so many were leavin' the gangs – because Gino was leadin' 'em to Christ. He'd become a threat to 'em. You need to know that sharing Christ and helpin' people get outta the gang life was more important to Gino than his own life.

"Here's what he told me just before he was shot. I asked him how many people, includin' you guys, he had helped get out of gangs since he started this effort. Anyone got any idea how many?" he asked rhetorically. "Forty-two! So far he's led forty-two people to quit that life – and most of 'em have come to Christ! But you know what else he told me? He said there were another 40 who are thinkin' about it.

"And you know what else he said? After he was shot, the very last words he said to me were, 'Chris, I'm gonna be okay. Whoever that was, I forgive 'em. Help 'em find God.' So if you wanna honor Gino, you need to have the same heart he had. We need to find that other 40 and help 'em leave the gangs."

After a few moments of silence, Maximus stood up. "Guys, Chris is right. If we wanna really honor Gino, we need to drop the hate and anger and pick up his mantle. Besides that, the best way to get back at the gangs for killin' him is not to go out and try to kill them. Havin' their work damaged by people leavin'll hurt 'em more. We need to do exactly as Chris is saying."

Typically, Maximus was one of the more reticent ones, but was also the most respected after Gino. Of course, now that they were not in the gang, they didn't have a leader as such, but all of 'em had looked at Gino that way anyhow. With him gone, Maximus became the one they looked to by default. When he spoke, they listened.

"Guys," Maximus continued, "we've all watched how Gino was so faithful in participating in the Bible studies, and how eagerly he soaked up the trainin' we've been gettin' from Levi. I know we've all been expressing our gratitude for all the people who've been helpin' us, and we've not been shy to let others know that the root of the change in our lives is Christ. I think now we need to go one step further and find those who want to follow in our footsteps and help 'em. What do you say?"

"You're right," Zander jumped in. "I was really angry when I heard about Gino, and I still am. But if we're gonna live out our relationship with Christ, we need to care about other people like Gino cared. And honestly, the best way to hurt the gangs is not to kill 'em with violence, but to kill 'em by getting' all their members to walk away – and only Christ in their hearts is powerful enough to pull that off. What do you say?"

Everyone looked around at each other, then Axel said, "I'm in." Then one by one all the rest followed suit. It was going to be a new day in Skeptopolis.

CHAPTER 67

THE REPORT

When his phone rang, Chris saw it was Connie. "Chris, I've been tryin' to get hold of you. I heard about what happened. Are you okay?"

"Connie, it's been an extremely traumatic day, but I'm doin' okay. Thanks for askin'."

"Listen Chris," Connie continued, "I hope you don't think I'm bein' insensitive, but would you be willin' to share with the community what happened today? Could I interview you about it?"

In some ways, Chris really didn't want to deal with that right then, but he also saw an opportunity to share with the community one more time the love of Christ. After all, Gino had died a martyr. He was killed because his witness for Christ had a profound negative impact on crime organizations in the city.

"Connie, I'm really exhausted after what's happened today, but I believe Gino's story's important enough that I'm willin' to work through my exhaustion. Can you be over here in half an hour?"

Connie was quite moved that Chris had accepted her request in the middle of his grief – and was deeply appreciative. She also knew his interview would turn a routine crime story into something that might really impact the city. "I'll be right over, Chris," she responded, then hung up the phone.

Connie arrived about 20 minutes later and sat down with Chris in his living room. As they began the interview, Chris let Connie know that he expected a certain level of decorum to surround the article. "Connie, this entire episode's been really traumatic for me, and my feelings are still very raw. I honestly don't feel like talkin' about this right now, but I know it's gonna be covered whether I give my input or not. So, I've made a decision to share it with you. But I do have a request."

"Sure, Chris," Connie responded empathetically, "I understand. What's your request?"

"Gino was killed because he was tryin' to help people get their lives straightened out, and he died as a hero savin' my life. I know in his past he was a criminal – a bad guy – but I don't want him to be remembered for his past wrongs, but for the person he became. He should be heralded as a role model for anyone who sees their life headed in a bad direction and has a desire to change."

"Chris," Connie replied, "I really hadn't thought far enough ahead to decide what spin to put on the story, but you've given me a great idea. His turnaround is really not just his story, but the story of everyone who's ever turned their life around. This horrible tragedy could be an inspiration for encouraging other people. I agree with you. I believe this is a case where we can use this very evil thing for good."

"I especially have in mind one particular group of people," Chris interjected. "The reason Gino was gunned down is because he was so effective at gettin' people to leave gang life. The gang leaders didn't like it. There are quite a number of gang members in the city that haven't yet made the decision to leave but are thinkin' about it. I especially want them to realize that there's still hope, and they can still make that decision. If that could be conveyed, I believe it would further Gino's positive legacy."

With that request, Chris went on to share the details of the shooting and answer all Connie's questions. After about 45 minutes, Connie felt she had all she needed, and said goodbye. She then went back to her office to write the article, which came out the next morning.

◆

𝔖keptopolis 𝔗imes

September 24   *Always There for You*   SkeptopolisTimes.com

Murder in the Streets

By Connie Granger

Yesterday, a horrific demonstration of gang violence rattled the streets of Skeptopolis. At about 4:00 in the afternoon, two members of the community were walking down Straight Street when a drive-by shooter came up from behind and opened fire. In the midst of this terrible act of violence was also an unbelievable demonstration of heroism.

Gino Chrysler had been known in this city as a gang leader for quite a few years. He was the former head of the Red Flag Pack. This gang has been involved in drug trafficking and extortion, as well as other kinds of organized crime activity.

As has been reported previously in the *Times*, Gino decided to leave gang life based on the influence of Chris Bel. Chris touched a spiritual nerve in Gino, who then became a Christian and sought to turn his life in a different direction. When he left the gang, nine other members left with him.

To help these former gang members change their lives, Chris arranged financial help from other Christian friends in Templeton. A pastor friend from his hometown also came over to help cultivate these new spiritual disciples. Additionally, Chris teamed up with the Universalist Church here in Skeptopolis to help with food and housing, as well as assistance in getting jobs and pursuing educational opportunities.

It seems Gino had a real heart for helping others involved in his former life to also get their lives turned around, so he began a personal mission to contact gang members throughout the city. He wanted to help any who also desired to leave gang life. As it turns out, his effort was so successful, it caught the attention of the various gang leaders throughout the community. Based on what Gino told Chris, he was warned to stop his efforts or more drastic action would be taken. Gino refused to quit, and shortly thereafter was gunned down.

The circumstances of the shooting itself were quite dramatic. I had the opportunity to sit down with Chris yesterday and get the story first-hand. According to Chris, the two were taking a stroll and talking about Gino's efforts to help gang members leave their life of crime, and about the threats he had received if he didn't stop. Suddenly, they heard the screeching of tires and Gino immediately pushed Chris to the ground and got on top of him. Apparently, Gino sensed what was about to happen.

A few seconds later, Chris heard gunshots, then a grey sedan sped past. Chris immediately pushed Gino off of himself and jumped up, not realizing at that moment Gino had been shot. He quickly did realize it, however, and called 911. When the police and ambulance arrived, Gino was still alive, but was in critical condition. The ambulance took him to the hospital where he died in surgery from a gunshot wound to the heart.

Based on Chris' information and description of the event, police were quickly able to find and apprehend Selena Torres, and have charged her with first degree murder. According to a statement from her attorney late in the evening, the killing was an accident. Selena claims she was only trying to send a message, but when Gino pushed Chris down, they fell into the path of the bullets.

What we have here is not only a terrible tragedy, but an amazing story of heroism. This is the story of a person who was not only working to turn his own life around, but also helping others do the same.

Gino actually had a degree from Skeptopolis University in Wildlife Management and had recently taken a job with the city's park service in their animal services division. He was using that as a means of earning an income, but desperately wanted to help other gang members get their lives turned around, as well. To do that, he began an effort to contact as many as he could and share with them how they could leave gang life. Based on information from Chris, he had already influenced 42 people to leave their gangs, and all of these were being helped and supported by the Skeptopolis Community Church and the Southside Universalist Church. Gino indicated to Chris that at this time, there are about another 40 who are considering leaving the gangs.

While Gino's previous life was one of crime, the legacy he leaves is of a community hero. He is about the best example this reporter has ever known of a person who made a decision to take their life in a new, positive, direction, and take others with him. His life is an example from which we should all learn a lesson.

Funeral services will be held at the Skeptopolis Community Church this coming Saturday at 10:00 am.

CHAPTER 68

THE FUNERAL

The story in the *Times* about Gino created quite a stir. You couldn't go anywhere that people weren't talking about it. Even the porch of Zorn Mercantile had a huddle of townsfolk who had decided to attend Gino's funeral in a show of support, mixed with curiosity. Though the town had very few Christians, the locals shared a sense that Gino was one of Skeptopolis' own, and what he had done was helping the city, and a credit to their reputation. Even people who didn't know him felt drawn to attend his funeral. Looking at the scene at the church, a huge number of cars filled the parking lot and spilled over onto undeveloped land on the church property. Anticipating a big event, the police department sent more than 15 officers to help with traffic control and parking.

When the time arrived for the funeral service to begin, more than 500 people packed out the church auditorium. They only had 350 chairs available, since the church was still new, and they had no way of anticipating such a crowd. On top of that, they hadn't had time to finish building out the auditorium. While the walls had been framed and drywalled, they were not yet painted, and the unfinished sheetrock, with its exposed spackling paste, made an interesting impression throughout the entire room of being "in-process." Still, Butch Grissom had done enough to make that space usable as an auditorium, and it was easily large enough to accommodate the 500 people who came – even if it was standing room only.

Those who attended represented quite a mixed bag. Of course, all the former Red Flag Pack members showed up. And, out of respect for Gino, a few leaders of the other gangs showed up as well. But that was not all. On the front rows, sat about 40 former gang members from other gangs whom Gino had influenced – most of whom had also received Christ. In addition to that, 30-40 more arrived who had gotten to know Gino through the weekly Wednesday evening Bible study.

A good contingent of others came to pay their respects, as well. Chris recognized some of the more prominent people, who had also become acquainted with Gino somewhat, especially noting Mayor Jill Gadsden from city hall with several of her staff. Gino's co-workers from Animal Services clustered together on the left side – in sadness and shock at the loss of someone they had quickly come to admire and befriend.

Dr. Albritton also made it a point to attend. Even though he didn't really know Gino, he felt a connection since his church was involved in helping him and his group get housing, jobs, and schooling. With him were Colleen, Melanie, and Jacob.

Beyond that, a noticeable delegation turned up from the business community – they had developed a deep appreciation for Chris and wanted to show him their sincere support. And finally, but most significantly, a couple hundred people from the community, who were moved or intrigued by Gino's story, made a showing. Then, of course, Connie was there to cover the story for the *Times*.

When the service started, Levi led the congregation in a couple of Gino's favorite songs with his guitar. He then read from Romans 8:35-39.

"[35]Who will separate us from the love of Christ? Will tribulation, or distress, or persecution, or famine, or nakedness, or peril, or sword? [36]Just as it is written, 'FOR YOUR SAKE WE ARE BEING PUT TO DEATH ALL DAY LONG; WE WERE CONSIDERED AS SHEEP TO BE SLAUGHTERED.' [37]But in all these things we overwhelmingly conquer through Him who loved us. [38]For I am convinced that neither death, nor life, nor angels, nor principalities, nor things present, nor things to come, nor powers, [39]nor height, nor depth, nor any other created thing, will be able to separate us from the love of God, which is in Christ Jesus our Lord."

When he finished reading, Levi led in prayer: "Father, today we're deeply saddened by the loss of our friend Gino Chrysler. Gino is a profound example of what you are able to do in a person's life when they give it over to you.

He lived most of his life with so many disadvantages, and where hopelessness ruled. But when he came to know you, he turned his life around – not only to better himself, but he dedicated his life to helping others leave their lives of hopelessness, as well.

"While we're sad today because of our loss, at the same time we're greatly heartened by the knowledge that he's now enjoying paradise in your presence. As we celebrate his memory in this service today, we ask that you also use this time to impress on others how you can change their lives. In the mighty name of Jesus Christ we pray. Amen."

After a brief pause, Levi shared with those in attendance. "I want to tell all of you some things about the amazing life of Gino Chrysler. Gino passed away three days ago on September 29 at the age of 29. He was a lifelong resident of Skeptopolis.

"He used to tell us that his life story was not very pretty. According to his own testimony, he never knew his dad, and his mom was a hooker. Gino was conceived when she got pregnant by one of her johns.

"Gino grew up not too far from here on Washington St., in a neighborhood filled with drug pushers and addicts. It was also the territory of the Red Flag Pack. He used to say, 'The gang was here way before me, and it's pretty hard for neighborhood kids to stay out of it.'

"In spite of all the bad influences in his life, his mom really did try to take care of him, and even tried to keep him out of the gang. She pushed hard for him to get his education. And in spite of the fact that he did ultimately join the gang, and even later became its head, he made it all the way through high school, and even attended Skeptopolis University where he got a degree in wildlife management.

"After his mother died, he didn't have any other family, and settled into gang life – which represented the only family he knew. And because of his education, the other gang members looked up to him. When their former leader was killed in a shooting incident with the police, Gino was tapped to take over.

"He remained in that life until he had a divine encounter with Chris Bel, who challenged him to explore a better way forward, and shared with him how a relationship with Christ could change his life. Gino decided to take that step and invited Christ into his life – and a more dramatic change you cannot imagine. Jesus Christ changed literally everything about his life – his desire to live a good life, his desire to help people, but most of all, his desire to know a deeper relationship with Jesus.

"In the process, he deeply wanted the other members of his gang to also know the inner peace and purpose he had experienced in Christ, so he told them about it, and announced he was leaving the gang. He invited the other gang members to follow him – nine did.

"But it couldn't have happened without the help of some other very loving people. Besides Chris, people in the Skeptopolis Universalist Church stepped up and helped provide housing, food, jobs, and educational opportunities. Gino even got a job with the City Park's animal services division.

"But he was not satisfied with that. He wanted to help others, as well, so he began going into the territories of other gangs and actively telling gang members how they, too, could have their lives changed by Jesus Christ and get a new start on life. As of the time he was killed, about 40 people followed him out – most of whom are here today.

"Sadly, one very disgruntled person felt threatened by what Gino was doing and took it upon herself to stop Gino from influencing other gang members. She ended up killing him. But he's left a legacy in Skeptopolis unlike anything ever seen here before. And I don't believe his influence is finished. Those whose lives he has touched will touch other lives. Gino will be deeply missed, but his legacy will live long into the future."

After telling Gino's story, Levi invited three people to share how he had touched their lives. Maximus represented the former gang members and shared how Gino's influence had given all of their group the possibility of fulfilling lifelong dreams that they never thought possible. Following Maximus, CJ shared how he had grown up in Gino's neighborhood, and how his life and testimony had changed the very environment of the neighborhood. Finally, Chris came up and shared how he had become such close friends with Gino and the inspiration he took from watching Gino radically live out his life for Christ.

When the three had finished, Levi came back up and read 2 Timothy 4:6-8:

"[6]For I am already being poured out as a drink offering, and the time of my departure has come. [7]I have fought the good fight, I have finished the course, I have kept the faith; [8]in the future there is laid up for me the crown of righteousness, which the Lord, the righteous Judge, will award to me on that day;

and not only to me, but also to all who have loved His appearing."

Levi then closed in prayer: "Our Father, thank you for the ties of love that bind your children together, and for all Gino did to leave a powerful and loving legacy for those who knew him. We are all hurting right now with grief, but we know that you are the God of comfort. I ask that even right now you show your special love and provide your powerful comfort to those of us who have been left behind. Give each of us a heart of understanding so that we may know your grace and comfort. We know that right now, Gino is standing in your very presence, and is facing an eternity of life together with you. I know it's his desire that we not mourn him, but that we take up the mantle he has left us to carry on in his footsteps. Lord, we thank you for your love and acknowledge our great love for you, in the name of Christ Jesus our Lord. Amen."

When Levi finished, the pall bearers came forward and carried his casket out to the hearse. His body was then taken to the cemetery where Levi committed his body to the earth.

CHAPTER 69

PAYING IT FORWARD

The Wednesday after Gino's funeral, all of his former gang members, plus those from other gangs who came to Christ by his influence, met at the church to talk further about Gino. Axel was particularly moved by Levi's challenge to continue Gino's legacy. So with Levi's permission, he called a meeting at the church for everyone who wanted to participate. About 50 showed up.

When everyone had gathered, Axel addressed the group, "Guys, you know I'm not the leader type, and I'm definitely not a good speaker. But at the funeral, when Levi was goin' back over what Gino had done, I got really choked up and felt God leadin' me to say somethin'. It made me think about my life in the gang. And even though I didn't realize it at the time, my life was miserable. Now that I'm out and can look back with a clear head, I feel like I've awoken out of a zombie trance. I have a purpose in my life like I've never experienced before. My relationship with Christ has completely changed me.

"Now, as I look back at it all, I clearly see that not only was Gino largely responsible for what happened in my life, I see how he did the same thing for so many others, and I can't let it go.

"Gino told us he was aware of probably another 40 people who'd expressed an interest in leavin' their gang but hadn't yet pulled the trigger. I bet there's a lot more than that. And we need to pick up where Gino left off.

"Over the last several weeks, we've been studyin' and trainin' about how to help people get their lives turned around. And we've all heard Gino tell how he did it. More than that, we've all heard each other's testimonies about what's happened in each of our lives. I say we hit the streets like Gino did and find those people who want their lives changed and bring 'em in. Who's with me?"

Hearing Axel's charge, Gunner spoke up, "I'm in. I didn't really know how to express it, but Axel laid out exactly what I was thinkin'. Levi, can you and Chris coach us up on how to best go about doin' it?"

Levi had been sitting in the back of the room just letting Axel lead out. Hearing his name, Levi got up and walked to the front. "Guys, I'm also absolutely all in. Chris and I'll do everything we can to support whoever wants to follow in Gino's footsteps. We're also always available to help you get people hooked up with food, housing, education, and jobs. In fact, if you guys are serious, we'll turn this into an official ministry of the church so you can have the church's full support."

Suddenly, Sybil's hand went up. "Can I say somethin'?"

"Sure Sybil. Go ahead."

Sybil stood up and spoke directly to Levi. "Levi, I don't know how effective I could be goin' out into the gang culture to talk to people. I'm not, and never have been, a part of that life, and I really don't think a lotta those people would listen to me anyhow. But I do have experience workin' with the support ministries. Plus, I know all the people at the Universalist church along with their systems. Do you need a coordinator to help with that part?"

Levi was stunned. He hadn't really thought that far ahead about the logistics. "Sybil, that's a brilliant idea. I hadn't even thought of that particular need, and I can't think of anyone more qualified than you to do it. If everyone really wants to go forward with this, you definitely have the job."

Levi then turned back to address the group. "So what about it? Do you guys wanna create this as an organized effort? Everyone in favor raise your hand."

Immediately hands shot up all over the room. Levi then addressed the room again. "Listen, I know not everyone here feels comfortable goin' out and talkin' to people on the street. And that's okay. To create a ministry of this kind'll require help in a lotta areas. Sybil's gonna need assistance in various areas to provide help for those who come in. Those of you who wanna be the 'Storm Troopers' out in the field are also prob'ly gonna need various kinds of help and training. And we'll need counselors and encouragers to talk to the people who come to us but are still not quite sure what they wanna do. As we begin this, we'll figure all that out so everyone who wants to participate will have a place. Does that sound good?"

Levi paused to let people respond. There were nods and affirmative chatter all over the room. "Okay then," Levi declared, "it is a done deal. Skeptopolis Community Church now officially has a gang outreach ministry. Let's take a few minutes to get some basic organization goin'. All who wanna go out and directly talk to people like Gino did, meet Axel over in the corner over there. Chris'll help you guys coordinate. Those who wanna work in support services, meet Sybil over by the table in the back. Sybil, I know you haven't had time to organize anything yet, but you do know the kinds of logistical elements that need to be put in place, so share those with your group and begin sorting out what needs to happen. Those of you who wanna do somethin' but are not quite sure where you wanna plug in, come meet me at the front. We can take some time to sort out your thinking."

Levi also realized that this kind of ministry was probably not for everyone. God has different plans for different people. "And guys," he picked back up," I also realize that there may be some of you who are not really comfortable with the idea of workin' in this particular ministry. That's okay, too. This won't be the only ministry our church does, and God may be wanting you to serve Him in a different way. If you're not sure and just wanna sit in and listen but not participate right now, that's fine, too."

The crowd broke into various groups and met for another 45 minutes or so to start getting organized on their specific areas of ministry. What had been intended to stop Gino's gang ministry, had only served to launch something even bigger.

CHAPTER 70

ON THE STREETS

Axel could not have been more fired up about continuing Gino's legacy, and he knew right where he wanted to start. With Gino dead and Serena in jail, the Red Flag Gang found themselves in total disarray and without a leader – numbers had dropped so low they could barely function at all. Since they had all been friends of his, he felt he might have some immediate influence there. And since he had been diligently learning from Levi how to effectively share his faith, he felt confident that he could do it.

So, the next morning, he made his way to the club house on Straight Street. When he arrived, the entire rest of the gang was there.

Axel walked up to the door and knocked. Immediately, Dillon opened the door with a gun in his hand, ready to defend himself and the others if needed. With the gang practically leaderless and in such disarray, they were increasingly antsy that some other gang might want to take advantage of their weakness. Seeing Axel, he immediately put the gun away and smiled. It was great to see a friendly face.

"Axel, what are you doin' here?" Dillon inquired with a look of shock on his face and a note of surprise in his voice.

"Hey Dillon, mind if I come in?"

"Yeah, of course. You're always welcome here. You know that. Just surprised to see you, that's all."

Axel smiled, "Yeah, I thought you might be. I just wanted to come by and see how you guys are doin.'"

"Hey everybody," Dillon yelled loud enough for everyone in the house to hear, "Axel's here."

Hearing it was Axel, everyone came out and greeted him like an old friend. After all the bad news of late, it was great to see a friendly face.

"Hey, Axel," Sarah called out as she walked into the room, "what brings you here. I thought you were done with us."

Axel looked over at Sarah and waited for her to get closer before speaking. "No, Sarah, I've never been *done* with you guys. In fact, I think about you all the time. And in spite of our recent disagreement about stayin' with the gang, you guys are still family. And now with Selena gone, I worry about you even more. With the gang weakened like this, I'm afraid the Checkers'll try to take the rest of you out in order to take over the territory."

"Well, for sure, we do stay on high alert all the time now," Dillon responded. We've thought of that, too."

With that, Axel began to share the reason he came over. "Guys, I know before you had your reasons for not leavin' the gang. And you had Selena pushing you to stay. But now you're in an entirely different situation. You've had a chance to see that there really is a way outta gang life, and there's people who'll help you with that. I remember when Gino first asked us if we had aspirations for our lives, and to a person everyone shared a dream they had growin' up. But then, when push came to shove, you decided you didn't feel it was really possible. Now that you know it is, what do you think? Would you like to take the step?"

Immediately when Axel made his offer, Sarah spoke up, "Axel, before I really was afraid. I didn't believe it was possible. But you guys've really done it. I, personally, would like to give it a shot. I've always wanted to become a pilot. Do you really think it'd be possible?"

"Sarah," Axel replied, "I think the only limitations are the ones you place on yourself. Our network can help you get in school, and I know there's a helicopter pilot school over at the technical college where a couple of guys are already studyin'. I don't see why you couldn't do it if you can pass the entrance exam – and we have people who can help you get ready for that, too."

"Then I'm in. I'm ready to leave this life!" Sarah responded.

"And what about the rest of you guys? Do you wanna make a move?"

One by one the entire rest of the gang told Axel they wanted to make the change. In fact, they were ready to completely disband the gang and move in a new direction.

Hearing that, Axel continued, "Remember when Gino first approached us about leavin' the gang and he, along with Chris, shared how there was a spiritual element to all this that'd allow us to not only have a different life path, but an entirely different perspective on life, as well?" Everyone definitely remembered that day and nodded their heads.

"Well," Axel continued, "I can tell you from firsthand experience, and in watchin' over 40 different people leavin' gang life, that the spiritual component really does make all the difference. You've heard the message of Christ already. Who of you'd like to take that step, as well?"

The first one to raise his hand was Dillon. Then the rest of them, one by one, raised their hand as well. So just as Levi had taught him, Axel led the gang members to personally invite Christ into their lives.

After they had made and confirmed their decisions for Christ, Alexander spoke up. "Axel, what do we do now? How can we go forward? I can think of several things that need to be addressed, and pretty quickly. First, we've gotta figure out a way to get rid of the gang affiliation, and get the Checkers, and other gangs, off our back. They're like sharks circlin' when they smell blood in the water. Then, we need to do somethin' with this house. If we're not makin' money to support it, we won't be able to keep it. Then, what do we do about movin' forward and makin' some money? And you mentioned school – what about that?"

"Guys, first let me call Levi and let him know what you've decided. He'll set everything in motion. We've got a network that'll help with all that – food, school, work, whatever's needed. As far as livin' space, I'm not sure, but maybe we can make the gang house a part of the housing network for former gang members. Since it wouldn't be a gang house anymore, maybe we could officially turn it over to the network and they could take over the support. And with that, I don't see any reason why you guys couldn't just keep livin' here. What do you think about that? Should we explore that option?"

"Wow!" Dillon responded with a sound of relief clearly coming from his voice. "You think that's really possible? We were thinkin' we'd eventually just have to abandon it and try to make our own way individually."

With that, Axel pulled out his cell, called Levi, and told him what was going on. Levi was beside himself with excitement. "Axel, we'll set the plans in motion immediately. Someone from the team'll be over there in about an hour to begin workin' out the details."

After they hung up the phone, Axel looked at Dillon and asked, "Well, what do you think? Shall we walk over to the Checkers' house and put the non-interference plan into motion? I'll go with you if you like."

"I'm really nervous about that," Dillon responded, "but if this is really what the group wants to do, I'll do it." Hearing him volunteer for this unenviable task, the rest of them affirmed that, yes, that's what they wanted."

"Don't worry about it one bit," Axel replied, "I've got your back." So, the two of them walked the four blocks over to the Checkers' club house.

When they got there, three of the Checkers gang were out in the yard. Seeing the Red Flag guys walk up immediately caused them to go into a defensive posture.

"Guys, "Axel called out, as both he and Dillon put their hands out where they could be seen, "we're not here to cause trouble. We wanna talk to George."

One of the guys in the yard immediately turned and ran inside to let George know what was going on. After about a minute, he emerged from the front door of the house and walked down to where Axel and Dillon stood, holding their hands up slightly, palms open, in a gesture of peace.

With a scowl on his face and as much gruffness as he could muster, he spoke to Axel, "What do you Red Flag losers want!"

Axel took a step forward and stood directly in front of George. "George, I don't know whether or not you remember me, but I'm Axel, a former member of the Red Flag Gang. We're not here lookin' for trouble."

"Okay then," George responded curtly, "what do you want?!"

"We wanted to let you know that we're disbandin' the Red Flag Gang. We'll no longer be involved in gang activities. All we ask is that you guys just leave us alone from here on out. We're gonna stay in our house, but we'll no longer be competing with you for business. Are you willin' to make that deal?"

For a moment, George stood there in stunned silence. Finally he spoke, "Did I hear you right? You're disbanding the gang? You're no longer gonna compete with us for customers?"

"That's right," Axel replied. "All we ask is that you leave us alone. We won't bother you and you don't bother us. Do we have a deal?"

Over the years, there had been a lot of bad blood between the Checkers and the Red Flag Gang, with even a certain amount of actual bloodshed. That kind of thing is hard to let go of, as there are always people who want to settle old scores. At the same time, those kinds of spats always put workers out of commission and hurt business. George thought to himself, *If gettin' rid of the competition only requires leavin' 'em alone, that'd be a pretty sweet deal.*

"Okay," George responded. "You have a deal. But if I catch you competin' with us on anything, the deal's off. Is that clear?"

"The threats are unnecessary, George," Axel responded. "All our people have found Christ, and we're just not into that kinda thing anymore. I hope someday you'll also experience the life changing transformation that comes from knowin' Jesus."

Hearing that kind of talk made George think back to Gino's funeral service. He thought to himself, *That's what that pastor Levi talked about – a life changin' experience. This religion talk is weirdin' me out.*

"Okay, just get outta here. And quit with the religion talk! I don't want my people bein' messed up by that."

"George," Axel replied, "I won't make any promises on that front. I promised not to compete with you and your gang business, and we'll keep our promise. But you'll have to guard the souls of your people yourself."

With that, Axel and Dillon turned around, went back to the house, and shared the news with the others – which provided a huge sense of relief to the entire group. Shortly after that, Sybil and Chris arrived and began to put a plan into motion to get the rest of the gang started on their new life.

CHAPTER 71

A DESIRE TO GROW

A few days later, Chris received a call from Jill. Since turning her life over to Christ, she had become a fixture in the new church, and quite vocal about her newfound faith in Christ – but it hadn't come without a cost. Many of her old friends had thrown her to the curb, and former allies had turned on her and become enemies.

"Chris, can we talk?" Jill asked. "I'm strugglin' with some things, and I need some advice and help."

"Absolutely, Jill," Chris replied. "When would you like to meet?"

"I'm at work right now, and I have a couple more meetings to go to, but I'll be done about 4:00 this afternoon. Could we meet then over at the church?"

"Absolutely," Chris replied. "I'll see you then."

At 4:30, Jill walked through the front door of the church. Chris was already there waiting for her. "Jill, is this private, or would it be good if Levi sat in, as well."

"Oh yeah, that'd be great. I can get the combined knowledge and wisdom of you both," Jill responded with a smile on her face.

"Okay then, go ahead and have a seat in the conference room and I'll go get him," Chris replied as he turned and headed toward Levi's office.

When he got there, Levi's door was cracked open, so Chris stuck his head in. "Levi, Jill's here and wants to talk. Can you join us?"

Levi jumped right up and headed toward the door. "Absolutely! Glad to do anything I can to help."

When the two entered the conference room, Jill was already seated at the table, so they walked over and sat across from her. "Hey, Jill," Levi greeted, "How's it goin'?"

"Well, things are goin' pretty well over all, but I do have somethin' I want to ask you guys about."

"Sure," Chris replied, "but before we jump into that, how's Tonya doin'?"

Hearing that question, Jill beamed. "She's doin' fantastic! Because she was bed ridden for so long, she's havin' to do therapy to get her strength back, but she's gettin' stronger by the day, and'll actually begin school next week. She may have to have some help gettin' around at first, but the way she's makin' progress, I don't think that'll last too long. I'm still breathless over what God did with her."

Chris and Levi, too, smiled from ear to ear. "We feel the same way, Jill," Chris gushed. "I get giddy just thinkin' about it. So what can we do for you today?"

"Chris, the reason I called is because I need some advice about dealin' with opposition. I've never seen anyone do it as well as you, and wanted to see what kinda tips you could give me. I've watched how you've done that with other people. Shoot, I've watched how you did it with me – and I've never seen anyone more effective than you.

"Ever since I came to know Christ, I haven't tried to hide it from anyone. I'm not tryin' to be 'in your face' about it, but my entire attitude and demeanor's changed since then, and people have noticed. And when they ask about it, I'm not hesitant to share.

"That said, a lotta the people I share it with get downright antagonistic. I get it, I really do. I used to be the same way. Chris, I was even that way toward you. But you always took the high road. You never hid your beliefs or backed down, but you were always respectful, and I noticed that. As I've interacted with people, I've really tried to imitate you that way."

"What kind and encouraging words, Jill" Chris replied feeling a little self-conscious. "Sometimes you just don't know how you're comin' across to people. But what you've just said affirms that doin' what's right is always right – and God'll use it. And when you do that with other people, he'll use you, too. You might not see the results right away, but it's happenin'."

"Yeah, I really see the attitude thing, and I can go with that. But there's one other thing I'm strugglin' with. I don't have a background as a Christian growin' up, and my ignorance is massive when it comes to talkin' about the Christian faith. I've been learnin' and growin' so much since I've been comin' to the church, but I'm still not far enough along to have a deep knowledge base. And that's where I am strugglin.'"

"Okay." Levi jumped in. "What in particular makes you feel that way?"

"Well," Jill continued, "when I credit Christ for changin' my life, some people immediately begin to jump on my Christian faith, and often ask questions or make comments about the Bible that I just don't know how to answer. How can I deal with that?"

Chris knew exactly what she meant and searched his mind for a way to explain what she could do. "Jill, I get it. People often do that with me, too. Fortunately, I've been in church long enough to have had the opportunity to learn the answers to a lotta those kinds of questions, and gain experience in how to handle 'em. But there's still a lot I don't know."

"Shoot," Levi jumped in, "I've been to seminary and there's a lot even I don't know. Learning about the Bible and how to interact with people is definitely a lifelong process."

Chris picked back up, "Absolutely! But here's another principle that should be helpful for you, as well. For people who are really antagonistic, answerin' their questions generally doesn't even matter. They're not lookin' for answers, they're looking to justify themselves. If they're actually attackin' you with an ugly attitude, I don't care how many of their questions you answer, they'll still keep badgerin' you with more. You probably know that from how you used to do it yourself. There's value in knowin' the answers, of course. It helps strengthen your own confidence, and it can help other people if they're really serious about wantin' to know the answers. But if not, you're pretty much wastin' your time doin' that."

Jill thought for a second about how she did, indeed, do that to other people – and it caused her to lower her eyes and feel a little ashamed. "Yeah," she replied, "you're absolutely right. That's exactly what happens. What, then, can a person do in that situation?"

"In that situation, there's a couple things you can do, Jill," Chris answered. "First, you can focus on what God's actually done in your life. In your case, there's two really big things you can share with 'em. First, you can tell 'em how you personally met God and how that changed your life. Antagonistic people can dispute a lotta things, but they can't dispute that. The second thing you can share is what happened with Tonya. That's an amazing and powerful story that even the doctors called a miracle. They won't have a way to dispute it. You can simply ask 'em how they'd explain those two things.

"But I realize there's also people who are so hateful they'll dismiss even your testimony. When that happens and they continue to attack your faith, you need to turn their argument back on 'em and make 'em tell you why their evaluation of your faith is valid. It's only right that if they're gonna blast your faith based on the assumptions of their faith, that they be forced to justify why *their* faith is the truth."

"Hmmm, that's an interesting approach," Jill replied thoughtfully. "So how do I do that?"

"Well, you were at the roundtable that evening when I had the discussion with the university professors," Chris replied. "I used that approach when dealin' with them. Here's the principle behind what I did.

"Most people who are Naturalists honestly believe they're not religious. They truly believe their beliefs are based on scientific facts. The truth is, though, that they're not!"

"Yes," Jill interjected. "I've heard both you and Levi talk about that in the training classes."

"Right," Chris continued. "Naturalism is a religious system as surely as Christianity. People who believe in it don't believe it based on science, because there's no science to back up their belief that the natural universe, operating by natural laws, is all that exists. So that's where you challenge your detractors. All you havta do is ask 'em 'why' they think their belief is true. And when they answer, ask 'em *how* they know it's true. Most'll probly try to tell you that science backs up their beliefs, but you and I both know it doesn't, and that's somethin' you can challenge.

"Specifically, it's impossible to empirically demonstrate **five basic things**. First, *that the universe began out of nothing or is eternal.* Based on naturalistic logic, the universe had to either emerge out of nothing or it had to be eternal, with no beginning. Obviously, neither of those can be demonstrated by science. Second, *that the matter and energy that make up the natural universe has a natural source.* Third, *that life can emerge out of non-life.* Fourth, *that less complex life forms can evolve into more complex forms.* And last, *that consciousness can* *emerge out of non-consciousness.* With that, you can point out that they're simply sharing their religious beliefs with you. There's no actual science to back up any of those points.

"I can tell you, though, when you do that, many of 'em'll be in total denial and think you're crazy. It's never occurred to them that they're religious in any way. But don't let 'em off the hook. To the greatest degree possible, make 'em answer. Then, when they can't, at the very least you'll have sown seeds of doubt into their minds that'll haunt 'em into the future. And at some point, who knows, that might lead 'em to recognize that the religion they follow's a false one."

"Chris, you're a genius," Jill exclaimed. "I totally get it. You've described my former life to a T. That's exactly the kinda thoughts and attitudes I once had. And when people made arguments like that to me, it didn't even make sense. But at the same time, it really did sow seeds of doubt in my mind – and now I see it. My beliefs simply were not true. And now that you've explained how that works, I know I can do that. I absolutely can!"

"Yes," Levi once again inserted himself into the conversation, "and you can save your effort in actually trying to answer questions about the Christian faith for people who are sincerely interested in hearin' what you have to say. Those answers'll be meaningful to them, and those are the kinda people who'll be patient with you while you search out answers you don't know."

"You guys, I've taken enough of your time today,"Jill said as she got ready to leave. "You've been so helpful. The light bulbs are going off like crazy in my head. I'm sure I'll have lots of opportunities, even over the next several days, to put this into practice."

Jill then got up, walked outside, and headed toward her car. Being the gentlemen they were, Chris and Levi walked with her to keep her company. "Jill," Chris said as she got into her car, "you feel free to call on us any time. We're here for you."

CHAPTER 72

PRISON

"Hey Selena," Delta said greeting her through the glass in the prison visiting area.

Chris also greeted her, "How are ya holdin' up, Selena?"

Hi guys," Selena responded. "Thanks for comin' by. I'm doin' okay."

Chris didn't know Selena very well, so he decided to bring Delta along to hopefully make things a bit more relaxed. The prison officials let both of them in at the same time to have a short chat. The meeting booth was not really made to accommodate two people, so he and Delta had to both put their ears to the single headphone to speak to her. Chris did most of the talking, and Delta mostly observed, not really knowing what to say.

Even though Chris didn't know Selena well, he did know her well enough that he felt a need to talk to her after she was jailed for killing Gino. He had first met her before Gino even received Christ. Sometimes when Chris would go by the gang house, she'd be around, and they made some small talk. He even managed to have one or two deeper conversations with her as he and Gino became friends.

The chances for a fairly long trial process loomed ahead and, no doubt, Selena would face a serious murder conviction. She would definitely spend a long time in prison – if she could even avoid the death penalty. And even though she had killed his friend, and came pretty close to killing him as well, Chris cared most about Selena's spiritual condition. So he got permission to speak to her, and she was willing to meet.

"I'll say this place is no walk in the park," Selena answered in response to Chris' question, "but no one's messin' with me."

I'm so sorry it's come to this," Chris told her with deep sadness in his voice. "I wish there was somethin' more I could do."

"Listen, Chris," Selena changed the subject, "first let me apologize to you for puttin' your life in danger like I did. I didn't really have anything against you. Gino was the one I felt broke trust with me."

"I appreciate that," Chris replied, "and I don't hold any animosity toward you. I do feel broken hearted about Gino though. You do realize, right, that he really loved you guys, and that was his entire motivation for wantin' to help you get outta gang life?"

"I know," Selena admitted. "He was definitely not bein' selfish in tryin' to do what he did. But I saw it as destroyin' my life, and at the time I wanted to stop what he was puttin' in motion. The gang life might not've been good for everybody, but it was good for me, and I was determined he wasn't gonna steal it from me."

"Looks like things haven't turned out the way you anticipated," Chris sighed. "Are you sorry about what you did?"

"Look Chris," Selena retorted, "I wasn't tryin' to kill Gino. I'm definitely sorry he's dead, and especially that I've ended up here. But I'm not sorry about takin' measures to protect what was mine. Gino was in the wrong, and he needed to pay."

At that point, Selena was starting to get a little worked up and Chris didn't want the conversation going that direction, so he changed the subject. "Well Selena, I didn't come here to get you worked up. I'm sorry if I've gotten you agitated."

"No, that's okay. I'm cool," Selena replied as she calmed herself down. "So just why did you come?"

"Selena, I know there's nothin' I can do for you to get you outta jail, but I did wanna see if there was somethin' else I could do for you. Back when Gino and I were sharin' with the gang about how your life could be changed from the inside through Jesus Christ, did you think about what it might be like to turn your life over to Christ at that time?"

Selena didn't really want to talk about that with Chris, but she also didn't want him to leave. No one else was going to come see her, and it was at least good to have someone from the outside to talk to. So, she decided to put up with the Jesus talk – at least for a little while. "Well, Chris, I'll admit there was a certain appeal to it. I mean, the gang life's definitely not warm and fuzzy ... and always havin' to look over your shoulder to avoid other gangs or the cops was stressful. But I was good at it and didn't wanna move into a situation where I was a 'nothin' again. Besides that, I just didn't believe any of that 'Christ' stuff."

"Well what about now?" Chris responded. "Now that your dream of livin' a gang life has pretty much ended, have you given any more thought about the inner peace and hope Christ can give to your life in the circumstances you're in now?"

"Chris," Selena replied, "I really appreciate the fact that you care about what happens to me. But just to be honest, no, I'm really not interested in goin' down that road. I've thought about it, and while the picture you paint's nice enough, deep in my heart I just don't believe it. I don't believe in God, and I believe that heaven's a pipe dream. I'm sorry to disappoint you that way. And besides that, there actually is a form of gang life here in lockup."

"I understand," Chris answered back. It's a decision you ultimately have to make for yourself. But while you don't believe it now, and think it's all a pipe dream, I wanna assure you it's not – it's absolutely real. And it's my personal sense of the profound reality of Christ that motivates me to care for you and want the best for you. And you might be interested in knowin' that since you've been in jail, the entire rest of the Red Flag Gang have given their lives to Christ, and they've decided to disband the gang altogether."

"Are you serious?! I can't believe they'd do that! You're not tryin' to yank my chain, are ya? Are you really serious?"

Chris replied, "Yeah, it's absolutely true. You're the only one left outside the spiritual family. Are you sure you don't wanna change your mind?"

Selena expelled a deep sigh as she tried to absorb what Chris had just told her. "I appreciate it, Chris," she said as she looked him squarely in the eye, "but in spite of everything, I simply don't believe. But I do appreciate your concern. I really do."

"So would you like for me, and some others, to come visit you periodically?" Chris asked.

Selena thought a second, then responded, "Yeah, that'd be nice."

"Now you do realize that when we come, we'll still talk to you about spiritual things, right? That's just our passion. You gonna mind that?"

"Well, I don't think you're gonna change my mind," Selena replied, "but once in a while it'd be nice to have someone to talk to from the outside."

"Okay then," Chris answered back, "I'll talk to the others and see what we can do."

"Listen, before I leave, do you mind if I have a prayer for you?" Chris asked.

"Suit yourself," Selena responded rather nonchalantly.

"Okay then, let's pray." Chris bowed his head and began, "Lord, I wanna lift Selena up to you today and ask you to protect her as she finds herself in such a dark environment. I know she's not ready, at this point, to open her life to you, but she's still one of your sweet creations and we know you love her very much. I wanna ask you to surround her life, and in the various ways that only you can, I ask that you'd protect her, and help her recognize your presence by putting in her a sense of inner peace, and even joy, that can only come from you. It's my prayer, Lord, that she recognizes this and ultimately knows you truly are real and are walkin' with her. I pray this in the name of our Lord Jesus Christ, Amen."

When Chris finished praying, he looked Selena in the eyes one more time and said, "Selena, we really do care about you, and we'll do all we can to support you."

With that, tears welled up in Selena's eyes. She tried to hide it, but Chris noticed. She knew he was sincere in what he was saying. "Thank you, Chris, for comin' by. You take care. And Delta, thank you for comin', too. It's good to see a friendly face."

They all then, said their goodbyes and hung up their phones. As Chris and Delta stood up to leave, they could see one of the prison guards on the other side of the glass come to lead Selena back to her cell. They felt very sad to watch her being led through the heavy steel door, and see it slam behind her.

CHAPTER 73

PRISON MINISTRY

After leaving the jail, Chris drove with Delta over to the church to share with Levi what had taken place. As the three talked, Delta asked if there was anything she could do to help Selena going forward.

As Levi listened to Delta's question, an idea popped into his head. "Delta, what do you think about the gang ministry we've started?"

"Well, I think it is fantastic! I wish I could do somethin' more, but right now I just don't feel I personally fit into it very well."

"And that is perfectly fine," Levi responded. "God equips and motivates people in very different ways to accomplish His purpose in the world. So tell me what you think about this. When you just asked if there was anything you could do to help Selena, an idea popped into my head. What would you think about helpin' start a prison ministry to help Selena and other women like her in prison?"

Delta's head jerked up, her jaw dropped, and her eyes popped open as she looked at Levi in surprise. "Huh? What'd that look like?"

"Well, it'd probably begin just by goin' to the jail and visitin' with Selena and encouragin' her – just like you and Chris did today. You could let her talk about her situation, but could also share, as appropriate, what's happenin' in your life and how you're growin' in Christ. There might be some others in the church who'd like to participate in that, as well. We could probly set up a plan to get a rotation of people to go visit her. What would you think about somethin' like that?"

"I like that!" Delta exclaimed. "Now that's somethin' I could get into." She then hesitated a moment and said, "But I wouldn't even know where to start."

"Delta, you know we'd never just throw you to the wolves. I'd work with you personally to train you in everything you need to know. And I believe God'll bring other people who'd like to do it, too. You won't be alone, and we'll help you every step of the way."

Levi continued, "Now just let me brainstorm with you for a minute. I'm actually envisioning something that could grow even bigger. What if we were eventually able to get a more complete prison ministry goin'. Maybe we could set up some courses to help those women get their GED, or maybe even some other kinds of classes like sewing or somethin'. In a place like that, there's bound to be a lotta people who feel a real sense of desperation and emptiness in their lives and would like to be able to do somethin' constructive to fill their time and give some hope. Even those things can cause 'em to open up to the gospel message. And even if Selena herself isn't interested in Christ right now, she might still be a key to gettin' somethin' goin' on the inside.

"Think of this. We start with just Selena, but we also make relationships with people at the jail and get permission to start a few activities inside, along with a Bible study. I bet there'd be a lotta interest.

"And to further expand the possibilities, we could not only share Christ with the ladies inside, but when they get out, we could plug 'em into the support system we already have set up for people comin' outta the gangs. I bet Sybil would jump at that, as well. Am I thinkin' too big for you, Delta?"

"Wow!" Delta replied, "It's actually breath taking. Just listening to you talk, I feel this excitement burnin' inside. You really think God could use me to help people like that?"

"I am absolutely sure of it," Levi replied. "If you're game, then, I'm gonna bring this up to the church next Sunday and get their approval. Are you in?"

"I'm all in!" Delta exclaimed enthusiastically. "I am definitely all in!"

CHAPTER 74

SURPRISE GUEST

The next Sunday as Chris looked around to see who might be in the worship service, he spotted someone who caught his attention. *Could that be Steve Craven over on the left side toward the back?* he thought to himself. *Could that really be him?* Chris was so shocked he did a double take to make sure his eyes weren't deceiving him. *Yep, that's Steve alright. What in the world's he doin' here? He was one of the most anti-Christian people I've ever met. Maybe he's here doin' some research.*

As soon as the service was over, Chris made a beeline in his direction and caught up to him in the foyer, Chris tapped him on the arm, "Steve, what a surprise. How ya doin'?"

Steve turned and faced him with a huge smile on his face. "Well hey, Chris. I was hopin' I'd run into you here," he said. "Actually, I'm here only reluctantly."

Chris wrinkled his brow and gave a little sideways glance. "Huh? How's that?"

"Chris, it's kind of a long story. Can I take you to lunch and tell you about it?"

"Well yeah, sure," Chris replied. "I don't have anything else going on. Where'd you like to go?"

"You like Indian food?" Steve responded. "There's a pretty good Indian restaurant just up the road – The Taj Mahal."

Chris loved Indian food and knew the restaurant well. "Yeah, I love that place."

"Okay then, that's what we'll do. You wanna leave your car here and ride down there with me?" Steve offered.

"Sure, that works," Chris replied. "Thanks for the invite. It's really good to see you again."

"On the short drive to the restaurant, Chris and Steve engaged in small talk just to catch up. When they arrived, they got out of the car, walked inside the restaurant, and waited for someone to seat them. A smiling Indian man almost immediately walked up, held up two fingers and tilted his head to the side as a way of asking if they were a party of two. Chris and Steve nodded and were led to a table and handed a menu. Both already knew what they wanted, so they went ahead and ordered and handed the menus back.

When the waiter left, Chris asked, "Well, tell me the story. You've been a bit cryptic."

Steve smiled. "Well Chris, you might not believe this, but I've become a Christian." Steve paused to let the full effect of that declaration sink in and watched as Chris' eyes bugged out and his jaw dropped open in disbelief.

"What?!" Chris exclaimed. "I guess you can tell you pulled a big surprise on me here. You could've blown me over with a feather."

"Well maybe I should've waited to pull that on you when we were facing each other at the dojo," Steve replied jokingly. With that, they both laughed out loud.

"Well, if you had, I can assure you, you'd have won that point," Chris replied as he continued to laugh out loud. "So tell me the story."

"Well, Chris," Steve began, "I suppose it all began when we first met at the karate workshop. I had read the article about you in the paper already and was pretty disgusted that you mentioned your faith in Christ. I felt that anyone who believed in God was just an uninformed ignoramus. I was so arrogant that it compelled me to ask that stupid question – which you brilliantly handled, by the way.

"I think you probly know I asked you to come speak to my class because I honestly thought you'd embarrass yourself in front of 'em, and that the word would get out to the entire city through the *Times* just what a fraud you were. Obviously, you handled yourself brilliantly, and that plan completely backfired.

"I'll admit it now, that while your performance in the class really frosted me, it also made me start thinkin' about the underlying beliefs of my Atheism in a way that I'd never considered before. Those questions continued to nag my mind well after that.

"But at the time, I was really frosted. Following that, I got together with doctors Everson, Gray, and Albritton, and we conspired to bring you down publicly. You may not realize this, but the roundtable was our attempt to do that."

Chris interrupted, "Actually, I did suspect that might be the case, but this is the first time I've had it confirmed."

"Well, I'm ashamed to say it, but it's true. But once again, you handled yourself brilliantly, and your arguments at the roundtable forced me to think even more deeply about the viability of my **atheistic faith**. From that time on I couldn't get it off my mind. What if my beliefs are not true? How can I prove it? So I began a deep dive into the claims of Christianity, as well as the evidence for the truth of my atheistic beliefs. In the end, I had to admit to myself that I was wrong, and that shook me to my very core. What could I do?

"So, one afternoon as I was takin' a walk around campus by myself thinkin' about it, I suddenly realized that I believed in Christ. I had to be the most reluctant convert to Christ since C. S. Lewis. And that's my story."

Chris just sat there with rapt attention, still not believing his ears. "Well," he asked, "how's that gonna affect your work as a sociology professor at the university?"

"Not 'will affect,'" Steve replied, "'DID affect!' I knew I couldn't keep hiding this. After all, teachin' what I teach pretty much requires that I hold a naturalistic worldview. The administration would never allow a Christian to teach a non-evolutionary theory of sociology at that school. I knew that, so before I blew the whistle on myself, I began makin' some inquiries as to where I might land if I left the school. Actually, I was just hired by a Christian think tank that focuses on social policy. Get the irony of this ... I was hired to write and speak on the shortcomings of evolutionary theory as it relates to sociology. I start next week, and it doesn't even require me to move. And Chris, all this is because of you!"

"I'm still flabbergasted!" Chris replied. "I had no idea. So how'd your colleagues handle it?"

Steve went on, "Well, the first ones I told were Everson, Gray, and Albritton. Actually, Dr. Albritton was okay with it. My belief, as I explained it, wasn't his cuppa tea, but he didn't really have anything negative to say. You know, right, that even though he's a religion professor and pastor, he still believes in naturalistic evolutionary theory, right?"

"I actually haven't talked with him directly about that particular topic," Chris replied, "but since the roundtable was totally about that, and it was his program, it certainly doesn't surprise me. That said, I have talked to him directly about theological issues, and his theological beliefs actually do have a naturalistic underpinning. So yeah, I can see that."

Steve continued, "Well, while Albritton's reaction was muted, the other two went ballistic! They couldn't believe I was serious – that I could possibly believe 'foolishness' like that. In fact, they were so mad that before I could even talk with the administration, they marched themselves over to the president's office and demanded I be fired. The crazy thing is, I'd actually already set up an appointment to talk to the president myself the next day. After bein' such close friends with those two for so long, it came as quite a shock to see 'em turn on me that way.

"Well, when I went into the president's office the next day, I can tell ya it wasn't pretty. They couldn't just up and fire me because I'm tenured. But I know how miserable they could make my life – and they'd do it. But I already had the new job, so I gave 'em my resignation letter right there on the spot. I already had it prepared."

After a short pause, Chris finally spoke again. "Steve, your story's taken my breath away. What can I do for you?"

"Well, Chris," Steve replied, "I'm a pretty quick study, so I understand a lotta the things I'll be dealin' with. But I'm still pretty new at bein' a Christian, so I feel certain there's a lot I don't know, and a lotta nuances about expressing the Christian faith in life that I'm simply not aware of. The think tank knows all this and they're willin' to work with me, and more importantly have patience with me, as I work with them. But I'll still need a learning venue. I plan to join your church and be baptized, but do you guys have some training opportunities there as well?"

"Absolutely!" Chris replied enthusiastically. "In fact, we do that every week. It's actually a central element of our church operation, and you're certainly welcome to come join us in that. And, of course, if there's anything outside of what's dealt with in that class I can help you with, you can call on me anytime – and on Levi, as well. We'll both do anything we can to help you. There's still a lot I don't know either. But I know people who know, and if you have things that are over my head, I can hook you up with others who can help.

"Oh, and there's another resource we can probly get you hooked up with, as well, if you wanna go even deeper – which you very well may need or want to do because of your new job. There are theology courses, and even degrees, that can be had online related to your focus. That may also be somethin' you wanna consider."

"Oh, that's fantastic!" Steve responded enthusiastically. "I hadn't even thought of that possibility. I'm really excited to embark on this new adventure. I just wanna thank you again for your part in my journey."

"Well, you're welcome in as much as I can take credit for anything," Chris replied, still dumbfounded at what he'd heard. "But God's obviously worked in your life far beyond anything I've done. I know you'll be a great asset to God's work here in Skeptopolis. I can't wait to see how he uses you."

As Steve shared his story, it got Chris' mind whirring. "Steve," Chris asked, "if you're gonna continue livin' in Skeptopolis, have you considered how you might still have some influence in the academic community at the university?"

"You know," Steve replied, "that thought keeps popping into my mind, but I don't know how it could even be possible. Those who used to be my closest friends and associates have literally turned their backs on me, the administration's pretty much made me persona non grata at the school, and now I don't really have much access to the students. I'd like to do somethin' to reach into that community, but I'm not sure it's possible now."

"Well what if I could come up with a way to make it possible," Chris responded. "Would you be interested in exploring it?"

Steve wrinkled his brow and looked Chris in the eye, "What do you have in mind?"

"Well," Chris replied, "as a result of my interactions at the university with your class and the roundtable, and a little bit at the dojo, as well, we have a small group of college students who are comin' to the church. Four of 'em have actually already accepted Christ. What would you think about helping to start a dedicated college ministry for the church, and perhaps even an actual campus ministry to reach more deeply into campus life. Might you be interested in that?"

Steve squinted his eyes as he thought more deeply about that possibility. "Well, maybe. But I'm not really sure I'd know what to do."

"Well, think of it this way," Chris continued, "you already know that doin' research and writing for the think tank is gonna be a vehicle for you to learn more about Christianity and its application in the field you'll be writin' about, right?"

"Absolutely," Steve responded. "Researching and writing are some of the best ways to learn for yourself."

"Well," Chris continued, "haven't you found, over the years, that teachin' your classes creates the same dynamic? I know I've personally found that when I teach, I end up learnin' more than anyone in my class."

Steve pondered that for a moment, then replied to Chris' question, "You know, you're absolutely right. Over the years, that's been a platform for some of my biggest insights."

"And you're already a skilled teacher," Chris continued his thought. "Doin' something like that could be right up your alley. And we could set you up with someone who'd work with you on that if it would help."

"Chris, I already mentioned that the kinda thing you're suggesting's been burning in my mind, but I just couldn't see a way to pull it off. But as we're talkin' now, that burning compulsion's bein' rekindled. Do you really think it's a possibility? Could we actually start somethin' like that?"

"Steve," Chris answered, "you don't have any way of knowin' this, but we've already been prayin' about how to help our college students more, and you may very well be the answer to our prayers. I don't know that you've personally met the church's pastor, Levi, yet, but would you be willin' to go with me and talk about this with him?"

"You know," Steve answered as he thought about what was happening, "this Christianity stuff's still so new to me, but it is so obvious God has His hand at work in all of this. I feel like I'm just along for the ride. But it's an exciting ride! Yeah, I'm ready to talk."

"Well, if you have the time right now, I could give him a call and we could do it this afternoon. What do you think?"

Steve replied, "Yeah, let's go for it."

With that confirmation, Chris pulled out his phone, called Levi, and gave him the one-minute version of his conversation with Steve. Then, he agreed to meet the two of them at the church.

After they finished eating, Steve took Chris back to the church to meet Levi. At that meeting, they set a plan in motion to establish a college ministry for the church that would include an outreach to the university campus. It was another affirmation that God was doing something profound in Skeptopolis.

CHAPTER 75

ONE LAST LOOK

I t was hard to believe that he'd be leaving Skeptopolis after all that had transpired. After he finished packing and putting everything in the rental trailer, Chris decided to take one last cruse around town for old times' sake. He first drove down the street past the dojo, then turned and headed into the heart of the gang district. Everyone there knew him and his car, so he knew no one would bother him.

From there he headed toward the Burger Barn. He was going to just drive past but decided to stop and get a vanilla malt. After ordering and picking it up, he went and sat at a corner table by himself. He thought about Gino and the celebrations he had enjoyed there with friends.

After about 20 minutes, Chris walked back to his car and headed toward the university. As he drove around campus, he especially noted Darwin Hall and the religion building. That's where so much of his adventure started.

From there he drove over to the *Skeptopolis Times'* building. As he drove by, he spotted Connie coming out the front door. Seeing her, he stopped in the street and had a short chat with her to say a final goodbye. "Chris," Connie said as they wrapped up their conversation, "I wanna hear from you after the national tournament, you got that? People in Skeptopolis'll be very interested in what you do, and I wanna write the story."

"Okay, I promise," Chris replied with a mischievous grin on his face. He knew how Connie loved to have those exclusive scoops. She didn't mention the surprise he was in for tomorrow.

From there, Chris drove downtown by City Hall and the court house. It conjured up lots of memories – of meetings with Jill and the trial. Continuing down the street he went by Mark's law office and further on past the sports arena where it all started. Going by there also brought back memories of the karate workshop.

Turning right off Main Street took him in front of Zorn Mercantile, then down by the country club where he'd attended the Chamber of Commerce meeting. And just a little further down that road was the cemetery where Gino was laid to rest.

When he got to the cemetery, Chris parked his car and got out to visit Gino's grave. Standing in front of his headstone, Chris knelt and touched Gino's name, voicing a prayer of thanksgiving to God for putting Gino in his life. He especially thanked Him for the way he used Gino to influence his own gang members, and then all the others who came to Christ because of his efforts. Before departing, he called out over Gino's grave, "Gino, I look forward to one day joining you in heaven with Christ."

Chris then walked back to his car and headed toward the church. When he arrived, he pulled into the parking lot and just sat there for about ten minutes thinking about all that had happened to make the church a reality.

When he finally pulled out of the church parking lot, Chris headed back home to his apartment for a little while longer. It had definitely been an exciting time – an unbelievable adventure of faith – especially to see how God had worked so mightily in his life.

CHAPTER 76

HEADING OUT

Chris had continued to train at CJ's dojo for the upcoming national tournament in Washington, DC. About a month before he was scheduled to leave for Washington, Chris began to get the same kind of feeling he had before the tournament in Skeptopolis – that maybe God was calling him to something special. And over that one-month period, he had, indeed, become totally convinced that God was leading him to do just that. When he began to feel more certain about it, he started making the necessary preparations to pull it off. It wasn't really that complicated because he just didn't have that much stuff. He could easily load up a rental trailer just as when he came to Skeptopolis.

Besides being the nation's capital, Washington was also a place where people generally didn't have much use for God. Most went there to immerse themselves in the center of the nation's power and wealth. And while, generally speaking, Washingtonians were not as overtly hateful toward Christians as the people in Skeptopolis, the entrenched nature of naturalistic beliefs was every bit as formidable.

Over his last few days in Skeptopolis, as the time approached to leave, Chris had many conversations with Levi about what he'd been feeling. "Levi," Chris once pondered out loud, "I know what's happened in Skeptopolis is very unique, and it'll never be duplicated exactly anywhere else. But do you think God might do somethin' similar in Washington, DC, as He's done here? I'm wonderin' if I should prepare to stay there after the tournament and see if God might use me in that place, too."

"Well Chris," Levi replied with a chuckle in his voice, "you'd have to win first. Ya think you can do that?"

Chris smiled. "Well, who knows. Maybe I'll be a huge bust. On the other hand, if God's wantin' to use me in that situation, I'm ready to offer myself to Him."

"Well, I'll tell you what," Levi responded, "if God opens the door, we'll be prepared to sponsor you livin' there for a while. And I'll also talk to Pastor Trumann. I know after what God's been doin' here, he'd be behind you 100 percent." Based partially on those kinds of heart-to-heart conversations, Chris finally felt led to take the step of moving to Washington.

Chris planned to drive to Washington in his car. He would leave on Monday. He planned to pull out about 10:00 in the morning and make it there in a single day. The night before, he and Levi packed up his car with the rental trailer behind it and was ready to go except for one bag he would need for his last overnight stay.

Levi left around 8:00 the next morning to head over to the church and said his good-byes before he left. After Levi left, Chris went into the kitchen and made himself some breakfast.

As he was eating, his phone rang. "Chris, this is Levi, It seems you left a bag of your stuff on the counter here in the office. You wanna swing by and pick it up on your way outta town?"

Chris was a little perplexed. He didn't remember leaving anything there, but it wouldn't be the first time he'd forgotten something. "Yeah, I'll swing by. I'm gettin' ready to head out now. I'll be there in about 10 minutes."

When Chris pulled up to the church parking lot, it was totally filled with cars, and there were a couple of hundred people screaming and holding signs that said things like: "Thank you, Chris." "We love you, Chris." "National Champion." And bunches of others.

As Chris pulled in, he was totally shocked. Not expecting anything like this, tears of joy began to spill down his cheeks. *How in the world did they pull this off without me knowin' anything about it,* he thought to himself.

When he got out of the car, masses of people mobbed him and started hugging him and cheering him on. They walked him over to the front of the building where Levi stood with everyone gathered around. Then Levi pulled out a microphone so everyone could hear and said, "Chris, this was not my idea. You know I'd never be for building your ego up like this," he said laughing out loud. "Seriously, though, these people love you so much they wouldn't allow me to let you leave without one last opportunity to say goodbye." He then handed the mic to Jill.

"Chris," she began, "God used you to change my life. I want you to know that both Tonya and I will never forget what you've done for us. I know I wasn't kind to you at all in the beginning, but you ignored that and shared God's love with me in spite of it all. You'll be greatly missed."

When she finished, she handed the mic to Gunner, who thanked him on behalf of the former gang members for believing in them when no one else did. "Chris, none of us could've ever imagined that our lives would turn out the way they have. God used you to make it happen for us. We'll all be forever grateful."

Gunner then handed the mic to Steve. "Chris," he began, "when we first met, I hated you. Well, really, I hated God, but I took it out on you as His representative. But your faithfulness to Him in the face of some really serious persecution was the catalyst God used to bring me to Him. I wanna thank you for bein' faithful, and I can't wait to see how God uses you in the future."

Then one after another, twenty different people spoke parting words of gratitude for how Chris had influenced their lives, and about how God had used him to turn their lives around.

When everyone had taken their turn, they gave the mic to Chris. As he stood before the crowd, tears flowed down his face. He was so choked up that, at first, he had a hard time saying anything. When he finally regained his composure enough to speak, he said. "You guys mean the world to me. My heart's overflowing with love and gratitude to God for you. Thank you for sharing your love and your lives. You'll always be family to me."

When Chris finished, Levi took the mic and said a parting prayer. He prayed especially that God would continue to use him in his next adventure.

When Levi finished praying, the whole crowd began cheering once again. They then formed a human corridor leading to his car. As Chris walked down that path, the cheering continued unabated.

As he was about to get into his car, he looked across the way and saw Connie standing where she could observe the whole thing. Unsurprisingly, she was making notes about everything going on. He caught her eye, smiled, and nodded to her. She smiled and nodded back. No doubt, there would be one more article in the next day's paper.

Finally, Chris got into the car and started it up one last time. As he pulled away, the entire crowd stood there and continued cheering and waving goodbye. No one even moved to leave as long as he was in sight. As he looked back in his rear-view mirror, he lifted a prayer of thanksgiving and petition to God, "Father, thank you for using my life in Skeptopolis to touch so many. As I move on from here, please use me again."

SKEPTOPOLIS GLOSSARY

Agnosticism - Agnosticism is the belief that nothing can be known about God or transcendent reality. It does not accept the beliefs of either Theists or Atheists.

American Civil Liberties Union (ACLU) - The American Civil Liberties Union is an American nonprofit human rights organization. Its stated purpose is "to defend and preserve the individual rights and liberties guaranteed to every person in this country by the Constitution and laws of the United States."

American Humanist Association - The American Humanist Association is a non-profit organization in the United States that advances **Secular Humanism**.

Anti-science - Anti-science is a set of attitudes or beliefs that oppose or reject empirical science.

Article of Faith - An article of faith is something that is believed without being questioned or doubted.

Atheistic faith - Atheistic faith is belief in the tenets of Atheism without having an objective basis for holding them.

Authority source - An authority source is a reference point that is recognized as reliable because its authenticity is widely acknowledged to be true and accurate.

Biblical sexual morality - Biblical sexual morality is a reference to the sexual moral values taught in the Bible.

Biblical values - Biblical values are the values derived from the teachings of Jesus Christ as found in the Bible.

Buddhists - Buddhists are people who are adherents of the Buddhist faith.

Center for Inquiry - The Center for Inquiry is a U.S. nonprofit organization that works to mitigate belief in pseudoscience and the paranormal, and to fight the influence of religion in government. It merged, in 2016, with Richard Dawkins' Foundation for Reason and Science to become the largest secularist organization in the United States.

Council for Secular Humanism - The Council for Secular Humanism is a non-profit organization that promotes secular values.

Discipleship Training Class - Discipleship training classes in Christian churches are training opportunities for Christians to learn how to more fully live life as a disciple (follower) of Jesus Christ.

Empiricism - Empiricism is a philosophy which holds that all knowledge is derived from experience and observation.

Evangelicals - Evangelicals are people who are adherents of the evangelical tradition of the Christian church. This tradition is an expression of Protestant Christianity that emphasizes the centrality of sharing the good news of Jesus Christ.

Existentialism - Existentialism is a philosophical theory which asserts that individual persons are free and responsible agents who are able to determine their own advancement based on acts of the will.

Faith - Faith is confidence or trust in something or someone.

Faith assumption - A faith assumption is a premise that is based on faith, as opposed to empiricism.

Faith in their underlying worldview beliefs - Having faith in one's underlying worldview beliefs is a recognition that an individual's worldview beliefs, by their very nature. are based on faith assumptions.

Faithful Church Community - The faithful church community represents the churches in a given community that remain faithful to the historic teachings of the Bible and biblical morality.

False Teachings - False teachings are doctrines that do not correspond to the teachings that are found in the Bible.

Far Eastern Pantheism - Far Eastern Pantheism is a worldview category that believes there is an objectively real transcendent reality, but that it is immaterial and impersonal.

Foundational belief - Foundational beliefs are those which are essential to any given faith system.

Hindus - Hindus are people who are adherents of the Hindu faith.

Historic Christianity - Historic Christianity is comprised of the beliefs that are historically common to all orthodox Christian movements and people.

Ignorant - To be ignorant is to lack knowledge of certain things.

Intolerance - Intolerance is a refusal to accept or acknowledge as valid views or beliefs that are different from one's own. It often carries the sense of being hostile to other's beliefs.

Liberal Theology - Liberal theology is an umbrella term that encompasses many churches and denominations that follow various liberal theological streams, such as Existentialism, Liberation ideology, and Postmodernism. It is an approach to interpreting the Bible based on naturalistic, rather than theistic principles. In practical terms, it promotes naturalistic beliefs using biblical vocabulary.

Marxism - Marxism is an economic and political theory developed by Karl Marx that puts a focus on the collective as opposed to the individual.

Modernism – Modernism is a philosophical viewpoint that emerged out of the 19th century Enlightenment. It affirmed the ability of human beings to create, improve, and reshape their environment using practical experimentation, scientific knowledge, and technology.

Moral beliefs - Moral beliefs are a system of beliefs for determining what is good and bad, right and wrong.

Moral values - Moral values are codes of conduct that are accepted by a society or group and form the basis for understanding morality.

Myth - A myth is a traditional story about the early history of a people or society that typically involves a supernatural element.

Naive- To be naive is to lack experience, wisdom, or judgment about a matter.

Narrow-mindedness - Narrow-mindedness refers to an unwillingness to listen to other people's point of view.

National Council of Churches - The National Council of Churches (NCC) is an ecumenical body that includes mainline Protestant, Eastern Orthodox, African-American, and evangelical churches. Its stated goal is to advance a shared agenda of peace, progress, and positive change.

Natural Laws or Laws of Nature - Natural laws are observable physical principles that govern the operation of the natural world.

Naturalism - Naturalism is the worldview category which asserts that the natural universe, operating by natural laws, is all that exists.

Naturalistic Atheism/Atheist - Naturalistic Atheism is the belief that God does not exist because of the overarching belief that the natural universe, operating by natural laws, is all that exists.

Naturalistic presuppositions - Naturalistic presuppositions are beliefs that assume in advance (before any objective evaluation is made) that the natural universe, operating by natural laws, is all that exists.

Original monotheism - Original monotheism is the belief that the original belief about God among humanity was monotheism, and that all other beliefs, that ultimately came to be, were corruptions of that original belief.

Paradise – Paradise is a reference to heaven or the afterlife.

Personal God - A personal God is one who is able to interact with human beings in a personal way.

Philosophy - Philosophy is the study of the nature of knowledge, reality, and existence.

Postmodernism - Postmodernism is a philosophy that emerged as a rejection of Modernism. It is characterized by skepticism, subjectivism, and relativism and involves questioning meta-narratives (grand narratives) and rejecting the certainty of knowledge (or truth).

Progressive ideology - Progressive ideology is a political philosophy that seeks to implement Marxist (collectivist) policies into society in a slow, progressive, manner rather than by means of an all-out revolution.

Religion - A religion is a particular system of belief that must be accepted by faith.

Religious belief - A religious belief is any point of view that is based on a faith foundation.

Science - Science is the use of observation and experimentation to study the structure and nature of the natural universe.

Scientific method - The scientific method is the process of using observation and experimentation to establish an understanding of the natural world. It involves making an observation, forming a hypothesis, making a prediction, conducting an experiment, and analyzing the results.

Secular Humanism - Secular Humanism is a philosophical position which believes that human beings are capable of living a moral and self-fulfilled life without belief in God.

Settled science - Settled Science is the belief that a particular point of view concerning some natural phenomenon is based on such strong scientific evidence that it does not require, or is not subject to, any more discussion.

Skepticism - Skepticism refers to the doubts someone has about the truth of faith system.

Social justice - Social justice is the attempt to define justice based on people's wealth or social privileges and their life circumstances, as opposed to what is actually or objectively just.

Testimony - A testimony is a Christian's story of how they became a Christian.

Theory of Evolution - The Theory of Evolution is a theory in biology advancing the belief that the great variety of life forms that exist in the world came about by naturalistic evolutionary processes.

Universalist Church - The Universalist Church was originally a Christian denomination in the United States. The basic belief of Universalism is that ultimately everyone will go to heaven. It no longer exists as a denomination.

MEET THE AUTHOR

Freddy Davis is the founder and president of MarketFaith Ministries (www. marketfaith.org). He is a 4th degree black belt in karate, and has a background as a pastor, university professor, speaker, and international missionary. He is the author of numerous books and is an expert in the field of Christian worldview.

Freddy is a graduate of Florida State University with a BS in Communications, and holds MDiv and DMin degrees from Southwestern Baptist Theological seminary. He is a popular speaker, particularly on the topic of worldview and its practical implications for the Christian life. He lives in Tallahassee, FL with his wife Deborah.

www.ingramcontent.com/pod-product-compliance
Lightning Source LLC
Chambersburg PA
CBHW071659120626
46550CB00001B/40